A WORLD MORE EQUAL

COLUMBIA STUDIES IN INTERNATIONAL AND GLOBAL HISTORY

COLUMBIA STUDIES IN INTERNATIONAL AND GLOBAL HISTORY

Cemil Aydin, Timothy Nunan, and Dominic Sachsenmaier, Series Editors

This series presents some of the finest and most innovative work coming out of the current landscapes of international and global historical scholarship. Grounded in empirical research, these titles transcend the usual area boundaries and address how history can help us understand contemporary problems, including poverty, inequality, power, political violence, and accountability beyond the nation-state. The series covers processes of flows, exchanges, and entanglements—and moments of blockage, friction, and fracture—not only between "the West" and "the Rest" but also among parts of what has variously been dubbed the "Third World" or the "Global South." Scholarship in international and global history remains indispensable for a better sense of current complex regional and global economic transformations. Such approaches are vital in understanding the making of our present world.

Julia Hauser, *A Taste for Purity: An Entangled History of Vegetarianism*

Hayrettin Yücesoy, *Disenchanting the Caliphate:*
A History of Secular Political Thought in the Early Abbasid Empire

Anne Irfan, *Refuge and Resistance: Palestinians and the International Refugee System*

Michael Francis Laffan, *Under Empire: Muslim Lives and*
Loyalties Across the Indian Ocean World, 1775–1945

Eva-Maria Muschik, *Building States: The United Nations, Development,*
and Decolonization, 1945–1965

Jessica Namakkal, *Unsettling Utopia: The Making and Unmaking of French India*

Michael Christopher Low, *Imperial Mecca: Ottoman Arabia and the Indian Ocean Hajj*

Nicole CuUnjieng Aboitiz, *Asian Place, Filipino Nation:*
A Global Intellectual History of the Philippine Revolution, 1887–1912

Mona L. Siegel, *Peace on Our Terms: The Global Battle for*
Women's Rights After the First World War

Raja Adal, *Beauty in the Age of Empire: Japan, Egypt, and the*
Global History of Aesthetic Education

Ulbe Bosma, *The Making of a Periphery:*
How Island Southeast Asia Became a Mass Exporter of Labor

Perrin Selcer, *The UN and the Postwar Origins of the*
Global Environment: From World Community to Spaceship Earth

Dominic Sachsenmaier, *Global Entanglements of a Man Who Never Traveled:*
A Seventeenth-Century Chinese Christian and His Conflicted Worlds

Perin E. Gürel, *The Limits of Westernization:*
A Cultural History of America in Turkey

Will Hanley, *Identifying with Nationality:*
Europeans, Ottomans, and Egyptians in Alexandria

Simone M. Müller, *Wiring the World:*
The Social and Cultural Creation of Global Telegraph Networks

Richard W. Bulliet, *The Wheel: Inventions and Reinventions*

Alison Bashford, *Global Population: History, Geopolitics, and Life on Earth*

Adam Clulow, *The Company and the Shogun:*
The Dutch Encounter with Tokugawa Japan

Samuel Moyn and Andrew Sartori, eds., *Global Intellectual History*

For a complete list of books in the series, please see the Columbia University Press website.

A World More Equal

AN INTERNATIONALIST PERSPECTIVE
ON THE COLD WAR

Sandrine Kott

Translated by Arby Gharibian

Columbia University Press
New York

Columbia University Press
Publishers Since 1893
New York   Chichester, West Sussex
cup.columbia.edu

Organiser le monde: Une autre histoire de la guerre froide
© Éditions du Seuil, 2021
This book was first published with support from the
French National Book Center (Centre National du Livre)
Translation copyright © 2024 Columbia University Press
All rights reserved

Library of Congress Cataloging-in-Publication Data

Names: Kott, Sandrine, author.
Title: A world more equal : an internationalist perspective
on the Cold War / by Sandrine Kott.
Description: New York : Columbia University Press, [2023] |
Series: Columbia studies in international and global history |
Orginally published as: Organiser le monde: Une autre histoire de la guerre
froide © Éditions du Seuil, 2021 | Includes bibliographical references and index.
Identifiers: LCCN 2023030895 (print) | LCCN 2023030896 (ebook) |
ISBN 9780231210140 (hardback) | ISBN 9780231210157 (trade paperback) |
ISBN 9780231558297 (ebook)
Subjects: LCSH: Cold War. | World politics—1945–1989.
Classification: LCC D843 .K63913 2023 (print) | LCC D843 (ebook) |
DDC 909.82/5—dc23/eng/20230925
LC record available at https://lccn.loc.gov/2023030895
LC ebook record available at https://lccn.loc.gov/2023030896

Cover design: Elliott S. Cairns
Cover image: Juliautumn / Shutterstock.com

In memory of my dear friend, and inspiring historian, Eric Weitz

CONTENTS

LIST OF ACRONYMS ix

ACKNOWLEDGMENTS xiii

Introduction 1

Chapter One
The Two Parts of Europe During the Postwar Period 11

Chapter Two
The Emergence of a "Second World":
Center and Periphery 38

Chapter Three
Internationalisms During the Cold War 68

Chapter Four
The Europe of Convergences 99

Chapter Five
The Third World and the New International Economic Order 129

CONTENTS

Chapter Six
From Internationalisms to Globalism:
The Slow Agony of the Cold War   163

Conclusion: Beyond the Cold War   194

NOTES   203

BIBLIOGRAPHY   251

INDEX   281

ACRONYMS

AFL	American Federation of Labor
AFL-CIO	American Federation of Labor–Congress of Industrial Organizations (trade union federation founded in 1955 via merger of the AFL and the CIO, which organizes less-skilled workers)
ARA	American Relief Administration (led by Herbert Hoover, active 1919–1923)
CEPES	UNESCO European Centre for Higher Education (founded in 1972 in Bucharest)
CGIL	Italian General Confederation of Labour
CGT	General Confederation of Labour, France
CIA	Central Intelligence Agency (founded in 1947)
CoCom	Coordinating Committee for Multilateral Export Controls (1949–1994)
Comecon	Council for Mutual Economic Assistance (founded in 1949)
CSCE	Conference on Security and Cooperation in Europe (1972–1975)
ECA	Economic Cooperation Administration (agency in charge of administering Marshall Plan, 1947–1951)

ACRONYMS

ECLA/ECLAC	Economic Commission for Latin America (since 1948) and the Caribbean (since 1984)
ECOSOC	Economic and Social Council of the United Nations
EEC	European Economic Community (created in 1957)
EPTA	Expanded Programme of Technical Assistance (1949–1965)
FAO	Food and Agriculture Organization of the United Nations (established in 1945)
FBI	Federal Bureau of Investigation
FRG	Federal Republic of Germany (1949–1990)
GATT	General Agreement on Tariffs and Trade
GDR	German Democratic Republic (1949–1990)
IAEA	International Atomic Energy Agency (founded in 1956 in Vienna)
ICC	International Chamber of Commerce
ICFTU	International Confederation of Free Trade Unions (founded in 1949 at instigation of the AFL and the CIA)
ICPED	International Center for Public Enterprises in Developing Countries (founded in 1974 in Ljubljana with UN support)
IIASA	International Institute for Applied Systems Analysis (founded in 1972 in Vienna)
ILO	International Labour Organization (founded in 1919)
NATO	North Atlantic Treaty Organization (founded in 1949)
NGO	nongovernmental organization
NIEO	New International Economic Order (presented and passed in 1974 at UN General Assembly)
OECD	Organisation for Economic Co-operation and Development (founded in 1961; succeeded OEEC)
OEEC	Organisation for European Economic Co-operation (founded in 1948 to administer Marshall Plan)
OFRRO	Office of Foreign Relief and Rehabilitation Operations
UN	United Nations (term, used to describe the nations at war against Nazi Germany, appeared in 1941; organization became active in 1945)
UNCTAD	United Nations Conference on Trade and Development (created in 1964)

ACRONYMS

UNDP	United Nations Development Programme (succeeded Expanded Programme of Technical Assistance and Special Fund in 1965)
UNECE	United Nations Economic Commission for Europe (founded in 1947)
UNESCO	United Nations Educational, Scientific and Cultural Organization (founded in 1945)
UNICEF	United Nations Children's Fund (founded in 1946)
UNIDO	United Nations Industrial Development Organization
UNRRA	United Nations Relief and Rehabilitation Administration (1943–1947)
USAID	United States Agency for International Development (founded in 1961)
USSR	Union of Soviet Socialist Republics
WEP	World Employment Programme (launched in 1969)
WFTU	World Federation of Trade Unions (founded in 1945, of Communist inspiration, especially after schism of 1949)
WHO	World Health Organization (founded in 1948)
WIDF	Women's International Democratic Federation (founded in 1945, of Communist inspiration)

ACKNOWLEDGMENTS

It all began in 2010. What was, in the beginning, simply a series of still vague intuitions took shape over the course of a long period of gestation. Throughout these ten years, I enjoyed excellent working conditions provided by the University of Geneva, as well as the kindness of my close colleagues. I owe much to those who helped make this book what it has become. I am especially grateful to Davide Rodogno for his extensive cooperation, always in equal parts and across numerous fronts. I would like to extend my warm thanks to Patricia Clavin, Michel Christian, Thomas David, Pierre Eichenberger, Madeleine Herren, Morgane Labbé, Jean-Frédéric Schaub, Jannick Schaufelbuehl, Cyrus Schayegh, Glenda Sluga, and Ludovic Tournès and for reading and commenting on the first version of some chapters. The young researchers whose research I oversaw—Paulos Asfaha, Simplice Ayangma, Camille Bolivar, Ondrej Fiser, Simon Godard, Olga Hidalgo-Weber, Maia Müller, Laure Piguet, Myriam Piguet, Véronique Plata-Stenger, and Alexandre Stefaniak—exposed me to new sources, subjects, and issues and pushed my reflections forward. This book bears the mark of our exchanges.

My research was supported and encouraged by the Swiss National Scientific Research Fund. Between 2012 and 2015, the Sinergia project entitled "Patterns of Transnational Regulation: How Networks and Institutions Shaped Markets and Societies Throughout the 20th Century" initiated fruitful cooperation with Thomas David, Jean-Christophe Graz, Matthieu

ACKNOWLEDGMENTS

Leimgruber, Martin Lengwiller, and Davide Rodogno on issues relating to regulation and international expertise in economic and social matters. The regular meetings, discussions, and informal exchanges made possible by the project helped to lay the important groundwork. Between 2014 and 2018, Michel Christian and Ondrej Matejka worked with me on the project entitled "Shared Modernities or Competing Modernities? Europe Between West and East (1920s–1970s)." The research conducted in connection with that project greatly nurtured the writing of this book. I owe a good deal of what I know about Czechoslovakia to my exchanges with Ondrej Matejka. Michel Christian conducted extensive research at the UN archives in Geneva and Vienna, the results of which he has broadly shared.

It was at the Work and Human Life Cycle in Global History center, where I had been invited to spend a number of months in 2010–2011, that this book gradually took shape. That is where I became aware of the importance of development-related issues, and where I discovered the abortive project for a new global economic order. Discussions with Ravi Ahuja, Dimitri van den Berselaar, Fred Cooper, Andreas Eckert, Jürgen Kocka, Prabhu Mohapatra, Lutz Raphael, and Marcel van der Linden were decisive.

During this decade I attended and participated in numerous seminars and conferences, at which I presented various aspects of my ongoing research. They provided an opportunity for encounters and discussions that enriched or revised my research prospects. It is impossible for me to mention all those I interacted with, but I would like to highlight what I owe to my exchanges with Miguel Bandeira Jerónimo, Patricia Clavin, Madeleine Herren, Isabella Löhr, Marieke Louis, Eva-Maria Muschick, Katja Naumann, Kiran Patel, Susan Pedersen, Elisabeth Roehrlich, and Cyrus Schayegh, the intellectual generosity of Glenda Sluga and members of the Program in International History at the University of Sydney, as well as the many initiatives pursued by Jessica Reinisch and her colleagues at the Reluctant Internationalists project at Birkbeck College, University of London. The discussions I had with colleagues at Bielefeld, Bochum, Bologna, Brussels, Florence, Leiden, Leipzig, Lisbon, Maastricht, Oslo, Padua, Prague, and Vienna, along with those at l'École normale supérieure in Paris, New York University, the University of California, Berkeley, Columbia University, Oxford University, Princeton University, Stanford University, Humboldt University of Berlin, and the Institutes of Political Sciences of Paris (CERI) and Toulouse have all, in one way or another, helped to refine my xv

ACKNOWLEDGMENTS

thinking. The editorial committees of the journals *Vingtième Siècle, Critique internationale, Le Mouvement social, La Revue d'histoire de la protection sociale,* and *Contemporary European History* provided me with the opportunity to assemble special issues and to deliver preliminary versions of my research. I would like to thank them for their trust, as well as the contributors to those issues for the fruitful exchanges that preceded and accompanied them.

My research required trips to numerous archival collections, where I enjoyed a kindly and informed welcome. This history book exists thanks to archival services. I think back with emotion at the hours spent in the magnificent archive room at the UN Palace in Geneva; the availability of Blandine Blukacz-Louisfert and Jacques Oberson was invaluable. Yet it was in the small archive room at the International Labour Office that everything began in 2010; I would like to extend my special thanks there to Jacques Rodriguez for his kindness and dedication, Remo Becci for his long and passionate discussions, and my friends Dorothea Hoehtker and Emmanuel Reynaud, who were valued and unerring guides in the maze of this organization now over one hundred years old.

This book would not have been born in 2021 without the support and interest of Patrick Boucheron and the editorial team at Seuil. Its publication in English was made possible thanks to the involvement of Caelyn Cobb at Columbia University Press and the directors of the Columbia Studies in International and Global History: Dominic Sachsenmaier, Cemil Aydin, and Thimothy Nunan. The translation was covered with research funds made available by New York University. Arby Gharibian proved to be an available, precise, and inspiring translator. To him my warm thanks.

Antoine Georges listened to my monologues with patience and bore with humor the long months of writing, during which I was fixed to my screen and little available for others. He offered unflagging support during moments of discouragement. This book owes him a great deal.

A WORLD MORE EQUAL

INTRODUCTION

This book grew out of my surprise when reading a report by David Morse, the director-general of the International Labour Office, who had once been close to U.S. president Franklin Delano Roosevelt. When the USSR withdrew from international organizations in January 1949, Morse traveled to Poland and Czechoslovakia to convince their leaders not to leave the International Labour Organization (ILO), of which they were founding members. The first draft of his visit report includes the following affirmation:

> In the US State there was a fear of the USSR but there was a terrible misunderstanding and misconception between East and West. In the United States there were two schools of thought, one of them wished a strong militaristic policy towards the USSR and the other to which he, the DG[,] belonged, which felt that conciliation was desirable and possible. This latter school was in ascendency and there would be a great difference visible in the US policy within the period of 12 months.[1]

It was crossed out in red upon review and ultimately left out of the final report. I found this trace, however fleeting it may be, intriguing, because it questioned the self-evidence of the Cold War, at least in terms of its simple definition as a global conflict between the United States and the USSR that

INTRODUCTION

dominated international affairs between 1945 and 1991.[2] The context and objective of the visit certainly called for words of appeasement, but they were nonetheless pronounced in what is considered a high point of the Cold War, and by a U.S. diplomat who was the head of a major international organization and therefore well aware of global political balances.

I could have ignored this observation, seeing it merely as a strategy to entice or the expression of wishful thinking, but I wanted to pursue the avenue it opened up. This avenue was attractive since it confirmed observations made from my long and intimate study of the German Democratic Republic (GDR), which convinced me that ideological oppositions notwithstanding, the elites of both parts of Europe shared a belief in modernity, as well as the objectives of economic and social progress. Recent research has supported this conviction. Numerous works have revealed the porousness of the "Iron Curtain," which some authors have even referred to as the "nylon curtain"; others have emphasized the convergence between capitalist and communist development models.[3] This porousness, and even convergence, is generally studied through the circulations and exchanges between two countries. Morse's comment suggested to me that international organizations could offer a good vantage point for taking a fresh view of Cold War oppositions and to question their centrality to the history of the period.

This book is therefore neither a linear account of the Cold War nor a history of international organizations during the Cold War.[4] My primary objective is to explore the period referred to as the Cold War through international organizations, grasped as prisms through which global balances and imbalances can be observed. This approach offers new perspectives on the period, which is all too readily reduced to "the Cold War," or to a confrontation between two blocks structured by opposing ideologies. Our current period also calls for doubt. The recent return of the term *Cold War* to interpret conflicts between the West and countries such as Russia and China once again obscures and simplifies the reality of conflicts that unfold on multiple levels—including economic, geopolitical, and cultural ones—which can hardly be reduced to opposition between clearly constituted ideological camps, although divergences and even oppositions in the representation of the world are indeed present. In this respect, international

INTRODUCTION

organizations have proven useful, both yesterday and today, in enabling us to rethink global imbalances and oppositions. This is also the case because they are spaces where, within narrow limits, solutions are discussed, developed, and proposed.

International organizations were and still are spaces in which diplomats can meet, along with experts, unionists, activists, and economic and cultural actors. They reveal the connections and circulations among individuals, groups, and states that run counter to the traditional Cold War ordering into "camps." Their secretariats facilitated, encouraged, and organized these meetings; they helped arrange discussions, exchanges, and even rapprochement that reveal or develop the deep convergence between groups of individuals, countries, and political systems perceived as being antagonistic. This role of multilateralism and the broader values of internationalism stand out all the more clearly, for they have been profoundly challenged in today's world in which competition has become the rule.

This book therefore seeks to provide a history of the period through the prism of internationalism understood as both a project and a social practice.[5] The Cold War did not prevent the development of international movements around common causes such as the environment or human rights, or the launch of major international campaigns for peace or the eradication of smallpox.[6] International organizations attest to this vitality, for in addition to the growing number of major international nongovernmental organizations (NGOs), the period was also marked by sustained activity by the United Nations and its agencies.[7] These internationalisms did not develop on the margins of, or in spite of, the Cold War but rather were a characteristic and specific expression of it. In fact, the two and later three worlds of the Cold War promoted their own internationalism that was structured around a series of ideas and values that were supposed to be valid for all people and all times, now and forever. These worlds and the diverging internationalisms they promoted were locked in combat with one another. Nevertheless, they also showed the same belief in the virtues of internationalism and projects for organizing the world for the benefit of all. This belief served as the basis for their coexistence within UN agencies, where they ultimately succeeded in working together.[8] Examining the sources of these organizations reveals how internationalism affirmed as an ideal could become a practice founded on the exchange of know-how and the existence or constitution of "international societies," which is to say networks of actors whose identity and activity are not entirely defined by their belonging to a national space.[9]

For all that, nation-states remain important actors in our history. The perspective offered by international organizations nevertheless encourages us to move beyond the Soviet-U.S. confrontation and shine a light on other countries: medium-sized powers such as France, Great Britain, and the Federal Republic of Germany (FRG) in the West, and Poland and Czechoslovakia in the East, assume their full role. A multilateral perspective places special emphasis on neutral countries such as Finland, Austria, Switzerland, and Yugoslavia, all of which served an essential function as bridges during the period. They also give voice to "small Central European countries." Despite their initial marginal position, they used international spaces to formulate a more differentiated and autonomous point of view than the one attributed to them by Western perceptions and a historiography too exclusively based on U.S. and Western European diplomatic archives.

Finally, and most important, viewing the period through the prism of international organizations entails leaving behind the simple opposition between the Cold War's First and Second Worlds and giving newly decolonized countries—and more generally what were referred to as Third World countries—their full role not as spaces in which proxy wars were waged, but as international actors that from the 1950s onward decisively shifted global issues and balances.[10] The discourses and demands they formulated in international arenas prompt us to rethink the very foundations of the Cold War, and to question its centrality.[11] It was leaders from countries in the Global South who, beginning in the 1950s, formulated human rights demands at the UN General Assembly, including defending economic and social rights. The decade between 1964 and 1974 ended with the Declaration on the Establishment of a New International Economic Order, which was adopted by a large majority at the UN General Assembly. The voices raised by actors from the Global South, which increased and expanded within international arenas, insistently questioned the global distribution of power and wealth. They challenged the discrimination and inequality suffered by these countries in the name of human rights. These global inequalities were the central concerns of the period and were at the heart of Cold War oppositions.[12] International organizations were places where governmental representatives, but also those from various NGOs, clearly formulated this issue. Until the 1970s, civil servants and

INTRODUCTION

international experts defended and promoted the idea that global inequalities had to be corrected and imbalances regulated in order to ensure peace. They believed that it was possible to organize a "world more equal."

This book is the fruit of a long journey through the archives of these organizations and the vast secondary literature covering them. This journey was not systematic, for even multiple lifetimes would be insufficient. Along the way I favored the sources of certain organizations while ignoring or neglecting others. In any event, the path taken was not arbitrary but was driven by an objective: to reveal and explore the economic and social issues at the heart—and even at the foundation—of what have been interpreted as Cold War divisions. This objective was based on a dual conviction. First, the Cold War was a period structured by heightened awareness of the injustice of global social and economic inequality. This gave rise to an ideological conflict between two models of economic development and social organization, between liberal capitalism and state socialism, as well as between the values asserted by each "camp": liberty and democracy, on the one hand, and equality and solidarity, on the other.[13] Culture has been a central field of research in this respect, as it was a medium for expressing and shaping these ideological rivalries, as well as a powerful instrument for diffusing and promoting them.[14] Second, the international discussions in which these diverging economic and social conceptions appeared, in addition to the global inequalities on which they were based, have been relatively neglected. I chose to focus on how these oppositions were developed, organized, and structured in international organizations through a variety of debates, such as those surrounding productivity and the organization of work, women's role in society, economic development choices, the spread of medical treatment and prevention policies, and human rights. All these debates were related to the central question of inequality, both national and international. My aim has been to observe how Cold War debates discussed, constructed, and transformed these topics, as well as whether they resisted the binary and oversimplifying logic that structured them, and if so, how. International sources clearly show that the Cold War should also be studied as an economic conflict between the U.S. elite and their Western allies, who dominated the global economy, and the Second and soon to come Third Worlds, who challenged this hegemony. This period began with the stormy debates surrounding the end of the United Nations Relief and Rehabilitation Administration (UNRRA), the launch of the Marshall Plan in 1947, and the implementation of the Coordinating Committee for Multilateral Export Controls (CoCom) in 1949. It continued through UN economic development programs and practices starting in 1949, the emergence and formulation of Third World demands for a New International Economic Order (NIEO) between 1955 and 1974, and finally the structural adjustment policies of the International Monetary Fund (IMF) and the World Bank from the late 1970s onward. These economic issues were well documented in the debates that occurred in various agencies within the UN system and Bretton Woods institutions, as well as major NGOs such as the International Chamber of Commerce (ICC) and global trade union organizations. They underscore that the economy was also a very effective weapon, as embargoes were used to weaken the enemy early on, and even ultimately to absorb it within the global market.[15]

To pursue my objective, I adopted a broad definition for international organizations. In addition to intergovernmental organizations and those belonging to the UN system, which are especially central to this work, I included regional organizations, nongovernmental organizations, and even major international foundations.[16]

This abundance of organizations called for selection, which was determined by the accessibility of archives and documents, by the questions I was exploring at the time, by my areas of expertise, and by my tastes. In addition to the UN secretariat, the commissions connected to the Economic and Social Council (ECOSOC) in particular, such as the United Nations Conference on Trade and Development (UNCTAD) or the United Nations Economic Commission for Europe (UNECE), I worked on documents produced by and about certain UN agencies, especially the International Labour Organization, which possesses exceptional archives, the United Nations Educational Scientific and Cultural Organization (UNESCO), the World Health Organization (WHO), and the United Nations Industrial Development Organization (UNIDO). While not absent, the Bretton Woods organizations—the World Bank and the IMF—play a secondary role in this account, for beginning in 1947 they essentially gave voice to Western actors and quickly became spaces for imposing a norm rather than forums for discussing diverging models. I used the secondary literature on regional organizations, such as the Council for Mutual

INTRODUCTION

Economic Assistance (Comecon) for socialist countries, and the Organisation for Economic Co-operation and Development (OECD) for Western countries, inasmuch as they were situated within—and took positions relating to—the global space. I also used documents produced by certain NGOs, especially major union federations: the World Federation of Trade Unions (WFTU), the International Confederation of Free Trade Unions (ICFTU), or the International Chamber of Commerce (ICC), and even documents from the Ford Foundation or international Communist and anti-communist associations.

When possible, I worked on the archives of these organizations, although I did not proceed with an exhaustive examination of their collections, which would have been impossible. This archival work primarily served to deconstruct a dominant interpretation of the period deeply marked by a Cold War discourse.

To venture on this terrain I had to equip myself methodologically.[17] Entering the world of international organizations is not easy, as they have established an elaborated and effective official discourse whose purpose is to legitimize their activity in the eyes of their sponsors: the public for international NGOs, and states for multilateral organizations. This discourse erects a rampart of sorts that conceals their contradictions from the outside world. Nevertheless, if one is attentive and cautiously studies the internal nonpromotional documents they produce, it is possible to move beyond this impression and gain access to a first inner circle where conflicting voices can be heard, including those of groups with diverging interests, such as workers and employers at the ILO, doctors and pharmaceutical companies at the WHO, and especially those of governments. Within the UN agency system, national delegates or representatives frequently have the leading voice, and for this reason these agencies have often been considered purely as diplomatic forums in which national governments, and the most powerful in particular, meet and oppose one another. International organizations offer a good vantage point for observing both the conflict and convergence among various countries or groups of countries. During the Cold War, UN General Assemblies, the ILO's Annual International Labour Conference, and the assemblies of the WHO or UNESCO served as spaces for staging and projecting the major ideological oppositions that structured the period; these oppositions are all the more visible given that many of these public debates were the subject of internal publications, which are now widely available on the websites of these organizations.

Yet it is also important to leave these public arenas and venture into the thicket of sources produced by permanent secretariats. This leads to a second inner circle, which I consider to be the beating heart of these organizations. This is where international knowledge and know-how is developed, as well as where the epistemic communities that coalesce around the sharing of knowledge and experience meet and even form.[18] The international civil servants employed within them, along with the many experts they recruited for specific projects, promoted these dynamics of internationalization, which is to say the constitution of international knowledge and know-how based on the gathering of national and local experiences. Only by working on the documents produced by secretariats (correspondence, reports, mission reports, etc.) can these dynamics and the diversity of actors contributing to them be grasped; they bear witness to the joint effort, as well as the conflicts and tensions, that accompanied them. These conflicts did not necessarily overlap with the national or ideological oppositions displayed in the first inner circle.[19]

Working on international organizations entails constantly moving between these two inner circles, but that is insufficient on its own, for in order to understand what was occurring and being said within them, one must be attentive to the many people who continually joined and left them, and who gave life to the organization. Diplomatic actors—"disciplined international forces,"[20]—and experts forming epistemic communities were temporary or more permanent visitors, and without them these organizations would be no more than deserted palaces. All these aspects—their specific architecture, the diversity of actors one could meet there, and the knowledge they produced—make international organizations fine focal points for exploring the period and for deconstructing the hegemony of the Cold War discourse.

This book emerged from these choices, with six chapters that are simultaneously thematic and chronological. Each one examines the Cold War from the viewpoint or activity of specific organizations and the issues discussed within them.

INTRODUCTION

Chapter 1 covers the postwar period. The perspective provided by UNRRA and UNECE underscores the existence and resilience of a pan-European project, one of whose objectives was to end the inequality between the two parts of Europe and to pull Eastern Europe out of the "semicolonial" situation in which it found itself. This project was supported by the antifascism networks that served as the very foundation for creating the UN system. This chapter highlights the importance of these networks and the role played within them by progressive and Social Democratic actors up through the late 1970s.

In chapter 2, which includes the period between 1949 and 1954, the international organizations of the UN system are grasped as platforms that exhibit the specific divisions between the First and Second Worlds of the Cold War. I show how they were established as spaces for Western domination, while the regional organizations that emerged from the Marshall Plan, such as CoCom, helped keep Central and Eastern Europe in a peripheral situation with respect to the developed world. Finally, they were spaces in which competing internationalisms were formulated and organized.

These competing internationalisms are the subject of chapter 3, which covers the years between 1955 and 1965, and in which I explore whether this decade can be seen as the golden age of internationalism, first through the growing intervention of major universal organizations, and second through the increase of regional organizations, sometimes in competition with one another. This was also when the Third World emerged. Yugoslavia served as a bridge between the three internationalisms being constituted at the time.

These bridges and convergences are the focus of chapter 4, spanning the years between 1965 and 1975. I examine the role of international organizations in the circulations and rapprochement between the two parts of Europe, and I show how cities such as Vienna, Helsinki, and Geneva were preferred locations for such encounters. Vienna was home to new international organizations that demonstrate how pan-European projects were concretely developed, while the Conference on Security and Cooperation in Europe (CSCE), held in Geneva and Helsinki, was the result and expression of these international projects, embodying this "new spirit." All these initiatives also attest to the limits of this convergence, as well as the persistence of ideological divisions and economic inequality between the two parts of Europe.

Chapter 5 extends the geographical range under consideration by following the entry of recently decolonized countries within international organizations in the 1950s, and by looking closely at the development of, and demands for, a New International Economic Order. In this context, I consider the constitution and nature of a third internationalism and analyze how it was defined in relation to the First and Second Worlds. I also show that making wealth inequality a central topic of the period deeply challenges our vision of the Cold War.

Chapter 6 examines how the failure of the New International Economic Order promoted by the Global South and the irremediable decline of the Communist world-system were accompanied by the weakening of international projects in the 1980s. Cold War internationalism gradually gave way to the logic of globalism, which put individuals, groups, and states in competition with one another. Entry into the neoliberal era was marked by important changes in paradigm that were quite perceptible within international spaces beginning in the late 1970s.

Chapter One

THE TWO PARTS OF EUROPE DURING
THE POSTWAR PERIOD

The year 1947 is generally seen as a pivotal moment during the postwar period.[1] A series of events relating to international history, national political balances, performative discourses, the reality of sociopolitical balances on the ground, fear of the other, and an expansionist desire inexorably led to a division of the continent into two blocs, on both sides of what Winston Churchill called "the Iron Curtain" in his famous speech delivered in Fulton, Missouri, on March 5, 1946.

In order for the U.S. Congress to pass his policy of intervention in Greece and Turkey, in March 1947 President Harry S. Truman announced the doctrine of containment for the USSR and communism. That same month, Communist ministers resigned from the Belgian government, and in May the French and Italian governments dismissed them. In June U.S. secretary of state George Marshall announced the Europe Recovery Plan, also known as the Marshall Plan. Political parties on the liberal right interpreted the large wave of strikes in France and Italy in November and December 1947 as an attempt to politically destabilize Western Europe. In October 1947 the constitution of the Information Bureau of the Communist and Workers' Parties (Cominform)—in addition to the affirmation of political Jdanovism, which declared the separation of the world into two antagonistic camps in the Polish city of Szlarska Poręba—marked the constitution of the Eastern bloc and the relaunch of the international Communist movement.[2] The Czechoslovak coup d'état in February 1948 bore witness to the broken alliance with socialist forces and the long-term installation of Communists atop the governments of people's democracies.[3] The Berlin Blockade in 1948–1949, which pitted the leaders of the United States and the Soviet Union, represented the height of Europe's entry into the Cold War. In this context, the new international organizations of the UN system became stages where verbal confrontations reflected the intractable opposition between the two blocs.

The history of these years, however, can be viewed and recounted differently when seen not from what followed—the Cold War—but rather from what preceded it—the aftermath of World War II. The wartime alliance against fascism brought victory but also formulated promises of a fresh start, of building European societies that were more just, solidary, and united. Communist, Socialist, and Christian Democratic Parties, which at the time accounted for nearly 70 percent of votes in major European countries in both the East and the West, developed programs to establish a broad economic democracy, generous social redistribution, the integration of marginal or excluded categories such as the working classes and women, and the implementation of large-scale economic modernization projects under the auspices of the state. Even after the right's return to power in most Western European countries, the state's organizing and planning role was not called into question, nor were the reform projects it oversaw.[4] UN and Bretton Woods organizations were the international expression of this promise.

Before it was established as an organization, the United Nations was initially a wartime alliance against fascism. Its founding text was the Atlantic Charter issued in August 1941, which was formulated by U.S. president Franklin D. Roosevelt and passed by British prime minister Winston Churchill. The leaders of nations entering the war alongside the Allies rallied behind the Charter, including Stalin in October 1943 on behalf of the Soviet Union. A text of circumstance intended to bring the United States into the war and to mobilize the population, the Charter nevertheless promoted the right of peoples to self-determination, economic cooperation among nations, and social security for all.[5] Despite being dominated by imperialist powers, the UN continued to convey this message, namely, the coming of a better world, one that international civil servants believed they could "organize."[6]

The tension between these two accounts—that of the aftermath of World War II and that of the beginning of the Cold War—is perfectly illustrated by the hesitation present in the documents that international organizations produced between 1945 and 1949. Through them emerges another history of Europe's entry into the Cold War, a tentative one marked by an abortive attempt at pan-European reconstruction, in addition to broken promises of economic equality between the two parts of Europe. Swedish economist Gunnar Myrdal, who had just assumed leadership of the secretariat for the new United Nations Economic Commission for Europe in 1947, clearly captured the hopes raised by this promise: "The West is battling to sustain its standard of living and to establish a firm foundation on which its future advance can rest, the East, already poor, and further impoverished by war is battling to overcome the heritage of an inefficient, mainly agricultural economy."[7] For Myrdal, reconstruction and prosperity for all—conditions for peace—were closely connected to the continent's balanced development.

In this chapter I reflect on how international organizations were spaces in which projects for advancing this prosperous and solidary Europe were developed and implemented. These projects revolved around three objectives that I will discuss in successive order—relieving, reconstructing, and organizing and developing—preceded by a brief overview of the war's aftermath, which revealed the growing imbalance between the two parts of Europe. These projects reflect the staying power of postwar internationalism, as well as continued relations and circulations between these two parts. This is demonstrated by the activities conducted within four organizations: the United Nations Relief and Rehabilitation Administration, the Rockefeller Foundation, the Food and Agriculture Organization of the United Nations (FAO), and UNECE.

UNEQUAL DEVELOPMENT, UNEQUAL SUFFERING

At the end of the war, Europe was in ruins. Numerous cities bombed by the Allies had practically been wiped off the map, and means of communication had largely been destroyed. Over thirty-six million people had died, including nineteen million civilians. More than twelve million displaced persons were accounted for: deportees returning from camps, prisoners of war, and forced laborers, who were joined by twelve million German-speaking people expelled from Central Europe, and those forced to abandon everything after changes to borders in the East.

At the end of the war, Europe was divided into victorious and vanquished countries, between occupiers and the occupied. The Nazi occupation had created divisions within each community, and populations everywhere had to learn how to overcome tenacious opposition between those who collaborated and those who resisted, those who took advantage of the war and those who suffered, victims and perpetrators. German occupations everywhere unleashed simmering social and especially ethnic oppositions, with the extermination of Jews being driven everywhere by long-standing anti-Semitism. Liberations themselves led to new ethnic and social violence. Men, weakened and diminished, found an opportunity to reaffirm a virility that defeat had challenged, especially by exerting brutal domination over women, who were raped en masse by Soviet soldiers, and to a lesser degree by Allied troops in Germany, during the campaign to recapture Italy, and even after the Normandy landings.[8] In France especially, but also in Italy and Germany, women had their hair forcibly shaved by members of the Resistance or former collaborators eager to establish a political virginity.[9] In 1945 the Red Cross counted thirteen million children who lost one or both parents, some of whom were left entirely to their own devices, roving the countryside in organized groups, while others gathered in the streets of major cities.[10] They all served as an alarming reminder of the upheaval of family structures.[11]

While every European country bore the scars of total war, not all suffered equally. Western European countries, more industrialized and wealthier, were exploited by Nazi leaders, who had an interest in maintaining their productive capacity. On the other hand, Eastern European countries, and Poland in particular, were pillaged. Six million Poles, including three million Jews, were massacred. "Words cannot describe what Poland suffered during World War II," exclaimed members of the FAO Commission of Inquiry in 1947, one of the many expressions that peppered reports from witnesses, members of the military, and international civil servants present on the ground after the war.[12] Other countries, such as Yugoslavia, Italy, and Greece, were ravaged by civil war, which lasted until 1949 in Greece.

THE TWO PARTS OF POSTWAR EUROPE

Practically nothing but ruins were left of insurgent Warsaw, while 27 percent of Budapest was destroyed. Between 25 and 35 percent of the industrial and agricultural production capacity of Poland and Hungary was destroyed, as was a substantial portion of transportation infrastructure, such as roads, bridges, and railroads, including 75 percent of Polish railroads, 70 percent of horses, and the vast majority of the truck and tractor fleet.[13] There were only two hundred trucks in Yugoslavia in 1944. Human losses were enormous, ranging between 10 and 20 percent for Yugoslavia, Greece, Poland, and the USSR. In the latter, accounts by UNRRA employees, who were unlikely to be sympathetic toward the Communist regime, painted a picture of a devastated country populated by survivors. In addition to the fourteen million soldiers who had died in combat or as a result of their wounds, or who were exterminated in Nazi prisoner camps, there were ten million civilian casualties of war due to repression by the German Army, malnutrition, and Stalin's purges. Some seventy thousand villages and seventeen hundred cities were entirely destroyed; thirty-one thousand factories were dismantled; and seventeen million cows and twenty-seven million goats and sheep perished.

Peace did not bring an end to destitution. In the East, many essential products were lacking, such as milk for children. In cities, rations were often below the threshold of one thousand calories per day. Malnutrition and even famine were accompanied by the risk of epidemics, which were exacerbated by the fact that retreating German armies had destroyed or pillaged hospitals. Tuberculosis was endemic, a typhus epidemic was incubating in Poland, and malaria was raging in Yugoslavia and Ukraine.

Reconstruction promised to be perilous. In the West, prewar social and political elites were facing criticism, but former structures were largely preserved.[14] In the East, society was deeply shaken by the war. Crimes and population displacement upset the already fragile ethnic and social balances of newly formed states. In Poland, the Baltic states, and Yugoslavia, the lack of labor primarily hindered reconstruction at first; Polish authorities counted approximately 250,000 war invalids and 350,000 civilian invalids, whose working capacity was sorely needed to rebuild the country.[15] This was compounded by the disappearance of most economic and cultural elites, whom the Nazi and Stalinist regimes had willfully eliminated. The annihilation of Jews and the expulsion of German-speaking populations represented a loss for the economies of these countries, one that is impossible to estimate: half of all Polish doctors had disappeared, as had a quarter of specialists in sectors such as telecommunications, along with the vast majority of urban craftspeople.[16] Future generations were not spared. It was in Eastern Europe that the issue of orphans was the most concerning, as 500,000 Polish children and 300,000 Yugoslav children had lost both parents. Establishing structures to house and reeducate children traumatized by the war was an urgent need in these countries.

Germany, whose permanent destruction was sought by both U.S. advisor Hans Morgenthau and Stalin, rebuilt quickly, prompting persistent and profound fear throughout the East. This was especially true in Poland, whose western border was definitively recognized only after German reunification via treaty in September and November 1990. On the other hand, the weakening of the former enemy presented a considerable threat for the economic balance of the entire continent, especially in Eastern Europe and the Balkans. These countries faced a strange paradox: they were freed of Nazi domination but dangerously destabilized economically by the loss of the German market, on which they had become highly dependent. UNECE observers stressed that the destruction of Germany would heighten inequality between the two parts of Europe.[17]

It was because Eastern European leaders, including in the Soviet Union, were painfully aware of their weaknesses and fragility that they accepted the founding of UNECE in 1947 and attended its first meeting in Paris in June of that year, where the forms and conditions of Marshall Plan aid would be discussed. What Eastern European countries expected was the aid promised by the Allied powers during the war.

OFFERING RELIEF FIRST

As was the case after World War I, aid initially came mostly from the United States. Under the resolute leadership of Herbert Hoover, the American Relief Administration (ARA) had implemented emergency assistance, which served as a major inspiration for the operations planned after World War II.[18] As in 1918, relief was initially directed toward Central Europe, which was seen as a sensitive area through which invasions, revolutions, and epidemics descended on Europe. Unlike the ARA, however, UNRRA was an international agency—it was simultaneously the first UN agency and the

THE TWO PARTS OF POSTWAR EUROPE

final initiative of Roosevelt's New Deal. Strangely forgotten in histories of the period, UNRRA nevertheless provides fertile ground for understanding some of its key issues. Its dissolution shines new light on this pivotal period, between the end of the war alliance and the beginning of the postwar world.

From One War to Another: Central Europe First

While UNRRA was in keeping with the tradition of the ARA, it was different in a number of respects. The ARA was criticized for its partiality, and for having openly pursued a political objective by supporting the Polish marshal Józef Piłsudski in his fight against the Red Army. It was also criticized for being overly bureaucratic, too exclusively American, and far removed from the reality on the ground, and for intervening too late.[19] The relief effort implemented in 1943 was different from that of 1918 with regard to these three points.

In August 1940, in a famous speech before the House of Commons, Churchill envisioned using the economic surplus of countries at peace—and that of the United States in particular—to assist, upon their liberation, those countries that had suffered Nazi occupation and pillaging. Attention turned once again to Central European countries.[20] Great Britain and the United States jointly discussed the first projects in 1941. Britain's Anthony Eden proposed establishing an agency that would guide the transition toward peace, while the economist Frederick Leith Ross assumed leadership of a committee tasked with estimating the needs of various countries and establishing an inter-Allied operational organization. In the United States, the Department of State conducted various studies beginning in September 1941 to assess the needs of occupied populations in terms of essential products such as food, clothing, and medicine. In November 1942 Roosevelt established the Office of Foreign Relief and Rehabilitation Operations (OFRRO), which was led by a close ally, Herbert Lehman, the former governor of New York. Initially under the supervision of the Department of State, in early 1943 OFRRO became an Anglo-American agency tasked with offering relief to war victims in the regions liberated by Allied forces. When contacted by Ross, Soviet leaders insisted on the need for an organization with multilateral governance in which they would be represented.[21] This would be UNRRA.

The new organization was created in November 1943 under the management of Herbert Lehman, five months after the UN Conference on Food and Agriculture, which brought together forty-four nations against the Axis in the small city of Hot Springs, Virginia, from May 18 to June 3, 1943. Confident of their victory, at the conference the representatives of these nations declared—in keeping with Roosevelt's speech on the four liberties—a war on hunger and misery.[22] The founding of UNRRA was in line with the dynamic of the Hot Springs conference: it made OFRRO, the first UN agency, international, including with respect to governance, and pursued the objective of economic and social justice from the beginning.

UNRRA: A Bridge Between East and West

The new agency aimed to assist liberated populations by providing emergency aid, and by promoting the reconstruction and development of war-torn countries. It also addressed the difficult issue of how to manage and return refugees. UNRRA was funded by a voluntary contribution from governments amounting to 1 percent of the gross domestic product (GDP) of unoccupied countries.[23] Due to its economic might, the United States was one of the new organization's primary backers, contributing approximately 73 percent of the value of shipments of essential products and equipment; with Great Britain and Canada, it accounted for 94 percent of contributions. In December 1946 UNRRA employed over twenty-one thousand people, including more than fifteen hundred volunteers, who were often women.[24] Britons made up 34 percent of the international staff and U.S. citizens 37 percent, including many New Deal experts.

While its governance was international, UNRRA was clearly a U.S.-British consortium. It broadly benefited from the technical know-how developed in the international organizations of the Geneva system; some of its leading figures came from the staff of the League of Nations, especially from its Health Section, including its founder and former director Ludwik Rajchman, who joined UNRRA as a representative of the Polish government.[25] The new UN agencies that took up the baton from UNRRA in 1948 took full advantage of the know-how accumulated by its staff. The relief agency thus served as a conduit between the Geneva system and that of New York, between the League of Nations and the UN.

THE TWO PARTS OF POSTWAR EUROPE

UNRRA intervened in seventeen areas or countries, chiefly in Europe, but also in China, India, the Philippines, the Middle East, and Ethiopia. In Europe, aside from Italy, which received the equivalent of $418 million in deliveries, it was countries in Eastern and southeastern Europe that were priority recipients of international aid, especially Poland ($478 million), Yugoslavia ($415 million), Greece ($347 million), and Czechoslovakia ($261.3 million), with Ukraine ($188 million) and Belarus ($61 million) receiving comparatively less. UNRRA provided people in these countries with emergency aid such as medicine, food, and clothing, as well as the means to ensure their subsistence over the long term, including seeds and tractors. UNRRA also launched programs for equipment for transport, agriculture, and even industry.

The choice of country was undeniably governed by the scope of the needs, but it was also in keeping with the cordon sanitaire tradition that began after 1917, as it was a matter of stemming epidemics, typhus in particular, and preventing misery from putting the population on the road to revolt. While the motivations were similar, the practices used on the ground by the organization's staff nevertheless show a different approach. UNRRA employees, who were social workers and sometimes also trained in anthropology, were more attuned to the realities on the ground, and more respectful of the distinctive social and cultural features of the population, as well as the policy orientations of their governments.[26] Unlike the practices developed by the ARA after World War I, UNRRA deliberately relied on local administrations, which were more in touch with the reality in the field and better able to deliver relief. In the words of its directors: "It was not within UNRRA provenience to regulate the domestic economies of the countries to which it rendered assistance. In the last analysis, recovery in each country depended on the way in which the government and the people managed their own affairs with the assistance of the supplies provided from abroad."[27] The agency thus served as a bridge between the East and the West, one that consisted of a fleet of ships and trucks continually circulating between the United States, Canada, Great Britain, and Europe. In late 1946 no less than eighty thousand trucks arrived in Eastern Europe from North America. This bridge was not easily built and remained fragile.

The Yugoslav and Soviet governments actually began by refusing the aid, which was seen as an intrusion into their internal affairs, before finally accepting it on the condition they could control its use. In the United States, and to a lesser degree Great Britain, UNRRA was quickly accused of "feeding" communism.

This suspicion reflected a powerful anticommunism in the United States, which assumed more compulsive forms from 1945 onward.[28] This is demonstrated in a report by Arthur Kemp, an aide to the former Republican president Herbert Hoover. Written in 1946, its purpose was to prepare the mission that Hoover, former head of the ARA, was undertaking at the request of President Truman: namely, to assess U.S. programs in Europe and the occupation of Germany.[29] Aside from its virulent anticommunism, the scathing criticism that Kemp directed at UNRRA activities was part of the challenge to multilateralism and international organizations in certain conservative circles in the United States. This criticism focused specifically on two points: its governance gave too much weight to recipient countries, which did not contribute to its efforts, and not enough to the United States, its primary backer; and its staff consisted of too many social workers, who were not qualified to manage its programs, and too few accounting administrators. This criticism was first and foremost political: for its enemies, UNRRA was chiefly an instrument in the hands of Communists; it fueled subversion inside the United States, while in assisted countries the delegation of power conceded to authorities helped fill, via the black market, the coffers of the Communist Parties installed in power by Soviet authorities.

The End of UNRRA and Promises of Prosperity for All

UNRRA had been conceived, from its very beginnings, as a temporary administration whose activities would come to an end in 1946. The sharp criticism leveled in the United States and Great Britain made this end unavoidable. When the U.S. Congress refused to pass additional funding, the organization was condemned. Its dissolution was pursued during the fifth session of its council in August 1946, despite requests from delegates from Central Europe and the Balkans—Poland, Czechoslovakia, Yugoslavia, and Greece—who argued for continuing aid programs. It was with astonishment and despair that former UNRRA employees, who could not be suspected of having sympathy for Communists, witnessed the severing of relations with Eastern Europe. As a result of rising anticommunism, which culminated a few years later in McCarthyism—with the House

THE TWO PARTS OF POSTWAR EUROPE

Un-American Activities Committee serving as its instrument since 1938—some of these former employees had to defend themselves before the various investigative committees created to assess the loyalty of civil servants in the Truman administration. A number of them even had to resign from positions in the U.S. government.[30]

The organization was dismantled between 1946 and 1948, leaving Eastern European countries, and Poland in particular, in a critical economic and social situation. To be sure, UNRRA helped check epidemics, famine, and absolute deprivation, but its early termination prevented the completion of programs for reconstruction as well as agricultural and industrial modernization, which were originally part of its mandate and had been partially initiated by its teams on the ground.[31] To the great regret of its defenders, UNRRA had offered relief but did not have time to reconstruct.[32] In February 1946 Jan Stańczyk, the Polish minister of labor and social welfare, introduced a resolution to the Economic and Social Council on the reconstruction of countries destroyed by the war.[33]

INTERNATIONAL NETWORKS AND RECONSTRUCTION EFFORTS

When the dissolution of UNRRA was being discussed in August 1946 in Geneva, it was decided that the new agencies of the UN would be entrusted with the various tasks previously performed by UNRRA: issues relating to health would henceforth be the remit of the World Health Organization, refugees would be the responsibility of the High Commissioner for Refugees, and agricultural issues would be handled by the FAO.[34] While Western governments could soon count on the Marshall Plan aid that would arrive in Western Europe beginning in 1948, those in Eastern Europe continued to depend on international, intergovernmental, and private aid. The connections and relations established before the war played an important role in gaining access to these, as demonstrated by the specific case of the Rockefeller Foundation.

The Rockefeller Foundation in Postwar Central Europe

Central and Eastern European countries, including the USSR, were the preferred recipients of international philanthropy during the interwar period. The Rockefeller Foundation was active in parallel and as a complement to the League of Nations.[35] In addition to a grant program, it supported the creation of multiple training centers for nurses and medical staff. After a long period of isolation due to the occupation, grant requests flowed in from the countries that had suffered the most during the war, with the most urgent need being to develop skills to tackle reconstruction. A foundation director emphasized "the list of fellowships and travel grants shows that many of them were granted to countries which are now classified as Communist, but no distinction was made for any political reason in awarding fellowships and travel grants."[36]

It was following requests from local staff, who were often former fellows, that the foundation assisted the health institutions it had helped found during the interwar period. Most of them were in a state of great material and human misery: buildings and equipment had been badly damaged and even destroyed, students had been dispersed, and some staff had disappeared. To contend with the emergency, in 1947 the foundation awarded $230,000 in aid, 65 percent of which was for health-related projects, with 57 percent of this total being directed to Yugoslavia.[37] Former fellows played an essential role in obtaining these grants, which generally passed through authorities, especially ministries of health. It was via this channel that the foundation's Health Commission provided support for reopening the nursing schools that it had helped found in the city of Zagreb in 1924.[38] Its involvement was event greater for the nursing school in Krakow—the first of its kind in Europe—that had opened with foundation support during the interwar period. The letters exchanged with surviving staff members are marked by great emotion and show the close ties that had been forged between on-site teachers and foundation representatives. Emergency aid of $12,000 was awarded in 1948, officially transiting via the new Communist government's Ministry of Health.[39] The National Institute of Hygiene in Warsaw, founded in 1922 under the direction of Ludwik Rajchman, who later presided over the Health Section of the League of Nations, received a total of $53,000 in funding between 1947 and 1950 to purchase equipment and books.[40] The institute in Budapest founded in 1927 also received a grant upon the request of its director.[41]

In July 1948 John Grant, director for Europe of the foundation's Health Division, provided an optimistic description of his trip to Eastern Europe, noting in particular that "the minister in Prague at the end of the first interview stated that whatever might be the differences of ideologies in economic

THE TWO PARTS OF POSTWAR EUROPE

and political fields, health should provide a cultural bridge in which the same universal ideology held throughout the world."[42]

Aside from the Rockefeller Foundation, other philanthropic networks were active during the immediate postwar period. This was especially true of the Young Men's Christian Association in the United States, which had developed important programs in Central Europe and Czechoslovakia in particular and maintained a correspondent on site. Once again, pivotal figures that were part of reform networks played a crucial role. For Czechoslovakia, this was the theologian Josef Lukl Hromádka, a founding member of the World Council of Churches in 1948. Hromádka served as a go-between until his death in 1969, doing so in the name of a humanist internationalism that transcended Cold War divisions.[43]

Antifascism: Rebuilding and Developing Together

The new international agencies hoped that the transfer of a substantial part of UNRRA staff would ensure the transmission of know-how and permit continuity in its activity. However, UN agencies hardly possessed UNNRA's logistical and material resources. For potential aid recipient countries, accessing their resources and know-how was once again highly dependent on prewar relations, in addition to the maintenance of international expertise. Poland, Czechoslovakia, and Yugoslavia were the only three people's democracies that were UN members.[44] The first two countries had been very active in Geneva organizations and still had international connections. For example, it was because he was very well informed regarding the state of malnutrition among Polish children that Ludwik Rajchman, the former head of the League of Nations Health Section and Poland's representative to UNRRA, took the initiative of establishing an international relief fund for children, which would be supported by UNRRA's remaining budget. This fund, the predecessor of UNICEF, provided powdered milk for children, especially in Poland, Romania, Czechoslovakia, and Yugoslavia, along with Greece and Germany.[45]

The extent of prewar ties was also behind the January 1949 visit to Poland and Czechoslovakia by the director-general of the International Labour Office, David Morse. For supporters of what some referred to at the time as "Iron Curtain theoricians," the visit may seem surprising. Morse was from the United States, and Soviet authorities had consistently shown hostility toward the International Labour Organization, which the USSR did not join until 1954.[46] However, Morse's lengthy report from his visit in the ILO archives, along with reports in the local press of both countries, show the great cordiality of relations. Actors from the International Labour Office—the organization's permanent secretariat—and from Eastern Europe emphasized the strong convergence at play, basing their dialogue on shared convictions, with social justice and above all antifascism serving as pillars.

Morse, who was close to Roosevelt, enlisted in the U.S. Army to fight Nazism, and for his Communist counterparts, he was also one of the liberators of the Mauthausen concentration camp, which was reserved for enemies of the Nazi regime, and in which numerous Communists had been detained. The reference to Mauthausen was thus used to open the discussion between Morse and Eastern European leaders; the Polish prime minister and former socialist Józef Cyrankiewicz mentioned that he had met Morse in Mauthausen, where he had been deported. This meeting is not documented and was probably invented, but it demonstrates the importance of the common fight against fascism in establishing and maintaining cordial relations between U.S. and Communist leaders during the postwar period. Nearly ten years later, in 1958, when Morse met the first secretary of the Communist Party of Czechoslovakia, Antonín Novotný, the latter cordially greeted him by saying that they had probably met each other in Mauthausen, where he had been detained from 1941 to 1945.[47] Once again, nothing attests that this meeting actually occurred, but it played an essential symbolic role. Antifascist solidarity, of which Mauthausen was a powerful symbol, provided a crucial basis for East-West dialogue: it reestablished the centrality of the wartime alliance and gave it meaning, representing a powerful counterweight to the new logic of blocs, which frustrated the internationalist values on which the UN itself was founded.

In addition to the symbolic expression of this shared antifascism, convergence was based on genuine biographical continuity. The people who prepared Morse's trip and accompanied him were already involved in multilateralism before the war; they were often former Social Democrats who had to join the ranks of the Communist Parties in power during forced mergers of the two parties. They put their skills in the service of their country and their new governments.

THE TWO PARTS OF POSTWAR EUROPE

In Poland, the ergonomist Jan Rosner, secretary of the Polish delegation to the International Labour Conference between 1930 and 1933 and later a civil servant at the International Labour Office in 1933, played a central role in reestablishing ties with the ILO. Rosner was the ILO's correspondent in Warsaw between 1946 and 1950 and as such planned Morse's visit.[48] The preservation of active ties between the Czechoslovak Ministries of Social Affairs and Foreign Affairs and the ILO was in keeping with powerful and long-standing relations, which can be explained by the special role Czechoslovak experts played in the field of social security during the interwar period.

Anton Zelenka, a member and later head of the social security department at the International Labour Office, played a pivotal role. He was born in Prague in 1903, where he completed his studies, and in the 1920s and 1930s held management positions in the First Republic's central social security administration. He then joined the office, where he worked in close collaboration with two other Czechoslovak experts who played an essential role in the field of social security during the interwar period: Oswald Stein, director of the office's Social Security Department from 1937 to 1943, and Emil Schönbaum, who helped develop the social security systems of numerous Latin American countries as an expert at the same organization.[49] Zelenka was the representative of the Czechoslovak government at the twenty-eighth International Labour Conference in 1946 and later returned to the office as a civil servant, but this time with Austrian nationality. With Leo Wildmann (who had also become Austrian) and J. Vanek, he was part of a group of exiled Czechoslovak Social Democrats who maintained close contact with their colleagues who had remained in Czechoslovakia, especially Evžen Erban, a former socialist who had become a Communist and served as minister of social affairs and later as director of the Social Security Service.[50]

It was the Zelenka-Erban duo who ensured that Czechoslovakia remained an ILO member when the most Stalinist Czech Communists envisioned its withdrawal.[51] Zelenka completed multiple technical missions to Prague in 1947 and 1948 to accompany reforms to the social security system and provide advice. He believed that this system, which he considered much better than French social security, could serve as an international model. In an unsigned article that appeared in the *International Labour Review* in 1948,

Zelenka affirmed that "the Czechoslovak National Insurance Act represents a step of primary importance in the social legislation of the country. At the same time, it has an important bearing on the development of social security on the international plane. It may finally be noted that the principles proclaimed by the Recommendations of the 26th Session of the International Labour Conference at Philadelphia form the basis of the new system of social security in Czechoslovakia."[52] For Zelenka, Czechoslovak social policy was not first and foremost communist but instead fundamentally international.

The international engagement of certain Central European countries is also reflected in their participation in the UN system, including financially. Poland, Czechoslovakia, and Yugoslavia contributed, despite their misery, to the United Nations Children's Fund and took active part in the work of the Social Commission, which functioned between 1947 and 1950 under the direct authority of ECOSOC. The latter was tasked with continuing the activities of UNRRA in three areas: advising governments, awarding fellowships, and diffusing technical documents relating to social services. It was tasked with developing training and programs for children and invalids, two fragile groups that were particularly important in Central European countries.[53] The commission consisted of eighteen representatives, including delegates from Yugoslavia, Poland, Czechoslovakia, and even the Soviet Union. It was presided over by the Czechoslovak socialist Klaus František, the former minister of social affairs, whom Morse knew well. Until January 1950 the commission had a representative in Warsaw who administered the remaining UNRRA funds in Poland.[54] Its primary objective was to develop a large program for the exchange and circulation among European countries of know-how relating to social work. For Central European countries, it funded a fellowship program that allowed a limited number of social workers specializing in the care and reeducation of war-disabled persons to visit Western European countries better equipped in these matters. This activity also served as a framework for the signing of an agreement between Poland and Czechoslovakia regarding information exchange in this area.[55] However, the commission's modest resources prevented it from effectively helping the institutions that cared for orphans and disabled persons in these countries.

THE TWO PARTS OF POSTWAR EUROPE

In reality, UN agencies had already initiated the transition from reconstruction to development. This is reflected in Morse's various declarations in Poland and Czechoslovakia, where he proposed making the organization's expertise available to these countries, but chiefly to help train their workforce. This same logic governed the FAO mission to Poland in 1947.

The FAO Mission to Poland in 1947

On February 8, 1947, the Polish government, which was facing a major food crisis, asked the FAO "to study the economic and technical issues relating to the rehabilitation of Polish agriculture and industry." The mission sent to Poland between July 4 and September 4, 1947, consisted of ten people (among them five from the United States and Canada, one from Ireland, and one from Holland) who were agriculture specialists at their respective ministries. Its goal was to provide a list of recommendations to improve food production, especially for children and youth.

The mission, which was accompanied by a Polish committee, traveled in UNRRA vehicles and conducted a meticulous field survey involving a series of visits and interviews. The mission's report emphasized the great freedom given to FAO delegates, as well as the "admirably constructive spirit" that presided over debates. In their conclusions, the experts identified the country's fertilizer needs in order to increase agricultural productivity, which were all the more pressing considering that the decimation of livestock had deprived peasants of natural fertilizer and children of dairy products, a deficiency that was poorly compensated for by emergency powdered milk.

The mission encouraged the Polish government to ask for an international loan. It stressed, however, that too much relief would impede productive efforts. As indicated in the introduction to the report, the goal of the FAO mission was to "encourage national action and development."[56] The UN had clearly entered a new phase, with the overarching logic now being one of development rather than reconstruction. This discourse was also that of UNECE, which was founded in 1947, and whose philosophy was largely in keeping with the pan-European planning projects of the interwar period.

ORGANIZING AND DEVELOPING EUROPE

Pan-European Plans from Wartime

Informed by the experience of World War I, the political leaders of powers hostile to Nazism became convinced quite early on that preparations for peace had to be coordinated internationally. In the United States, numerous political leaders were persuaded that the treaties emerging from World War I failed essentially due to a lack of international planning and an inability to correctly address the global problems that grew out of the war.[57]

In May 1940 Arthur Greenwood was tasked with coordinating reconstruction plans in Churchill's war cabinet. More broadly, the goal of reconstruction provided an opportunity for long-term international mobilization and inspired a planist and modernizing turning point within postwar internationalism. In this context, some agencies from the Geneva system that were present on the American continent succeeded in imposing themselves as important actors despite drastic cuts to staff and resources.[58] This was especially true of the League of Nations Economic and Financial Section, which was set up in Princeton in 1940 thanks to support from the Rockefeller Foundation and the ILO, and whose secretariat was housed by McGill University with assistance from the Canadian government.[59]

In late October 1941 the ILO, which was the only international organization from the League that was still functioning, held an international conference in New York with support from the U.S. government, and especially Secretary of Labor Frances Perkins. This conference was in keeping with the Atlantic Charter of August 1941: it sought to mobilize the people of the American continent to combat Nazism, and to organize international solidarity for the postwar period. The event was important symbolically, as demonstrated by the large number of countries present: representatives from thirty-five states, including eight European governments in exile, made the trip.[60] Those from the governments of Eastern European and Balkan countries issued a joint declaration emphasizing the scope of the exactions committed by German armies and authorities and calling for international solidarity for future reconstruction. Relying on commitments made in the Atlantic Charter, U.S. representatives loudly proclaimed their solidarity with the countries most affected by the war—those in Eastern Europe—and promised to act in favor of a more just world. In his opening speech, the Democratic governor of New York, Herbert Lehman, the future director of UNRRA, stressed that the preservation of peace depended on better distribution of resources among nations.[61] In his closing speech, President Roosevelt appealed to the solidarity of the people of the United States, promising genuine economic cooperation among nations for the postwar period, equal access to raw materials, and just trade policy in order to ensure the prosperity of all.

The conference entrusted the ILO with shaping reconstruction policies and ensuring "full collaboration between all nations in the economic field."[62] In 1942 the Eastern European governments in exile submitted reports detailing their needs.[63] Following the conference, the Central and Eastern European Planning Board, which between 1942 and 1945 consisted of representatives—often with a past in the socialist movement—from the governments in exile of Czechoslovakia, Greece, Poland, and Yugoslavia, developed plans for economic recovery and the constitution of a political federation.[64]

In 1943 the Royal Institute for International Affairs in Great Britain held a seminar led by Polish economist Paul Rosenstein-Rodan to establish figures for the destruction in Eastern Europe and identify economic recovery projects for the governments of these countries. Beyond strict reconstruction, these plans sought to bring the region out of its state of underdevelopment, with a view to creating the conditions for a lasting peace based on harmonious economic development in Europe. Rosenstein-Rodan defended its objective in two articles published in 1943 and 1944, in which he argued for priority aid for Eastern Europe, whose development could subsequently serve as a model for the rest of the world.[65]

Dirigiste ideas, based on the values of social justice, also permeated the report from the Political and Economic Planning group in Great Britain. The authors once again emphasized the need to couple reconstruction and development in Eastern and Southern Europe, in order to promote the good economic health of these countries as well as that of the entire continent.

For that matter, it was in hopes of having specific reconstruction and development plans proposed for them that representatives from Europe's eastern periphery (Yugoslavia, Czechoslovakia, Poland) took part in Bretton Woods negotiations in 1944. There they formulated pressing requests for financial assistance to rebuild their countries and expressed support for development aid based on industrialization policies overseen by the state.[66]

Conceived of as replicas of the New Deal, such projects were strongly supported by U.S. secretary of labor Frances Perkins, along with the progressives from her team.[67] They were in keeping with plans to combat the economic crisis of the 1930s implemented in the United States and European countries and that were developed in international arenas. To pull Europe out of the crisis, in the early 1930s Albert Thomas, the first director of the International Labour Office, proposed major pan-European works projects financed by the Bank for International Settlements. These projects gave prominence to equipping the underdeveloped European peripheries of the south and east. The projects never saw the light of day, nor for that matter did those developed between 1942 and 1945.[68] A number of reasons explain this failure, well before the outbreak of the Cold War, with changes to power relations in the United States playing a decisive role. Beginning with the U.S. entry in the war, the planist solution promoted by Roosevelt's team ran into strong opposition. In August 1943 Congress decided, by a small majority, not to renew funding for the National Resources Planning Board, anticipating the end of the New Deal.[69] This vote reflected a change to the political balance in Washington, where members of the military and major industrialists now joined forces to block planist projects.[70]

Planning Reconstruction or Liberalizing Trade

These political changes actually reveal the outlines of a new world in which the social and solidary message of the Atlantic Charter had already lost its force. The ILO was gradually stripped of all power in postwar planning, while projects for free trade—initially developed by experts from the Economic Section of the League of Nations with the support of British authorities—emerged as a solution for organizing economic recovery. These plans saw the liberalization of global trade as a guarantee of peace and a solution to the unemployment that demobilization would cause. However, they exposed less economically developed countries to competition from more advanced economies.[71] To meet the demands of these countries, especially given Latin America's involvement in the war effort, the project for an International Trade Organization was discussed in Havana in 1947–1948. In line with the promises made during the war, this organization was supposed to promote oversight of global free trade, as well as to encourage international social policy and development aid. Its failure to pass in the

THE TWO PARTS OF POSTWAR EUROPE

U.S. Congress between 1948 and 1950, however, condemned the project. At the same time, the development plans discussed at Bretton Woods were abandoned, as economists closer to the world of finance rose to the leadership of the World Bank and the International Monetary Fund.[72]

The planist debates during wartime ultimately gave rise to a world "organized" by free trade. In this world, less industrialized countries, those on the periphery—the Global South and to a lesser degree Eastern Europe—found themselves in a global market competing with more powerful and developed economies.[73] For Eastern European countries, the situation was aggravated by the Cold War logic that prevailed in the international economic organizations dominated by the United States. For instance, the Polish government's loan request at the World Bank in 1947 was rejected despite support from the FAO and UNECE.[74] Czechoslovakia, which was accused of concealing information, was forced to withdraw from the World Bank in 1954.

Planist solutions—projects for organization and development—were not entirely abandoned within international organizations. The pan-European discourse of economic rebalancing was maintained within UNECE, as were projects organizing economic exchange.

The Pan-European Projects of the Economic Commission for Europe

UNECE was the first regional UN agency and initially included eighteen countries: UN member countries along with the United States and Turkey. Non-UN member countries, as was the case in the East with Hungary, Bulgaria, Romania, and later the GDR, were invited to take part in the discussions as observers.

Created in March 1947, UNECE took over for the previous organizations that had emerged to manage the transition from a wartime to a peacetime economy: the European Coal Organization, which emerged from Allied military organizations; the Solid Fuel Division of Supreme Headquarters Allied Expeditionary Force; the European Central Inland Transport Organization; and the Emergency Economic Committee for Europe.[75]

The need to merge these organizations into a single enduring structure became pressing with the dissolution of UNRRA, and it was not by chance that Polish representatives played a crucial role in this respect. Jacek Rudziński, who directed the Polish delegation to the UN, insistently requested the creation of a pan-European economic organization in which Poland could maintain its economic relations with Eastern and Western Europe, and that would protect against potential and dreaded German revanchist aggression. Aside from the Poles, Czechoslovak political leaders, who wanted to protect their export economy, were very favorably disposed toward such an organization. Czechoslovakia, the only Central European country to be a member of the General Agreement on Tariffs and Trade (GATT), actually conducted the majority of its foreign trade with Western Europe until the 1960s. Rudziński was at the intersection of pan-European movements and networks. From the time of his exile in London, he had kept numerous contacts in the West with representatives on the left. In Poland he was an influential economist, vice president of the Planning Committee, and an advisor to Hilary Minc, the minister of industry and commerce until 1956; he subsequently played an important role in establishing the Council for Mutual Economic Assistance (Comecon), which served as a framework for coordinating economic exchange in Eastern Europe. In the West, this project was supported by Keynesians, who were dominant at the time in international arenas, and who stressed the need for economic complementarity between Eastern and Western Europe. The U.S. economist Walter Rostow, who referred to himself as the brains behind UNECE, indicated he was part of a movement favorable to pan-European reconstruction that avoided the bias of diplomacy.[76] He supported the nomination of Swedish economist Gunnar Myrdal as the head of the new organization's secretariat in August 1947 and became his aide before stepping aside for his brother, the legal scholar Eugene Rostow. Myrdal was a representative of planism and was open to the experiment being conducted in Eastern Europe; as minister of commerce of Sweden between 1945 and 1947, he encouraged trade relations with the USSR.[77] He embodied a current of social democracy well represented within the Internationale Gruppe Demokratischer Sozialisten (International Group of Democratic Socialists), of which he had been a member alongside Willy Brandt and Bruno Kreisky. Within this resistance movement, which was created in 1942, he frequented Central European socialists in exile, some of whom joined Communist Parties in the East during the forced merged of Social Democratic and Communist Parties between 1946 and 1948. These socialists in exile defended the economic, social, and political promises made by the Atlantic Charter. They were attached to internationalism and the preservation of the wartime alliance and were united by antifascism.[78] UNECE was one of the spaces where this spirit endured.

Myrdal, Walter Rostow, and Nicholas Kaldor, the chief economist at the new UNECE, who believed that political preconceptions and opposition could be overcome by developing a common language, contributed to what has been defined as technocratic internationalism.[79] This technicization of problems enabled UNECE to function as a space of communication between the East and the West. Myrdal carefully avoided any publicity during the meetings of technical committees in connection with coal, wood, transport, and housing, which became spaces where a shared language was developed over the course of meetings.[80] For instance, the Coal Committee established a classification and an international typology for coke that is still in use today. This common technical language was the basis for exchange between European countries.

For Walter Rostow, UNECE's raison d'être was genuine complementarity between the economies of Eastern and Western Europe. In 1948 he declared: "The economic basis for the ECE rests in the fact that, beneath the surface of national and regional economic plans, beneath the surface of exacerbated political tension, there exists an important range of common European economic interests which it is to the advantage of no European government to deny."[81] In the context of the postwar period and the economic ruin of Germany, this complementarity was particularly obvious in the coal industry.

The UNECE secretariat insisted on the need to develop the production and export of Polish coal to Western Europe, and it was incidentally Jan Ciszewski of Poland who directed the coal division, one of UNECE's most important and effective ones. Polish involvement in this commission was in line with Eastern European demands regarding the reconstruction of devastated countries; in fact, the Polish delegation included an amendment stating that the future UNECE should prioritize the reconstruction of the countries that suffered the worst damage during the war, with the reestablishment of the coal industry being an essential objective for Poland.[82] Beginning in 1948, Polish experts tried to use their presence on this subcommittee, as well as the preservation of trade relations with the West, as counterweights to Soviet dominance over their country's economy.

In the initial phase, the enemy was still Germany, with Polish and Soviet representatives seeing the development of trade with the West as a way of avoiding renewed German monopoly over the economies of Europe's eastern periphery.[83] Guided by the same objective, Walter Rostow encouraged economic cooperation between Eastern European countries, as well as multilateral rather than bilateral trade relations between the continent's east and west. Even though the commerce commission was only created in 1954, the development of commerce between the two parts of Europe became an essential objective of the UNECE secretariat's policy. There were also precise technical projects for promoting connections between the two parts of Europe, for instance in the road and electricity sectors.[84] This policy was governed by the resumption of exchange on a multilateral basis. Western Europe received approximately a fourth of its imports from Eastern Europe in 1938, but this proportion fell to one-fourteenth in 1949; while there were bilateral agreements between Great Britain and Poland (for coal), or between Switzerland and Czechoslovakia, they remained modest in relation to the quantities exchanged before the war.[85]

The decline of pan-European exchange led to the excessive dependence of Western European countries on the United States. For Rostow, as for Myrdal and in general for UNECE economists, reestablishing a pan-European market was essential to liberating Western Europe from the economic domination of the United States, and Eastern Europe from Soviet domination. Until 1953 the USSR was not very present at UNECE, whereas the people's democracies were well represented. During his trip to Poland, Czechoslovakia, and Yugoslavia in August and September 1948, Rostow stressed the importance that officials in the Ministries of Commerce and Foreign Affairs ascribed to reestablishing and developing trade relations with the West and noted their concern regarding the increasingly hostile policy of U.S. authorities. Overall he emphasized—often with surprise— the seriousness and competence of the officials he met, in addition to their curiosity and generally very warm welcome.[86]

Trade was not an end in itself, however, and Myrdal believed that the resumption of trade relations was closely linked to ending "underdevelopment." In his speech opening the first meeting of the ad hoc committee for industrial development and commerce in September 1947, he emphasized: "The committee has been established in order to achieve practical measures for the restoration and expansion of Intra European trade . . . it is only by fostering economic development throughout Europe both between East and

West and between advanced and backward countries that rapid improvement in production and living standards could be achieved."[87]

In keeping with the reflections of Rosenstein-Rodan during the war, he insisted on the need to overcome unequal development in Europe and to promote rapid industrialization, which would enable these countries to overcome underdevelopment: "Europe is going forward not back and Poland Czechoslovakia and Yugoslavia particularly will and should be more industrialized than before, a new balance between East and West must come. But it will not be the old one that left the East in a semi-colonial state."[88] Likewise, during his trip to Central Europe, Rostow stressed in discussions with Polish and Czechoslovak officials the need for a policy of economic development based on encouraging certain industrial sectors: Poland should develop its coal production, and Czechoslovakia could provide spare parts for agricultural machinery and trucks across Europe.

These projects met with the expectations of Communist leaders, for whom industrialization—and economic development in general—were the very foundation on which socialism was constructed. The Soviet Union's delegate insisted on having industrial development be closely linked to the development of trade.[89] But with the launch of the Marshall Plan, the U.S. representative rallied the votes of the Western European countries that had remained reluctant, Sweden included, thereby ensuring the failure of the Soviet proposal.[90] In return, the Soviets opposed the creation of a trade committee, which was ultimately established only in 1954. Deprived of its development component, this committee became, against Myrdal's wishes, a multilateral platform for organizing trade relations within the European space. This evolution, which was in line with the policy reorientation observed globally, de facto placed Eastern bloc countries, which were economically less developed, in a dominated position.[91]

The point of view offered by international organizations provides a different account for the period between 1945 and 1949. It is clear that 1947 did not represent a clean break: as we have seen, UNECE, the FAO, the International Labour Office, and even the Rockefeller Foundation launched numerous international and pan-European projects in 1947 and ensuing years. One could no doubt cite more examples by including other international spaces. Because international organizations—and their secretariats in particular—were essentially places of circulation and exchange, this "break" in 1947 had to contend with the preservation of networks and solidarities from the war, and even from the interwar period. These enabled the pursuit, even when hindered, of pan-European projects, which continued alongside the emergence of blocs. They were inspired by an internationalist ideal that had its roots in the struggle against the crisis in the 1930s, and then in the common fight against fascism during the war. They found concrete expression in the plans developed during the war. This ideal was driven by networks of actors, with the socialist/social democratic movement playing an essential role in both Eastern and Western Europe.

In both parts of Europe, and especially in the East, these actors tried to escape the domination of the hegemonic powers that were the United States and the Soviet Union. The Poles and Czechoslovaks in the East, and the Swedes and Norwegians in the West, played a particularly important role in this respect. This first group was joined by U.S. nationals from the New Deal administration, who were gradually marginalized in the United States and sought to diffuse their projects for organizing the economy and society on the international level. They were initially part of UNRRA in large numbers, and later in UN agencies, especially the ILO, WHO, and FAO. The representatives of this broad socialist and progressive movement, who were often Keynesian economists, were united in preserving an antifascist orientation in keeping with the Atlantic Charter, which reinforced their belief in the need to organize a more harmonious and solidary world.

While they were dominant in international spaces, they were nevertheless not alone. The end of UNRRA underscored the difficulties faced by activists for a powerful multilateralism. Within the Bretton Woods institutions dominated by the United States, actors opposed to national and international regulation could see the division of the world into two blocs as an opportunity to preserve the domination of economically and politically less powerful countries. Seen as intergovernmental agencies and diplomatic forums, international organizations were not exclusively "enchanted palaces," spaces for building and spreading the internationalist ideal they claimed to personify. They were also instruments for preserving the domination of the most powerful states, in this case the United States and Great

Britain, and to a lesser degree the Soviet Union.[92] This is demonstrated by the role of major powers within the UN Security Council, as well as the thorny discussions that preceded its implementation.[93] It is in this respect that they can also be seen as spaces of—and instruments for—the unfolding of the Cold War.

Chapter Two

THE EMERGENCE OF A "SECOND WORLD"

Center and Periphery

Between 1948 and 1953 Asia became the epicenter of conflicts between two political systems. The victory won by the Communist leader Mao Zedong over the Nationalist troops of the U.S.-backed Kuomintang paved the way for the proclamation of the People's Republic of China in October 1949. It was immediately recognized by the USSR, with which it signed a "friendship, alliance, and mutual assistance" treaty in February 1950. However, it did not join the United Nations and the Security Council until 1971, when it did so in place of Taiwan, which had the support of Western governments. Following the aggression of North Korea on June 25, 1950, the armies of the two Korean states engaged in a deadly war that continued until July 1953. North Korean armies were supported by a Sino-Soviet coalition, and those of the South by an alliance under the military command of the United States, which provided nearly 90 percent of troops but fought under the UN flag.[1] The division of Korea in Asia mirrored that of Germany in Europe. The creation of the German Democratic Republic in October 1949 was a response to the establishment of the Federal Republic of Germany in May of the same year. It was only in 1973 that the two German states joined the UN, although during the 1950s the FRG was admitted to all of the UN's specialized agencies, where, in conformity with the Hallstein Doctrine promoted by the country's Christian Democratic political leaders, it claimed to represent all of Germany.[2] The FRG became a full-fledged member of

THE EMERGENCE OF A "SECOND WORLD"

UNECE in 1956, while the GDR possessed observer status and continued to be referred to as the "Soviet occupation zone."

These examples illustrate the imbalance of power, as well as how the UN functioned as a space and even an instrument of the Cold War, to the benefit of the Western bloc. With this in mind, repeated use of the veto by Soviet authorities—and even the empty chair policy in the 1950s—was first the expression of their relative powerlessness.[3] It is this imbalance that I will explore first, by asking how the UN, which was born from the wartime alliance, became a space in the late 1940s for the marginality of socialist states, which were relegated to the periphery of the world. By *periphery* I mean a marginal and even dominated position within the international system. I have borrowed this term from development economists, who, beginning in the 1950s, shed light on the relation between geographical periphery and economic dependence.[4] The term underscores the relation between the political marginality of Eastern Europe within the international system and its relative underdevelopment over the long term, as well as its economic dependence on the continent's west, Germany in particular.[5] During the Cold War the Communist leaders of Eastern European states affirmed that they had been freed of this dependence, but their peripheral position endured in renewed forms. In this chapter I will draw attention to some of these forms of dependence. The establishment of regional international organizations in the wake of the Marshall Plan made it possible to organize an economic embargo against the East, as well as to structure a powerful and protected economic space in contradiction to the ideology of free trade, which was nevertheless the foundation of the Bretton Woods agreements and continued to shape the economic discourse of Westerners.[6] Regional organizations in the East were an imperfect response to Western initiatives; Comecon, which was founded in January 1949 in response to Marshall aid and the creation in April 1948 of the Organisation for European Economic Co-operation (OEEC), essentially served at the time as a framework for bilateral economic relations between the USSR and people's democracies.[7] The signing of the North Atlantic Treaty in April 1949 made the constitution of a Western military bloc official; the Warsaw Pact provided a partial and belated response in May 1955. While they were not equivalent, these regional organizations nevertheless played a role in the constitution of blocs and became instruments for affirming two competing socioeconomic models of organization, each claiming universality in the name of specific values: liberty and justice for the West, peace and equality for the East. It was on the basis of these values—on the creation of a political and social countermodel—that socialist states escaped their marginality within international organizations.

While the previous chapter analyzed international organizations as active spaces for pan-European construction during the late 1940s, this chapter will explore how they became spaces for and instruments of Cold War oppositions during the years 1949–1954. This inversion of my aims was inspired by a change in chronology but was especially driven by a methodological shift. The previous chapter focused on what organizations did through the activities of their permanent secretariats; this chapter first grasps them as diplomatic forums subject to power relations, constituted as instruments of domination by more powerful states.

Due to these oppositions between states, symbolized by repeated Soviet vetoes at the UN Security Council, contemporary observers often described this period as that of the paralysis of the international system. I would like to explore the hypothesis that the Cold War helped strengthen the visibility of international organizations, which in return "organized" and staged the Cold War.[8]

COMMUNIST STATES ON THE WORLD'S PERIPHERY

Between 1949 and 1954 the pan-European initiatives that still existed, such as those of UNECE, collided with the reality of Europe's division. This challenging of internationalist projects that had emerged from the wartime alliance reflected a fear, shared by both Soviet and U.S. political leaders, directed toward an international system that they saw as a possible check on their sovereignty and power. In line with the Wilsonian project and the Geneva institutions established in 1919, however, the international system was largely organized by and for countries of the Atlantic Arc. Between 1949 and 1954 the socialist states gradually constituted a Second World on the periphery of the First.[9]

Who Is Afraid of Internationalism?

Stalin clearly showed his opposition to any kind of international project, including within his own bloc.[10] This is demonstrated, for example, by the

THE EMERGENCE OF A "SECOND WORLD"

incomplete nature of the Cominform founded in 1947, whose role was quite different than that of the Comintern, as well as by the hesitations surrounding the launch of Comecon, which truly functioned only from 1961 onward.[11] Stalin was also opposed to any federative type of construction or delegation of power within the western periphery of the USSR.[12] Instead of federalism and multilateralism, he preferred a bilateral policy of submission and control of the Communist Parties and elites of Central Europe, military and police elites in particular. This was done by sending Soviet "advisors," whose chief function was to implement security institutions: police and army based on the model present in the USSR.[13] This blockage was also the expression of the deep mistrust among Soviet elites toward international networks, which they feared they could not control.[14] In the people's democracies, the Communists who were the most connected internationally and exposed to "foreign influence" were the first victims of purges. The accusation of "cosmopolitanism," behind which lurked a state-sanctioned anti-Semitism, was at its apex.[15]

In general, Soviet political elites, and those who rose to power in people's democracies, had a limited international culture and were ill-prepared to be part of circles that required knowledge of foreign languages and familiarity with multilateral diplomacy.[16] The various ministries were poorly equipped to respond to the requests for documentation and expertise emanating from UN specialized agencies, which made no effort to adapt to the cognitive or cultural frameworks of leaders from socialist countries. Soviet diplomacy was decapitated after the Stalinist purges, and new diplomats who trained on the job had poor mastery of the profession and foreign languages, especially the English that took hold in international organizations.[17] Amazasp Arutiunian, the head of the Soviet delegation to the UN, had studied in the United States during the interwar period and was one of the rare Soviets able to express himself in this language. During discussions in Geneva and New York, he repeatedly emphasized that he struggled to have his colleagues in the USSR understand the type of cooperation expected of them.[18] For the very same reasons, the USSR's domination over countries on its western border—which was violently imposed on the ground—assumed incomplete and paradoxical forms on the international stage. This is reflected, for instance, in the social activities division of the UN's Economic and Social Council. Beginning in 1948, leaders of Eastern European countries began to favor the exchange of expertise with the USSR, in an effort to yield to Soviet leaders.[19] Soviet authorities, however, seemed incapable of meeting these demands: they struggled to provide experts and were in no rush to open borders to specialists from the new people's democracies. The negotiations conducted by Henri Laugier, the assistant to the secretary-general of ECOSOC, and Andreï Gromyko, the Security Council ambassador, proved especially complicated and ultimately unsuccessful.[20] These failures attest to the difficulty Soviet leaders had in conceiving and establishing relations other than pure domination with the countries on their western periphery.[21]

The defiance and even hostility of Stalinist Soviet elites toward the international system had immediate repercussions on the everyday functioning of the organizations in which these countries were still present. The International Labour Office could no longer obtain the information needed to monitor the international labor agreements adopted by these states, or to conduct the major annual survey of social security costs, while the documents used to chart trade were no longer sent to the UNECE secretariat. Myrdal signaled that some civil servants in his secretariat had difficulty obtaining visas to travel to Central Europe, and those who were originally from there feared retaliatory measures if they returned.[22] In spite of these restrictions, however, Poles and Czechoslovaks continued—even during the Stalinist period—to maintain economic ties with Western Europe and strove to continue activity with UNECE. Czechoslovak delegates were active in the committees for electricity, steel, transport, and wood and successfully negotiated an agreement on steel with the Belgian government.[23] Like their Polish colleagues, they nevertheless complained about the growing difficulty imposed by Western partners with respect to trade with the East.

Soviet leaders' mistrust of the international organizations of the UN system was broadly shared by large groups within the U.S. political world, which harbored the long-standing suspicion that such organizations were dens of spies in the pay of the USSR and Communists. In 1943 the Federal Bureau of Investigation (FBI) launched a campaign against international institutions. Under the Truman administration it gradually overtook the entire state apparatus and assumed extreme forms between 1950 and 1954 under McCarthyism.[24] Anticommunism turned into an instrument for discrediting multilateralism and its defenders. In 1945 the FBI suspected Harry White, the architect of the Bretton Woods system, of spying for Soviet authorities during World War II. The House Un-American Activities

THE EMERGENCE OF A "SECOND WORLD"

Committee, the armed wing of the anticommunist campaign since 1938, questioned him in August 1948, but no definitive charges were brought against him. In November 1953, however, the U.S. attorney general declared that he had irrefutable evidence against White. These allegations would be confirmed in 1997 by the Moynihan Commission on Government Secrecy.[25]

The context of the early 1950s was highly favorable to such suspicion. In 1950 Senator Joseph McCarthy affirmed that the UN secretariat and its agencies had been infiltrated by Communists. The FBI expanded its surveillance of international civil servants and engaged in a genuine witch hunt. It could count on the cooperation of the UN secretary-general, Trygve Lie of Norway, who accepted the systematic investigation of U.S. staff members. In 1948 Lie refused to renew temporary contracts, and in 1952 he dismissed nine permanent civil servants, who invoked their Fifth Amendment protection and refused to submit to the investigations.[26] UNESCO's Paris secretariat had also been under close State Department surveillance since 1949. Twenty civil servants were investigated, and in 1954 seven of them were dismissed under pressure from the United States, with the assent of Director-General Luther Evans of the United States. The Swedish sociologist and Social Democrat Alva Myrdal, who led the Social Sciences Department, was refused entry to the United States in March 1953.[27] Many other international civil servants from the United States were targeted by this campaign, including the sociologist and physician Milton I. Roemer, a renowned specialist in public health and an indefatigable defender of a social security system. In 1951 he was serving as a WHO medical advisor in Geneva but was stripped of his passport and had to take refuge in Canada, where he helped implement a public health system.[28] Morse, the director-general of the International Labour Office, firmly opposed FBI investigations, but the ILO—which U.S. employers believed was hostile to their interests—was not spared from attack. It was the target of a defamation campaign strongly supported by employer circles, which lasted until 1957.[29] These repeated attacks from various U.S. actors deeply shook the secretariats of international organizations.

Major philanthropic foundations, especially the Rockefeller Foundation, which had a long tradition of exchange with Eastern Europe, did not escape this climate of suspicion. Between 1952 and 1954 the foundation had to respond to the Cox-Reece Commission, which was investigating its activity in the Central European countries that subsequently became Communist.[30] The new fellows who were nationals of these countries faced more difficulty obtaining U.S. visas. The foundation subsequently suggested to the Polish nurses with whom it had long-standing ties to turn to Canada. The nurses did not hide their hostility toward the Sovietization of their country and expressed concern regarding a situation that only increased their isolation.[31] Already in July 1947, a U.S. supplier worried about sending scientific equipment to a country "dominated by the Soviet Union."[32] These difficulties affected major figures close to the Rockefeller Foundation that had long-standing relations with the United States. The Czechoslovak literary critic Dagmar Eisnerova, a specialist on Franz Kafka, received a fellowship but was worried about obtaining a visa, as her preceding application had been denied. She described this as a particularly humiliating experience.[33] Andrija Štampar, a Croatian public health doctor and Rockefeller fellow in the United States between 1931 and 1933, who was later very active in the League of Nations Health Section, served as president of the WHO's first international conference in 1946. Yet in 1947 he secured a visa only with great difficulty, and his spouse was not authorized to travel with him.[34]

In general, Rockefeller Foundation directors, who were perfectly aware of the political situation in Central European countries, were alarmed by these restrictive measures that helped isolate the elites in the East and push them into the arms of the Soviet Union. This was particularly true of Czechoslovakia, where intellectuals, who had not forgotten how their country was abandoned after the Munich Agreement in September 1938, felt betrayed by the West once again.

As a result, the foundation found itself the subject of criticism on the ground. Beginning with the interwar period, its medical policies focusing on disease eradication were criticized as being poorly adapted to the social realities of countries on Europe's peripheries. During the late 1940s Communists, and even some of their socialist allies, increasingly saw it as a representative of "American imperialism." In Yugoslavia, Štampar, whose conception of social medicine developed from his experience in rural Macedonia and from his contact with Chinese peasants during technical assistance missions for the League of Nations Health Commission, criticized it for seeking to "enforce an American Standard of nursing."[35] In this tense climate, foundation directors felt that the commission could no

THE EMERGENCE OF A "SECOND WORLD"

longer peacefully conduct its mission.[36] Facing hostility from local authorities and blockage from the U.S. administration, the foundation withdrew
from Central Europe in the early 1950s.

The U.S. campaign against Eastern European countries was largely based
on the idea that the Communist world represented a "monolith," a united
bloc dominated by the Soviet Union's imperialist desires.[37] International
organizations instead, however, show the withdrawal and gradual marginalization of Communists, as well as their renunciation of the conquering
internationalism of the 1920s.

International Organizations and the Triumph of Liberal Internationalism

Myrdal, who was a fervent supporter of dialogue with the Communist leaders of Eastern Europe, stressed in a 1953 letter to Adrian Pelt, director of
the UN office in Geneva, that Eastern European countries had generally
not taken part in the technical work of UNECE since 1950, and as such he
had had little contact with the political authorities of these countries, other
than encouraging them to participate more in his organization's work. This
affirmation was exaggerated, but between 1949 and 1953 Eastern European
countries—even those that were the most present on the international
stage—did gradually withdraw from specialized agencies. In early 1950 the
UN's director of social affairs for Eastern Europe left Warsaw, and all international organization offices in the city closed.[38] Czechoslovakia and
Poland, the two Eastern European countries that were the most active in
the Geneva system during the interwar period, ended their participation
or withdrew from the FAO, the WHO, UNESCO, and even UNICEF.[39]
After turbulent discussions, however, they did remain members of the ILO.
These discussions reveal that the Communists in power hoped to turn the
ILO into a platform for convincing trade unionists in the West of the superiority of the socialist model. They also demonstrate the existence of groups
strongly attached to an organization with which they had long-standing
ties, and where they preserved contacts that they hoped could serve as
resources.[40]

The departure of the people's democracies that had been the most
involved in the different international arenas and networks before the war
can also be explained by the marginalization, disappearance, and defection
of the competent experts and politicians who did not join the Communist

ranks, or who distanced themselves from them. There were of course exceptions, such as the economist Oskar Lange, a former professor in the United States and representative from Poland to the UN, or the ergonomist Jan Rosner, who remained connected to the ILO after World War II. The Polish economist Adam Rosé, however, a member of the International Labour Office during the interwar period who was very active at UNECE between 1947–1949, left Poland in 1949; Anton Zelenka, the Czechoslovak government's delegate to the International Labor Conference in 1946, declined the offer made in 1948 to join the Ministry of Social Affairs in Communist Czechoslovakia and took Austrian nationality instead.[41] In January 1950 Professor Alexander W. Rudzinski, a Polish diplomat to the UN, sought asylum in the United States. His article published in the journal *International Organization* the following year expressed the concern of internationalized Eastern elites with respect to growing Soviet hegemony, and the Stalinization of Communist Parties and people's democracies.[42]

Overall, the Communists in power in Eastern bloc countries echoed the long-standing hostility of Soviet authorities toward liberal international organizations. The founding of the League of Nations and the ILO in 1919 was clearly a response to what Westerners perceived as the danger of revolution. Bolshevik Russia was not invited to join the new international organization, and in return Lenin and Trotsky formulated virulent criticisms of what they saw as a diplomatic forum in the service of European imperialist interests. This was especially true for the ILO, which they saw as the enemy of the international labor movement. In 1920 the Executive Committee of the Cominform declared:

> The illustrious League of Nations, which is in fact a league of imperialist robbers, convened in Washington, and later in Paris, a farcical conference on "international labour protection," at which two-thirds of the votes were given to the bourgeoisie, and one-third to bourgeois agents like Legien, Jouhaux, and co., who call themselves the "workers' representatives." These conferences of representatives selected by the bourgeoisie have tried to put a strait jacket on the regenerating labour movement.[43]

After World War II and West Germany's early entry in 1951 into a number of UN agencies, such as UNESCO, the FAO, the WHO, and the ILO, the exclusion of East Germany until 1973—and the fact that Taiwan continued

THE EMERGENCE OF A "SECOND WORLD"

to represent China at the UN until 1971—proved the partiality of UN internationalism in the eyes of Communist leaders. For Soviet leaders, the UN Security Council, in which Westerners had the majority of the votes, was actually a kind of "annex of the U.S. Department of State," and even a "U.S. rubber stamp."[44]

In the early 1950s Communist leaders could do no more than note their powerlessness in different international forums, in which the United States and its Western allies had a large majority of the votes. They tried to circumvent this situation at UNECE by proposing, in vain, to give voting rights to countries with simple observer status, such as Bulgaria, Albania, Finland, Hungary, Italy, and Romania. More fundamentally, socialist countries struggled to integrate within an international system that had not been designed for them. This was especially true of the international economic system, with the World Bank and the International Monetary Fund. Molotov and Soviet representatives were quite present at Bretton Woods in 1944, but they withdrew from the negotiations and did not recognize the agreements that concluded them.[45] Shortly thereafter, the Soviets also did not participate in the negotiations for an International Trade Organization, which ultimately led to the General Agreement on Tariffs and Trade.

The U.S. diplomatic documents that have served as a basis for numerous studies indicate that the Soviet withdrawal was motivated by a desire to avoid the control of other states. Soviet leaders, and Stalin in particular, of course distrusted international organizations, which was partially motivated by not wanting to reveal the weaknesses of the Soviet economy, but they also gave substantive reasons to justify their abstention. The Soviets especially underscored that the free trade promoted by the Bretton Woods system—in addition to GATT between countries whose economies were unequally developed—was fundamentally unjust, as the most-favored-nation clause governing trade always worked to the advantage of the most economically powerful nations. They also quickly pointed out that declarations in favor of spreading free trade had never prevented preferential economic agreements between Western countries, as demonstrated by the implementation of the European Coal and Steel Community (ECSC) in 1952 and the Single Market in 1957. In comparable contexts, the elite of recently decolonized countries would use a similar argument, and it would also be behind the organization of the first United Nations Conference on Trade and Development, under the presidency of the Argentinian economist Raùl Prebisch in 1964.

In the end, Soviet abstention effectively favored the implementation of economic organizations whose architecture corresponded to the rules of trade between developed countries with capitalist market economies. The negative expression "nonmarket economy countries,"[46] used to refer to countries with centrally planned economies, emphasized their exteriority with respect to the international economic system centered on the transatlantic area and dominated by the United States. Poland's withdrawal from the World Bank and the IMF in 1950 as its loan request was about to be refused, and the expulsion of Czechoslovakia from the same organizations in 1954 on the pretext that it was not submitting the required economic information, reinforced this marginality.[47] Furthermore, while Czechoslovakia had been a member of GATT since 1947, it was not spared the embargo affecting all Communist countries.

The incompatibility between the internationalism of the liberal tradition and the social and political structures of Communist regimes was especially clear in connection with the ILO. Explicitly founded in 1919 to offer a reformist alternative to "violent revolutions," it was organized according to the principle of tripartism, which was incompatible with a Soviet nationalized economy that did not recognize the autonomy of employers or workers.[48] The representatives for workers and employers from socialist countries were quickly marginalized within the organization.[49] In 1937 the representative of Christian trade unionism, Petrus Serrarens of the Netherlands, questioned the representativeness of the Soviet workers' delegate attending the conference.[50] The sidelining of Soviet "employer" representatives clearly took the form of an ideological crusade against the nationalized economy. In 1953 employers questioned the legitimacy of the mandate of their Czech counterpart Pøemysl Tomášek, who was from the Ministry for Heavy Industry.[51] The situation deteriorated further when the Soviet Union joined the organization in 1954, as employers contested any legitimacy on the part of delegates from countries led by Communist Parties, which they believed solely represented their government. The organization's board of directors established a specific committee tasked with reflecting on the actual notion of an employer. The McNair Committee concluded that it was impossible to exclude public sector employers at a time when various forms of a mixed economy were spreading in all countries.[52] This did not defuse the opposition of U.S. employers, who were against any international social regulations, and whose chamber of commerce used the conclusions of this report as a propaganda argument against the ILO in general.[53]

Until 1955 socialist countries were thus clearly pushed to the margins of international organizations, as demonstrated by the exclusion from the UN of China, the GDR, Albania, Bulgaria, Hungary, Romania, and Mongolia. When Dwight D. Eisenhower rose to power in January 1953, leaders at the Department of State did not hide their intention to use the UN as a platform for combatting communism, as stressed by a memorandum from May 1953, which indicated: "In the Cold War the UN has become a major means for diplomacy and propaganda in combatting the political warfare of the Soviet Union and in rallying the strength of the free world through a wide variety of measures."[54] Even more than the UN, however, it was the constitution of a solid Western bloc structured around a project of reconstruction and economic prosperity that rejected the countries of Europe's eastern periphery.

ECONOMIC WAR AGAINST EASTERN EUROPE

The Cold War was, especially in its beginnings, also an economic war waged by the United States and its allies against Europe's eastern periphery. The debate among historians has focused less on U.S. intentions than on the conflicts within its state apparatus with respect to the intensity of this war, as well as the actual degree of submission of European allies. They all agree that the Marshall Plan, which replaced UNRRA, helped build and reinforce a shared economic space directed against the East. Moreover, the economic embargo conducted within the Coordinating Committee for Multilateral Export Controls raised a considerable obstacle to the reconstruction and economic development of Eastern Europe.[55]

The Marshall Plan and the Division of Europe

In June 1947 Secretary of State George Marshall announced, in fairly general terms during a speech at Harvard University, the launch of an economic assistance program for the countries destroyed by the war. This program proclaimed to be open to all: "Our policy is directed not against any country but against hunger, poverty, desperation, and chaos." Unlike with UNRRA, it was designed to be administered solely by U.S. actors, but based on cooperation among European nations: "The program should be a joint one, agreed to by a number, if not all European nations." Passed by the U.S. Congress in April 1948, the program provided $12 billion in economic assistance until 1952, which was distributed in each country by the U.S. Economic Cooperation Administration (ECA). Coordination among the different European countries participating in the recovery program was provided by the OEEC, which gave rise to the Organisation for Economic Co-operation and Development (OECD) in 1961.[56]

The Marshall Plan was announced in a context of economic and social crisis in Europe, which was compounded by a political crisis connected to the dismissal or resignation of Communist ministers from governments in France, Italy, and Belgium between March and May 1947. From the winter of 1947 onward, upon order of the Cominform, Communist Parties conducted a ferocious campaign against the American program, which Stalin promised to sabotage. In countries where Communist Parties were powerful, such as France and Italy, the Marshall Plan was the culmination of a civil Cold War of sorts.

The historiography on the Marshall Plan is as divided as its contemporaries were.[57] It is impossible and unnecessary to summarize this diversity here, but I will mention the following aspects. U.S. historians have explored the intentions and motivations of U.S. decision makers, as well as the effects that the aid had on economic prosperity and growing U.S. power.[58] In parallel, European historians have tried to measure the economic influence of U.S. aid on European reconstruction. The low estimates of Werner Abelshauser for the FRG or Alan Milward of Great Britain—who believe that U.S. aid made minor contributions to the recovery of European countries—stand in contrast to the more positive assessments by the economists Barry Eichengreen of the United States or Marc Uzan of France.[59] The role of the ECA in the Americanization of European countries and the real impact of the productivity programs that the agency implemented are explored with nuance.[60] Finally, historians of the construction of Europe have explored the role played by the Marshall Plan in spurring the construction of Western European institutions.[61] Beyond these divergences, all these works emphasize the Marshall Plan's role in constituting a zone of economic prosperity in Western Europe dominated by the dollar.

THE EMERGENCE OF A "SECOND WORLD"

However, its negative effects on Eastern European economies remain underexplored.[62]

In his speech in 1947, Marshall signaled that aid was available to all, but neither U.S. authorities nor their European allies intended for the USSR or Communist-led countries to receive Marshall Plan aid.[63] The U.S. Congress, which was dominated by Republicans, would never have passed funding to aid the Communists they were combatting at home. The various actors at the Department of State who were behind the plan—Secretary of State George Marshall, ambassador to the USSR George F. Kennan, and Under Secretary of State for Economic Affairs William Clayton—insisted that the plan was clearly in keeping with the logic of containment and the struggle against communism. The rapid economic recovery of Europe was seen as a rampart against the exploitation of misery by the Communists. Soviet leaders quickly developed a negative view of the plan, which they saw as a means for intensifying U.S. economic power, and for attracting those considered to be part of its "natural" sphere of influence.

When Georges Bidault and Ernest Bevin, respectively the French and British ministers of foreign affairs, invited the Soviets to Paris to discuss the plan in June 1947, it was to calm—as they indicated in a letter to the U.S. ambassador—their own opposition from the left. Stalin and Soviet leaders, who were aware of their country's economic weakness, thought they could use this opportunity to once again raise the issue of war compensation and German reparations. It was to this end that Stalin agreed to send Minister of Foreign Affairs Molotov with a large delegation to encourage the Czechoslovaks and Poles to join them. Soviet representatives, however, required two conditions to begin negotiations: settling the issue of German reparations, and renouncing the implementation of a multilateral organization that they saw primarily as an instrument of U.S. diplomacy. These two conditions, which were clearly contrary to the spirit of Marshall's speech and the goal of German reconstruction, were rejected by British and French negotiators, prompting the departure of Molotov and the Soviet delegation. Soviet authorities subsequently exerted pressure on the Czechoslovak and Polish governments to renounce Marshall Plan aid. Stalin's responses to the Marshall Plan were a meeting with Szlarska Poręba, in which Jdanov affirmed the existence of two irreconcilable camps, and the founding of the Cominform, which was presented as a way to strengthen the cohesion of Communist Parties but was chiefly an instrument for their

Stalinization. Comecon was created in 1949, initially as a symbolic gesture, with no genuine path to economic integration in the East.[64] The constitution of an Eastern European economic space was profoundly contradictory to the traditions of autarky espoused by Eastern European leaders since the interwar period.[65] Finally, leaders of Eastern European countries, especially the Czechoslovaks and Poles but also the Soviets, did not want to renounce trade with Western European countries, to which they sold raw materials, and from which they bought the equipment urgently needed for their economic development, the very condition for the construction of socialism.[66] In 1949, during the founding conference for Comecon, two goals were clearly reaffirmed: reconstruction had to be accelerated, and the maintenance of trade with the West should be encouraged; this second objective was a constant preoccupation throughout the organization's existence.[67] Eastern European countries were nevertheless quickly confronted by an economic war that forced them to withdraw into themselves.[68]

While the Marshall Plan was conceived of as an instrument of Truman's policy of containment, it also pursued the goal of diffusing the values specific to liberal capitalism. The ECA was led by a team of businessmen who were part of the liberal movement, joined by U.S. trade unionists from the American Federation of Labor (AFL), who were closely associated with the policies of Roosevelt and the New Deal, namely, by promoting a mix of state interventionism and free trade. In various Western European countries, the ECA was not content with distributing aid as it also sought, with more or less success, to reorient the organization of the economy in order to ensure the free play of the market, and to simultaneously foster the development of regulated forms of social democracy in the tradition of Anglo-American industrial relations. It especially sought to promote collective negotiation and to this end encouraged the development of a reformist trade unionism, especially in Italy and France, countries where the Communists were powerful. With the financial assistance of the AFL and the CIA, the Marshall Plan's ECA helped create competing trade union federations in these countries, for instance in France with the Force ouvrière, which splintered off from the Confédération générale du travail dominated by the Communists.[69] The ECA also made sure that the aid dispensed in Western Europe benefited the U.S. economy and companies. With regard to the lack of dollars in circulation, the deliveries provided U.S. companies with an export market, while certain specifications—such as the fact that transport was provided by U.S. ships, or that grain was ground into flour in the United States—ensured that companies there also benefited.[70]

On the other hand, the Marshall Plan quickly became a weapon against economies in the East. Raw materials, which represented 52.7 percent of Marshall Plan deliveries, were in direct competition with traditional trade coming from the East, with Czechoslovak representatives bitterly complaining about this at UNECE.[71] During the discussions that occurred within its coal division, the representatives of European producer countries— Belgium and especially Poland—accused "subsidized" American coal of engaging in unfair competition. It was in this context that the Polish delegate Adam Rosé presented a resolution on May 13, 1948.[72] He explained that the committee should "consider as one of its primary duties the creation of a situation in which European countries would be self-sufficient with respect to their coal needs." He believed that European coal was more expensive because producer countries—he mentioned Great Britain, Germany, and Poland—had greatly suffered during the war, and the arrival of American coal created a dangerous situation by deepening the trade deficit of European importers.[73] Some U.S. economists, such as William Diebold, Jr., shared this criticism; for Diebold the reconstruction of Western Europe was linked to preserving trade with the East, and he even saw it as a condition for the Marshall Plan's success.[74] At UNECE, Walter Rostow also insisted, in the context of a dollar shortage, on the need to develop intra-European trade to promote reconstruction.[75] For these international actors, the true question was determining whether it was better for importers to procure coal at a better price "with more or less fictional dollars" or to "lift (all) of Europe and place it . . . in a state of self-sufficiency?"[76] The issue was at the heart of debates within UNECE, whose secretariat hoped to continue developing pan-European commerce at all costs. This goal was threatened less by the plan itself than by the fact that it quickly became an instrument for the U.S. secretary of commerce to impose embargoes against Eastern Europe. One of the amendments inserted in the Marshall Plan's Economic Cooperation Act stipulated that countries receiving Marshall aid that were members of the OEEC had to refuse to deliver merchandise for which American authorities had not granted an export license. Averell Harriman, the businessman and former secretary of commerce who was coordinating the ECA, campaigned for a total interruption of trade with the

Embargo and Economic Cold War

In 1948 Rosé, the Polish delegate to UNECE, stressed that productivity gains could lower the price of Polish coal, but this would require importing from the United States new machines, whose delivery was blocked by the embargo imposed by the U.S. Department of Commerce. The first economic embargo measures were adopted in 1947. Beginning in November, Kennan, who was head of the Policy Planning Staff, a Department of State think tank, recommended generalizing export licenses toward Eastern European countries, a policy that became harsher with the nomination of Charles Sawyer as secretary of commerce in 1948.[78] Despite resistance from Marshall himself, he decided to extend the embargo to include "sensitive" equipment, with mining falling under this category.[79] When Rostow visited Poland and Czechoslovakia in 1948, he was the powerless witness of the anger of officials he met, who bitterly emphasized that this practice of restrictive licenses greatly hindered economic reconstruction, even as the German aggressor was receiving Marshall Plan funds. With regard to U.S. policy, Rostow added: "unless the US straightens up and flies right, We (that is the Secretariat) must open fire."[80] The same embargo policy contributed to the failure of other pan-European economic projects, such as the one from 1949 to 1950 to connect the electricity networks of Czechoslovakia, Poland, and southern Germany. This plan, which was led by UNECE, had to contend with blocked shipments of U.S. and Western European electrical equipment heading to Central European countries. This equipment was on list 1-B of CoCom, which included "equipment of lesser strategic importance," whose export in large quantity toward Eastern Europe represented a threat.[81]

The discussions that led to the creation of CoCom began in 1949. The goal was to establish a single list of goods prohibited from export to the East for all North Atlantic Treaty Organization (NATO) countries, in order to prevent U.S. embargoes from being circumvented via intra-European trade. In 1949 there were still many trade agreements between the East and the West, and some countries, such as Great Britain, Italy, and Switzerland, conducted a substantial portion of their trade with countries in Communist Europe.[82] Seen from the West, the primary issue revolved around the

THE EMERGENCE OF A "SECOND WORLD"

capacity of U.S. leaders to impose their embargo policy and their list of restricted goods on allies highly dependent on their economic aid. In Western Europe, German partners historically inclined to trade with the East enjoyed no political autonomy at the time and could not openly oppose this policy.[83] In Great Britain, however, there was considerable resistance, as the country had become the primary economic partner of Eastern Europe; while this trade represented at most approximately 6 percent of the British trade balance, some companies, medium-sized ones in particular, were highly dependent on these trade flows. Immediately afterward, representatives from other countries—especially neutral countries such as Sweden and Switzerland—formulated objections to this policy.[84] To overcome this reluctance, Harriman first initiated bilateral negotiations in connection with the ECA, after which Marshall Plan recipient countries tried to establish their own lists. CoCom, which officially met for the first time in January 1950, represented a space for the harmonization of these efforts. Until 1954 U.S. representatives were able to impose on their NATO allies a gradual alignment of the lists generated by CoCom and the U.S. Department of Commerce. Nevertheless, it is important not to overestimate CoCom's activity, for its history is primarily one of seeking difficult compromises in establishing lists of goods subject to embargo: European representatives, especially from Great Britain, France, and Denmark, who were joined in the late 1950s by the Japanese and Germans, had always shown resistance to U.S. demands, with more or less force and unity. In the United States, powerful representative associations for economic interests, such as the National Association of Manufacturers or the National Industrial Conference Board, were concerned about the negative consequences of the measures on U.S. companies and came out in support of easing the embargo in 1953.[85]

Nevertheless, the creation of CoCom was an important moment in Europe's division. For the West, it was a space, among others, for economic experts to meet and helped strengthen a culture for the Western bloc, while in the East it marked an additional stage in its marginalization and exclusion from international circulations. Reading the lists also clearly shows that only a small portion of the goods placed under embargo directly threatened the security of Western allies.

Representatives from Eastern European export countries, such as Poland and Czechoslovakia, repeatedly expressed their concerns regarding an embargo that slowed an economic reconstruction that was already laborious and heightened their dependence on the USSR. The real impact of this policy on the economies of Communist countries should still be assessed, but it undeniably contributed to the establishment of two economic spaces: a first structured around dynamic organizations, initially the OEEC and from 1952 onward the European Coal and Steel Community; and a second in Eastern Europe that was structurally less developed, and impoverished by the war.

In spite of this economic marginality, however, this peripheral Europe successfully used international forums to project an alternative discourse that gradually constituted it as a Second World.

THE INTERNATIONAL AFFIRMATION OF TWO SOCIETAL MODELS

International organizations were spaces in which a hegemonic discourse was produced, but they also enabled the expression of challenges to it. They served as stages on which states projected images of themselves. In this sense, the organizations of the UN system were privileged spaces for the ordering of Cold War worlds.

International Organizations and the Ordering of Blocs

To function, if only financially, international organizations needed to maintain the principle of universality on which they were founded, and they subsequently developed strategies for establishing or conserving ties with the largest possible number of countries. David Morse, director-general of the International Labour Office, who was concerned about the announced departure of Czechoslovakia—a country that had provided important social expertise during the interwar period—made the trip to Warsaw and Prague, where he gave reassuring speeches and was seen as an "open man." His efforts helped keep Poland and Czechoslovakia in the organization. The director-general of the WHO, Brock Chisholm of Canada, used shrewdness: he proclaimed that the Communist countries that wanted to leave would simply be "suspended" and could once again become full members upon request. To maintain these ties, international civil servants, and the directors-general of agencies in particular, used intermediaries; those at the

THE EMERGENCE OF A "SECOND WORLD"

Office could rely on a network of long-standing correspondents and collaborators, who were often socialists and had joined Communist Parties after the forced merger of the two parties between 1946 and 1947. Those who were exiled could convince their former colleagues to pursue their collaboration with the ILO. Relying on networks of practitioners loyal to the organization, the WHO director-general proposed visiting the country to convince the Soviet government to remain a member of the organization. In general, contrary to actors of U.S. international policy who constructed the Soviet "bloc" as a monolith, international civil servants strove, as part of their everyday work, to deconstruct this foregone conclusion.

At the same time, international organizations, and their general assemblies in particular, became spaces for staging the division of the world into two camps. The alternating speaking format sanctioned by votes fostered the solidification of blocs. The homogeneity of the Eastern bloc was marked by perfect voting discipline, which reflected Soviet domination over the people's democracies; this was mirrored in the West by OEEC countries organized around the United States. This discipline was sometimes fostered by the institutional functioning of organizations: in 1955 the USSR became a member of the ILO Governing Body and spoke there in the name of the entire bloc.[86] The Soviet Anatoly Koudriatzev became an aide to the director-general in 1956 and was replaced by Pavel Orlov in 1960.[87] While the former was specifically in charge of relations with the Soviet Union, the latter accompanied the director-general on all his trips to people's democracies and read everything that was published regarding socialist countries in order to "avoid problems."[88] Soviet domination over the people's democracies was in a way institutionalized within the ILO. For the bloc to speak with a single voice, it quickly became necessary to develop spaces for discussion in advance of conferences, at which the representatives of various countries could develop a common line. After Stalin's death in 1953 and the UN admission of Albania, Bulgaria, Hungary, and Romania in 1955, multilateral meetings became systematic. Upon the request of representatives from the people's democracies, in 1956 Soviet authorities accepted to hold consultations, which were often located in the capitals of Central European countries, along with Geneva and New York. Their minutes show open debates, as well as the development of a multilateral culture within the bloc. This is demonstrated by the especially acrimonious discussions between representatives from Comecon countries before UNECE meetings. It was therefore within international arenas in Geneva and New York—and not in Moscow—that the "bloc" gradually took shape during the 1950s and 1960s.[89] Delegates from Western European countries and their U.S. allies had active multilateral spaces to develop common strategies, especially the OEEC. As with those for Eastern Europe, these organizations were also places for discussion that show the limits of U.S. domination over its Western allies.

Finally, the general assemblies of the UN and some of its agencies were stages on which states projected a discourse about themselves to the world, one that emphasized publicity and propaganda. While they provide little information regarding the social and political realities they promoted, these discourses outline worlds organized around diverging values.[90] Competing values such as liberty/equality, democracy/peace, and solidarity/humanitarianism emerged in the late 1940s. They made it possible, within international organizations, to attract countries and large groups. Various networks and organizations, international union federations, and international nongovernmental organizations could drive, relay, and challenge these values, thereby fueling debate. Finally, organizations opened up spaces for reform that transcended the binary logic of the Cold War.

Women and Children First

After World War II, traditional family structures were challenged. The imbalance between men and women, the role women assumed during the war and continued during reconstruction, and the thirteen million total or partial orphans in Europe all contributed to a reevaluation of traditional family organization.[91] Because the family is the foundation of social organization, it became an important issue in the Cold War ideological conflict, as well as one of the topics where opposition between the socialist East and capitalist West was forcefully expressed. Nevertheless, the discussion regarding the family should not be limited to the Cold War discourse to which some actors sometimes sought to reduce it.

The preamble to the United Nations Charter recognizes gender equality: "We the Peoples of the United Nations determined to . . . reaffirm faith in fundamental human rights . . . in the equal rights of men and women." Soviet representatives played an important part in the inclusion of this

THE EMERGENCE OF A "SECOND WORLD"

passage in the preamble. In 1972 the Women's International Democratic Federation, of Communist obedience, suggested the idea for what would eventually become the decade for women.[92] The federation, which was founded in Paris in 1945, gradually became one of the Communist movement's international organizations, although its initial attractiveness was its connection to the tradition of a women's internationalism of the left. This internationalism organized in 1907 as part of Socialist International Women, under the impetus of the German socialist Clara Zetkin. In 1910 Zetkin and the Russian feminist Alexandra Kollontai proposed celebrating an International Women's Day on March 8, when social demands (equality at work) and civic demands (right to vote) would be highlighted. Zetkin, who in 1919 joined the ranks of the Communist Party of Germany, was part of the pantheon of Communist heroes. In the GDR and other socialist countries, March 8 was observed with emphatic celebrations but long remained ignored in Western countries.

Women's socialist internationalism and the Communist discourse on women therefore largely predated the Cold War. In continuity with Marxist discourse, it raised the issue of gender equality in economic and social terms.[93] By eliminating the economic foundation of inequality, socialism would give equal place to women and men, with the state seeing to the protection of the weakest members, children in particular.[94] The Soviet Union and some European socialist states mobilized this tradition, presenting themselves as the defenders of gender equality and child protection in international arenas. The USSR joined the ILO in 1934, and in 1937 the unionist Eugenia Egorova headed the delegation of Soviet workers at the International Labour Conference, the only woman in this position at the time. She embodied and publicly defended what was doctrine in the USSR and would become so in the people's democracies: under socialism, gender equality is achieved in and through work.[95] The representatives of socialist states, especially Soviet and Polish ones, were highly active in the Commission on the Status of Women, created in 1946 within ECOSOC. In 1947 Polish delegates requested that the issue of equal pay for women be added to the agenda for the International Labor Conference. Adopted in 1951, Convention 100 on Equal Remuneration was the subject of emulation between the Communist-leaning World Federation of Trade Unions and the reformist International Confederation of Free Trade Unions.[96] The defense of gender equality in the workplace allowed representatives of socialist countries to demonstrate their commitment on behalf of groups dominated in the capitalist world, as well as to affirm the superiority of socialism.[97]

While it is important to confront the discourse of equality emphasized by the Communists with the reality of the inequalities that remained in state socialist countries, two opposing conceptions of women's role in society were nevertheless presented on the international stage. For instance, following their survey of Poland in 1947, FAO experts, who were mostly from Canada and the United States, suggested that female farmers be "freed from working in the fields and concentrate on their home, where they should develop better practices in terms of nutrition"; they incidentally recommended that women be educated in becoming good housewives.[98] This vision, which reduced women to the role of mother and wife, was clearly contradictory to the one being diffused at the time in Communist-led countries; it also conflicted with the policies of integration and equality through work that were being promoted there.[99] This contrast in the conception of women's role found its strongest expression in the international meeting spaces represented by the occupation zones in Germany until 1949. Women's work was underscored in the Soviet occupation zone, and the women who cleared the ruins (*Trümmerfrauen*) were encouraged to pursue training and become professionalized. In short, they were considered heroic figures. These very same women were seen as a temporarily necessary aberration in Western occupation zones, where political authorities strove to send them back to their homes as quickly as possible. In the 1950s, when a large majority of women returned to their homes in the FRG, their counterparts largely remained active in companies in the GDR.

More broadly, it was the question of each person's role within the family—and the family's role within society—that was at the center of debates. The dominant international discourse of the early 1950s was based on a traditional conception of the family, as demonstrated by the UN Convention Relating to the Status of Refugees in 1951, which declared that "the unity of the family, the natural and fundamental group unit of society, is an essential right of the refugee" and recommended that governments take the necessary measures to protect the refugee's family, notably for the purpose of "(1) Ensuring that the unity of the refugee's family is maintained, especially in cases where the head of the family has fulfilled the necessary conditions for admission to a particular country."[100] The Declaration of the Rights of

THE EMERGENCE OF A "SECOND WORLD"

the Child of 1959 stressed that the child "needs love and understanding. He shall, wherever possible, grow up in the care and under the responsibility of his parents . . . a child of tender years shall not, save in exceptional circumstances, be separated from his mother." The traditional role of the woman as a mother was thus reaffirmed, one that was incidentally not questioned in either of the two blocs. Nevertheless, the Communists emphasized the role of public actors in the protection and education of children. During the discussions surrounding the declaration on the rights of children, Soviet representatives insisted that this collective responsibility be included in the convention in order to ensure social policies for child protection. Representatives from Western countries were opposed, insisting instead on the need to secure and protect the young child's relation to its mother, in order to ensure his or her harmonious development. This point of view was justified by the work of psychoanalysts such as André Spitz in the 1930s and John Bowlby in the early 1950s, both of whom emphasized the mother's decisive role in the young child's emotional and intellectual awakening. The WHO actively contributed to the international diffusion of this research and the representations it promoted.[101] The Christian churches around which a vast coalition of actors came together stepped in to condemn the work of married women and the early socialization of young children. Mobilizing a Cold War discourse, these defenders of the traditional family accused Communists of wanting to deprive children of maternal love, and even seeking to destroy the family by forcing women to work and sending their children to collective institutions where they would undergo "brainwashing."[102] It was probably within a divided Germany that these oppositions were expressed the most clearly. In the FRG, churches and Christian Democracy, with the help of associations of psychoanalysts, established a "countermodel" to East Germany, where they believed that the children who were sent to nurseries lagged intellectually and emotionally. This allowed them to justify a traditional maternalist discourse, and to oppose any collective management of childcare.[103]

This Cold War discourse distorted reality. In Eastern European countries, the creation of collective institutions was initially a response to the painful question of orphans, who were very numerous in Poland and Hungary. The spread of nurseries was also a condition for integrating women in the labor market. While hygienist objectives still largely took precedence in educational missions during the 1950s, this was far from being a distinctive feature of socialist countries. In fact, the leaders of these countries were not indifferent to the emotional care of young children in orphanages or nurseries. Polish authorities repeatedly applied for grants from the ECOSOC social fund to visit Western institutions.[104] In the Budapest suburb of Lóczy, the pediatrician Emmi Pikler founded an orphanage where she developed an innovative teaching method. She encouraged close ties between the child and one or more dedicated adults, and she promoted the independence of infants thanks to free activity. These two elements were the foundation for what has since become the Lóczy-Pikler model, which numerous nurseries across Europe adopted. In the GDR, the pediatrician Eva Schmidt-Kolmer was a driving force in the late 1950s in emphasizing the educational role of nurseries in East Germany. No more than Pikler can she be accused of serving a collective education project in the service of dictatorship. The situation of nurseries and orphanages improved with the economic recovery, and with the diffusion of new pedagogical concepts in the 1960s.[105]

Both Pikler and Schmidt-Kolmer came from the world of Viennese social pediatrics and were part of a broad European reform movement reflecting on the development and education of young children, especially within a difficult context. This movement found international expression with the creation, in January 1950 in Paris, of the International Children's Center by the French pediatrician Robert Debré and the Polish doctor Ludwik Rajchman. This organization, supported by UNESCO, was an international space for studying early childhood care.[106] In June 1949, in a note to the minister of foreign affairs, Debré affirmed that the social pediatrics course that would be the nucleus of the future center "represented the most important intellectual link, and sometimes the only one, between France and doctors on the other side of the Iron Curtain: Poles, Czechs, Yugoslavs, and Bulgarians in particular."[107] Representatives from these countries, especially those from Yugoslavia and Poland with a lively social pediatrics tradition, joined voices with representatives from France, Switzerland, and Greece in support of creating the center, while the Soviets abstained, and U.S. representatives voted against it. These associations and movements did not advocate the destruction of the family, nor did they question the role of the mother, but they established early childhood as a subject for public policy and promoted reflection on collective childcare in underprivileged environments.

THE EMERGENCE OF A "SECOND WORLD"

Others went further and stressed—in opposition to these dominant maternalist arguments—the benefits of early socialization for young children and the importance of peer groups within this socialization. The Communist movement played an important role in diffusing this view of education. In France it was led by the Communist-leaning psychologist Henri Wallon, while his student Irène Lézine promoted it in the world of nurseries.[108] They were not the only ones, as the Pikler model was imported to France in the 1960s by Myriam David and Geneviève Appell, neither of whom were Communists.[109]

Because it was used and distorted within a Cold War context, the debate surrounding the family was deeply polarized in the 1950s. Within international institutions, Communist countries presented a discourse of equality between men and women, especially in the working world, adopted a position supporting collective childcare, and more broadly emphasized public policies beneficial to children. Their Western adversaries used Cold War political arguments stating that Communist dictatorships wanted to destroy the family to ensure state control over all of society. This hardening of the models could have paradoxical effects in the field. In some countries, such as the FRG, it delegitimized family policies, while in others, such as France, the debate, on the contrary, sustained and stimulated long-standing reflection on early childhood care.

The Working World Divided

Like the family, work was central to the ideological conflicts between the socialist East and the capitalist West.[110] Since the outbreak of the Russian Revolution, the announcement of the creation of a workers' state in which exploitation would no longer exist proved seductive to European working classes. The founding of the ILO in 1919 was a reformist response to this revolutionary enticement. In the 1920s the civil servants of the International Labour Office seriously studied what was happening in the USSR and circulated information to counter Communist propaganda.[111] Upon joining the ILO in 1934, the Soviet delegation used the International Labour Conference to emphasize the Communist model of a workers' state where exploitation no longer exists, and where workers in power—via the Communist Party—would enjoy more extensive social rights.[112] In fact, it was precisely to use this platform that the Czechoslovaks and Poles remained members of the ILO in 1949, as demonstrated by the discussions that took place within the Central Committee of the Communist Party of Czechoslovakia. The minister of foreign affairs, Vlado Clementis, stressed that the ILO represented "the most favorable international base for waging the political and propaganda battle with representatives of imperialist policy. It is all the more important given that the Anglo-American block is trying to transfer (thanks to the right of veto) important social issues from ECOSOC to the ILO."[113]

The minister alluded to the debates on forced labor that had been held at the ILO since 1947 at the request of the U.S. labor union, the American Federation of Labor (AFL). They represent a striking episode of what could be called the trade union Cold War. In 1945 the AFL refused to join the WFTU, which included all unions of Communist and socialist obedience under the leadership of Walter Citrine, head of the British Trades Union Congress. At the same time, the AFL actively prepared, with the help of the Office of Strategic Services and later the Central Intelligence Agency (CIA), the global division of trade unions that occurred in 1949, and that led to the creation of the ICFTU, which was home to reformist unions.[114] This break was rooted in diverging conceptions of the role of unions, which were seen as an instrument for redistribution and collective bargaining on one side, and as a place for organizing protest—and even fighting and revolution—on the other. Nevertheless, in the form it assumed, this break was undeniably the result of activism on the part of the AFL and U.S. intelligence, representing an episode of the Cold War.[115] It was a disaster for the pro-Communist federation, whose secretariat, which was expelled from Paris in 1951, settled in Vienna before once again being expelled in 1956, ultimately taking refuge in Prague. Despite still being led by Western unionists—Giuseppe di Vittorio of Italy was president and Louis Saillant of France secretary-general—this dual shift toward the East clearly pushed the WFTU under the domination of the Soviets and the socialist bloc, whose model it defended, and whose arguments it loyally conveyed.[116] It was also an important setback, however, for Soviet leaders, who had tried via the WFTU to transform ECOSOC into a global union parliament in order to circumvent the ILO, which was seen as a bourgeois organization.[117] After the break in 1949, the union federations affiliated with the WFTU were not represented at the ILO, which went without the presence of France's General Confederation of Labor (CGT) and the Italian General Confederation of Labour (CGIL), the largest union forces in both countries at the time. In the 1950s the management of the reformist ICFTU led, under the influence of the AFL, a resolute struggle against Communist influence. This militant anticommunism sometimes placed it in an awkward situation with some of its federations, such as the one for railroads, and even with parts of its union base and civil servants at the International Labour Office.[118] Jan Shuil, who nevertheless came from reformist unionism, was indignant in 1952 that Czechoslovak and Polish workers' representatives were systematically excluded by their colleagues from the industrial committees, despite every reason to include them given their technical expertise.[119]

As during the interwar period, the ILO represented a platform for systematically questioning the social accomplishments of state socialist countries. On a more fundamental level, what was being challenged was the very logic on which the organization of work was based in these countries. The freedom of association that guarantees relative equality among the signatories of an employment contract in the liberal tradition was reinterpreted as a human right against the intrusion of the state.

In 1948 the ILO adopted the Freedom of Association and Protection of the Right to Organise Convention, which emphasized that "public authorities shall refrain from any interference which would restrict this right or impede the lawful exercise thereof."[120] The Committee on Freedom of Association, created in 1951 to oversee compliance with this convention, soon received complaints regarding interference with the freedom of association in Eastern European countries on the part of unions affiliated with the ICFTU, especially the Trades Union Congress (Great Britain) and the AFL (United States). It is true that in direct keeping with the Leninist conception of the union as a "transmission belt," unions were closely linked to the Communist Party and the state.[121] The debates that took place before the Committee on Freedom of Association sometimes allowed for reflections regarding the conditions for exercising this freedom. The minority U.S. union, the Industrial Workers of the World, which was widely attacked under McCarthyism, denounced the limitations to the freedom to organize and protest resulting from passage of the Taft-Hartley Act in 1947, which restricted the right to strike and other union prerogatives.[122] As for Latin American unionists, they emphasized that it was less the state than the excessive power of employers that restricted their freedom.

In the end, what was discussed was the concrete possibility of exercising union freedom within power relations unfavorable to workers. The company, and even the workplace, were seen as essential places for exercising this freedom. An organization such as the ILO, however, had no direct influence over production spaces. On the question of work, the binary thinking of the Cold War finally gave rise to a nuanced reflection regarding the role of trade unions and workers' freedom of expression in the company. It also prompted emulation that reform groups could eventually use to their advantage.

Can international organizations serve as a platform for observing the Cold War under a different light? Three provisional answers can be formulated.

From 1948 to 1955 these organizations were indeed spaces of "Western domination," in which Communist Eastern Europe was constituted as a "Second World" on the margins of the First. The Marshall Plan and the regional organizations connected to it became instruments for economic embargo against countries with Communist governments, hindering their reconstruction and increasing their dependence on the Soviet Union. Economically dominated since the nineteenth century, these states were clearly cut off from Europe's developed spaces.

This position as a Second World on the periphery of the First nevertheless gave the leaders of Communist countries legitimacy in openly formulating demands for justice and equality, as well as for proposing an alternative vision of progress. The defense and promotion of these values took on aggressive propagandistic forms, making dialogue difficult within international arenas, which became privileged spaces for the staging and ordering of blocs. International organizations thus helped to promote, within each of these blocs, a culture and practice of the multilateralism spreading within regional organizations.

International organizations were not the only sites of pointless confrontation between the two blocs. The discussions that took place in the assemblies of these organizations were also an opportunity to question dominant models—often Western ones—regarding fundamental issues such as the family or the organization of labor relations. This questioning cannot simply be reduced to Cold War oppositions, and it paved the way for the views and even reform projects that emerged in the ensuing decades.

In this regard, when viewed from the vantage point of international organizations, the Cold War did not solely express the division of the world by the United States and the Soviet Union, for it was also a moment in which competing internationalisms developed. These were structured and strengthened within and through international arenas and assumed their full importance in the decade following Stalin's death in 1953.

Chapter Three

INTERNATIONALISMS DURING
THE COLD WAR

In 1953, the year Stalin died and the Republican Dwight D. Eisenhower became president of the United States, Dag Hammarskjöld of Sweden succeeded Trygve Lie of Norway as the head of the UN Secretariat. He immediately put an end to the inquiry conducted by the Federal Bureau of Investigation against U.S. civil servants, reestablishing a more peaceful environment within the secretariat. The rise of Nikita Khrushchev within the Communist Party and state apparatus of the Soviet Union, and the beginning of de-Stalinization with the Communist Party's Twentieth Congress in 1956, were accompanied by reaffirmations of the need for "peaceful coexistence." International organizations were privileged spaces for this coexistence, as most countries from the bloc assumed or reassumed their place in the World Health Organization between 1956 and 1958.[1] In 1954 the USSR joined the International Labour Organization and the United Nations Educational, Scientific and Cultural Organization.[2] In 1956 the Soviet government ratified twelve ILO conventions; that same year, a branch of the World Federation of United Nations Associations was established in Moscow. In the United States, this Soviet openness was viewed with concern. It was accompanied by pressure exerted on UNESCO director-general Luther Evans emanating from circles close to the government. With the end of Senator McCarthy's activity in December 1954, however, the U.S.

anticommunist crusade changed in nature: the struggle against the domestic enemy was succeeded by a strategy of subversion, making subtle use of various international networks. This strategy was continued after John F. Kennedy was elected president in December 1960.

In 1955 discussions within the UN General Assembly grew more peaceful, making it possible to reinitiate the admission process for new members, which had been blocked since 1950. That same year, sixteen new countries joined the UN, including four people's democracies (Albania, Bulgaria, Hungary, Romania), along with Mongolia in 1957. The Eastern bloc remained numerically in the minority but came out of its isolation. The admission of fifty new members between 1955 and 1969, essentially countries that had recently emerged from colonization, changed the balance of power, as demonstrated by the election of U Thant of Burma as UN secretary general in 1961. Other factors also contributed to the influence of the USSR and the Eastern bloc. The launch of the first artificial satellite, *Sputnik 1*, in October 1957 appeared to demonstrate the advances of Soviet science and technology. That same year, the head of the Central Intelligence Agency, Allen Dulles, affirmed before the United States Congressional Joint Economic Committee: "If the soviet industrial growth rate persists at eight or nine percent per annum over the next decade, as is forecasted, the gap between our two economies . . . will be dangerously narrowed."[3] The Eastern bloc appeared to be victorious in the economic war being waged against it, with this success proving highly attractive to newly independent countries.

This emergence from marginality was accompanied by a return of Communist internationalism. The latter was based on three pillars: the cohesion of the Eastern bloc, the existence of numerous dedicated nongovernmental organizations, and especially the attractiveness of the Communist discourse among leaders from newly decolonized countries. This attractiveness was met with an international anticommunism led by various networks, in which powerful philanthropic organizations such as the Ford Foundation were actively involved. Nevertheless, the period can hardly be reduced to this confrontation. As an example, I will focus on the role of Yugoslavia. Excluded from the Cominform in 1948, it never abandoned the model of socialism and served as a bridge between the East and the West, thereby giving it a role in international arenas that was much more important than its actual political and economic weight. Yugoslav leaders also

INTERNATIONALISMS DURING THE COLD WAR

knew how to speak to elites from recently decolonized countries, those that, following Alfred Sauvy in 1952, were referred to as the "Third World." These elites had specific demands that could not be reduced to the Cold War logic of confrontation between the First and Second Worlds. They were primarily guided by their efforts to shed the political dependence to which their economic underdevelopment condemned them.

These two—and soon to be three—internationalisms were clearly heard in the arenas of UN international organizations, albeit in distorted fashion. To document their abundant forms and heterogeneity, it is important to consider the activity of international NGOs, and to examine their autonomy from either bloc. This chapter will use the vantage point of various international organizations and major international associations to interpret the period as a moment in which the world was organized around the affirmation of international values.

DIVIDED TOGETHER

Together at the UN

Between 1955 and 1961 the United Nations experienced a series of political and diplomatic crises that were not necessarily Cold War conflicts but led to opposition between the two worlds of the Cold War.[4] As violent as the verbal confrontations in international confines may have been, they never halted the development of multilateral practices, and international organizations actually seemed to emerge from each new crisis with renewed strength. For instance, when Soviet tanks rolled into Budapest in 1956 to crush the Hungarian Revolution, the Hungarian prime minister, Imre Nagy, appealed to the UN; the secretary-general did not respond, but via the High Commissioner for Refugees (UNHCR) he deployed a substantial aid package for the two hundred thousand Hungarian refugees. It was the UNHCR's first intervention on the ground.[5] The abstention of UN authorities in Hungary was almost contemporaneous with their armed intervention in the Suez Canal to end the war opposing Egypt and the French-British-Israeli alliance reacting to the canal's nationalization. It led to the creation of the first UN Emergency Force in November 1956 and served as a model for the "peacekeeping" interventions that succeeded it, especially in Congo in July 1960. During the Congo crisis, the Soviet and U.S. representatives to

INTERNATIONALISMS DURING THE COLD WAR

the Security Council both voted to send troops under the UN flag to push the Belgian Army out of Katanga, and it was not until the ensuing months that this unanimity was shattered. Soviet leaders supported Patrice Lumumba, while the CIA planned his elimination. Although it has been largely obscured in the literature, Secretary-General U Thant acted as a mediator in the de-escalation of the Cuban Missile Crisis in October 1962.[6] These different moments attest to the UN's role as a space for dialogue and as an instrument for conflict resolution during this decade of the Cold War. Each of these crises was an opportunity to enhance the UN's activities and broaden its area of intervention. The UN's nation-building efforts were largely a response to the risks of social conflict (in Bolivia), or the dangers of war (in Congo).[7] In similar fashion, and still with the same goal, various UN agencies played a decisive role in promoting a less fragmented economic space.

A World Economy

With Stalin's death, Soviet leaders abandoned the dogma of economic autarky: "The world was globalizing, and the Soviets along with it."[8] To develop their economy—the very condition for building socialism— authorities in the Soviet Union and in people's democracies knew that they had to expand relations with the capitalist West. In 1952 a major international economic conference intended to bring together partners from the two blocs was held in Moscow. While it enjoyed only mixed success, it shows the openness of Communist leaders even before Stalin's death. In 1956 Soviet leaders requested, in vain, to join the International Chamber of Commerce.[9] In 1957 Poland and Romania requested and were granted observer status to GATT, with Hungary following in 1958.[10] The Soviet Union did not join GATT but in 1953 developed trade agreements with Western countries, initially with Iceland, somewhat later with France, Greece, Argentina, and Denmark, and in 1954 with Belgium, Norway, Sweden, and Finland. These agreements were made despite repeated warnings from U.S. leaders who, with the end of Marshall aid, lost part of their influence. Under pressure from business circles, Western European governments successfully reduced CoCom lists in 1954.[11]

These trade relations were facilitated by the resumed activity of the Trade Committee of the United Nations Economic Commission for Europe, which became an important space for meetings and mutual acculturation between leaders and economic actors from the two blocs. Economic leaders, especially those from Poland and Czechoslovakia, were particularly active.[12] In 1957 the Polish economist Oskar Lange paid tribute, upon Gunnar Myrdal's departure, to the role played by the commission and its director in maintaining relations between the East and the West: "During the cold war when the countries of Europe were divided between East and West the ECE succeeded not only in surviving, but also in continuing its positive work. In that period the Commission was practically the only meeting ground where countries of eastern and western Europe met and cooperated. Much of this success was due to the personal efforts of its Executive Secretary, Professor Myrdal."[13]

In 1953 the UNECE Secretariat organized annual consultations to develop and discuss lists of products and selected experts likely to promote trade relations between Eastern and Western Europe. The representatives from the Eastern bloc came very well prepared, with numerous bilateral agreements between Eastern and Western European countries originating at UNECE. Myrdal also traveled to Moscow to discuss the expansion of intra-European economic relations in 1956.[14] These discussions at the commission provided an opportunity to identify both administrative and political issues hindering the development of trade, including the protectionist measures implemented by countries in Western Europe: Eastern European countries criticized the establishment of the European Coal and Steel Community in 1952 and the European Economic Community (EEC) in 1957.[15] This criticism was also fueled by the fact that representatives from the Council for Mutual Economic Assistance were not received in Geneva before 1959, even as UNECE maintained close relations with economic organizations from Western Europe.[16] Moreover, the Federal Republic of Germany was admitted in 1956, whereas the German Democratic Republic, which was still referred to as the "Soviet occupation zone," conserved observer status until 1972. The technical work of the committees, however, especially the Transport Committee, provided support for East-West trade.[17] In 1953 the quantity of products traded between the two parts of Europe barely reached two-thirds of 1938 levels, although it on average grew 15–25 percent per year between 1953 and 1957.

In addition, countries in the Eastern bloc sought to develop economic relations with countries that had recently gained their independence. Trade relations remained modest—less than 10 percent of the trade volume with the USSR during those years—but were encouraged by Comecon. The development programs promoted by the UN beginning in 1949 also provided an incentive for such efforts. The Soviets became involved upon Stalin's death: in July 1953, during the United Nations Economic and Social Council's sixth session, the Soviet delegate Amazasp Arutiunian announced that his country would contribute four million (nonconvertible) rubles to the United Nations Expanded Programme of Technical Assistance, and then in 1959 Soviet leaders financially committed to the Economic Development Fund.

The role of Eastern European countries in development programs, however, clearly shows their ambiguous position in the world economy and within the international system. Leaders from Eastern bloc countries officially refused the notion of underdevelopment, which they felt was inspired by a capitalist vision of the world, although they were aware of their lagging economies, with some of them—the Poles, Romanians, and Bulgarians in particular—hoping to take advantage of the Expanded Programme as underdeveloped countries. These calls came the earliest from Poland, where the new elites inherited know-how and staff trained in requesting aid from philanthropic agencies and international programs. This was carried out by key figures well-versed in relations with international organizations since the interwar period.[18] As part of the Expanded Programme, the Polish government hosted experts in 1958 to help it rationalize family housing.[19] In 1959 the deputy permanent representative of Poland to the UN European Office requested that a social worker be sent for one year, and that a grant program be established for information exchange among Austria, Yugoslavia, and Poland in the field of handicapped child rehabilitation.[20] Similarly, between 1957 and 1961 the ILO provided funding for a dozen Polish grant recipients, who visited rehabilitation centers for handicapped workers in Western Europe.[21] Finally, in 1958, and once again in 1961, the Polish representative in Geneva wrote to the UNECE secretary requesting that economists from the Polish government's Planning Committee take advantage of the expertise produced by his organization.[22] These requests show that the economic and social planning model of the Central European Communist elite was far from stabilized during the 1950s, and that the USSR was not the only inspiration for countries within its sphere of influence. They also bear witness to the permanence of the subordinate

The Enduring Marginality of the Second World

Aside from their economic marginality, Central and Eastern European countries remained underrepresented in international organizations, in which civil servants from Eastern European countries generally represented no more than 3 percent of staff. Communist leaders interpreted this underrepresentation as a deliberate segregation: it was no doubt connected to suspicion of these regimes and their nationals among international civil servants, the large majority of whom were from countries in the capitalist West. It could also be explained by the primary recruitment criteria of the time in international organizations, as mastering various Western languages (English and French in particular) and possessing specific economic knowledge automatically favored Western candidates. In addition, the practices of socialist governments did not foster the integration of their civil servants. Being highly concerned about the loyalty of their nationals, they strove, often in vain, to control the recruitment of their nationals. The latter were most often on secondment from their original administration, thereby helping maintain strong ties with the authorities of their country of citizenship. This strategy was common in Eastern bloc countries but not specific to them, as many civil servants from Western countries were also on secondment. Civil servants from the East, however, were subject to a specific status: their salary was paid to their governments, which provided them modest compensation in exchange. When it was not for political reasons, economic motives prompted international civil servants from socialist countries to try to defect to the West. To limit this, the governments of these countries imposed a regular rotation on their nationals in the secretariats of organizations; during the 1950s they rarely stayed more than three to five years and lived in reserved buildings where they were carefully isolated from their colleagues from the West. This fueled the mistrust of the latter, who often considered them to be the emissaries of their national governments—and even spies in the pay of their country's intelligence services—rather than full-fledged international civil servants, thereby limiting the influence of civil servants from the East and heightening their marginalization.[23]

In general, the involvement of political leaders from the Soviet Union and people's democracies remained critical, prudent, and selective. Representatives from these countries denounced the domination that those in the West had over the functioning of international institutions, monopolizing 75 percent of positions in international civil service in 1955. This domination fueled recurring criticism by representatives from both socialist and Third World countries, hence explaining why they often voted against the UN budget. Similarly, they refused international courts, which they deemed directly inspired by a "bourgeois" conception of justice, and participated little in the central missions of these organizations, in particular their development programs. Their financial contribution remained below 5 percent of the total budget, as opposed to approximately 70 percent for Western countries. Ultimately, even though they joined most of the UN agencies, the leaders of socialist countries continued to see major international organizations as an emanation of liberal internationalism, and as instruments in the hands of capitalist powers. In 1961–1962 the UN's muddled involvement in the Congo crisis—and the assassination at the hands of Belgian authorities of Patrice Lumumba, the former prime minister, who had the support of Soviet leaders—fueled this negative view. Nikita Khrushchev apparently said at the time that he "spit on the United Nations."[24]

THE COMMUNIST WORLD-SYSTEM

In addition to their engagement within organizations in the UN system, socialist countries reactivated a competing internationalism organized around three groups.[25] The first involved interstate and supranational institutions, such as the Warsaw Pact and Comecon, which served as a foundation for the bloc and reinforced the perception that there was a Cold War opposition. The second was the support provided by the governments of socialist countries for national liberation movements in the Global South, as well as the close ties of "solidarity" they had with many of the governments of these countries. Finally, in keeping with an older internationalism, the third group involved strengthening the "international Communist movement," which is to say the Communist movement's various associations and international organizations. Their degree of dependence on the Communist Party of the Soviet Union was the subject of Cold War polemics.

Communist Internationalism

The founding of the Comintern in 1919 is traditionally seen as the birth of Communist internationalism, although to understand its conflictual relation with international institutions, it should be seen more in line with the socialist response to liberal internationalism. During the first half of the nineteenth century, free trade advocates such as Richard Cobden saw liberal capitalism as the natural foundation for peace and internationalism. The global revolution called for by Karl Marx was formulated in response to this first internationalism and the domination of capitalism, which Marx already saw as global.[26] The International Workingmen's Association, founded in 1864, and the Second International, established in 1889, were the first international socialist organizations; their goal was to internationally organize labor resistance to the oppression of global capitalism. They were flanked by a multitude of sister organizations serving as spaces for political mobilization, and organizing labor solidarity and sociability as a counterpoint to "bourgeois" organizations.[27]

It was based on this model that Communist internationalism developed. In 1919 the Comintern brought together the new parties that had emerged from the division of the socialist parties. However, Lenin's Twenty-one conditions, which required Communist Parties to submit to the objectives of the Russian Revolution and the pyramidal organizational structure adopted by the Third Communist International, placed it more under the close control of the new socialist state. The latter served as the center from which the global revolution would spread. The leadership of the Communist International, as well as that of some of the organizations connected to it, was incidentally headquartered in the USSR: the Red International of Trade Unions (Profintern), founded in 1921; International Red Aid (or the Communist Red Cross), founded in 1922; Young Communists, etc. However, organizations in the Communist movement cannot simply be considered as the armed wing of a new workers' state. Workers' International Relief was established in Berlin in 1921 and was based in that city until 1933 under the direction of the German Communist Willi Münzenberg. This organization developed large-scale international solidarity actions thanks to its vast international network, which, unlike liberal internationalism, included countries that were still colonized.[28]

INTERNATIONALISMS DURING THE COLD WAR

Communist internationalism conveyed, in its beginnings, a message of emancipation that was subject to various forms of national and local reappropriation in the 1920s. It especially spoke to colonized or dominated peoples, whose demands had not been met by the promises of U.S. president Woodrow Wilson after 1919. With the failure of revolutions in Europe—and basing itself on a Leninist analysis of colonialism, seen as a kind of imperialism—the Comintern endeavored from the early 1920s onward to internationalize its anticapitalist discourse by turning toward colonized peoples. In 1920 the Congress of Peoples of the East brought together in Baku representatives from Communist Parties and national liberation movements in countries that remained colonized. In 1921 the Commissariat of Nationalities of the future Soviet Union founded the Communist University of the Toilers of the East in Moscow, which, via its satellites in Soviet Asia, became a school for the cadres of national liberation movements. Numerous cadres from these movements emerged from this melting pot, including Ho Chi Minh of Indochina, Deng Xiaoping of China, and the Communist Manabendra Nath Roy of India, along with the cadres of the South African Communist Party. They spread a message that closely connected national liberation and anticapitalism. These appeals to colonized or dominated peoples of course served propaganda purposes, but the emancipating message cannot be reduced to its manipulation by Soviet Communists, as it profoundly influenced a number of leaders from nationalist movements and explains the Communist model's influence among the elite of new countries up through the 1970s.[29]

For all that, in spite of the hope it aroused among the elite of colonized countries—and the concern it caused among leaders of Western powers—Communist internationalism could not compete with the liberal international institutions established following World War I. Communist influence remained marginal in Latin America and Africa, and most especially, the Communist movement gradually lost its internationalist momentum after Lenin's death in 1924.[30] The Comintern slowly came under the close control of leaders of the Communist Party of the USSR, and then of Stalin himself, becoming an instrument for the Stalinization of Communist Parties.[31] The scope of the purges of the 1930s in internationalist Communist circles and the dissolution of the Comintern in 1943 demonstrate Stalin's obsessive suspicion of anything emanating from abroad, and of internationalism of any kind. The Cominform, whose founding was announced in 1947 in response to the Marshall Plan, did not represent a Communist international organization; it stopped meeting in 1950 and was officially dissolved in 1956. It nevertheless gathered and mobilized the international Communist "forces" organized within a multitude of associations: the World Federation of Democratic Youth, the International Students Union, the Women's International Democratic Federation, the International Association of Democratic Lawyers, and so on, which were all more or less closely controlled by the Communist Party of the Soviet Union.[32]

This was especially true of unionism of Communist inspiration, which was pivotal for the strategy of winning over the working masses. Following its forced move to Prague in 1956, the World Federation of Trade Unions clearly became the voice of the Soviet "camp," as demonstrated by the contradictory responses of its secretary Louis Saillant regarding the intervention of Warsaw Pact armies in Prague in the summer of 1968. After a prudent condemnation, the WFTU aligned with the Soviet position, despite repeated calls from the Czechoslovak Confederation of Trade Unions during the summer of 1968.[33] However, when observed via the archives of its competing organization, the International Confederation of Free Trade Unions, the WFTU cannot be reduced to a pro-Soviet office. ICFTU leaders showed genuine concern regarding the growth of its international influence. The WFTU launched a charm offensive among reformist trade unionists in the West and organized trips to people's democracies for the leaders of federations affiliated with the ICFTU, doing so despite repeated prohibitions from its leadership since 1950. Most especially, it supported causes that the reformist trade union federations in the West acknowledged having abandoned. The WFTU was clearly more active in the anticolonial struggle and developed relations with unions in the Global South, the vast majority of which joined it after independence. The federations affiliated with the ICFTU recognized that they were highly dependent on traditional imperial channels, which explains why they were not very attractive for their colleagues in new countries.[34] The WFTU was also deeply involved in advocating for women's rights in the workplace. Leaders of the ICFTU repeatedly expressed their concerns regarding the positive impact of the World Conference of Women Workers held in Budapest in 1956, and later in Sofia in 1966.[35]

INTERNATIONALISMS DURING THE COLD WAR

Advocating for women's representation and role in society was, as we saw earlier, a topic around which Communists developed an international discourse early on. The Women's International Democratic Federation (WIDF), founded in Paris in 1945 and led by the Communist scientist Eugénie Cotton, was an organization that worked for women's rights. It brought together a broad coalition of forces on the basis of antifascism, peace, and the promotion of women's role in society. In 1950 the House Un-American Activities Committee forced the U.S. branch of the WIDF to dissolve. In 1951 the organization's secretariat was expelled from Paris, taking refuge in East Berlin. This clearly increased the WIDF's dependence on the social-ist bloc. It would be going too far, however, to simply consider the organi-zation as a docile executor of Soviet policy: in the 1960s Italian women emphasized that the organization's struggle for peace had to free itself from Soviet diplomatic objectives, while the Czechoslovaks mobilized against the Warsaw Pact intervention in 1968. After securing its advisory status at the UN and other agencies of the UN system, in 1967 the WIDF developed issues more clearly revolving around demands for greater civil and profes-sional equality: in 1972 it proposed at the UN to make 1975 International Women's Year, a celebration that the liberal feminist movement later tried to appropriate for itself. The WIDF was also behind the UN Convention on the Elimination of all Forms of Discrimination Against Women in 1979. Finally, like any international Communist movement, the organization developed its activity with women from colonized or recently decolonized countries.[36]

Similarly, the Peace Movement, generally considered an organization of the Communist movement—a "third-drawer" one to use Annie Kriegel's expression—mobilized forces beyond exclusively Communist ones. The movement was born in 1948 in France, and while it was supported and encouraged by the Cominform, it did not directly emerge from it, as it ini-tially grew out of an initiative by a circle of Resistance members, which included members and fellow companions of both the French Communist Party and Christians on the left. Following the Wroclaw Congress, held that same year in Poland, an International Liaison Committee of Intellectuals in Defense of Peace was created, led by the Communist physicist Frédéric Joliot-Curie. Organized according to the pyramidal structure specific to international Communist organizations, it developed positions that unde-niably served the interests of Soviet foreign policy, although the movement was never exclusively limited to Communists, especially in France, where it included representatives from the full "progressive" spectrum. In addition, the Stockholm Appeal launched in 1950, which demanded a ban on atomic weapons, was well received far beyond the Communist movement.[37] The peace movement and the Stockholm Appeal helped internationalize the issue of peace, so much so that President Eisenhower voluntarily used the pacifist phrasing of the Stockholm Appeal when he announced his Atoms for Peace program in 1953, which provided for the creation of an International Atomic Energy Agency (IAEA). Anticommunist movements themselves quickly took pride in the struggle for peace. Communists successfully showcased the attractiveness of their internationalist practices and messages during the major international festivals they regularly held. The World Festival of Youth in 1951, which took place in East Berlin in the midst of the Korean War, drew thousands of youth from Western Europe, who braved prohibitions from their country's authorities.[38]

For at least two decades (1954–1975), the international Communist movement was able, in the context of Cold War ideological competition, to bring together groups that exceeded Communist forces alone. It especially internationalized, and even universalized, certain issues led by Communists, in particular women's rights, promoting peace, and supporting anticolonial struggles.[39]

The Eastern Bloc: Between Sovietization and International Space

The terms Eastern "bloc" or Soviet "bloc" were part of the Cold War vocabulary and were initially used by British and U.S. journalists and politicians to denounce the dominance of Soviet political leaders over the Central and Eastern European countries liberated by the Red Army. The creation of the Cominform in 1947, Comecon in 1949, and the Warsaw Pact in 1955—in addition to the military interventions in countries where the power of the Communist Party appeared under threat, such as the GDR in 1953, Hungary in 1956, and Czechoslovakia in 1968—was seen as proof of a bloc dominated by the Soviet Union.[39]

During the 1940s and 1950s Soviet leaders exported broad swaths of their system to Eastern European countries, with priority being given to security, intelligence, and political control.[40] With the support of Soviet advisors and experts, Communist Party cadres long exiled in the USSR played

INTERNATIONALISMS DURING THE COLD WAR

an essential role in exporting the Chekist model to countries liberated by the Red Army.[41] The Communist Parties that seized control of the state apparatus in people's democracies in 1947–1948 were organized according to the model of the Communist Party of the Soviet Union; they largely used its by-laws as the basis for their own and made uniform the curricula of the Communist Party Schools for training the cadres of new regimes. Severely purged during the Stalinist period, the most docile of these cadres were systematically sent to the Higher Party School in Moscow.[42] Economically, nationalizing the means of production and exchange, along with centralized planning, was at the very foundation of economic coordination within Comecon, which began to function in earnest only in the early 1960s.[43] In the field of culture, artistic production was subsidized everywhere and encouraged as an instrument in the construction of socialism; centralized cultural associations such as Writers' Unions could control production and organize artistic circulations in all countries. Until the 1970s socialist realism was a requirement for all the bloc's artists.[44] Soviet Friendship Societies and trips to the USSR for the most deserving were signs of this desire to establish the bloc as a specific and unified space of circulation, with the USSR at the center.

Nevertheless, while the Soviet Union was seen as a monolith by its enemies, its leaders initially struggled to "imagine" this bloc.[45] The Soviet model only partially imposed itself and was called into question beginning in the mid-1950s. The leaders of various countries tried to assert and implement, in varying ways, national pathways to socialism. The desire for independence and an early affirmation of nationalisms are demonstrated by Gomulka's Polish October in 1956; the Czechoslovak reforms of the 1960s; the Romanian refusal to participate in the International Socialist Division of Labor within Comecon in 1964; Kadar's national policy in Hungary; and the aggressive campaign of East German leaders to establish a sealed border between the two blocs.[46] These nationalisms were reinforced by the overwhelming power of national states, the sole political, economic, and social actor in state socialist countries.[47] As for the Soviet Union, it struggled to establish itself as a positive model; trips to the USSR, which were offered as a reward to the most ardent Communists, were often counterproductive given the disappointing Soviet reality. In addition, while Russian was the bloc's official language, it did not truly take root either in societies—where rejection of Russian instruction has been widely documented—or at the top. Artists and political or economic leaders from Eastern Europe who could express themselves in Russian were rare. The meetings of Comecon or the Soviet Writers' Union generally were held with the help of interpreters.

The USSR was therefore not the beacon that its leaders glorified, with its cultural and civilizational influence certainly being less than that of the United States over Western European countries, although the imposition of a model for political and economic organization constituted a specific space in Eastern Europe. This space, however, was not exclusively structured by bilateral ties between the USSR and people's democracies. Beginning in the late 1950s, the latter developed numerous relations among themselves in the fields of culture and the economy. The bloc's institutions served at the time as spaces for exchange and circulation and can be studied as regional international organizations, like their liberal competitors in Western Europe. Relations between national writers' unions encouraged book translations and circulations within the bloc, chiefly but not exclusively involving Russian literature. Meetings and festivals promoted the development of interpersonal relations that led to the creation of networks, especially in the field of art.[48] Comecon never became a "single market" in the East, but it served as a framework for bilateral exchange and played a role in the international organization of the bloc by serving as a melting pot, giving rise to a group of economic experts focused on developing projects for integration. While these projects failed, Comecon nevertheless became a place for organizing the economic interests of people's democracies, initially with respect to the USSR, later with their economic partners in the West, and ultimately with the Global South.[49]

The GDR, the bloc's most developed country, which suffered from its lack of international recognition, played a driving role in this regard.[50] The authorities of this country organized events that attracted representatives from across the globe and projected themselves as the leaders of an alternative internationalism. The International Leipzig Festival for Documentary Film was a regular platform, with more occasional events also taking place.[51] To celebrate International Women's Year in 1975, the East German government hosted the International Congress of Women, which after the World Festival of Youth in 1973 enjoyed the presence of charismatic figures such as Angela Davis. These events show the attractiveness of this alternative internationalism, especially among newly independent countries.[52]

"Friendship" with the Third World

In his speech during the Twentieth Congress of the Communist Party in 1956, Khrushchev again insisted, clearly in keeping with the Leninist tradition, on the relation between revolution and the anticolonial struggle. At the time the UN served as a platform from which Soviet leaders spread a message of anticolonialism and international solidarity toward oppressed peoples.[53] In September 1959, during his first speech before the UN General Assembly, Khrushchev took a position in favor of independence for colonized peoples. From 1954 onward, the Soviets took active part in the United Nations Trusteeship Council, which since 1945 had been tasked with administering the dependent territories placed under its supervision. They also became more involved in the work of the United Nations Economic Commission for Asia and the Far East (ECAFE), and even the Economic Commission for Latin America (ECLA), demonstrating their concern for developing relations with the Global South.[54] This new internationalism primarily took place—as it did during the Leninist period—via an education program for the Third World elite. The founding of Patrice Lumumba People's Friendship University in 1960 was firmly in keeping with this Leninist tradition.[55] The governments of various people's democracies also developed education programs geared toward the Global South and successfully attracted a growing number of students thanks to grants, and even the establishment of training institutes on site, such as the Galal Fahmy Advanced Technical School founded by the East Germans near Cairo.[56] This academic diplomacy was conceived during the 1950s and 1960s as an important instrument for standing and influence in African and Asian countries; it was supported and driven by Comecon's Technical Assistance Commission, which from 1962 onward centralized the educational activities of people's democracies directed toward Southern Mediterranean countries.[57]

These relations were part of a strategy of influence in connection with the Cold War, although they should be situated in longer-term genealogies. Countries in Eastern Europe and the Middle East had long-standing relations, which were fostered by geographical proximity, lengthy cohabitation within the same Ottoman space, and even the continued presence of Muslim culture in the cases of Albania, Bulgaria, and Yugoslavia.[58] In fact, since the interwar period, Islam had been a strong instrument for connecting the

USSR and the Arab world via the republics of Central Asia or the Kazan Tatars.[59] In addition to Muslims, there was the Armenian diaspora that had settled around the Mediterranean rim, Lebanon in particular, and had privileged relations with the Soviet Republic of Armenia. In 1970 all ninety-eight of the Lebanese students who enrolled at Yerevan State University thanks to a Soviet scholarship were Armenian.[60]

In addition to this geographic and cultural proximity, there were similarities with respect to their state of economic and social development, as well as their shared peripheral position in relation to the developed West.[61] This proximity explains why the writings of economists from Eastern European peripheries received the welcome they did in Latin America from the interwar period onward. This was true, among others, of the Romanian economist Mihail Manoilescu, who during the 1930s emphasized the negative effects of the international division of labor for "lagging" countries and challenged the notion that international trade could automatically be a factor in development. According to Manoilescu, inequality in terms of trade would reinforce inequalities in development, an idea that had a lasting influence on development economists in Brazil and Latin America, including Raùl Prebisch, the future director of UNECLA, and the first secretary-general of the United Nations Conference on Trade and Development.[62]

Within international arenas, Eastern Europe, which was seen as an underdeveloped European periphery, represented a laboratory of sorts for development issues from World War II onward. This is demonstrated by the previously cited article by the Polish economist Paul Rosenstein-Rodan, a civil servant at the World Bank between 1947 and 1954.[63] At international organizations such as the World Bank or UNECE, a group of economists belonging to the socialist movement advocated, beginning in the late 1940s, for development policies for Eastern and Southern Europe. Most of them, such as Rosenstein-Rodan, Nicholas Kaldor, Władysław Malinowski, and Michał Kalecki, were émigrés from these countries. They established these European peripheries as spaces for experimentation, and as models for exporting development policies to Latin America, Asia, and later Africa.[64] Due to their early emergence from decolonization, Latin American countries enjoyed a special role in these exchanges. Relations expanded between Central European and Latin American countries beginning in the 1950s; they of course had a political dimension, but they were also based on the

INTERNATIONALISMS DURING THE COLD WAR

exchange of economic know-how that was in keeping with a shared vision of development issues.[65]

The Soviets were late to join the international debate on development, although in 1955 the four million rubles provided by Soviet authorities for the Expanded Programme of Technical Assistance enabled the development of various projects, especially in India. In coordination with UNESCO, Soviet experts founded the country's second institute of technology, in Bombay. They also helped fund more modest projects in connection with various UN agencies. They cooperated with the ILO to establish a training institute, with the WHO as part of a health program, UNESCO for the development of a geology institute, and the FAO for a fishery. During the same period, Soviet engineers were sent as part of the Expanded Programme to Burma, Ceylon, Afghanistan, Indonesia, and Yugoslavia.[66]

However, most Soviet aid—especially the most spectacular—was provided as part of bilateral relations. This was particularly true in China, where the first five-year plan enjoyed broad financial support from both Soviet and Central European authorities. This was also the case in India, where the large Bhilai steel plant kept over eight hundred Soviet technicians busy and represented the most important of the seventy facility projects created in India with Soviet aid.[67] This was also true of the famous Aswan Dam in Egypt, for which the Soviets replaced the World Bank as sponsor and expert, after the latter rejected the loan request Nasser submitted under pressure from U.S. authorities. Beginning in the late 1950s, there were also a multitude of initiatives involving all countries in the bloc. Some of them were part of the UN Development Programme, such as the loans provided by Czechoslovak authorities to Afghanistan to build factories in 1955, or the one provided by the GDR to Indonesia to establish a sugar refinery.[68] Educational and cultural initiatives increased from the late 1950s onward in the form of bilateral agreements in 1956 between the USSR and Syria, as well as Egypt and Czechoslovakia. The Soviet Society of Friendship and Cultural Relations with the Arab Countries and its East German equivalent were created in 1958. These cultural and educational relations accelerated in the 1960s.

In 1961 Comecon created a Standing Committee for the Coordination of Technical Aid, which organized educational activities in member countries directed toward the Third World. Comecon leaders tried to implement a concerted aid and development policy and sought to promote "a socialist economic development model" based on the nationalization of large swaths of the economy, state planning, and the development of industry.[69] This model proved highly attractive for the political elites of underdeveloped countries, precisely because the USSR and countries from the first European periphery apparently proved one could emerge from situations of dependence and underdevelopment without deepening social or racial inequality. In addition, this model seemingly promised endogamous development without recourse to Western capital, and with no risk of creeping recolonization. Finally, elites from these countries were won over by the possibility of implementing a centralized, state-led development, which would enable them to expand their own power.[70] Beginning in the period, however, this development model came up against the limits of the USSR's economic capacity—which, economically speaking, was a midsized power—as well as the limits of centralized planning. This is demonstrated by the ongoing difficulties experienced by Soviet engineers and technicians when building the large Bhilai steel plant in India, which was in the end mostly equipped with Western technology. The failure of Soviet projects in Ghana, Congo, Guinea, and Togo in the early 1960s also reflect these challenges.[71]

Finally, while Western leaders interpreted the intervention of Eastern European countries in their former colonies as a Cold War offensive, field studies show that recently independent countries generally had a more pragmatic relation to development aid. They strategically sought aid from the East and the West based on their economic and political interests. For instance, political leaders from the most conservative Arab states accepted sending their students to Eastern European countries despite courses on Marxism-Leninism, which were reintroduced in 1968, because the cost of study was more reasonable. They quickly learned how to play the competition between the blocs to their advantage, with a view to generating more offers. Finally, it is difficult to assess the real effects that educational policies implemented by socialist countries had on the elites of the Global South. These effects were always less extensive than claimed by ideological discourses.[72] For representatives of these countries, it was less a matter of choosing between two models than of making them compatible and even complementary.

This is demonstrated by the debate that unfolded at the International Labour Office regarding the definition of *employer*. In response to attacks from employers in capitalist countries directed at those from countries with nationalized economies, the office created a committee to draft a report for debate at the Thirty-ninth International Labour Conference in 1956. The conclusions of the report, and those of the discussions surrounding it, underscored the artificial character of the radical oppositions highlighted by employers from capitalist countries.[73] The growing importance of forms of mixed economies—and by correlation the need to distinguish between an employer and a private owner—was clearly emphasized by representatives from developing countries, especially by the Indian delegate, who affirmed:

> In past controversies, many among us tended to believe that the countries of the world could be divided into two groups: those where workers' and employers' organizations were independent and free of government control, and those that were not. . . . There are varying degrees of control. . . . Today, the section that represents nationalized industry is of course still small, but it continues to grow, and if we decided in advance to ignore the role it can play, then perhaps we will prevent elements useful to the cause that we hold dear from taking part in the ILO's activities.[74]

The governments and dominant groups in the West did not necessarily appreciate the pragmatism of the elite from the Global South, whose relations with socialist countries they saw as a threat. More generally, the apparent success of Communist internationalism from the late 1950s onward led to concerted international responses from the anti-Communist networks that established themselves as an international counter-movement.

FIGHTING COMMUNISM: AN INTERNATIONAL PROJECT

As an ideology and practice, anticommunism developed beginning in the second half of the nineteenth century. It was structured and organized around an international movement after the outbreak of the Russian Revolution and the fear of revolutionary contagion it sparked.[75] The Cold War, and especially the 1950s, was a pivotal moment in the international struggle against communism, which was generally conflated with the Soviet Union and the Eastern bloc. This confusion served as an effective means for discrediting the international Communist movement, which was presented as an instrument of Soviet foreign policy.

Much more so than the communism it was fighting, anticommunism was a heterogeneous movement, with disparate ideological inspirations. Anticommunist associations, mobilizations, and international movements included political sensibilities ranging from the far left to far right. It also involved very different groups: émigrés, White Russians from the interwar period or exiled after World War II, played a driving role but were far from the only ones to do so. Finally, even though the centrality of the USSR within the Communist "world-system" can be questioned, anticommunism was not dominated by the United States either, even though U.S. actors organized its internationalization via the CIA and the Ford Foundation.

Anticommunism: A Multifaceted Movement

The International Anticommunist Entente founded in Geneva in 1924 by the lawyer Théodore Aubert and the Russian doctor Georges Lodygensky was one of the first international associations whose explicit goal was to respond to the Communist project of global revolution. Its aim was to systematically fight the Communist International, or Comintern, through propaganda, and by trying to influence political leaders. The Entente was originally a pan-European movement with considerable influence on political elites, especially in Switzerland, although its role in the United States remained limited.[76] The rhetoric of the Entente and the various organizations connected to it shows, from its very beginnings, the multifaceted nature of anticommunism. The ideological corpus was disparate, and while some emphasized the values of liberty and democracy, other underscored defense of Christian civilization. This Christian inspiration was led by sister associations such as Pro Deo, founded in 1934, or Moral Rearmament, founded in 1938, both of which served during the Cold War as the spearhead for a conservative Christian anticommunist movement directed against atheistic socialism.[77]

Cold War anticommunist movements extended the legacy of Aubert's movement, all while globalizing and diversifying it.[78] Non-European organizations also emerged, such as the Asian Pacific Anti-Communist League in 1954, which became the World Anti-Communist League in 1966. Protestant churches played an important role in the movement's internationalization, such as the International Council of Christian Churches founded in 1948, in response to the liberal branch organized by the World Council of Churches.[79] The more conservative fringe of international Catholicism organized via the International Committee for the Defence of Christian Civilization, which became a major actor in anticommunism.[80]

Unlike the interwar period, U.S. actors, and the CIA in particular, played a crucial role in organizing this anticommunist internationalism. The U.S. intelligence agency provided funding for a multitude of organizations, including the Congress for Cultural Freedom founded in Berlin in 1950, the International Commission of Jurists founded in 1952, and the various national branches of the Peace and Freedom movement.[81] Nevertheless, the CIA proved unable to exert a lasting influence on their orientations. For instance, the Cultural Freedom movement swung, with respect to its French component, toward the left of the political spectrum and became a platform for East-West resistance to totalitarianism, as well as a driver of cultural circulations between the two blocs.[82] Similarly, the International Jurists Commission transformed into an organization that fought everywhere to protect political and human rights on the basis of well-documented studies. The Peace and Freedom movement shows the diversity of anticommunist inspirations. Its French branch was founded in 1950 by the deputy and former Resistance member Jean-Paul David, and it collaborated with the German branch on the basis of European solidarity against Bolshevism. This collaboration was nevertheless complicated by the quite clear nationalsocialist inspirations of the Volksbund für Frieden und Freiheit (People's League for Peace and Freedom). Financed by the U.S. and FRG governments, the Volksbund was largely inspired by the anti-Bolshevism of the Nazi Party, of which its founder, Eberhardt Taubert, had been an active member since 1931.[83] In fact, Taubert was one of the linchpins of anticommunist propaganda under Nazism, as the leader of the anti-Comintern league and a civil servant of the Ministry of Propaganda, where he actively spread the theory of Judeo-Bolshevism. Until the mid-1960s the German association was in keeping with the legacy of Nazism and functioned on principles of organization largely inherited from the Nazi Party (Führerprinzip). This direct or indirect legacy of Nazism helps explain the emphatic anticommunism of numerous West German actors in various international bodies, such as the ICC.[84]

Over time, however, the antitotalitarian branch on the left assumed an increasing role in the vast network of anticommunist movements; its strength was based on its informed criticism of state socialism. Unlike traditional anticommunism or the anti-Bolshevism of the Nazi tradition, it did not play on fears but instead based itself on accurate analyses to emphasize the gap between the promises of an equal and just society, and the reality of the people's exploitation by a new class of cadres, who under the cover of collectivization actually appropriated the country's resources.[85] Beginning in the late 1960s, in close relation with dissident movements in Eastern bloc countries, the New Left provided a more effective and mobilizing criticism of state socialism than traditional anticommunism. It also represented a new bridge between the East and the West.

The Ford Foundation and Subversion from Within

After 1953 the anticommunist struggle assumed new forms. In response to the political orientations of President Eisenhower, who declared his intention to fight—and not just contain—communism, two strategies emerged. Supporters of a defensive anticommunist approach revolving around the FBI and its director, J. Edgar Hoover, believed that anyone from a country led by Communists was suspect, whereas the Department of State, led by John F. Dulles (since 1952), developed an offensive strategy seeking to weaken the Eastern bloc and to undermine communism from within.[86] This strategy, which was actively encouraged by the British Ministry of Foreign Affairs, was also supported by the political leaders of Western European countries. Alongside an offensive cultural diplomacy personified by Radio Free Europe, which broadcast from Munich beginning in 1950, the Ford Foundation's program for Eastern Europe was a tool for this second strategy.[87]

In agreement with the Department of State, the foundation conducted an unofficial policy of openness beginning with the Polish October of 1956, which was interpreted as a rebirth of Polish nationalism and the expression of a desire for independence.[88] The foundation's leaders sought to take advantage of this window of opportunity to reestablish contact via a policy of aid and intellectual exchange, in an effort to detach Polish elites from the USSR and instead foster their attachment to the values of the West, or, to use the language typical of those years, of "free nations." The foundation's leaders had no doubt regarding the superiority of their political and social system, believing that "the primary basis of this program was the conviction that first hand exposure of Polish leaders to [the] Western World, particularly the United States, would have a profound and positive effect upon the leaders and people of Poland."[89]

In December 1956, with the agreement and support of the Department of State, the foundation planned its pilot program with Poland to "develop relations between the East and the West on a democratic basis." In January 1957 representatives from the Ford and Rockefeller Foundations were invited to visit Poland, with the former releasing $500,000 to fund exchanges between professors and students in the fields they deemed the most likely to convince their adversaries, namely, the social sciences, the humanities, and economics. In return, they planned to send professors from the West to teach these disciplines in Polish universities. These funds were also intended, but in a more limited manner, for sending books and equipment to accelerate the country's economic development.

In May 1957 sixty-four of the three hundred candidates who applied were selected to travel to the West, with thirty-six going to the United States and twenty-eight to Western Europe. They essentially consisted of professors or doctoral students strategically from two specific fields, economics and sociology, along with journalists and high-ranking civil servants.[90] After some hesitation, Polish authorities accepted this aid program, seeing it as a way of gaining access to the Western expertise they needed to overcome the development gap hampering the country's economic performance. They nevertheless tried to negotiate a reorientation of the priorities. In 1961 the Polish minister of education demanded that one-third of the travel grants offered to Polish academics and experts be allocated to technical fields.[91] This gap between the intentions of aid providers and the uses made by recipients was entirely characteristic of the "misunderstandings" caused by the rigid ideological framework of those Cold War years.

In 1959 other countries from the Eastern bloc were added to this program under varying terms based on their political evolution and state of economic development. Yugoslavia received the same type of funds as Poland, but the programs intended for Hungary aimed in particular to help the refugees of the Hungarian Revolution, which was crushed by Soviet tanks. The USSR received funds and special treatment highly encouraged by the U.S. State Department, which in February 1957 signed a cultural agreement with the government involving doctoral students in the sciences; another exchange agreement came in 1959, this time between high-level scientists from the academies of science of the two countries. Unlike the stated objectives for people's democracies, it was less a matter of promoting internal subversion and more of promoting exchange in expertise, with Soviet fundamental science rightly being seen at the time as highly advanced. This exchange program developed during the 1960s, with the Ford Foundation working in close cooperation with the Inter-University Committee on Travel Grants (IUCTG), a governmental program partially funded by the Carnegie Foundation.[92] Numerous exchanges were funded in this way, always in the strategic fields of the economic and social sciences, and involved various institutional actors, especially universities in the United States and later in Western Europe as well. For instance, the École pratique des hautes études in Paris received, via the Ford Foundation, multiple Polish academics. In the East, aside from Poland and Yugoslavia, nationals from almost every country in the bloc, including the GDR, took advantage of these two exchange programs. In 1968 they were combined within the International Research and Exchange Board (IREX), whose funding was jointly provided by the American Council of Learned Societies, the Ford Foundation, and the Social Science Research Council, under the auspices of the Department of State.[93] The objectives were later changed, but until the early 1960s anticommunism remained the primary motivation. These exchange programs were hence clearly in keeping with a Cold War logic, as also demonstrated by the activities intended for Yugoslavia.

THE YUGOSLAV THIRD WAY

Building Socialism with Help from the West

Yugoslavia was the first socialist country, after the break between Tito and Stalin in 1948, to receive international aid led by the United States. The World Bank guaranteed a loan of $3 million, which was followed by a first line of credit from the International Monetary Fund in the amount of $9 million in March 1950, followed by an additional sum of $20 million.[94] This "international aid" was to a great extent prompted by the U.S. government, which in 1950 succeeded in having Congress pass a financial package of $38 million to assist Yugoslav Communist leaders. Against the argument of Republican senators, who opposed support for the Communist government, President Harry S. Truman and State Department officials stressed that supporting Yugoslavia first and foremost meant weakening the bloc, and thereby communism. The Republican administration of President Dwight Eisenhower would maintain this position between 1953 and 1961.[95] In 1950 U.S. authorities sent emergency aid in the form of food and developed economic exchange by lifting the export restrictions applied to other Eastern bloc countries in connection with CoCom. In 1953 goods from the United States represented approximately one-third of the country's imports.[96] This was accompanied, between 1950 and 1956, by substantial military aid to ensure the country's territorial integrity. Finally, U.S. authorities supported loan requests from the Yugoslav government made to the International Bank for Reconstruction and Development (a branch of the World Bank). For Yugoslav authorities, this aid fulfilled a dual function: it enabled them to circumvent the embargo of the Soviet Union and the Eastern bloc and in the long term helped ensure the country's independence by promoting its economic development. Some of the U.S. aid was distributed by the International Cooperation Administration (ICA), the forerunner to United States Agency for International Development (USAID), and in 1953 passed through the Expanded Programme. The U.S. government supported, via the UN, an impressive number of one-off programs involving all branches of Yugoslav industry. Equivalent programs were implemented by other UN agencies, and then by the OECD from 1961 onward. They were designed to train Yugoslav engineers and technicians in fields as diverse as the extractive industries, steelmaking, machine tools, the hydroelectric industry, the textile and leather industries, and the agri-food industry. They also involved the acquisition of know-how in creating transportation networks, with roads, railroads, and waterways being encouraged in particular. The engineers selected in Yugoslavia were sent to all Western countries, including the United States and especially Western Europe, namely, Germany, Sweden, Holland, Norway, Italy, and France. In return, experts from these countries went to Yugoslavia to help local authorities modernize their means of production and increase labor productivity. In addition to know-how, equipment was also exported, with Yugoslavia receiving textile machines from England in 1953.[97]

INTERNATIONALISMS DURING THE COLD WAR

In the early 1950s Yugoslavia conducted two-thirds of its trade with Western countries, European ones in particular, with which the Yugoslav government signed numerous bilateral treaties. This opening of trade with the West was recognized by its becoming an associate member of GATT in 1959 and a full member in 1966. In 1955 Yugoslavia secured observer status at the OEEC and as such took advantage of the U.S. productivity agency's programs from 1957 onward. Its experts took part in the OEEC's various technical committees.[98] This dependency on technical expertise and trade relations with the West undeniably promoted an early Westernization of Yugoslavia, which had an effect on the country's economic and social orientations.

The Internationalization of the Yugoslav Model

Yugoslav economists were sent to the West beginning in the 1950s. This was the case for Branko Horvart, who after studying in London directed research at the Planning Bureau in Belgrade (1958–1963). Between 1952 and 1965 these economists helped develop and implement a series of reforms that initiated what was referred to at the time as "market socialism." They introduced greater flexibility in state planning, giving more freedom to the heads of state-owned companies. In addition, unlike those from other state socialist countries, Yugoslav companies gradually used consumption indicators to develop their economic policies. This also came, at least on paper, with a less vertical organization in the chain of command, as well as the introduction of workers' councils, which were granted the power of coparticipation.[99] These solutions were favorably received by part of the non-Communist European left, which saw them as an alternative to authoritarian Soviet socialism, and as a third way between capitalism and state socialism.[100] This perception largely resulted from promotion on the part of Yugoslav economists and politicians, who were very active in international organizations. It also helped establish the Yugoslav experience as a model for economic success, including at GATT and the World Bank.[101] At the ILO, the Yugoslav experience was presented in the 1960s as a virtuous example of self-management.[102]

At the OECD, however, Yugoslavia was not involved in programs that were at variance with the letter of socialism, and in international organizations Yugoslav representatives most often voted with Eastern bloc

INTERNATIONALISMS DURING THE COLD WAR

countries. The Yugoslavs did not abandon socialism as a model of economic and social organization. The resumption of relations with the USSR and Comecon countries after Stalin's death was of course marked by recurring conflict, but the Yugoslav government sent an observer to Comecon in 1956, and economic relations with countries of the bloc resumed proportionally as Yugoslav leaders, like those of the Eastern bloc in general, grew very concerned about the protectionist measures associated with the implementation of the Single Market in 1957. In 1964 Yugoslavia became an associate member of Comecon, all while developing its relations over time with the EEC.[103] Members of the various regional organizations of which it was a part used the presence of Yugoslav representatives to establish and develop ties with countries from the opposing bloc. Yugoslavs especially provided Comecon representatives with easier access to the information and deliberations unfolding within UNECE.[104]

This intermediate position was marked by unusual tensions that reveal the limits of grasping the period through the prism of rigid Cold War categories. For example, among the projects managed by the Expanded Programme that involved Yugoslavia, in 1957 there was a request for aid to develop civil nuclear energy, which provided for sending a group of young scientists to the Argonne National Laboratory in the United States; the document explicitly signals that the program would proceed alongside the agreements that Yugoslavia signed in 1956 with the USSR. In 1957 the Expanded Programme, which was largely funded by the United States, sent Soviet experts to Yugoslavia.[105] This example once again shows that the period can hardly be reduced to the confrontation between two economic, social, and political models. In this respect, international organizations simultaneously served as Cold War actors and as spaces for questioning it.

The rhetoric of nonalignment used by Yugoslav leaders incidentally allowed them to secure numerous positions of responsibility within international organizations, a privilege they shared with their Finnish colleagues.[106] It was a Finn, Sakari Tuomioja, who succeeded Gunnar Myrdal as secretary of UNECE in 1957, before a long Yugoslav period that saw Janez Stanovnik (1968–1982) succeed Vladimir Velebit (1960–1967). The position of Yugoslavs within international organizations was promoted by the great skill of the diplomats and experts who were sent there. In return, they were able to negotiate economic agreements they hoped would ensure greater economic independence for their country.[107] In 1954 a first agreement between Yugoslavia and Austria, concluded under the auspices of UNECE, established control over the waters of the Drava River, a first step toward developing joint hydroelectric energy.[108] Yugoslavs were also present at the World Bank. After working at the National Bank of Yugoslavia, Dragoslav Avramović joined the World Bank in 1953 and held a number of management positions in the field of economic development.

Socialism and Third-Worldism

Aside from their intermediary position between the two blocs, Yugoslav authorities defined their country as "less developed," which allowed them early on to give voice to the demands of countries that had emerged from colonization. Even before the emergence of the Non-Aligned Movement, Tito and Yugoslav leaders supported within international forums a position promoting peace, disarmament, decolonization, and more equitable economic exchange for nations that were less developed and placed at a disadvantage by forms of economic integration. The meeting between Nehru, Nasser, and Tito on Brioni Island off the coast of Croatia in July 1956 attracted broad media attention, and the Brioni Declaration unofficially launched the Non-Aligned Movement, which was officially created during the Belgrade Conference in 1961. The only nonaligned international organization—the International Centre for Public Enterprises (ICPE), established in Ljubljana with UN support in 1974—constituted and strengthened Yugoslavia's centrality in this movement. Aside from a desire to secure allies and economic partners, for Yugoslav leaders the Non-Aligned Movement was also a space where they could promote a socialist model of development, with the ICPE serving as a showcase, and the Yugoslav government's initiatives in Ethiopia representing a concrete implementation.[109]

Was the decade between 1955 and 1965 the golden age of internationalism? The accession of new countries gave shape to the UN's universalist ambition, with the General Assembly becoming a platform that the governments—including from the least powerful states—seized upon to have their voice heard, and to call for UN mediation and even intervention in connection with multiple conflicts, thereby enhancing the organization's prestige. These calls and interventions drove the conviction that world peace would be best secured by multilateralism and internationalist ideals. The

INTERNATIONALISMS DURING THE COLD WAR

implementation of technical assistance programs in the 1950s and those relating to national construction[110]—and later the launch of the first Development Decade in 1960—strengthened the notion that while international organizations did not govern the world, their secretariats could organize it for the common good.

UN universalism, however, did not strike the same balance with all actors and came up against the deployment of regional organizations and competing internationalisms. The international Communist project gained new strength after Stalin's death. It could rely on Communist Parties, a vast network of organizations that promoted a language of peace and solidarity, as well as the declared "friendship" with the Third World. It was rooted in older histories and networks based on geographical and cultural proximity—as well as economic calculations—more so than genuine ideological convergence. The fear sparked by this Communist project was behind the constitution of a network of anticommunist organizations, which assumed ambiguous forms and in the FRG fostered the persistence of a Nazi anticommunism. While heterogeneous, this anticommunism nevertheless sought, like the enemy it was fighting, to convey a universal message: that of liberty.

Despite the fear it sparked, Communist internationalism was fragile. Solidarity with the Global South did not lead to the acceptance of the Communist political project on the part of these countries. There were numerous divisions within the bloc, with the Yugoslav schism of 1948 and the break between the USSR and China—and later Albania in the early 1960s—representing other manifestations. More underground forms of division emerged in the late 1950s within the bloc's organizations. The countries that spoke for Communist internationalism were actually more economically dependent on the developed West than they were in competition with it. This is demonstrated by the uneven involvement of people's democracies in GATT and UNECE during the 1950s. Paradoxically, the survival and reputation of the Yugoslav socialist experience were secured with Western support, while international organizations circulated this aid and helped build the reputation of the alternative model of Yugoslav socialism.

The Cold War therefore did not represent an obstacle to internationalism but on the contrary fueled it. International organizations were spaces of negotiation that were always available in moments of diplomatic crisis between representatives of major powers, which they used to avoid wars threatening planetary annihilation, as demonstrated by the Cuban Missile Crisis.[111] But most especially, Cold War oppositions were also firmly anchored in universalisms that may have been competing, but were highly dependent on one another, and shared the same belief in the modern project. The Cold War convergences that unfolded in the ensuing years were based on this dependency.

Chapter Four

THE EUROPE OF CONVERGENCES

In 1967 Eugene S. Staples, a former cultural advisor at the U.S. Embassy in Moscow who had recently been recruited by the Ford Foundation, visited Europe to explore the creation of a Center for the Study of Common Problems, designed to discuss the issues facing political and economic officials in both Eastern and Western Europe, and doing so beyond differences in political system.[1] This mission shows that a new period had begun, one that actors from the time and the ensuing historiography have generally summarized with the term *détente*. This decade of détente (1965–1975) was marked by the resumption of diplomatic relations between the Cold War enemies and was accompanied by intensifying economic and cultural exchange between countries with different political and social systems.[2]

Cold War historiography has extensively explored the chronology, forms, and reasons for this resumption: authors have highlighted the immediate reasons for the resumption of these relations, especially the concerns caused by the Cuban Missile Crisis. They have also emphasized the role of leaders from midsize powers in this evolution, such as Charles de Gaulle of France or Willy Brandt of Germany.

In this chapter I will explore this decade of détente from the perspective of international organizations, seen as spaces of circulation, with a focus on their role in this rapprochement. The major organizations of the UN

THE EUROPE OF CONVERGENCES

system—such as the United Nations Economic Commission for Europe, the International Labour Organization, and the United Nations Educational, Scientific and Cultural Organization, along with the Ford Foundation—whose importance in understanding East-West relations I emphasized earlier, will be joined here by the UN and non-UN organizations that were founded in the late 1950s, such as the International Atomic Energy Agency in 1957, the United Nations Industrial Development Organization in 1966, and the International Institute for Applied Systems Analysis (IIASA) in 1972. One could say that their creation grew out of this resumption of relations, although they also represented new spaces in which experts and civil servants from the two blocs met and developed shared knowledge and know-how.[3] Alongside these organizations was a vast network of NGOs and think tanks that brought together economic, cultural, and religious actors engaged in pan-European dialogue. These actors pursued varied objectives, ranging from promoting peace to searching for new markets. Yet beyond their immediate objectives, these international platforms were also places for developing and diffusing an international discourse of modernity shared by both blocs. This discourse was based on a common belief in the benefits of progress—economic and social, as well as technical and scientific—in addition to the importance of education as a condition thereof.[4] This shared discourse of modernity enabled a multitude of cooperative efforts in the educational, scientific, and technical fields within or on the margins of international organizations. It served as the basis for the idea, which circulated widely in the Western intellectual and political circles of the time, that there was growing convergence between capitalist and socialist societies and systems, one that went beyond ideological differences.

Relations between the two parts of Europe facilitated these contacts and discussions. Slowed but not entirely suspended between 1949 and 1953, they were continued in a more reserved manner thanks to the activity of certain groups of actors, such as those in exile. International spaces proved to be favorable places for these actors to pursue their activities as go-betweens. The permanence of a shared intellectual and social breeding ground fostered by the preservation of pan-European networks enabled and encouraged diplomatic relations in the economic, cultural, and political domains. These networks served as the foundation—and even the condition—for the resumption of relations. In the following chapter I will therefore explore the role of international organizations, associations, and networks whose activities were often less visible than those of governmental actors in resuming contact. More specifically, I will determine whether and how they served as facilitators, and even as drivers for these intensifying exchanges. I will first revisit the notion of convergence and will then examine how this joint effort proceeded within the international organizations located in Vienna—a genuine bridge between the East and the West—along with the principal actors involved. Finally, through what I call the "spirit of Helsinki," I will try to understand the reasons behind the cooperation and convergence between Eastern and Western Europe, as well as their limits.

MODERN CONVERGENCE

The Staples Mission of 1967 may seem to be an anecdotal example of the many such initiatives between 1965 and 1975, but as we saw earlier, the Ford Foundation was a major international actor of U.S. soft power, and Staples can serve as a valuable guide for identifying certain international actors, along with the issues related to this new policy. The project shows a change in the perception of the other bloc and renewed interest for the economic and social changes occurring there on the part of Ford Foundation leaders, and more broadly by some Western elites. After attracting fellows from Eastern Europe to Western countries in order to convince them of the superiority of capitalism beginning in 1956,[5] these leaders supported, from 1966 onward, a grant program for U.S. academics to visit Eastern Europe, with a view to increasing their knowledge of the economic and social systems of socialist countries. In the same vein, in 1969 the foundation funded a detailed study of the health systems of these countries, which revealed the advantages of a broadly accessible subsidized medicine based on preventive care in clinics, doing so as U.S. president Lyndon B. Johnson's ambitious social project was being challenged in the United States.

CONCEIVING CONVERGENCE

The idea for a Center for the Study of Common Problems was launched by the Ford Foundation's president, the Democrat McGeorge Bundy, upon the request of Johnson, in the context of the Great Society project, which in 1965 initiated a program of far-reaching social reforms. It was in keeping with an intellectual movement that emphasized growing convergence between the two economic and social systems. Convergence theory was based on the idea that there was a de facto rapprochement between modern industrial societies, and that political divergence was secondary to the similarities between their deep social and economic structures. This theory, which was formulated in 1960 by the Russian-born U.S. sociologist Pitrim Sorokin—and one year later by the Dutch economist Jan Tinbergen—was based on debates and dialogue that unfolded among reform-minded economists and social scientists in both parts of Europe during the 1950s. This dialogue was especially active within international organizations.

These social scientists placed great emphasis on the existence of technological convergence that would pave the way for a shared "postindustrial" knowledge society.[6] The two economic and social systems were characterized by the multiplication of large monopolistic companies, led by directors/managers working closely with a state technocracy. These synergies allowed for rational organization of the economy and society through tools for economic planning and management, whose development was fostered by technological improvements. In the name of the common good, this new technocracy implemented a rational policy that reduced social inequality and fostered redistribution, made possible by a general rise in wealth amid a context of strong economic growth. The converging evolution of societies in Eastern and Western Europe was marked, among other things, by a decline in fertility and the development of women's work.[7]

Convergence theory did not garner unanimous support. It was challenged by certain liberals, such as Raymond Aron, who stressed that the differences in political regime—and especially the absence of liberty and democracy in the East—represented an essential difference and curbed long-term economic and social convergence.[8] Soviet Communists saw this idea as a way of delegitimizing the Communist project, according to which only socialism and later communism could resolve the contradictions and crises of capitalism and pave the way for a more just world.[9] Going against this vision, they insisted that the structures of property prevented capitalist societies from evolving toward greater social equality, and they contested the idea that a proletariat could be "absorbed" by the middle class. Finally, the development of capitalist monopolies would lead, according to Communists, to increased power for those controlling the means of production and financial capital and would weaken the regulatory power of states.

THE EUROPE OF CONVERGENCES

Despite these objections, convergence theory spread in the European and North American social sciences, while the political programs of the reform movement drew inspiration from the experiences or ideals promoted by the opposing "camp." In the East, the economic reforms defended during the late 1950s by Evsei Liberman in the USSR—and put into practice in the 1960s in Poland, Czechoslovakia, and especially Hungary, albeit with generally limited results—were part of this evolution. In all Eastern bloc countries, these reforms pursued the goal of loosening the vise of centralized planning and giving greater power to local decision makers, the directors of companies in particular, but also producers and consumers, who were even promised the coming of a socialist consumer society.[10] In the West, the economic theorists behind welfare capitalism and Keynesian economists emphasized the need for mechanisms of redistribution, protectionary legislation, and spaces for collective bargaining, which were seen as the necessary conditions for the balance and growth of the welfare society. In both cases, the other model of society, or the ways in which it was promoted and interpreted, represented an inspiration or incentive for reform. While their reasons may have been very different, observers deduced from these meetings of the mind that it was possible to foster rapprochement between the two systems, and this would promote, beyond political differences, the emergence of shared solutions in economic, social, and technological matters.

Theories of convergence were, unsurprisingly, well received within international civil service. Some of the most prominent figures who rallied behind these ideas were Gunnar Myrdal and Nicholas Kaldor at UNECE and Jan Tinbergen at the United Nations Development Programme (UNDP).[11] The Ford Foundation helped diffuse the thought of these economists: in 1960 it organized, at the request of Soviet authorities, a conference on development issues that was attended by representatives from the West such as Jan Tinbergen, Nicholas Kaldor, Gunnar Myrdal, and the American John Kenneth Galbraith, in addition to Prasanta Chandra Mahalanobis, the father of Indian planning.[12] In 1967 the foundation supported, in collaboration with the Social Science Research Council in the United States, a conference in Cambridge, Massachusetts, on the economy of socialist countries, which was attended by the economists Abram Bergson, a specialist on the Soviet economy, and Simon Kuznets, a specialist on growth. The economic reforms underway in Eastern European countries were central to the discussions, with Kuznets arguing that they could even represent an inspiration for other countries emerging from underdevelopment.[13]

For these international circles, convergence theory offered a shared frame of reference that facilitated the international conversation. By insisting on the predominance of economic and technical factors in the evolution of societies, and by relegating political opposition to the background, it provided the basis for an international expertise. Consequently, convergence theory not only received a positive reception in international circles, but the latter also implemented programs to promote such convergence.

Identifying Common Problems

The Staples report can serve as a guide. It helps to identify the various international movements and initiatives that, without openly laying claim to convergence theory, drew on it for inspiration and attempted to develop exchange. Staples met with numerous figures in the worlds of business, senior national and international civil service, and academic circles who, one way or another, were in relation with or financially aided by the Ford Foundation. Raymond Aron, who was contacted for France—and whose skepticism regarding convergence we saw earlier—argued for developing joint ad hoc projects and emphasized that cooperation should not pose a problem with the Czechoslovaks or Poles, who he believed were entirely "nonideological." Other actors echoed this vision during meetings. Different speakers generally emphasized that Eastern European leaders were more interested in relations with the West than the other way around. The U.S. ambassador to the international organizations in Geneva even regretted that the U.S. envoys had shown reserve and even hostility toward their counterparts from socialist countries. The same ambassador emphasized that the absence of a clear message in high places complicated the adoption of an open stance toward proposals made by Eastern European countries within UNECE or the OECD.

As a whole, the specifically Western institutions created in the wake of the Marshall Plan had little or no relations with state socialist countries, which was true, for example, of the European Economic Community created in 1957 by the Treaty of Rome, an organization that Staples incidentally did not contact. This was also the case for the OECD. The British

THE EUROPE OF CONVERGENCES

sociologist Ron Gass, who was the head of the OECD's research service, affirmed that "contacts with the East have been negligible, and solely on a personal basis." The Swedish economist Göran Ohlin, head of division at the Swedish industrial federation, underscored, however, that the OECD was the natural place for developing these relations. On the other hand, in the East leaders from the Council for Mutual Economic Assistance (Comecon), who continued to assert that they wanted to develop trade relations with the West, increased overtures beginning in the 1960s.[14] This asymmetry attests to the openness of Eastern bloc countries during the 1960s, and especially to their long-standing dependence on countries in the West. The Western representatives who were the most interested in cooperation generally emphasized the need to develop contacts not with political leaders, but rather with the economic cadres of regimes, directors of major state companies, or any persons in a supervisory position and exercising a local activity, including certain academics. They believed that these cadres were less bound by Communist orthodoxy. This remark reflects greater knowledge of Communist societies, which were in reality much less monolithic than the image of them projected by traditional anticommunist propaganda.

The report also helps to clearly identify the topics that were central to the common concerns of modernizers. The management of private companies and public services apparently dominated all other issues, along with common concerns regarding the education and training of youth and issues relating to the environment, infrastructure, and urban planning. The latter was the subject of a project jointly financed by the Ford Foundation, the U.S. Department of State, and the Yugoslav Federal Council for the Coordination of Scientific Research. Launched in 1967, it studied issues relating to urban planning based on the example of the Yugoslav city of Ljubljana. According to one of the project's participants, Professor Myer Wolfe from the University of Washington, "We are not going to make plans for Ljubljana. . . . We're using it as an experimental lab. . . . Whether it's Ljubljana or Milwaukee, we are concerned with a network of cities." Ljubljana was in reality established as a "gathering place for Europe's planners," with the research team's director stressing that the planning studies based on this specific case could be extended to larger regions.[15] In 1968 these meetings were attended by representatives from Czechoslovakia, Poland, Bulgaria, Hungary, Austria, Italy, Switzerland, Greece, and West Germany, in addition to those from Yugoslavia and the United States. Communicating in "broken English," all these urban planners stressed the importance of promoting cooperation in order to find common solutions stretching beyond differences in political system.

This is one example among many of the initiatives listed in the Staples report. Certain organizations played a particular role in these contacts and convergence, such as UNECE in Geneva, the Institute for Theoretical Physics in Trieste, and the IAEA in Vienna. The Staples report also mentions more occasional ad hoc meetings: a conference in 1966 on social welfare held by the Danish Institute of Social Research under the auspices of UNECE, which was attended by Yugoslav and Polish representatives; a meeting in 1967 between managers from the East and the West regarding economic issues, held by the European League of Economic Cooperation, founded in 1948 by private industrial actors; and the activities of the Center for the Study of Economic and Sociological Problems (Centro ricerche economiche e sociologiche dei paesi dell' Est, CESES). The latter represents a particularly interesting focal point and actor. Founded in 1964, it was funded by the large confederation of Italian industry, Confindustria, to conduct research on the reality of socialist economies and to plan conferences and publications to combat the influence of Communist ideas among the Italian intellectual left and some economic elites. Led by a former Communist, Renato Mieli, it welcomed reformers often from the left, along with exiles and dissidents from the East. Over time the center became a space for dialogue with economic actors from the Eastern bloc. The identification of convergence soon gave rise to a political project for a "third way" between liberal capitalism and state socialism.[16] Other spaces within the UN system pursuing similar objectives emerged between 1965 and 1975.

WORKING TOGETHER: THE VIENNA PLATFORM

New International Spaces

The Center for the Study of Common Problems envisioned by McGeorge Bundy at the request of Lyndon B. Johnson was finally created in 1972, in the form of the International Institute for Applied Systems Analysis. As suggested by Sigvard Eklund, director-general of the IAEA, it was based in Vienna, a neutral country near Eastern Europe where German was spoken,

THE EUROPE OF CONVERGENCES

a language still broadly used by the elites of these countries. Vienna was also the capital of a country led since 1970 by the Social Democrat Bruno Kreisky, who had previously served as secretary of state and minister of foreign affairs between 1953 and 1966.[17] He took refuge in Sweden during the war and, like the West German chancellor Willy Brandt or UNECE secretary Gunnar Myrdal, was active in the Group of Democratic Socialists. Also like Brandt, Kreisky never hid his opposition to the Communist regimes of Eastern Europe, but both nevertheless encouraged the persistence of Social Democratic antifascist networks, which played an important role in preserving ties between the two parts of Europe.[18]

The new institute wanted to primarily be seen as an East-West organization: the Soviet and U.S. institutions participating in the project provided its funding in equal parts. Its director was Howard Raiffa, a professor of managerial economics at Harvard University, while the chairman of the Board of Directors was Djhermen Gvishiani, a member of the Academy of Sciences of the USSR, who had been highly involved in East-West dialogue since the 1960s. The institute hosted representatives from the academies of ten other countries, four of which were from the Eastern bloc, including the GDR, a country that at the time was excluded from all international organizations. The inspiration for IIASA was the activity of the RAND Corporation, a U.S. military think tank founded in 1948 to improve the decision-making process by developing operational research and strategic analysis in line with the research conducted by the British Army during World War II.[19] In focusing its activity on systems analysis—in other words, the mathematical modeling of decision-making based on the breakdown of social and environmental issues—the new center promoted the ultimate form of policy technicization, as well as a shared language fostering dialogue between specialists and experts from different political systems.[20]

This modeling of economic and social problems, in addition to decision-making, enabled this common effort, but it was based on diverging visions of the utility of such approaches among the elites of both political systems. For U.S. teams, beyond its technicist neutrality, IIASA should diffuse decision-making and governmental practices inspired by rational choice theory, which they believed was the basis for the proper functioning of Western economic and social systems. Communist leaders hoped that the center's activities would help them find solutions to the impasses of centralized planning by gaining access to Western management techniques.

They also saw it as a way to secure IT tools and computers, whose technology they did not yet master, by circumventing the embargo imposed by CoCom.[21] While international civil servants and experts were able to work together, the expectation of political leaders from the two blocs remained quite asymmetrical up through the end of the Cold War.

In Vienna, IIASA was neither the only nor the first international organization of this type. The "sciences of war" were already located there in the form of the International Atomic Energy Agency, an organization of the UN system officially founded in 1957.[22] The IAEA's primary function was to conduct research on atomic energy and to diffuse the results; it also exercised control over its use. While the speech given on December 8, 1953, by U.S. president Dwight D. Eisenhower to the UN General Assembly—advocating for "atoms for peace"—is seen as the starting point for the project, the discussions that occurred at the UN General Assembly beginning in 1945 represent its prehistory. The Soviets and Indians played a crucial role in the negotiations and launch of the organization. This involvement shows the interest in the civil nuclear industry on the part of governments from recently decolonized countries.[23] They were, for that matter, the first beneficiaries of the on-site missions dispatched to implement civil nuclear programs. The agency's first director, who served until 1961, was Sterling Cole of the United States, although the governments of socialist countries, and the Soviets in particular, sent qualified civil servants from the very beginning. The Soviets represented the second group after the U.S. group, a remarkable situation when compared to the former's role in UN agencies during the same period. Beginning in 1961, under the presidency of the Swedish scientist Sigvard Eklund, the IAEA became an important space for exchange between scientists from all three worlds of the Cold War.

The concern for economic and technological development that Communist elites shared with those from the Third World was especially marked by their involvement in another Vienna agency, the United Nations Industrial Development Organization. Founded in 1966, it sought to help the least economically advanced countries increase their industrial potential, which was seen as a key condition for economic development. UNIDO was a late response to a request for an industrial development program formulated by Soviet representatives at UNECE in 1948. Its first director-general, who served until 1974, was Ibrahim Helmi Abdel-Rahman of Egypt, who was

THE EUROPE OF CONVERGENCES

succeeded in 1975 by Abd-El Rhaman Khane of Algeria. Both were from countries with friendly relations with the Eastern bloc. From the very beginning, representatives from socialist countries were members of the organization's industrial development executive committee. Leaders from East Germany, the bloc's most developed country, were highly involved in UNIDO, which they saw as an opportunity to develop relations with Third World countries.[24] In 1974 Vienna also became home to the International Council for New Initiatives in East West Cooperation, which developed in the wake of the Helsinki process and aimed to promote economic relations between the two parts of Europe, and to work on a certain number of common problems, especially in environmental matters.[25] There was also the Wiener Institut für Internationale Wirtschaftsvergleiche (Vienna Institute for International Economic Studies), founded in 1973 as a private institute in the service of companies; it published an annual report on Comecon economies, held symposia, and in the 1970s produced numerous studies on East-West economic relations. The Vienna Institute worked in close synergy with UNECE in Geneva and developed relations with the International Chamber of Commerce. Other initiatives also bear mentioning, such as the Vienna Institute for Development founded at the initiative of Bruno Kreisky, which promoted a space of cooperation with the Global South in response to the growing influence of Communist actors in that part of the world. Finally, UNESCO was also represented in Vienna thanks to the European Coordination Centre for Research and Documentation in Social Sciences, or the Vienna Center, which was created in 1962 during the twelfth session of the organization's General Conference. This new institution, under the authority of the International Social Science Council, sought to promote comparative research in the social sciences in Europe by establishing international teams of researchers from the East and the West. The new center was chaired until 1982 by the linguist Adam Schaff, who was a member of the Polish Academy of Sciences. Schaff studied in Paris at l'École nationale des sciences politiques, had a fine grasp of Marxism, and engaged in dissent beginning in the mid-1960s. He embodied the bridge between the East and the West that served as the center's mission. A careful balance between members of the two parts of Europe was maintained: the executive board included fourteen members, seven of whom were from Eastern Europe; each international research team was chaired by two directors, who were respectively from the two parts of Europe.[26]

Shared Epistemes

These organizations represented spaces for the international discussion of issues relating to economic, social, and technological organization. They helped develop and promote a representation of modernity, one that is well illustrated by the evocatively titled bulletin *Industrialization and Productivity*, published from 1962 onward by the UN, which included articles from various technical agencies as well as from the World Bank and the International Monetary Fund. This modern project was based on the belief that it was possible to organize and improve societies, and to even plan the future. It relied, from the 1960s onward, on the use of computers, thanks to which both supporters of operational research and Soviet planners thought they could "calculate" the world by including elements of uncertainty.[27] In the 1960s this concern fueled enthusiasm for cybernetics, an approach that corrects programs by integrating the effects of past decisions, and by implementing what are known as feedback loops.[28] Cybernetics became the methodological framework for studies by IIASA, and it was via this approach that participating researchers carefully explored selected topics such as urban planning, health systems, and especially environmental issues and pollution, which were global by nature.[29] These topics were the subject of studies conducted by international teams, with a view to developing solutions that could be reproduced in different political and social contexts. This type of approach corresponded precisely to the ongoing practices of the international bureaucracies striving to create development plans that could subsequently be replicated in as many countries as possible.

UNESCO's Vienna Center promoted international research of a different kind, one that was in keeping with long-standing forms of cooperation based on comparative methods and previously explored topics. The socioeconomic issues placed on the agenda were shared by different European countries in the process of modernization, but they were studied on the basis of research conducted in strictly national contexts, with the results being compared afterward. Of the twenty projects studied between 1962 and 1976, a number involved questions relating to youth or education, while others focused on the social consequences of development: time use, social hierarchies, innovation in agriculture, and tourism were the subject of comparative studies. The issues were selected and studied by research teams from different countries, each one being involved in the project on a voluntary basis. The center, which had very limited resources, suggested topics, coordinated teams, and organized meetings. The comparative method had the goal of accumulating data, all while revealing the differences in the solutions adopted by various countries. This bottom-up approach was seen as a way of developing models closer to social realities, which would ultimately inform policy decisions without producing a model of intervention applicable for all situations, as was the case with IIASA.[30]

The list of countries respectively involved in the Vienna Center and IIASA illustrates another important difference between the two centers. While the latter was dominated, at least in the beginning, by the involvement of two major powers, the Vienna Center saw large-scale involvement on the part of researchers from medium-sized powers such as France, Czechoslovakia, Poland, and Italy, countries that had developed long-standing intellectual cooperation and had a rich sociological tradition, Poland in particular. The USSR played a more limited role, with the United States being absent. In this respect, the Vienna Center reflected the desire to develop independent research that was more respectful of European specificities and existing intellectual convergence. Teams from the East brought together researchers who were accustomed to European cooperation, while those from the West often had an ideological inspiration on the left, but not necessarily Communist.

These two institutes thus reflected the diverse forms of action adopted by international organizations and stakeholders, with a view to rapprochement between the countries of Europe. They also show the polysemic nature of the term convergence: a feeling of a shared modernity, as well as the need to foster it through cooperation.

Beyond their differences, however, these centers demonstrate that this convergence was based on and encouraged by the existence of "espistemic communities" whose members shared knowledge and references, for which international organizations offered a space for discussion. Rather than actual communities, it often involved groups with fairly blurry outlines—consisting of researchers from higher education institutions playing the role of experts—and whose political divergences could be compensated for by a common belief in the possibility of organizing and guiding society, and even planning the economy. The two institutes produced publications and reports, but their results remained fairly limited; their importance had less

THE SPIRIT OF HELSINKI:
CONVERGENCE, COOPERATION, DIVERGENCE

to do with their impact than with the fact that they promoted contact and simultaneously revealed and fueled a certain "spirit of the times."

The Conference on Security and Cooperation in Europe in Helsinki closed with the signing of the Final Act on August 1, 1975. The act was not legally binding for signatory states and was limited in scope, and it can therefore be seen as a simple declaration of intention. The CSCE's importance cannot be reduced to its Final Act, as it sheds light on the nature of ties and cooperation as well as the actors promoting them, all while clearly revealing the dependence and divergence between the two parts of Europe. This is what I am referring to when I use the term the *spirit of Helsinki*.

Much more than a simple conference, the CSCE was actually part of a long process. It was held over a period of two years and eight months and unfolded in three successive phases. Multilateral talks occurred between November 22, 1972, and June 8, 1973, in Helsinki, ending with the first phase of the conference itself, which in July 1973 brought together the ministers of foreign affairs from the thirty-five countries involved. The second phase of negotiations took place between September 18, 1973, and July 25, 1975, at the Palace of Nations in Geneva and was attended by over six hundred representatives and experts, who were divided into a dozen commissions. Finally, the third phase, which was very short, was that of the signing ceremony for the Final Act in Helsinki on August 1, 1975, by representatives from thirty-five countries, including all European states except Albania and Andorra, the United States, the USSR, and Canada. The act thus brought to a close a long period of shared acculturation for the various actors present and was extended by the follow-on conferences that were held in Belgrade in 1977–1978, Madrid in 1984–1985, and Vienna in 1987–1989.

The conference's Final Act consisted of multiple parts, or baskets. The first focused on security: first that of borders, and second of respect for sovereignty and issues relating to disarmament. The second basket involved cooperation in the economic, technological, and environmental fields. The third basket concerned humanitarian cooperation and cultural exchange.[31] The content of these three baskets was unanimously adopted by those present and was the result of meticulous discussions in Geneva. The latter

The International Breeding Ground

were made possible by the ties between negotiators and experts, who for the most part had already rubbed shoulders during various international meetings.

The International Breeding Ground

There is a long diplomatic prehistory of the CSCE that recent literature on the subject has amply explored.[32] However, the initiatives developed by various international organizations in the years that preceded the Helsinki conference are less well known. The presence at the final conference of the UN secretary-general, the director-general of UNESCO, and the executive secretary of UNECE was not solely symbolic, as it reflected the fact that UN organizations played a driving role—both direct and indirect—in the content and negotiations surrounding Helsinki.

The discussions that took place in the General Assembly during the 1960s, especially those initiated by recently decolonized countries with regard to human rights, border security, and sovereignty, served as both an inspiration and an invisible albeit highly significant framework.[33] More specifically, European rapprochement was fostered by meetings within the various UN agencies. The work of UNECE was essential in establishing and monitoring the economic provisions of the second basket. Other pan-European initiatives were encouraged by the ILO and UNESCO, and played an important role in putting new topics on the agenda, as well as constituting a group of actors well-versed in collective discussion and the development of common expertise.

In June 1972 UNESCO organized a meeting, once again in Helsinki, with representatives from twenty-nine countries in Eastern and Western Europe.[34] It was the culmination of a history that began in 1956, when the French commission for UNESCO held a pan-European conference of ministers of education and culture.[35] In 1965 the resolution on Europe gave carte blanche to Director-General René Maheu to organize a conference of European ministers on issues relating to higher education.[36] They met in Vienna in 1967 and again in Bucharest in 1973. UNESCO had established, in that same city in September 1972, the first international organization based in the East: the European Centre for Higher Education (CEPES). This was a response to the wishes formulated by the Romanian government and cultural elites to develop relations with the West.[37] Among the various recommendations adopted by these different UNESCO conferences was the development of cultural relations between the two parts of Europe via three channels: bilateral agreements among governments, Academies of Science and higher education institutions, and NGOs such as the "Pen Club." These different proposals were included with no changes in the Final Act of the Helsinki Conference on August 1, 1975.[38] These UNESCO conferences and recommendations were based on a multitude of private initiatives—translations, film coproductions and festivals, and exchanges of theater troupes and orchestras—that created fertile ground for international discussions and decisions.[39] The results of the UNESCO study in 1972 nevertheless show that socialist countries tended to be more engaged than their Western partners in these cultural relations. The 11 Eastern European states concluded 59 cultural agreements among themselves and 77 with Western countries; conversely, the 21 Western countries concluded 145 agreements among themselves and only 79 with Eastern European countries.[40] This asymmetry cannot be exclusively explained by the blockage resulting from the Cold War, as it was in keeping with a long history in which Eastern European cultural productions received a limited reception in major Western countries. As we saw earlier, this same asymmetry was present in the economic and technological fields as well but was to a certain extent inverted when it came to social fields, as suggested by the trade union dynamic.

Aside from UNECE and UNESCO, civil servants from the International Labour Office had been involved in East-West activities since the late 1950s and in 1974 planned the organization's second European Regional Conference in Geneva. Initially scheduled for 1968, it was postponed due to the events in Prague, and was held after lengthy preparations and a meticulous study conducted between 1968 and 1970 by Wilfried Jenks, the deputy director of the International Labour Office.[41] Like the Ford Foundation's Staples report, the Jenks study revealed and emphasized the extensive relations between Eastern and Western Europe during the 1960s and expressed the hope of seeing them develop. Economic and union leaders, especially in the East, shared this hope. Beginning in the late 1950s, trade unionists in the East sought to establish relations with their colleagues in the West, on whom they counted to convey a message of protest in capitalist countries.[42] It was unions from Eastern Europe and the Communist-leaning World Federation of Trade Unions that argued in favor of a European regional

THE EUROPE OF CONVERGENCES

conference at the ILO. By using the internal divisions of Western unionism, they successfully convinced their counterparts from other international confederations—the International Confederation of Free Trade
Unions (ICFTU) and the reformist International Federation of Christian
Trade Unions (IFCTU)—to formulate a joint declaration on the subject in
1967.[43] This policy met strong resistance at the ICFTU, especially on the
part of the highly anticommunist American Federation of Labour, which
left the confederation in 1969. There was strong East-West convergence in
certain union federations, such as those for railroads and typographers,
and even sympathy on the part of unionists from Australia, Japan, Israel,
India, France, Italy, and Finland for their counterparts in socialist countries.[44] After the AFL's departure, ICFTU leaders ultimately resolved to
plan a joint meeting with the ILO in a reassuring setting. Rapprochement
was thus formalized in connection with the ILO's European Regional
Conference in 1974.[45] On January 19 of that year, after meeting one
another, European trade union leaders created a platform highlighting
common problems, especially in connection with the globalization of
the labor market, and emphasized the need to fight together.[46] In both
the East and the West, unions were concerned about the bolstering of
European institutions, in which they had not found a role, as well as the
growing presence of multinational corporations.[47] Unionists from the
West also feared the influx of foreign workers, including from countries in
Eastern Europe. In 1972 the director of the ILO's local office in Bonn
revealed that a substantial number of Romanian and Polish workers were
already present on the Federal Republic's territory and were employed by
companies engaged in subcontracting, as well as practices of wage and
social dumping.[48]

In advance of the Helsinki Conference, international organizations represented privileged spaces for discussions aiming to identify common
issues, which were then taken up in preliminary negotiations. These international initiatives could rely on pan-European social movements, whose
visibility and mobilization they could promote.[49] I will argue that these
movements encouraged the engagement of European diplomacies promoting rapprochement. Research is lacking on this point, although UNECE
documents mention an Assembly of Representatives of Public Opinion for
European Security and Co-operation, whose secretariat was located in
Brussels. This assembly, which held its first meeting in June 1972, continued

to meet at irregular intervals. It brought together, on a national basis, representatives from associations in twenty-nine European countries. It included political movements and parties that were generally on the left of the political spectrum (socialists and Communists), in addition to a vast Christian social movement and representatives from peace movements. After the signing of the Final Act, it drew active involvement from union, political, and cultural representatives from socialist countries, as well as from neutral ones, with the most numerous unsurprisingly being Finnish.[50] There was also the continuation of long-standing solidarities born from the common fight against fascism. Movements for veterans, Resistance members, and deportees were remobilized in the 1960s and 1970s to discuss questions relating to security in Europe.[51] These citizen mobilizations, and the involvement of social actors from the two parts of Europe, played an important role in the success of the Helsinki process, especially with respect to peace and security.

Security: A Common Goal

The goals of peace and security defined in the first basket were behind the holding of the Helsinki Conference. In 1954 Soviet leaders had proposed holding a conference on European security. In July 1955 in Geneva, leaders from the four powers occupying Germany (the USSR, the United States, Great Britain, and France) had discussed conditions for establishing peace and security in Europe, and for developing better trade relations. The Geneva Conference did not lead to any tangible decision, but it initiated a "first détente," with the Helsinki Conference being a culmination of sorts.[52] The Final Act of Helsinki met the expectation of leaders from countries in Comecon, especially the Soviets, Poles, Czechoslovaks, and East Germans, by guaranteeing the intangibility of borders. It went further, however, echoing the efforts made in international nuclear arms control, declaring that "the participating States recognize the interest of all of them in efforts aimed at lessening military confrontation and promoting disarmament."[53]

This declaration was in keeping with an older international dynamic. In October 1957 the Polish minister of foreign affairs, Adam Rapacki, had proposed to the UN General Assembly a plan for a denuclearized zone including Central European countries and the German federal state. These proposals, taken up by Soviet leaders in 1958, were not pursued, and the first

THE EUROPE OF CONVERGENCES

official talks began in earnest only after the Cuban Missile Crisis in 1962. They led in July 1963 to the Partial Nuclear Test Ban Treaty signed by U.S., British, and Soviet political leaders. The arms control movement continued with the signing of the Treaty on the Non-Proliferation of Nuclear Weapons in July 1968 and culminated with the SALT I Anti-Ballistic Agreement in May 1972, which provided for limiting—but not reducing—the nuclear arsenal.[54] These diplomatic efforts followed on the provisions from Article 1 of the UN Charter. It gave the new organization the goal of maintaining peace and international security and gave the General Assembly the possibility of studying the principles "governing disarmament and the regulation of armaments." In 1946 the General Assembly used this power to establish an Atomic Energy Commission, tasked with controlling atomic weapons; it was followed in 1947 by the creation of a Commission on Conventional Armaments. Between 1946 and 1948 representatives from the United States and the USSR presented before the Atomic Energy Commission plans for the international control of nuclear weapons, albeit with no results; the commission stopped meeting in 1949 and was dissolved in 1951. However, it was by relying on this mandate—as well as the experiences and expertise produced at the UN—that Secretary-General U Thant played a crucial role in resolving the Cuban Missile Crisis, as well as implementing long-term negotiations.[55]

Other international collective actors also contributed to this culture of disarmament. As we saw earlier, the mobilizations for peace from the 1950s were a visible manifestation of the shared concerns of European populations and compelled governments to affirm their commitment to peace: Eisenhower's "Atoms for Peace" speech was in keeping with this context. Movements more specifically opposing the development of nuclear weapons were organized in Europe during the 1950s. They were rarely spectacular but were based on the constitution of an active network of scientists opposed to atomic weapons—but not to civilian atomic energy. It played an important role in the prehistory of negotiations, as well as the freeze and later the reduction of armaments in the 1970s.[56] This movement was initiated in the 1940s by scientists involved in military programs and assumed public form in 1955 with a joint declaration by the physicist Albert Einstein and the philosopher and mathematician Bertrand Russell warning about the dangers of nuclear weapons. It was behind the Pugwash movement, named after the Canadian city were scientists from the two blocs met for the first time, essentially Soviet and U.S. physicists involved in nuclear research. The group study on disarmament initiated by Pugwash had considerable national and international influence thanks to the direct relations some of the group's scientists maintained with leading political figures. The movement played a major role in the success of negotiations that led to the Partial Nuclear Test Ban Treaty in July 1963. Between 1964 and 1969 the scientists who had gathered in Pugwash met nearly twenty-five times and helped prepare the SALT I agreements of 1972.[57]

The provisions of the first basket from Helsinki were thus the result of joint efforts on the part of diplomatic, national, and international actors, as well as mobilizations for peace by activists and scientists. The existence of international organizations promoting a culture and rhetoric of peace and disarmament broadly contributed to this dynamic.

Cooperation and Economic Dependence

Similarly, the negotiations that began surrounding the second economic basket were facilitated by the fact that the economic experts involved in them had already met in other international arenas, such as UNECE and the General Agreement on Tariffs and Trade. In addition to their active presence in UNECE, socialist countries gradually engaged in GATT in the 1960s. Yugoslavia became a member in 1966 (observer since 1961), Poland in 1967 (observer since 1957), Romania in 1971 (observer since 1957), and Hungary in 1973 (observer since 1958), while Czechoslovakia had been a GATT member since the beginning.

This presence in international economic organizations reflected a resumption of economic and technological exchanges, which were strongly encouraged by the work of the UNECE secretariat.[58] In 1969, when commerce between Eastern and Western Europe represented barely 6 percent of all intra-European trade, the organization included among its priority objectives the development of economic relations between the two parts of Europe, in addition to technological cooperation, long-term planning, and environmental issues. The research UNECE conducted during this period had a decisive influence on the negotiations surrounding the second basket, which were held in Geneva. More fundamentally, by encouraging the development of East-West exchange since the 1950s, it helped create an environment that was favorable to discussions.[59]

THE EUROPE OF CONVERGENCES

While in 1960 there were just a few dozen industrial cooperation (or interenterprise) agreements between socialist countries and those in capitalist Europe, by 1977 there were approximately two thousand. These contracts concerned most branches of industry and all countries of the bloc, including technological transfers and even more long-term forms of coproduction. There were also vast projects with the USSR, involving the installation of major facilities such as mining operations or oil pipelines, in exchange for raw materials. Between 1955 and 1975 trade between the two blocs rose considerably. Soviet imports increased by a factor of twenty in terms of value. In 1975 more than 40 percent of these imports were from countries in the capitalist West, and within the European Community in particular.[60] This evolution, which was fostered by sustained economic growth, revolved around 6 percent in the 1960s and was even greater for small Eastern European countries. The foreign trade volume of Comecon countries with Western countries increased 10 percent per year until 1970, and then by 23 percent between 1970 and 1975. This trade, however, which was vital for the former, remained secondary for the latter. In the West, Finland, which conducted 7.6 percent of its trade with Comecon countries, was the only economy that was truly dependent on trade with Eastern Europe.[61] In general, Eastern European countries received finished products and in return provided semifinished products, raw materials, and sometimes even inexpensive and docile labor, an imbalance that perpetuated Eastern Europe's long-standing economic dependence on Western Europe.[62]

In Western Europe, it was primarily private actors—major companies and their international representation such as the ICC—that, driven by specific economic interests, developed exchanges with the East. In 1952 large German employers, organized in the Federation of German Industry (Bundesverband der Deutschen Industrie), successfully created an Eastern Committee of German Industry (Ost-Auschuss der deutschen Wirtschaft), even as Chancellor Adenauer had aligned with the U.S. position and remained reluctant.[63] During the 1960s these exchanges developed at the instigation of major companies in Western Europe, especially in the automobile industry.[64] Economic representatives from socialist countries were invited, from the 1960s onward, to take part in discussions of the ICC, which in 1969 created a Liaison Committee with the Chambers of Commerce of Socialist Countries. This committee, which worked with UNECE, was unsurprisingly directed by a representative of German employers, M. Schröder.[65] In 1974 West German companies alone accounted for nearly 40 percent of trade with Eastern bloc countries. In the field, the reality of economics over politics fostered the continuation of the traditional policy of German openness and economic expansion toward the East.[66]

Since the economic interest of U.S. actors had always been negligible in Eastern Europe, they easily renounced pursuing trade there and until the 1960s accommodated themselves to the embargo policies applying to Communist countries.[67] Those who were the most opposed to developing exchanges with socialist countries asserted that these exchanges first and foremost sustained the Soviet military-industrial complex and represented a threat to peace, while others, relying on the declarations of Lenin and Khrushchev, believed that developing trade with the East would eventually help consolidate socialism.[68] Beginning in the early 1970s, free trade business leaders applied pressure to ease embargoes on trade with countries in the East: they were behind the tentative opening that culminated in the trade agreements of 1972 and 1974 with the USSR.[69] At the same time, U.S. political actors rallied behind the idea that these economic exchanges could provide political leverage. In 1974 they inserted a provision in their trade agreement with the USSR facilitating the emigration of Soviet Jews who requested to do so. In Helsinki, French negotiators even saw the development of trade between the two parts of Europe as a way of promoting the convergence of systems, and ultimately helping to delegitimize the Communist revolutionary project.[70]

A combination of political objectives and economic interests explains why Western leaders accepted to take part in negotiations with their counterparts in the East on economic matters, which were crucial for the latter. They saw exchanges as a way of compensating for the older technological gaps that the rigidness of the centrally planned economy did not allow to make up, or in the case of Czechoslovakia and the GDR, even tended to exacerbate.[71] Over the longer term, communist leaders also hoped to develop their consumer goods industry to ensure domestic political stability by meeting the population's demand for manufactured products. Leaders saw international trade, a state monopoly in socialist countries, as an instrument for building socialism.[72]

The political leaders of the two blocs converged in seeking to develop exchanges, but negotiations were complicated by the constraints on cooperation imposed by the difference in economic and social systems, as well as by the imbalance in power relations. While Communist leaders insisted on respecting the equality of rights between governments, their counterparts in the West were especially concerned by greater transparency in the exchange of economic data, as well as guarantees of freedom of movement for businessmen from their countries. What is more, because they depended on the pace of five-year plans, Communist elites favored long-term agreements and large-scale industrial projects that linked partners over long durations, whereas the governments of Western countries championed more flexible solutions. Finally, to compensate for their difficulties in research and development and to circumvent various embargos, Comecon leaders insisted on technology transfers, whereas those in Western Europe tried to promote adherence to certain environmental standards.

In negotiations, representatives from the East were in the position of requesting and found themselves part of an unfavorable power relation, even more so as they feared that the merger of the various European communities and the launch of joint trade policies would seriously impede the trade relations they had developed with their partners in Western Europe. To counter the power of the EEC, Soviet and Comecon leaders attempted to organize a collective answer, as well as to develop relations between the two blocs via their respective economic organizations.[73] While Soviet leaders continued to feign the unity of the bloc, during the 1970s those in Eastern Europe, including the Soviets themselves, ultimately negotiated bilateral treaties with countries within the European Community. The implementation of the EEC's common policy toward Comecon countries in 1971 facilitated this process.[74] These agreements show the inability of Comecon countries to develop a genuine regional economic policy, as well as their dependence on the capitalist West.

Ultimately, the economic basket from Helsinki was a rubber stamp for rapprochements already underway within other international arenas, namely, the ICC since 1967, and especially UNECE, which was tasked with implementing the provisions of the second basket.[75] The difficulties and conflicts that peppered the discussions reveal the limits of cooperation, as well as of social and economic convergence between the two systems. They document the persistence of economic inequality between the two parts of Europe.[76] It was especially with respect to human rights, however, that the

The Redefinition of Human Rights

Among the ten "principles guiding relations between participating States" that open the Final Act of the CSCE from 1975, article 7 pertains to "respect for human rights and fundamental freedoms, including the freedom of thought, conscience, religion or belief." It states general principles, with special emphasis on respecting individual freedoms.[77] This seventh principle was addressed by the third basket from the Final Act, which included three series of recommendations. Contacts between people should be encouraged, especially for families separated by the Wall; tourist and professional trips should be simplified, although freedom of movement was not proclaimed; the free flow of information was recommended, but the provisions adopted primarily involved protections for journalists sent to a third country. In general, the cultural cooperation that was encouraged broadly repeated the provisions that had been discussed at UNESCO since the 1960s. These articles were already well short of the Universal Declaration of 1948, but they drew the attention of contemporaries—and later that of historians—who saw them as an inaugural moment for human rights diplomacy of liberal inspiration, and even as a "return" of human rights as an issue in the 1970s.[78] This "return" is reflected in the awarding of the Nobel Peace Prize in 1977 to Amnesty International and the founding of the NGO Human Rights Watch in 1978.[79]

Article 7, however, was not really a "return" of the liberal tradition of human rights in the 1970s but was instead in keeping with the discussions at the UN General Assembly and demands issued by states in the Global South against racial discrimination and religious intolerance beginning in the early 1960s, often against the advice of the governments of major powers in the West. These discussions culminated in 1968 with the International Year of Human Rights.[80]

The mobilizations encouraged by major Western NGOs such as Amnesty and Human Rights Watch attest to a redefinition of human rights, as does the nature of negotiations surrounding the third basket, along with the final form it assumed. Human rights were henceforth centered on the defense of individual political rights, breaking with the definition prevailing since

THE EUROPE OF CONVERGENCES

the end of World War I.[81] In 1919 minority treaties had recognized collective rights by granting minorities the opportunity to petition the League of Nations when they felt they had been the victim of discrimination.[82] In the context of the fight against Nazism, in August 1941 paragraph 5 of the Atlantic Charter promised peoples engaging alongside the UN "the fullest collaboration between all nations in the economic field, with the object of securing for all improved labour standards, economic advancement, and social security." The ideological battle against Nazi barbarism was fought on the grounds of social rights; the "totalitarian" social model of the Nazis was contrasted, by the International Labour Office civil servants located in Montreal, with the social rights guaranteed by social security based on the Beveridge model.[83] In 1944 the International Labour Office's Declaration of Philadelphia, which opened the period of liberation from the Nazi yoke, firmly proclaimed that "labour is not a commodity" and made the protection of workers an element in the affirmation of human rights against the widespread use of forced labor in the Third Reich.[84] Finally, the Universal Declaration of Human Rights of 1948 granted a role, albeit a subordinate one, to social and economic rights. Articles 22–26 added to political liberties the right to social security, to work, to equal pay for equal work, to just compensation, to organize, to rest, and to an adequate standard of living, a list that drew inspiration from the creation of the ILO in 1919. These rights were reaffirmed specifically in the International Covenant on Economic, Social and Cultural Rights in December 1966. The inclusion of social rights in the declaration of 1948 was a response to the demands made by representatives from Chile and recently decolonized countries such as India or the Philippines, with the support of socialist countries, especially Yugoslavia. They also enjoyed the support, despite his Gaullist tendencies, of the French jurist René Cassin, who for this reason was accused by the U.S. Department of State of playing into the hands of the Communists.[85]

While countries in the Global South insisted in the 1950s on the indivisibility of human rights—in other words the importance and even primacy of economic and social rights—restricting the scope of human rights to individual political liberties became an instrument of self-definition for the Western bloc.[86] This was demonstrated by the European Convention on Human Rights of 1950, which, unlike the Universal Declaration, did not include social rights. This absence was generally justified by the fact that European human rights were guaranteed by the existence of actual mechanisms of recourse—the European Commission of Human Rights and the European Court of Human Rights—and that these bodies could not adjudicate on social rights that were matters for states.[87] In fact, the absence of courts for social rights was essentially related to political choices, as shown by the discussions surrounding the development of the European Convention. It was British conservatives in particular who systematically opposed the inclusion of social rights in the convention, doing so for domestic political reasons.[88] More broadly, this "omission" of social rights reveals how, within a Cold War context, human rights became an instrument for promoting liberal values specific to the Western "camp" against socialist states, and especially against demands from the Global South for a right to development.

This is clearly demonstrated by the long debate surrounding the ban on forced labor that took place between 1947 and 1957. In November 1947, the AFL denounced the massive practice of forced labor by the Soviet Union before the United Nations Economic and Social Council (ECOSOC). These accusations—like the allegations that were brought to the council's knowledge in the ensuing months and years by various private actors and associations—sought to document and condemn the serious human rights violations of Eastern bloc countries and Communist China.[89] To conduct an investigation by circumventing the Soviet veto, UN officials proposed to the ILO—of which the USSR was not yet a member—to establish a joint special or ad hoc committee on forced labor, under the direction of the Indian jurist and politician Ramaswani Mudaliar. The committee operated from 1951 to 1953, and its conclusions were taken up and reworked by a dedicated commission of the International Labour Office between 1954 and 1959. In the ILO Governing Body, it was unsurprisingly the AFL representative Philip Delaney who was the most aggressive, with support from the British unionist Alfred Roberts. They had the strong backing of employers' representatives, who added that forced labor represented unfair competition.[90] Even though Communist authorities denied it vigorously, there was no doubt that labor camps were a common practice in people's democracies, especially in Czechoslovakia, and even more so in the Stalinist Soviet Union.[91] Free labor was a particularly thorny issue for leaders in Communist countries, where work was an obligation for all citizens, who had to commit to building socialism. Re-education through labor was even institutionalized in the 1960s, when asociality became an official offense.

THE EUROPE OF CONVERGENCES

It is nevertheless interesting to observe how the extensive study conducted by international civil servants as part of the ad hoc committee ultimately freed the debate regarding forced labor from the strict binarism imposed on it by the Cold War. It opened a space for reflecting on the nature of free labor and the importance of social rights in guaranteeing this liberty, and human rights more generally; it especially involved actors from the Global South, who underscored and documented the existence of new forms of segregation and human rights violations.[92] The committee's civil servants gave voice to a wide variety of actors, such as the Workers Defense League from the United States, which gathered vast documentation on peonage and forced labor for debts in Latin America and some states in the southern United States.[93] The committee's hearings, individual witnesses, and associations for the defense of colonized populations emphasized that the creation of a formally free labor market was in reality accompanied by new forms of forced labor that were not explicitly forbidden by law. They emphasized the role of economic and social inequality, along with ethnic differences, in maintaining and even strengthening forced labor. They stressed that in the absence of social rights, human rights remained formal promises. In this context, representatives from the USSR—which had joined the ILO in 1954—and from people's democracies tried to impose a new interpretation on forced labor: it resulted primarily from the very nature of capitalist exploitation, with the ultimate form being unemployment, which deprived workers of their freedom of choice.[94] This economic and social conception of forced labor cannot be reduced to Communist propaganda, as it was actually part of a long socialist tradition in which genuine free labor was based on the guarantee of social rights, especially the right to work. Representatives from the USSR were inspired by declarations and analyses on the part of reformist unions, especially those from representatives from the Global South, in an effort to report on actual cases of forced labor affecting some categories of populations in situations of social inferiority or ethnic segregation, such as black Americans, in addition to legal inequality for certain categories of migrant workers.[95] This example illustrates how actors in the Global South seized on, to their advantage, notions of human rights and discrimination between 1947 and 1957. In the ensuing years, representatives from Western countries sought to avoid international discussions on human rights. In 1950 U.S. and British representatives tried, with support from various Western powers, to dissolve the UN

Commission on Human Rights, as well as the Sub-Commission on the Prevention of Discrimination and the Protection of Minorities. They feared that these would become weapons for denouncing the violation of fundamental freedoms in colonies, and forms of discrimination experienced by the black population in the United States.[96]

The "return" of human rights in the late 1970s was actually a pared-down reinvention without collective economic and social rights.[97] When representatives from nonaligned countries and the Group of 77 mobilized in the 1970s at the UN Commission on Human Rights for collective rights to development and basic health care in the name of human rights, representatives from Western countries refused in the name of respecting individual liberties. The lengthy discussions finally produced the declaration of 1985, adopted in December 1986, which renounced any obligation of reparations on the part of Northern countries in favor of an obligation to cooperate, while reaffirming the responsibility of each state to develop its population and respect the political rights of each individual.[98] The CSCE consequently did not invent human rights diplomacy but was a decisive stage in its redefinition and reduction to individual civil rights.

The Helsinki Conference was an international moment that grew out of a long practice of diplomatic, economic, and cultural exchanges promoted by international organizations and associations. For some Western leaders, these exchanges had to foster convergence between the two economic and social systems and eventually weaken the Communist project. The "spirit of Helsinki," however, reflected the limits of theories of convergence and the end of ideologies. The emphasis on a "humanitarian" and human rights discourse focusing on the protection of individual liberties did not take into account the economic and social conditions that actually limited these liberties. At the same time, the issue of the free flow of information was contested at UNESCO by representatives from new states, whose independence was effectively limited by the financial power of major Western press agencies and the monopoly they had over means of communication, satellites in particular.[99]

International organizations—universal or regional, intergovernmental or not—represented privileged spaces for developing relations between the two parts of Europe. They were actors and focal points for what is referred to as détente. Within these international spaces, representatives from medium-sized European powers such as France or the FRG in the West and

THE EUROPE OF CONVERGENCES

Romania and Poland in the East could be heard more clearly and could even play a role consistent with their objectives, namely, the constitution of a common space for developing exchanges and stabilizing borders. In this context, neutral countries—Austria, Finland, Switzerland—became bridges between actors in Eastern and Western Europe, and cities such as Vienna, Helsinki, and Geneva became the site of privileged encounters.

Scholarly "epistemic communities" or groups of actors gathered around common causes organized internationally and worked together in organizations that served as places for discussion, the implementation of joint projects, and even epistemic convergence. These actors did not represent a homogeneous group and pursued diverging objectives. The executives of companies in the ICC were driven by economic interests; scholars and peace groups aware of the nuclear threat sought to promote peace; representatives from the world of culture and education met at UNESCO; sociologists and economists came together around joint projects within the European Coordination Centre for Research and Documentation in Social Sciences, or the Vienna Center, and defended a universalist vision of culture, education, and the social sciences. The trade unionists involved in global confederations, whose meetings were fostered by the existence of the ILO, had diverging visions regarding their role but agreed on the need for giving voice to labor and for avoiding social dumping. Finally there were international civil servants, who encouraged the circulation of information and dialogue between the two parts of the world. All these actors took part, in one form or another, in ordering the world.

This project of organizing the world was based on a shared belief in modernity and progress, and in the possibility of planning the future, thereby driving the notion that the societies of the two parts of Europe could develop together. The research conducted at IIASA, which was founded in 1972, shared this belief and helped develop intervention models for policy issues, such as the environment, that were reproducible in different contexts. In contrast, the comparative approach adopted by the teams working together at the European Coordination Centre for Research and Documentation in Social Sciences suggested that differences subsisted, and that it was these differences that should drive exchanges. International discussions, including the Helsinki Conference, were a culmination of sorts, reflecting the tension between these two logics, as well as the reality of differing worldviews and expectations on the part of leaders from both blocs. Economically, Eastern bloc countries, which inherited a relative situation of underdevelopment, were much more dependent than those in the West on pan-European exchange, especially in matters of technology, a dependence that was clearly marked by their marginal position within international economic institutions, GATT in particular. The economic fragility of these regimes increased their legitimacy deficit with respect to their populations. Ideologically, in the context of a liberal redefinition of human rights from which social rights were excised, socialist countries were in a position of relative weakness. This imbalance in favor of the West was ultimately demonstrated by the Final Act of the Helsinki Conference. Often seen as a diplomatic victory for the USSR, which successfully imposed recognition of the bloc's borders, it was a first step in the triumph of an economic organization and a human rights system that consecrated Western predominance and the liberal model. Challenges to it during this period often emanated from newly independent countries, with specific demands being formulated by what is referred to as the Third World.

Chapter Five

THE THIRD WORLD AND
THE NEW INTERNATIONAL ECONOMIC ORDER

On December 14, 1960, the UN General Assembly passed resolution no. 1514, the Declaration on the Granting of Independence to Colonial Countries and Peoples, which stated that "immediate steps shall be taken . . . to transfer all powers to the peoples of those territories."[1] This signaled the arrival of the Third World on the international stage. The declaration and the committee of twenty-four members tasked with overseeing its implementation bear witness to an important change in the meaning and role of the UN. When it was created in 1945, the UN was still dominated by colonial and imperial powers, which left their mark on its functioning. The Trusteeship Council established to supervise eleven territories and to guide their transition to autonomy or independence was in keeping with the League of Nations Permanent Mandates Commission. Like the latter, it embodied the permanence of colonial logic within the UN, which helped maintain the domination of colonial powers. This very council, however, and more specifically the UN Secretariat and General Assembly—especially its committee on non-self-governing territories—were places where this domination was called into question.[2] The UN included 76 countries in 1955 and 144 twenty years later. With a few rare exceptions, the newcomers were all countries emerging from colonization, sometimes after lengthy and lethal wars, for instance in Algeria (1954–1961), Indochina and Vietnam (1946–1954,

1955–1974), and Mozambique (1964–1975). The victories of these movements proved the limits of the all-powerful West, but a number of these new countries were exhausted and divided, and their governments struggled to establish sovereignty over territories that they administered with difficulty. Given this position of relative weakness, major international organizations could appear in the eyes of the new political elite of these countries as spaces of legitimization—arenas in which they could have their voice heard—as well as resources for national construction.

The UN General Assembly, where each country has one vote, became a platform for the leaders of these newly independent countries, who in 1964 established a new group within the organization: the G77. It provided visibility to those who were henceforth referred to as the Third World. In 1974, when Amadou Mahtar M'Bow of Senegal, a practicing Muslim, became director-general of UNESCO, he presented his election as "a manifestation of consideration and esteem toward regions and peoples—those from the Third World—who were long kept far from universal centers of decision-making and influence."[3]

Leaders from countries that joined the UN wanted to make a specific voice heard, namely, one that was independent of the logic governed by blocs. They nevertheless shared, with both Western and Communist elites, the conviction that in order to exercise full and undivided sovereignty, they had to promote the economic and political development of their country.[4] International organizations, which since the interwar period had developed genuine expertise in matters of technical assistance, offered invaluable resources in this respect. During the first General Assembly in 1946, the representatives for Colombia and Lebanon raised the issue of inequalities in development. In 1948, at the initiative of countries in the Global South that were already independent, the UN General Assembly decided to establish a budget to "arrange for the organization of international teams consisting of experts . . . for the purpose of advising those governments in connexion with their economic development programmes."[5] What would become the Expanded Programme of Technical Assistance in 1949 was an essential instrument of economic policy directed toward the Third World at the UN and Bretton Woods organizations. It was accompanied by the emergence of numerous international NGOs, which implemented development projects on the ground. This chapter will set out from programs led by the WHO, UNESCO, and the ILO in order to explore the ideologies and

THE THIRD WORLD

development practices of organizations within the UN system, especially how the civil servants and experts in charge of these programs "ordered" the world based on criteria for economic development and helped reinterpret the conflicts that divided it.

At the same time, the issue of development revealed and generated new oppositions. In the years following World War II, it was closely linked to decolonization and therefore can appear to be closely related to North-South conflicts.[6] However, when President Harry S. Truman announced on January 20, 1949, that the United States was ready to broadly contribute to the UN Development Programme, it was primarily to combat the revolutionary danger caused by misery; this contribution was seen as a way to combat the dreaded influence of Communists in countries that had just broken free of direct Western political domination.[7] Representatives from socialist countries proclaimed that since they were not associated with the crimes of colonization, they had no obligation to provide development aid; they stressed that U.S. actors and their Western allies were actually seeking to export their model of modernity and, as part of a capitalist logic, to take advantage of new economic opportunities. This critique connects with another present in some of the recent literature, namely, that development aid prolonged earlier forms of economic exploitation and served as a vector to export economic and social models that were specifically Western, at the expense of local cultures and balances.[8]

Development aid became a major issue in the Cold War, even when deployed independently from the logic of confrontation between the blocs. In different local settings, economic aid was used as a means to create a clientele and served as a vector for exporting a specific model of economic and social organization.[9] Countries in the Global South knew how to exploit this competition to increase the aid they received from governments in each bloc. For instance, the Syrians skillfully took advantage of the rivalry between the two Germanies.[10] In fact, while development could be a vector through which countries in the Global North imposed their model of modernization, it was primarily the elite of the Global South that demanded, within the forum of the UN, a right to development as reparation for the crimes of colonization. This right was part of what would later be formulated as a demand for a New International Economic Order (NIEO) and was meant to allow newly independent countries to take full part in global economic competition. While it was mainly related to an opposition between developed and underdeveloped worlds, this project for an NIEO also met the interest and aspirations of certain countries in the Council for Mutual Economic Assistance because it challenged the rules of the Bretton Woods system. Cold War discourse and practices were thus grafted onto North-South relations and the issue of development, and not the other way around. Finally, this history in return challenges the nature of oppositions between the blocs. The ideology of development was rooted in a representation of modernity and progress that was, for the most part, measured by indicators of economic growth, a belief that the technocratic leaders and elites of socialist and capitalist countries shared.[11] In this sense, development policies and practices enable us to further explore the nature of the differences between the two systems.

DEVELOPMENT AS AN INTERNATIONAL PROJECT

The Institutionalization of Development

Beginning in the late 1920s, the League of Nations and the International Labour Organization launched technical assistance programs that were the precursors for policies of development. Their goal was to circulate knowledge and know-how. With financial support from major private foundations, the Rockefeller Foundation in particular, the League sent experts to various countries across the globe, including China, which at the time was transformed into a development laboratory of sorts.[12] The League's Permanent Mandates Commission, which supervised the territories administered by the major powers in Africa, the Middle East, and the Pacific, promoted these activities with a view to establishing politically and economically viable states, especially from the ruins of the Ottoman Empire.[13] From the 1920s onward, international organizations implemented development plans for "backward" European regions, namely, Southern Europe and the Balkans.[14] The Bruce Report, named after Stanley Bruce, the Australian politician who proposed it, provided in 1938 for an extension and institutionalization of the economic, social, and humanitarian activities of the League of Nations.[15] During these same years, the ILO sent experienced civil servants and experts into the field to diffuse the standards and technical know-how produced by the organization in three primary areas: social insurance, industrial hygiene, and labor law.[16] They were

THE THIRD WORLD

initially sent to the European periphery and later to China, Egypt, and Latin America, in particular Cuba in 1934, Brazil in 1936, and Chile in 1938. The reports submitted by Western social policy specialists on missions reveal their imperfect local knowledge, as well as the gap between the goals of the organization that sent them and the expectations of local actors. With a few exceptions, the results of these missions were disappointing for contemporaries, but they are of interest to historians because they help identify the logic that already governed technical assistance, and later development aid.[17] They helped export know-how produced in the West, strengthened the organization that circulated this knowledge, and could ultimately also serve a political function. ILO civil servants, who had taken refuge in Montreal during World War II, set out on missions in Latin American countries to implement social security systems, with a view to countering the propaganda efforts of Nazi authorities designed to influence public opinion in these countries.[18]

After World War II, and in the wake of President Truman's speech on January 20, 1949, development aid assumed a new dimension. The objectives nevertheless remained the same: in keeping with their experience in Latin America, U.S. political actors expected international experts to circulate know-how and expertise produced and developed in North Atlantic and other developed countries, with a view to combatting the misery that fostered the spread of Communist ideas.[19] In November 1950 the U.S. Congress passed a first package of $30 million to fund the Expanded Programme created in November 1949 within the United Nations Economic and Social Council. The Permanent Committee of Technical Assistance distributed resources between the different UN agencies tasked with selecting and sending experts on missions in the field; these experts diffused technical know-how and helped train local managers and elites. Soviet authorities immediately interpreted Truman's appeal as a declaration of war. By offering, via their policy of development, a "Marshall plan to the world," U.S. economic and political actors were seeking to secure economic markets and political allies.[20] While Paul Hoffman, who directed the Economic Cooperation Administration in Europe, quickly joined the UNDP, which was dominated at the time by U.S. staff, Truman's Point Four Program did not provide for direct economic aid, unlike the Marshall Plan.[21]

Beginning in the early 1960s, with the acceleration of decolonization, development became a priority for international organizations.[22] When the

Organisation for Economic Co-operation and Development took over for the Organisation for European Economic Co-operation in 1961, the goal of development was naturally accompanied by that of cooperation, as reflected in its new name.[23] U.S. actors played an essential role in the international diffusion of this ideology of development, and this was especially true of economists, through the success enjoyed at the time by the theory of modernization. According to these "mandarins of the future"—Walt Whitman Rostow and his colleagues at the Harvard Department of Social Relations or the Massachusetts Institute of Technology Center for International Studies—all countries go through the same stages of economic development. Aid programs for Third World countries simply acted as a trigger.[24] The first International Decade for Development was incidentally launched in September 1961 with a speech by U.S. president John F. Kennedy, which was echoed in 1962 by UN secretary-general U Thant. Various U.S. administrations regularly served as the primary backers for these programs.

Rostow was aware that the very notion of development was based on an evolutionist view of society shared by leaders from both competing economic systems and therefore strove to establish a rigorous distinction between U.S. and Soviet growth models.[25] Reciprocal influences also existed, however. In the United States, the experiences from New Deal economic planning, which were partly developed based on the example of the USSR, served as an inspiration for development policies directed toward the Third World.[26] Lenin did not hesitate to call on U.S. engineers to accelerate industrial development in the USSR during the 1920s.[27] In the postwar years, theorists of modernization in the United States drew inspiration from—all while establishing contrasts with—the Soviet example, which they saw as a successful development project.[28] The capitalist modernization project shared numerous characteristics with its socialist rival with regard to the representation of the world on which it was founded—a single historical model oriented toward progress—as well as the practice it generated, namely, projects led and funded by state agencies. The ideology of development was actually in keeping with the history of a right to self-determination jointly formulated by leaders from the two major Cold War powers on the occasion of the two World Wars. In 1919 Wilson and Lenin both proclaimed the right of peoples to self-determination, and in 1941 the powers that signed the Atlantic Charter reiterated the same promise. Both Soviet Communists and U.S. political leaders were well aware that this

THE THIRD WORLD

political independence truly existed only insofar as peoples could establish sovereignty over their territory via institutions and a stable economy. The development policies promoted by international organizations clearly pursued the objective of establishing the foundations for this sovereignty.

For international organizations, these development programs, which were presented as the very condition for peace, served as an important factor of legitimacy. They helped strengthen the collective sense of belonging of international civil servants by justifying their mission, namely, that of organizing a better world for all.[29]

The civil servants who joined the UN system following World War II, who were often economists, were in keeping with this tradition, as were those working at the World Bank. It was a restricted group whose coherence was based on strong convictions inspired by their analysis of the economic crisis of the 1930s and its horrible political consequences. They believed that global economic imbalances led to wars, and being faithful to the Atlantic Charter, they were convinced of the need to promote and establish the political independence of less economically advanced countries. Generally part of the Keynesian or even Social Democrat movement, they were favorable toward indicative national planning and were convinced that public actors, enlightened by expert know-how, were best positioned to develop and implement rational development policies over the long term.[30] Economists active in the UN's regional economic commissions, especially the most dynamic among them, the Economic Commission for Latin America based in Santiago de Chile since 1948, shared these convictions.

The ECLA's secretary-general, Argentinian economist Raùl Prebisch, promoted the hypothesis of the secular deterioration in the terms of trade, which in the 1960s gave rise to the "theory of dependence," according to which North-South inequality was fueled by the perpetuation, in renewed forms, of colonial exploitation. This conviction fostered the engagement of UN economists in support of a right to development for poor countries and a change to the rules of international economic exchange. Hans Singer, who held successive positions within international organizations, was an important figure in this trend. After studying with Joseph Schumpeter, he had to leave Germany in 1933 and pursued his Ph.D. degree in Cambridge under the supervision of Keynes. In 1947 he joined the UN Department of Economic Affairs, where he rubbed shoulders with David Owen, another

Keynesian economist. The latter, who was executive director of the UN Technical Assistance Committee, became the assistant secretary-general for economic affairs in April 1946. He recruited two Polish socialist economists to the Department of Economic Affairs, Władysław Malinowski and Michał Kalecki. After working at the United Nations Economic Commission for Europe, the former played an essential role in founding the United Nations Conference on Trade and Development in 1964. In 1949 Owen and Singer were the architects behind implementation of the Expanded Programme, which had limited resources provided on a purely voluntary basis and chiefly worked toward the circulation of knowledge and know-how. Compensating experts accounted for 70 percent of the Expanded Programme's budget: eight thousand of them were sent to 135 countries between the beginning of the program and 1958; the remaining resources were devoted to a fellowship program awarded to approximately sixteen thousand individuals between 1949 and 1959.[31] In 1959 the Special Fund was added to the Expanded Programme, with a view to increasing resources for development aid by attracting private and government investment to the most important projects. It enabled the creation of the development agencies that offered training for the planning and programming of economic development in Latin America in 1962, Asia in 1963, and Africa in 1964.

In 1965 the UNDP unified and replaced the Expanded Programme and the Special Fund and was placed under the direction of an Executive Board elected by ECOSOC, in which representatives from developing countries were in the majority. Between 1966 and 1972 Jan Tinbergen—as we saw earlier, another neo-Keynesian economist won over by the notion of convergence between the two blocs—presided over ECOSOC's Committee for Development Policy.[32] Unlike the Expanded Programme, the UNDP authorized contributions in nonconvertible currencies, which allowed Comecon countries to participate more easily. This was the context in which the first two Development Decades unfolded between 1961–1969 and 1970–1979. During this period, the increasing activity of UN agencies depended on the financial involvement of the World Bank and the International Monetary Fund, which became major actors in international development policy. The role played by the Bretton Woods institutions represented a Western response to requests from countries in the Global South and the socialist bloc, which sought the creation of a special fund for development within the UN. To counter this request, in 1960 Western countries created the

THE THIRD WORLD

International Development Association connected to the World Bank, over which they exerted nearly total control, thereby giving them power over the funds invested, unlike at the UN. Between 1968 and 1981, under the presidency of Robert McNamara, the value of subsidized loans granted by the World Bank increased tenfold; these loans were joined by those made by major private Western banks. UN development economists were constantly confronted with this contradiction: they wanted to promote the independence of countries in the Global South, but funding for development remained at the goodwill of the developed countries providing money and expertise.

Development as an Issue

Development remained a de facto Western endeavor, as up through the late 1960s, 80 percent of contributions to the Extended Programme, the Special Fund, and later the UNDP came from Western countries, especially the United States, which provided approximately 40 percent of the funds. Great Britain and France were the leading European contributors but were soon surpassed by countries in Northern Europe, which provided up to 15 percent of the total in 1970 (Sweden nearly 9 percent on its own), followed by Canada and the Federal Republic of Germany.[33] Three-quarters of experts were from these countries during the 1950s, and two-thirds during the 1960s. For the overall period, 55 percent of experts were from Western Europe, particularly from the former colonial powers; the United States provided 17 percent of experts in 1953, a share that was far below its financial contribution.

The financial and human commitment of Western countries in UN development programs naturally led to a transfer of economic and social models from these countries toward those in the Global South. When the UN director-general Dag Hammarskjöld of Sweden launched the OPEX programme in 1956, which involved sending executive and administrative operational staff to help recently decolonized countries create robust administrations, there was no doubt that this assistance should promote the implementation of state administrations based on the model of Western liberal democracies and should pave the way for capitalist economic development.[34] Development policies were therefore closely dominated by representations forged in former metropoles, and until the 1960s they remained highly inspired by the choices made by them. The policies were oriented toward increasing agricultural productivity, which was one of the goals of the first Development Decade (1961–1969).[35] A quarter of the funds for UN development programs at the time were devoted to agricultural projects, and only 12 percent to industrial development. The Food and Agriculture Organization (FAO) received 38 percent of the UNDP's funds in the 1960s, while just slightly above 10 percent were used for UNESCO education programs or ILO professional training. There was tension between these choices and the orientations of the international economists who oversaw the establishment of these programs, whether they were Keynesians or dependency theorists, or both.

The orientations of this first Development Decade were, for this reason, the subject of sustained criticism from leaders from the Global South, especially countries in Central and South America, which were supported by leaders from Eastern Europe. As they had done during the immediate postwar years, when they themselves were dependent on international aid, the latter emphasized the importance of development policies that ensured genuine economic independence through a diversification of sectors of activity. The need to create specific industrial development aid was one of the demands made in 1948 by Soviet representatives at UNECE, a request that representatives from Western countries rejected.[36] The latter were ultimately forced, due to the changing power relations at the UN, to accept the creation of a Centre for Industrial Development in 1961. Announced in 1964 during the first United Nations Conference for Trade and Development, in 1966 the Centre became the United Nations Industrial Development Organization. In 1967 the new organization symbolically set up in Vienna, which, as we saw earlier, served as a bridge between the East and the West.[37] Its research director was Hans Singer, whose role in the launch of the UNDP was discussed earlier. The goal of UNIDO was to promote the industrialization of countries in the Global South, essentially in connection with the UNDP, receiving 7.3 percent of its funds in 1969. It embodied an alternative vision of development centered on industrialization as an engine for economic independence and political sovereignty; this conviction was driven by elites from the Global South, as well as those from socialist states. While Western developed countries provided the bulk of funding and expertise, leaders in socialist countries were actively involved in UNIDO from its creation.[38]

THE THIRD WORLD

The ILO's World Employment Programme, launched in 1969 to inaugurate the second Development Decade, also bears witness to this change in paradigm. It sought to combat underemployment and unemployment throughout the world and offered those countries that requested it its expertise in developing and implementing structural reforms.[39] Representatives from Communist countries were favorable toward the program's orientations because it made a central goal of reducing unemployment, which served as a key propaganda argument in support of their economic system. Economists from Communist countries were invited to submit a report on the role of agri-food industries in reducing rural unemployment or underemployment.[40] Overall, however, these Communist experts were little involved in creating and implementing the employment program. Codirected by Hans Singer and the labor economist Walter Galenson, it was highly inspired by theories on deterioration in the terms of trade. The program's overarching philosophy was inspired by the research conducted at the Institute of Development Studies at the University of Sussex, with the very same Hans Singer becoming its director in 1968, and a new generation of development economists emerging from there.[41] Dudley Seers, who directed the first major project in Colombia, developed arguments in his final report that clashed with those formulated by World Bank experts during a survey they conducted there in 1952. To pull Colombia out of misery, the World Bank had bet on high rates of growth and strong agricultural productivity obtained at large semi-industrial farms. On the other hand, the Seers Report emphasized the need for large-scale agrarian reform, which would give rise to a more productive class of average farmers. It recommended modifying the tax base in order to develop a vast education and public hygiene program.[42] The program was never implemented due to resistance from the country's economic elite, but it nevertheless attests to a reorientation in thinking connected to underdevelopment. Indicators for "human development" appeared alongside those for economic growth; they were detailed and clearly presented during the Conference on Employment held in Geneva in 1976, at which participants emphasized the importance of meeting the basic needs of populations lacking in food, clothing, and access to education.[43] The promoters of the Employment Programme celebrated the 1976 conference as a major moment of innovation in conceptions of development, despite the fact that McNamara, the director of the World Bank, had already stressed the importance of meeting the basic needs of populations in 1972.

While Comecon countries were associated—albeit vaguely—with the World Employment Programme, its inspirations and the discussions surrounding it gradually moved away from Communist points of reference. The importance ascribed to meeting basic needs during the second Development Decade tended to replace demands for redistribution and social rights, which were central to the discourse of Communists.[44] At the same time, Eastern bloc regimes were facing competition from a different source, namely, a Chinese development model "from below."

Global Health and the Emergence of the Chinese Model

Within the WHO and the ILO, numerous civil servants were favorable toward universal health coverage, a goal that was quickly countered by a coalition of forces: representatives from colonial powers such as Great Britain and France; from what was referred to as liberal medicine; and from the pharmaceutical industry. When Milton Roemer, a U.S. civil servant at the WHO, came out in favor of equitable access to health care, his opponents mobilized a Cold War discourse and accused him of promoting "socialized" medicine.[45] The USSR and people's democracies had already left the WHO in 1949 on the pretext that it was too closely dominated by U.S. actors, who at the time were practicing an active policy of boycotting penicillin from Eastern European countries.[46] More fundamentally, these same actors promoted, from the very beginning, specific health policies that primarily involved curing and combatting disease through targeted medicinal treatments, which were accompanied by eradication campaigns that were not always successful, as demonstrated by the failure of malaria eradication.[47] Contrary to targeted measures, representatives from socialist countries declared their support for "social hygiene" policies managed by states.[48] While the systematic opposition of the Soviets may often seem fruitless, the position of Communist leaders cannot be reduced to Cold War discourses. As early as the interwar period, the League of Nations Health Committee—and experts from Eastern Europe and the Soviet Union in particular—advocated for local measures of control for malaria, breaking away from the Rockefeller Foundation.[49] This orientation resonated with a branch of social medicine, which was also represented in the United States, and for which the struggle against the disease should be based on a vast public infrastructure and measures of prevention. In 1949 Brock Chisholm of Canada, the first director-general of the WHO, expressed his desire to preserve the principles of social medicine rooted in the organization's constitution. The Croatian doctor Andrija Štampar, a founding member of the WHO, emphasized that it should continue to consider four principles in its approach to disease: social and economic security, education, nutrition, and housing. In the ensuing decades, after the return of socialist countries within the organization, this debate was once again on the WHO agenda. It concluded and culminated with the Alma-Ata Declaration of 1978 regarding primary health care. The declaration promoted a public preventive medicine service that was in proximity to populations, contrary to major centralized and targeted eradication programs. This vision, which Soviet representatives defended, was driven by a broad coalition of actors. The group included certain reformist civil servants at the WHO, such as Kenneth W. Newel or the new director-general Halfdan Mahler of Denmark, who was elected in 1973. They garnered support from politicians from the Social Democrat movement, which had rallied around a public health model inspired by the report from Marc Lalonde of Canada in 1974, as well as activists who were part of the Catholic and Protestant Christian Social movement (such as the World Council of Churches). Finally, an entire Third-Worldist movement promoted the new international model of "barefoot doctors."[50]

Between 1963 and 1989 the Chinese government sent medical teams to more than forty African countries and created a training program for young doctors. The elites of these countries were won over by the advantages of a health system that could provide care at lower cost to a large rural population by using traditional know-how.

It was in 1970 that this Chinese medical model made its "official" entry in the West. It was publicized in articles by the journalist Edgar Snow upon the departure of the first delegation of U.S. doctors, who had been invited by the Chinese medical association. Convinced by the scope, quality, and reduced cost of Chinese health and medical care, public health experts drew inspiration from it for medicine in the United States as well as in the Global South. This positive reception inspired the documentary film shot in 1972 by researchers from Stanford University, entitled *The Barefoot Doctors of Rural China*. A new model was born. The WHO, under the direction of its new director Halfdan Mahler of Denmark, greatly contributed to its diffusion. In response to a proposal by Chinese authorities, the latter organization accepted to hold an international conference on primary health care.[51] Due to pressure from Soviet authorities concerned about Chinese influence in Third World countries, the conference was ultimately held in the Soviet Kazakh city of Alma-Ata.

The Chinese government boycotted the conference in retaliation, but it nevertheless brought together three thousand representatives, primarily from the ministries of health of 134 countries, who were joined by representatives from 67 international organizations. It resulted in a declaration that closely linked health and development and emphasized the need to promote medicine that is free and accessible to all by increasing the number of public health centers, where a preventive medicine based on local know-how would be dispensed.[52] The controversies that followed the Alma-Ata gathering greatly weakened the euphoric declarations formulated there. Supporters of a holistic approach favored long-term programs that tried to identify and provide solutions for the economic and social roots of problems but were unable to win out against supporters of a selective approach, who favored concrete results within the framework of limited projects. The fundamental question involved was the funding of health programs within a market economy and the role of public insurance and social security systems. Historically, it was such systems that enabled the funding of social medicine; the fact that the ILO, which was tasked with implementing these social security programs, had been sidelined from discussions regarding global health care, bears witness to competition among organizations, one that was fueled by but not reducible to Cold War oppositions. Specialists in health and social protection had struggled to work together since the 1920s. In the years following the Alma-Ata conference, this competition doomed the establishment of a global health program.

As in the field of health, development policies quickly came up against diverging interpretations that were not connected to the Cold War but were rapidly reinterpreted according to Cold War categories. The abandonment of primary health care in favor of more targeted actions and the focus on combatting deep poverty in World Bank or ILO programs were ultimately part of a development approach that sought to preserve existing global economic balances.[53] It was to break out of this status quo, which was fostered by the development policies implemented internationally, that political elites in the Global South formulated demands in the 1960s for a new international economic order.[54]

THE THIRD WORLD

PROJECTS FOR A NEW INTERNATIONAL ECONOMIC ORDER

In May 1974 the UN General Assembly adopted the Declaration for the Establishment of a New International Economic Order (NIEO) by an overwhelming majority. The declaration consisted of two major parts: a guarantee of better redistribution of global wealth, and regulation of trade in raw materials. The declaration also emphasized protection for the economic sovereignty of Third World countries, especially their capacity to protect access to their natural resources; to this end, instruments such as the right of nationalizations and control over the power of multinational enterprises were not ruled out.[55]

This declaration was led at the UN by the Algerian president Houari Boumédiène, who at the time was secretary-general of the Non-Aligned Movement and issued demands for "reparations" from former colonial powers and U.S. dominance. While some leaders of the Non-Aligned Movement, such as the Group of 77 at the UN, adopted offensive language, it initially presented itself as an offer to engage in dialogue. The demands formulated in the declaration of 1974 were not revolutionary and did not represent a challenge to the capitalist order but all the same emphasized the interdependence between the economies of the South and the North. Supporters of the NIEO sought to strengthen the economic sovereignty of Third World countries by reducing the dependence of economies in the Global South on those in the Global North, as well as global inequality. International organizations, and the UN General Assembly in particular, were seen as actors that could channel and even oversee this interdependence to attain this greater equality.

The idea for an NIEO was therefore not an invention on the part of UN civil servants, but rather a response to concerns that some of them had, with the UN serving as a sound box. The new UN secretary-general, Kurt Waldheim, attended the Fourth Summit of the Non-Aligned Movement held in Algiers in 1973, and in the ensuing years the idea of an NIEO was the subject of discussions at various agencies. At UNESCO, requests for a new communication order were issued against domination by Western press agencies and media; they led in 1978 to the Declaration on Fundamental Principles concerning the Contribution of the Mass Media to Strengthening Peace and International Understanding, to the Promotion of Human Rights and to Countering Racialism, Apartheid and Incitement to War, which reaffirmed the freedom of information, but also emphasized that to guarantee this freedom, "it is necessary to correct the inequalities in the flow of information to and from developing countries, and between those countries."[56]

The declaration of 1974 was formulated as the economic crisis spread; it met with strong resistance from most of the economic and political elites in Western countries and with no real support of the Soviet Communist Party. The NIEO never saw the light of day, but the genealogy of this idea and the discussions surrounding it are interesting for what they tell us about new international utopias and hopes—and the opposition they sparked—as well as about the appearance of new actors in global power relations.

The Prehistory of the 1974 Declaration: From Bandung to UNCTAD

The 1974 declaration was a high point in the expression of a new internationalism, namely, that of countries emerging from colonialism, which since demographer Alfred Sauvy's article in 1952 were referred to as the Third World.[57] It was more of an idea than a reality, given the divisions that marked the group. In the mid-1970s some countries were at war with one another, such as India and Pakistan or Vietnam and its neighbors. In addition, the differences widened between the rich oil-producing countries that took part in formulating the NIEO and those that gradually sank into deep poverty, partly due to the rising price of oil. After a short period of euphoria, the group of Third World countries became deeply divided with respect to the price of raw materials.

Third Worldism nevertheless became a new international movement that attracted broad support. Its core consisted of Third World countries that organized, between 1955 and 1975, into multiple groups that formulated a discourse of solidarity and anti-imperialist demands.[58] In 1955 representatives from twenty-nine countries who met in Bandung, Indonesia, agreed on the need to develop economic and cultural cooperation between countries in the Afro-Asian space by circumventing the colonial powers: they relied on the UN Charter to condemn colonialism and racism, came out in support of UN membership for all newly independent countries, and counted on international organization to promote disarmament and cooperation.[59] The UN and its foundational ideas thus represented, from the

THE THIRD WORLD

very beginning, an important reference for this new internationalism. In a second phase, the Non-Aligned Movement was created in Belgrade, Yugoslavia, in 1961. A Yugoslav observer had already been present at Bandung, and Tito undeniably played an important role in structuring the movement. In addition to Yugoslavia's particular position between the blocs, Tito shared numerous convictions with Nehru, who succeeded Gandhi in 1948, as well as with Nasser, who had been in power in Egypt since 1953.[60]

The UN General Assembly provided an institutional framework and a stage from which the leaders of these countries could speak to the world. In 1964 they gathered within the G77, which brought together the Afro-Asian countries present in Bandung and Belgrade, who were joined by a number of Latin American countries. In 1966 eighty-two countries from Africa, Asia, and Latin America participated in a tricontinental conference in Havana, whose resolution adopted an offensive rhetoric of struggle against colonialism and economic imperialism. The conference became a launching pad of sorts for a Third Worldist movement that challenged the international capitalist order. It resonated in Western countries, where some movements on the left saw these newly decolonized countries as locales for a revolutionary hope that had faded in the North.[61]

The Bandung conference and those that followed were a launching pad for a political movement, a time for formulating and structuring economic demands that garnered international recognition with the first United Nations Conference on Trade and Development in 1964. Its goal was to create a new framework for global trade, one that was better adapted to the needs of the Global South. The economic discussions held in the aftermath of World War II resulted in the Havana Charter in 1947–1948, which recommended the creation of an International Trade Organization to oversee free trade policy and offer support to less developed countries. As the U.S. Senate did not ratify it, the International Trade Organization was never created, with the General Agreement on Tariffs and Trade—originally conceived as a transitional institution—serving as the institutional framework for global trade until 1995.[62] GATT, which organized free trade, provided for protectionary customs arrangements for less developed countries but did not include specific arrangements for direct foreign investment, or for the exchange of commodities such as sugar, coffee, and cotton. It also preserved the most-favored-nation clause, which in effect favored the most economically powerful countries.[63] In this context, the volatility of raw material prices perpetuated the dependence of Third World countries on more developed ones.

UNCTAD sought to respond to these structural inequalities. In 1964, for the first time, it brought together representatives from 120 countries in Geneva, including 80 from developing countries.[64] Władysław Malinowski, who was the secretary of ECOSOC at the time and one of the masterminds behind UNCTAD, managed to convince Raúl Prebisch to serve as conference secretary.[65] Following the gathering in Geneva, the conference transformed into a permanent body under the supervisory authority of the UN General Assembly and had a General Secretariat led by Prebisch.[66] UNCTAD carried out a number of functions. It offered training sessions for the economic elite of the Global South. The Trade Center created in 1967 in partnership with GATT collected documentation and offered support to governments in the Global South during trade negotiations with the Global North, encouraging exports.[67] Last but not least, regular conferences provided a space for discussing global trade agreements by product, with a view to protecting the economies of the Global South by ensuring more stable income. Prebisch celebrated the sugar agreement negotiated in 1968, which grew out of negotiations conducted over time, as a success.[68] While all these negotiations primarily underscore the diverging interests between the Global North and South, they were also marked by Cold War logic, as demonstrated by the sugar agreement, which was in keeping with the broader context of a U.S. embargo on Cuban sugar.[69] Tito, who affirmed socialism and maintained privileged relations with the Eastern bloc, played a pivotal role.[70] The economic demands formulated by underdeveloped countries converged, on a number of points, with those expressed in international arenas since 1947 by representatives from Communist countries. For the former, it was a matter of reestablishing greater equity in economic exchange, and for the latter, of bringing an end to the various forms of economic discrimination to which they were subject. It was on the basis of this convergence of interests that in 1962 representatives from the USSR and ECOSOC proposed a text calling for the creation of an international trade organization. Subsequently taken up and amplified by G77 countries, which added calls for a right to development, this led in 1964 to the passing of a UN resolution. The latter sought to foster the reorganization of international trade in favor of countries on the periphery and subjected developed capitalist countries to "structural adjustment" policies, requiring them to import

THE THIRD WORLD

more goods from underdeveloped countries. As we saw earlier, this goal had the support of UN civil servants—with Malinowski playing an active role—as well as the leaders of UN Regional Commissions: UNECE, headed between 1960 and 1967 by Vladimir Velebit of Yugoslavia, and especially the United Nations Economic Commission for Latin America (ECLA). The latter apparently served as a model for UNCTAD.

The Power of Multinational Corporations

The dangers that powerful multinational corporations posed for the sovereignty of states had been discussed within UNCTAD since the late 1960s, as part of a context of repeated interventions by U.S.-based multinationals in the affairs of Central and South American states during the postwar period. The coup d'état in Guatemala in 1954 at the instigation of United Fruit with the involvement of the CIA, or the intervention of the American Telephone and Telegraph Company in Chilean affairs in the early 1970s in order to overthrow the Allende government, are the most familiar examples. In 1972 the Chilean delegation to the UN General Assembly asked for an investigation into the role of multinationals in international relations. It led to the constitution of a Group of Eminent Persons tasked by ECOSOC with making recommendations for an international action to regulate the activity of multinationals. This group issued a report in 1974, which concluded that there was a need to create a documentation center, and to establish a code of conduct with respect to the investments of multinational companies abroad, especially in Third World countries.[71] This was the goal of the United Nations Centre on Transnational Corporations established in 1974. In addition to the code of conduct, the center, which was directed by the Finnish diplomat Klaus Sahlgren, was tasked with developing and providing information on multinational enterprises, as well as offering legal and technical assistance to developing countries during their negotiations with these enterprises. The center's creation was not an attack against multinational enterprises; it instead saw itself as a reassuring response to the concerns expressed by leaders after the NIEO declaration, with economic actors being involved in the discussions, especially via the International Chamber of Commerce.[72] However, the idea of holding a discussion on potential regulations, at a time when the demands of the NIEO seemed to resonate widely, was seen as a danger by these economic actors and some political circles, especially in the United States, where most of these enterprises were based. It prompted a counteroffensive that assumed different forms. Executives from multinational enterprises organized within various organizations, especially the International Organisation of Employers, the Employers' Confederation of Europe (UNICE), the International Christian Union of Business Executives (UNIAPAC), and the International Chamber of Commerce (ICC) in particular. Within these spaces, they organized their opposition to restrictive codes of conduct by emphasizing that misdeeds were the doing of isolated actors and promoted a voluntary and ethical response in the form of corporate social responsibility.[73] In addition, these associations served as powerful interest groups within international bodies, including at the UN Centre, where some of their representatives were full-fledged members. One of them, the Business and Industry Advisory Committee to the OECD (BIAC), played an important role from 1976 onward in the drafting of a nonrestrictive code of conduct at the OECD. Its drafters hoped that BIAC, conceived of and presented as a model, could orient thinking at UN agencies.[74] This strategy appears to have had an effect on the discussions held at the ILO at the time.

In January 1976 a symposium was held to reflect on the social implications of the NIEO. Its participants called into question inequalities in trade and exports in connection with development policies—Western solutions ill-adapted to the economic and social conditions of the Global South—as well as the increasing and concerning concentration of capital and technology in the hands of multinational corporations more powerful than many states.[75] This reflection led in 1977 to a Tripartite declaration by the Governing Body on multinational enterprises and social policy, which promoted corporate social responsibility as a voluntary response by employers to demands for social justice. The discussions that took place at the ILO show that the concerns and demands formulated by countries in the Global South were shared by other groups and were not exclusively connected to the opposition between developed and underdeveloped countries. The declaration in 1977 also grew out of meetings held since the late 1960s at the initiative of global trade union confederations and in particular International trade secretariats. They denounced the repeated violations of national social and economic legislation by major multinationals, and not just in the Global South. The declaration, which sought to respond to the concerns of both groups, nevertheless adopted a moderate formulation. It affirmed that multinationals had to honor their economic and social responsibilities toward their workforce and "respect the sovereign rights of states," but no monitoring measures ensured its application. Trade unions emphasized the negative effects of the OECD code on the ILO declaration.[76]

The UN Commission on Transnational Corporations was dissolved in 1992 and brought under UNCTAD in 1993, without managing to hold a vote on the code of conduct it had developed in 1982 and that was behind its creation.[77]

The failure of negotiations surrounding the UN code, as well as the difficulties encountered by the trade negotiations of UNCTAD, brought an end to the hopes that elites from the Global South had placed in the economic regulatory power of the UN. It also illustrates how Cold War rhetoric was mobilized to counter the demands made by governments in the Global South.

The NIEO and the First and Second Worlds of the Cold War

For neoliberal economists, who made their entry in the U.S. Economic Policy Board created by U.S. president Gerald Ford in 1974, the NIEO proposed by G77 countries was a direct attack on liberal democracy and the market economy. They believed that demands for sovereignty through expanded power for states, including in economic matters—in addition to requests to control multinationals and for a right of nationalization—were clearly inspired by Communist ideas.[78]

At first, however, Western diplomats did not directly oppose the requests of G77 countries and showed themselves to be open to dialogue. This openness was driven by prudence, as in the case of U.S. secretary of state Henry Kissinger, or political leaders from the former colonial powers of France and Great Britain. It was based on the apparent convictions of some political leaders from the Social Democrat movement who were active in international organizations.[79] In 1974, on the occasion of his Nobel Prize in economics, Gunnar Myrdal gave a speech entitled "The Equality Issue in World Development," in which he argued for redistribution of global wealth through greater aid to underdeveloped countries.[80] In 1976, at the request of World Bank director McNamara, the former German chancellor and winner of the Nobel Peace Prize, Willy Brandt, established a commission on underdevelopment and poverty. Its heterogeneous composition included numerous progressive politicians, such as Olaf Palme of Sweden and Edgard Pisani of France. It issued a consensus report that proposed, in particular, a transfer of resources to countries in the Global South via taxes on armaments and better regulation of global trade, solutions that had incidentally been proposed since the 1950s by representatives from countries in the socialist bloc. The report also promised that pursuing the economic growth of developed countries could help meet basic needs in the Global South.[81] By signing the first Lomé Convention in 1975 with forty-six countries from Africa, the Caribbean, and the Pacific, the governments of countries in the European Economic Community (EEC) provided a first collective response to global inequality: they opened their market with no customs duties to agricultural products from their former colonies (but not all countries in the Global South) in order to contain price variations for raw materials; established delivery quotas for certain products; and created a development fund designed to cushion price variations.[82]

While the U.S. government and the World Bank did not directly attack the NIEO project, they attempted to contain it. Leaders at the World Bank responded to the requests of the Third World with a program to combat poverty and meet "basic needs," which was intended for the most disadvantaged populations but offered no pathway out of dependence for the countries that were home to these populations.[83] U.S. leaders at the Department of Commerce worked to restrain the new group's capacity for action by furthering divisions. They also promoted specific international spaces in which representatives from developed capitalist countries could henceforth discuss global affairs among themselves; this was especially the role of the G7, created in 1975 in response to the declaration for an NIEO, or the OECD's Development Assistance Committee. The latter, which was established in 1962, saw its role expand in 1964 in reaction to the first meeting of UNCTAD.[84]

The prudence exhibited by political leaders from Western countries with respect to demands in support of an NIEO can be explained by international power relations, as well as by the existence of an organized anticolonialist and Third Worldist public opinion. The latter was structured in the 1960s within the anti-Vietnam committees in the United States that formulated a coordinated condemnation of the war. They served as powerful vectors during the late 1960s for the internationalization of revolutionary movements and utopias within the North Atlantic space and played an important role in the global diffusion of the aspirations and demands made by May 1968 movements. The Third Worldist movement was organized in the 1960s based on a dual Marxist and Christian inspiration, with its supporters seeing wars of independence and the demands that accompanied them as the pursuit of a revolutionary project and as an ideal of social justice, for which the USSR and Eastern bloc countries had ceased to serve as a possible model.[85]

Representatives from the Eastern bloc at the UN were not opposed to the NIEO, but they knew that it could not become an instrument for global revolution. In their relations with the Global South, Soviet leaders adopted a pragmatic stance, as demonstrated by the formulation of a Non-Capitalist Path of Development in 1961. It provided for an evolution in three stages: independence, "national democracy," and the adoption of socialism. Soviet economic aid was incidentally never provided on the condition of adopting socialism.[86] In reality, the NIEO program agreed on numerous points with the most long-standing aspirations of socialist countries. This was especially the case with demands for a right of nationalization, the establishment of more stable international prices, increased aid for industrial development, and free access to technological progress, in addition to the need to regulate the activity of multinational corporations expressed during the third session of UNCTAD in 1972. Beyond its strategic dimension, support from certain Comecon countries can be explained by this real convergence of views between two groups of countries that were late to join an international system organized by and for developed capitalist countries, and dominated by them.[87] Finally, Chinese competition also played an important role.

Since the Sino-Soviet split of the early 1960s, Chinese leaders tried to export their development model to the Global South and enjoyed limited but decisive support among public opinion in the Global North.[88] In the early 1970s this "Chinese model" had numerous defenders within international organizations. In addition to the promotion of "barefoot doctors" by various actors at the WHO, the FAO sent a mission to China in 1975 to gather information regarding Chinese approaches and to study people's communes as an example of integrated rural development. For the drafters of the report, rather than exporting Western solutions, Chinese agricultural techniques could be a possible source of inspiration for development policies designed for Third World countries.[89]

The convergence between the objectives of countries in the Global South and the Communist project was obvious when, during the first session of UNCTAD in 1964, Raùl Prebisch and Che Guevara both emphasized the importance of international trade for the development of poor countries, in accordance with the arguments of Lenin.[90] As we saw earlier, UNCTAD was not a space in which the dominant economic system was challenged. It rather sought to offer alternatives to the domination of economies in the Global South by those in the Global North, and to promote economic relations between the Global South and Eastern Europe. Trade relations between Comecon countries and those in the Global South increased substantially during the 1970s, although they remained secondary in the international trade of socialist countries. At the time, Comecon countries conducted 20–30 percent of their foreign trade with countries in the West and no more than 15 percent with those in the Global South, while the inverse was even truer.[91] Nevertheless, there was a marked interest on both sides for developing trade relations: for Comecon countries, the trade surplus with the Global South could finance their imports from the West and, from the mid-1970s onward, especially pay back their debts in convertible currency. Third World countries admittedly received manufactured products of mediocre quality, but at lower cost, and did not necessarily have to pay in hard currency, as Comecon countries favored barter arrangements. In addition, trade with countries with planned economies was more predictable and ensured price stability. Finally, socialist countries guaranteed loans with low rates and long terms: in 1964 Comecon secretary Nikolai Fadeyev proposed to Prebisch the creation of an international development bank that would have served as a kind of socialist world bank. These exchanges were in connection with what Communist leaders called the "international socialist division of labor," which was discussed within Comecon in 1958.[92] This division distinguished itself from its capitalist equivalent in that it did not lead to exploitation of the weakest but rather encouraged their development thanks to genuine economic cooperation and a systematic policy of technology transfer.[93] Economically, trade with the Global South was not always immediately profitable for Comecon countries, and some governments of Sub-Saharan African countries paid their debt by sending workers to Eastern bloc countries, part of whose salaries directly reimbursed Comecon countries.[94]

Despite this rapprochement, at the UN leaders from Third World countries did not necessarily differentiate between countries with market economies and others. They believed that socialist countries—which were more developed—and those from the West had an obligation to contribute to development aid. In the discussions surrounding the establishment of a code of conduct, they likened major combines from countries with planned economies to multinational enterprises. The discussions that occurred at UNCTAD'S Commission for Trade Among Countries Having Different Economic and Social Systems also reveals diverging interests, especially with the most developed socialist countries.[95] For instance, the leadership of the delegation from the GDR acknowledged that they were often more in agreement with the propositions of developed capitalist countries than with those from the developing countries, to which they were nevertheless ideologically closer.[96]

Unlike those from Comecon countries, Chinese leaders loudly affirmed their belonging to the Third World and referred to themselves at UNCTAD as an "underdeveloped socialist nation." They also emphasized that under the cover of solidarity, Comecon was practicing political predation on the poorest.[97] China's accession to the UN in 1971 enabled its delegates to publicly condemn the USSR's policy in the Third World. During the UNCTAD session from October 1975, the Chinese delegate declared:

> Developing countries should be on their guard against the propaganda of a super-power relating to the so-called experience of "economic integration" and "the international division of labour." In his country's view, such propaganda was merely an attempt to reduce the developing countries of Asia, Africa and Latin America to sources of cheap raw materials, affiliated processing mills, and markets for capital exports and outmoded equipment.[98]

Beyond its propaganda aspect, this declaration reminds us that Communist leaders often had an ambiguous position with respect to the Global South. The language of friendship and solidarity often concealed genuine economic asymmetry and the pursuit of clearly defined interests. Within the international system, the leaders of Eastern European countries took advantage of the position as intermediaries that international civil servants had ascribed to them since the interwar period.

THE SECOND WORLD, A BRIDGE BETWEEN WEST AND SOUTH

Leaders of Comecon countries refused the "underdeveloped" label that Soviet Communists saw as an invention by economists from capitalist countries, one that was imposed on other "worlds" as part of a theory of modernization automatically applied to former colonies. At UNCTAD, Comecon countries were grouped together under the name "socialist countries." However, even though Communist leaders long opposed development programs, they became beneficiaries of them as soon as the 1950s. The Ford Foundation clearly perceived this evolution and quickly adapted to it. In 1968 David E. Bell, executive president of the Ford Foundation—after serving at the U.S. development agency USAID between 1962 and 1966—drafted a report on the orientations of the foundation's programs directed toward Eastern Europe. He immediately emphasized that "a reformulation of Foundation objectives in Eastern Europe involves a shift of emphasis from politics to development . . . the support of institution-building projects, based on the adaptation of American methods and achievements to east European conditions."[99] For the new head of the foundation, development became another tool for subverting socialism through the diffusion of U.S. and capitalist economic and social models.

Western Economic Aid to Socialist Countries

Within international organizations, some Eastern bloc countries deliberately put themselves under the category of developing country in order to take advantage of Western aid. As we saw earlier, this was the case from the late 1940s onward for Yugoslavia, and from the 1960s onward for Romania, which in 1976 joined the group of Third World countries at the UN, the G77. In 1971 the United Nations Development Programme opened a regional office in Romania, an opening that was in keeping with the independence demanded by Romania since the 1960s with regard to Comecon, one that leaders of Western countries encouraged.[100] Charles de Gaulle visited Romania in 1968, followed by Richard Nixon in 1969, with the goal of weakening the bloc, as was the case with Yugoslavia beginning in the late 1940s or Poland during the late 1950s. Yet these relations were also part of longer histories, especially with regard to relations between France and Romania.

THE THIRD WORLD

Poland was nevertheless the first country to benefit from UN aid programs, initially in connection with reconstruction, and later with development. This example spread widely during the 1960s and 1970s, as all Comecon countries except for the USSR and the GDR applied for UN development aid programs. The implementation of the planning project for the Vistula Basin between 1968 and 1973 at the request of the Polish government clearly illustrates the specific expectations of leaders from countries in the first European periphery. The direct involvement of UNDP personnel remained limited, with the Polish government taking charge of most of the infrastructure and management for the project. The UNDP sent a director on site, and various agencies—the FAO, the WHO, and the World Meteorological Organization—selected qualified experts from Western European countries who stayed on site for short periods. At the same time, fourteen Polish engineers were sent as fellows to Western countries for training. According to the UNDP manager, "the project could be termed as one of 'intellectual cooperation' rather than 'technical assistance' in the conventional sense."[101] The projects implemented in Comecon countries all bear witness to the specific position they held in the mental map of UN experts and civil servants, namely, an intermediary position between the developed West and the underdeveloped South. Most of the requests for development aid by socialist countries involved industry and were ultimately handled in the UNDP's Europe and Middle East offices by the ILO and UNIDO. Unsurprisingly, between 1969 and 1980 it was Romania that made the greatest recourse to UNIDO aid with seventy-one financed projects, followed by forty-four for Hungary, thirty-three for Bulgaria, and twenty-eight for Poland.[102] These programs chiefly involved light industry (food, textiles) in which the economic cadres of Comecon countries were little or poorly trained. But they were especially crucial in acquiring computer technology, which was instrumental to the modernization of their industry and the implementation of centralized planning. Bulgaria is a good illustration of the role played by UNDP programs in Eastern bloc countries. In the 1960s the country's leaders undertook a policy of development for the computer industry and with UNIDO aid created the Research Institute for Instrument Design (NIPKIP) in 1966, which they hoped would develop the country's capacity for innovation.[103] Bulgaria became a kind of Japan of the Balkans, with almost half of Comecon computer hardware being produced there in the 1980s. To acquire computer technology, the Bulgarian government developed relations with Japanese companies like Fujitsu and pursued a policy of industrial espionage, but it also acquired this technology entirely legally through international development programs and UNIDO aid.[104] Beginning in the early 1970s, the organization supported the efforts of the Bulgarian government by establishing a training program that promoted sending Western experts to a number of specialized centers, such as the Institute of Industrial Cybernetics and Robotics, and by following the development of NIPKIP.[105] UNIDO thus circulated computer technology, but not without resistance from various Western political partners, who refused to host Bulgarian engineers. To circumvent these difficulties, local UNIDO officials sometimes proceeded with exchange with countries in the Global South that had previously benefited from such programs, India in particular.

The desire to acquire computer technology embargoed by CoCom provided a strong motivation for development aid requests on the part of Comecon countries, including in the highly important management program led by the ILO, which underscores the similarities between the two blocs in the rationalization and organization of production. In 1952 the organization sent its first productivity mission to Israel, which was followed by missions to India, Egypt, Pakistan, Yugoslavia, Brazil, Bolivia, Greece, Hong Kong, and Ceylon.[106] Wherever governments requested it, the ILO established productivity centers for training the country's managerial staff.[107] These productivity missions were soon joined by a management program whose goal was to train local staff in charge of promoting productivity gains.[108] Communist leaders applied to these programs early on, with the first mission being sent to Poland in 1958.[109] The experts appointed by the International Labour Office recommended creating a management center and awarding fellowships to train the regime's economic cadres. This program, which was put in place in 1960, became a model for similar initiatives in Eastern Europe, and later in newly independent countries. Fellows were sent to Western European states, and management centers were created in the capitals of these countries via cooperation agreements between the governments and the International Labour Office, which provided the required expertise. The National Management Development Center Poland (CODKK) was established with its own building in 1960 and was followed by its Hungarian equivalent in Budapest in 1966 (OVK) and its Bulgarian and Romanian equivalents in 1967 (CEPECA).[110] From the late 1960s onward,

THE THIRD WORLD

all these centers housed computers purchased via the UNDP from British firms, and more rarely from U.S. ones. In general, reformist actors in these countries, who were often Social Democrats who had been forced to join Communist parties, played a crucial role in initiating negotiations with international organizations. This was the case for what International Labour Office experts called the "men of October" in Poland, who were followed by other reform figures in different countries. In Czechoslovakia, Karel Padevět, a member of the State Committee for Technological Development, Professor Pernica from the economics school in Prague, and Zdeněk Mošna, the dean of the Faculty of Management, were better connected and successfully secured the dispatching of Western experts.[111] Similarly, in Romania the mathematician and philosopher Mircea Malița, who at the time worked for the Ministry of Foreign Affairs, played an essential role in launching CEPECA.[112]

These programs, which effectively diffused management cultures developed in Western countries, were intended for a substantial portion of the economic elite of Eastern European countries. In 1962 the course held at the Warsaw center brought together over one thousand participants, mostly executive directors of ministries and major industrial combines.[113] These centers trained a new generation of Communist managers in connection with the economic reforms of the early 1960s. Between 1967 and 1972 more than sixteen thousand managers took part in the training programs of the Romanian CEPECA.[114] In Bulgaria, the reports sent to the International Labour Office indicate that virtually all individuals in a position of responsibility in the economy (industrial or agricultural enterprises), politics (within a trade union, party, or the Communist youth), or the state administration attended these training centers.[115] This new "class" trained in Western management methods seems to have had no difficulty communicating with experts from the West, as they shared the fundamental notion that economic development was primarily based on productivity gains. Highly aware of the potentially subversive aspect of this training, in the 1960s Ford Foundation leaders developed a fellowship program to train managers in the United States, who were initially from Hungary and later from Czechoslovakia.[116] In the 1970s this program was extended to all countries in the bloc.[117]

Even though the political elites of socialist countries used the instruction of these management programs selectively, they diffused specific practices to the capitalist world and gave rise to stormy discussions between leaders of Comecon countries in the early 1970s. Leaders in the GDR, who were the most faithful to the letter of the socialism on which their country was founded, were the most strongly opposed. They emphasized, and not without reason, that these programs helped convert the cadres of socialist countries to capitalism.[118] Various economic actors, especially European ones, saw a genuine interest in them, as they enabled exchange with the East by circumventing the export bans imposed by U.S. political authorities in connection with CoCom. Most of these programs were in effect Western endeavors, often on the part of Great Britain and the United States, which provided the materials and equipment used.[119]

In Bulgaria, UNDP development programs had two components: training the workforce and developing the tourism industry.[120] Locally, they were led by John McDonald, a U.S. civil servant from the Department of State in charge of relations with international organizations. In Bulgaria, McDonald worked with a team of eight people, including five British experts. He organized training sessions for Bulgarian managers, using "business games" created by his friends for this purpose. He also maintained very good relations with the local representatives of the British company International Computers Limited (ICL), which provided the hardware and programmers to computerize the hotel reservation system for the Bulgarian Ministry of Tourism. Local authorities had reservations regarding the de facto monopoly created by ICL's position, but McDonald effectively protected the British company's interests in the region, and the Bulgarian government looked the other way as long as it gained access to the technology it was seeking. McDonald appears to have enjoyed great popularity in Bulgaria. Despite the fact, according to reports by experts on the ground, that Bulgarians were the most "ideological" of the bloc, their objectives accorded well with the pursuit of private British interests.

International organizations, one of whose functions was to develop and diffuse models, promoted these circulations and exchanges. For UN civil servants and experts, countries in the East played a specific role in these circulations, that of a go-between linking the West and the South.

Socialism: Alternative Model or Imperfect Copy?

Under pressure from U.S. authorities, international civil servants were initially reluctant to call on experts from the East for development programs intended for the Global South. In 1956 Evžen Erban, the Czechoslovak minister for social security, asked International Labour Office management to hold a seminar on social security as part of the UN assistance program, a request justified by the fact that since the interwar period, Czechoslovakia had been a model country for social security and had provided numerous experts to the ILO. It nevertheless met with a negative response, on the pretext that Communist leaders were primarily seeking to use development programs for propaganda in support of socialism.[121] It was only after repeated requests, and support from the head of the Social Security Department Anton Zelenka—a former Czechoslovak citizen who was a Social Democrat, like the minister Erban, whom he knew well—that Czechoslovak leaders were able to plan a seminar on social security in Prague using the ILO's own money. Representatives from a number of countries in the Middle and Far East attended, and Czechoslovak experts promoted a social security system organized by the state but managed by trade unions, which was in perfect agreement with the model promoted by civil servants from the International Labour Office in the decades following World War II.[122]

Leaders of Middle and Far Eastern countries called for expertise from the East, which they deemed well-adapted to their needs. In September–October 1966 the Czechoslovak government organized a seminar on Small Scale Industry within the Framework of Overall Economic Development Planning. In the final report, participants emphasized:

> While recognizing certain advantages of a market oriented economy, most participants felt that in view of the range of problems facing the developing countries, including the shortage of capital and foreign exchange, they could not afford to rely wholly on the interplay of market forces. There should be a central authority of the government responsible for planning activities in major economic sectors of the national economy.[123]

Similarly, Comecon countries took advantage of industrial expertise via UNIDO and helped develop and diffuse this expertise; a number of seminars on industrial techniques were held in Poland, the USSR, Hungary, Czechoslovakia, and Romania, especially in the field of petrochemistry between 1969 and 1975.[124]

Beginning in the mid-1960s, international institutions and civil servants even started to show a particular interest in diffusing the social and economic knowledge produced or developed in Central Europe toward underdeveloped countries. In continuity with practices from the interwar period and the aftermath of the war, they even established Eastern Europe as a transition zone between the First and Third Worlds.[125] For instance, Jean Fauchon, the head of the Institute for Rural Studies and a specialist in agronomy at the International Labour Office, believed "that the experience of these countries in the field of rural development could be usefully applied to numerous developing countries."[126] In 1970 Jean Ozet, who was from the same department, encouraged the creation of a rural development center in Bulgaria, which could become the center of a network of similar institutions in less developed countries.[127] In the eyes of international civil servants, the collective agricultural experiences of Eastern European countries were similar to the solutions implemented by agricultural development experts, who since the interwar period had seen agricultural cooperatives as a solution to rural underdevelopment.[128]

With UNDP support, some training and management centers created in Central Europe were soon established as relays for training the elites of developing countries. In this context, Czechoslovak authorities held a seminar in 1970 on management in the Prague suburb of Jiloviste. In 1973 CEPECA in Romania launched an international program designed for business managers from the Global South. In 1974 the course was attended by fifty-three participants from nineteen African and Asian countries. ILO experts stressed that Romania, which had industrialized more recently, was in an ideal position to understand the difficulties encountered by the elites of developing countries and to transmit to them this newly acquired knowledge.[129] In 1983 the British expert George Boulden gave a course to Bulgarian managers in Varna that was immediately reused to train Cuban colleagues. Managers from socialist countries thus became, via the development programs implemented by the ILO, vehicles for diffusing the productivist model and managerial practices developed in Western countries. Similarly, UNIDO used some of its training centers to circulate a knowledge produced in the West toward countries in the Global South via Eastern bloc countries, especially with respect to Bulgarian computer expertise. Multiple training courses were held in this country during the 1970s and 1980s, initially to train Indian engineers, and later for engineers from Arab countries.

THE THIRD WORLD

The importance of these transfers should not be overestimated, but they serve as a reminder that on the basis of a shared belief in the virtues of economic development, there could be genuine proximity between the organization of work in countries in Eastern and Western Europe. This proximity was encouraged by international civil servants and experts, who organized the world according to development hierarchies, without necessarily considering differences in political systems. With this in mind, countries of the Second World were not primarily Communists: they were especially less developed and represented a resource as spaces for testing solutions that could potentially be applied more widely.

During the period that began in 1955 with the Afro-Asian Conference of Bandung and ended in 1974 with the proclamation of an NIEO, international organizations served as privileged spaces for the appearance of new nation-states by offering them a framework for collective organization as well as a forum. They are therefore a good vantage point for exploring the role and specific place of countries from the Global South in the Cold War. Within UNCTAD in particular, but also other UN agencies such as the WHO, UNESCO, or the ILO, the issue of better distribution of international resources, redistribution models, and paths toward development were clearly explored. Encouraged by part of international civil service, Third Worldism organized there and presented itself as a third internationalism. The demands it formulated in support of greater social justice met with those of other organized groups, such as global unionism. Together they succeeded in making an alternative voice heard.

These demands were reinterpreted through the vocabulary of the Cold War by those who opposed them in the West. It is true that they often—but not always—enjoyed the support of Communist leaders, who saw them as a strategic opportunity, as well as a way to reinforce the demands they had made within the international economic system. At the same time, they shared with leaders in the West a belief in progress, growth, and productivity. For this reason, beginning in the 1950s they were the recipients of Western development programs. Chinese Communists, who affirmed a genuine proximity with poor countries, boasted about implementing solutions rooted in the field, ones that were more in touch with the true needs of the populations of these countries.

Like those from the Communist world, the leaders of Western countries did not adopt a uniform reaction to the demands of the Global South. Nevertheless, the Declaration on the Establishment of a New International Economic Order challenged the economic balance from which Western actors benefited, especially major capitalist enterprises. Through various channels, the latter mobilized against what their leaders and part of the Western political class saw as joint attacks against free enterprise, which they interpreted—deliberately or not—as a Communist offensive. Third Worldism, which established itself as an internationalism within the UN, prompted a reaction from powerful global economic actors who, in concert with anticommunist political elites, developed a neoliberal response to the demands expressed by elites from the Global South. This reaction underscores the limits of the influence that international civil servants and experts had when faced with the interests of those who backed these very same organizations.

The victory of these backers translated into the triumph of globalism, an ideology that emphasizes widespread competition, including between nation-states. During the 1980s it gradually replaced Cold War internationalisms and their program for organizing the world.

Chapter Six

FROM INTERNATIONALISMS TO GLOBALISM

The Slow Agony of the Cold War

At first sight, the end of the Cold War was primarily due to the military and diplomatic victory of the United States and its allies following a resumption of tensions during the late 1970s.[1] Ronald Reagan, who was elected U.S. president in 1980 and reelected in 1984, saw the USSR as an "Empire of evil" and substantially increased military spending.

In 1983, in response to the deployment of Soviet SS-20 missiles, the North Atlantic Treaty Organization set up Pershing II missiles with nuclear warheads in Europe.[2] In 1979 the Red Army entered Afghanistan to rescue the Communist Party in power but became bogged down in a war against mujahedeen resistance supported by the U.S. government, via the CIA, and its allies Saudi Arabia and Pakistan.[3] The Soviet intervention was condemned at the UN in 1980 and 1981 and was, in particular, widely rejected by the Soviet population, such that Mikhail Gorbachev ordered the withdrawal of troops beginning in February 1988, which was completed in February 1989.

However, these confrontations and the Soviet defeats were the symptoms—rather than the causes—of a long decline that ended with the disappearance of regimes led by Communist Parties in Europe. This decline was rooted in the weakening of the political and economic model on which these regimes were built. In the late 1970s their incapacity to offer their populations the affluent society and equality promised by leaders further undermined their weak political legitimacy. I will not revisit these points, which concern the history of communism.[4] Pursuing the international perspective adopted, I will analyze this decline in the context of the profound transformations in global ideological and economic power relations, which were reflected in the debates that took place in international organizations and spaces, especially within the UN system. We saw earlier how some UN agencies, especially the UNCTAD, UNESCO, the ILO, and the WHO, served as spaces of discussion and proposal for the New International Economic Order. These very agencies were deeply weakened in the ensuing years. In 1982 the WHO had to face a major budgetary crisis due to a reduction in the U.S. contribution. The United States left the ILO in 1977 (returning in 1980), and UNESCO in 1984 (returning in 2002). Aside from the financial difficulties they created, these departures signaled and encouraged a challenge to multilateralism. When the United States left the ILO in 1977, its leaders criticized the growing Communist influence over the organization, and the fact that tripartism was no longer respected there. In 1984 the withdrawal from UNESCO was justified by the "failure to respect Western values." These arguments challenged the validity of the practices that founded internationalism: collective discussions and the production of knowledge and expertise by transnational epistemic communities.

As the ILO, the WHO, and UNESCO were weakened, other international agencies, such as the IMF and the World Bank, gained the upper hand.[5] The decline of UN internationalism unfolded within the context of an evolution in global economic policies. The Bretton Woods Agreement of 1944 was supposed to guarantee, according to its architect John Maynard Keynes, political and economic stability by establishing a system to control financial and capital flows.[6] Beginning in the 1960s, the British and U.S. governments unilaterally broke the commitments made at Bretton Woods by promoting free financial flows—initially on the European market, and later in the United States (1974) and Great Britain (1979)—by abolishing controls over the free movement of capital. What's more, encouraged by economists such as Gottfried Haberler, in 1971 the U.S. government suspended the convertibility of the dollar and in 1974 allowed it to float, which enabled market forces to play currencies—and even states—against one another, thereby encouraging international speculation. This speculation was incidentally facilitated by the rise of information systems. In this context of

FROM INTERNATIONALISMS TO GLOBALISM

deregulation, the increasing volume of petrodollars, which led to the rising price of oil in 1973, resulted in an economic imbalance. These petrodollars were invested in developed countries but also served to finance loans to developing countries, especially via the World Bank. They fueled the debt crisis of Latin American countries in the 1980s.

During the same period, and without it being possible to establish simple correlations, new paradigms achieved hegemony within the international space, especially that of human rights.[7] This is how the demands for a "right to development" formulated by Third World countries were transferred during the 1980s to the United Nations Commission on Human Rights and were requalified as individual rights, losing their social and collective dimension in the process.[8] This commission, and the Conference on Security and Cooperation in Europe that grew out of the Helsinki process, attest to this reformulation, to which major NGOs such as Amnesty International and Human Rights Watch actively contributed.[9] There was also emphasis on humanitarian language and practices, which had existed for a long time but gained new energy with the founding of major NGOs, including Doctors Without Borders in 1971. These organizations shared the characteristic of the individualization of both donations and aid.

The end of the Cold War was therefore in keeping with a long decade marked by the conjunction of two phenomena that fed into each other.[10] There was the gradual triumph of economic deregulation and the decline of a radical critique of capitalism. Demands for collective social justice gave way to a humanitarian and human rights discourse, which was grasped in its political and individual dimensions.[11] This chapter will explore the end of the Cold War as the slow dissolution of forces that had driven the discourse on social justice, equity, and equality. I will first show how Keynesian solutions were gradually marginalized within international organizations in favor of a discourse and practices of deregulation. This was characterized by the declining role of UN agencies to the benefit of other organizations such as the IMF, the World Bank, and later the OECD, which were firmly dominated by North Atlantic states. During a second phase, this model gradually spread to the managers of state socialist countries confronted with the failure of their economic model. This abandonment of the economic orthodoxy of state socialism anticipated and accompanied the economic and political crisis of countries where it was practiced, as well as the dissolution of the Communist world-system. In a third stage, this

THE NEW LIBERAL INTERNATIONAL ECONOMIC ORDER

The Declaration for the Establishment of a New International Economic Order in 1974 and the discussions it gave rise to were the swan song of the Third Worldist movement, and more broadly of the idea that the stability of the world is based on a better sharing of wealth and greater equity, both nationally and internationally. Keynesian or Social Democratic solutions dominated the international development agenda and served as a foundation for establishing and diffusing measures for redistribution and social rights in connection with national social states. The Willy Brandt Report drafted at the request of the UN following the 1974 declaration embodied this alliance between the Third Worldist and Western Social Democratic movements, one that was fostered by the existence of a discourse critical of capitalism.[12]

Beginning in the late 1970s, this alliance dissolved following the powerful counteroffensive sparked by concerns surrounding the NIEO and the mobilizations that followed it, more so than the economic crisis that followed oil shocks.[13] Neoliberal discourse and solutions gradually imposed themselves at the time. At the same time, protecting established social rights in the West prompted the national leaders of Social Democratic Parties and trade unions to abandon international solidarity and to instead fall back on the short-term interests of their members and voters.

The Triumph of the Neoliberal Paradigm

Despite not having proven their effectiveness, neoliberal solutions became the language and instrument of "reform" in the late 1970s and early 1980s in Margaret Thatcher's England and Ronald Reagan's United States, as well as at the OECD, the World Bank, the IMF, and the General Agreement on Tariffs and Trade.

Neoliberalism established itself as an international movement during the interwar period, and more particularly during the years of crisis.[14] Initially marginalized in the postwar world, it was nevertheless well-organized

FROM INTERNATIONALISMS TO GLOBALISM

internationally, especially in the Mont Pelerin Society in Switzerland, which the economist Friedrich Hayek founded in 1947. Some of its eminent representatives occupied important positions in the 1950s in certain countries, the United States and the Federal Republic of Germany in particular.[15] This was true of the ordoliberal Wilhelm Röpke, an influential advisor to the West German government, who was behind numerous measures adopted between 1949 and 1963 by Minister of Economic Affairs Ludwig Erhard.[16] Until the 1960s German ordoliberals represented a more statist and more social wing; Röpke's departure from the Mont Pelerin Society in 1962 accompanied and promoted the neoliberal movement's evolution toward deregulation.

Neoliberals were characterized by opposition to socialism and suspicion of state intervention in the economy. They had an unfavorable view of planning of any sort, even indicative. They expected the state to perform its legal responsibility to establish and ensure the rules for an undistorted market economy, in which prices are the only mechanism of adjustment.[17] While neoliberals were not strictly speaking antistatists, they saw the sovereignty of nation-states as an obstacle to the deployment of the free market and had a favorable view of international organizations, insofar as they could ensure proper functioning on the global scale. Confronted by what they called "Keynesian orthodoxy" in international organizations, beginning in the 1940s they sought allies in economic circles and were particularly active at the International Chamber of Commerce, which brought together and represented part of an already globalized economic elite.[18]

Neoliberals were firstly "globalists," and this globalism was not an internationalism.[19] It was chiefly directed against the regulatory power of states and international organizations when they became involved in establishing conventions and rules, which were seen as obstacles to the free movement of goods and capital flows. Globalism encouraged competition and noncooperation between states; it was characterized by the trust that its representatives placed in a government of the wise, and experts protected from immediate pressure from the masses.[20] Globalism was not guided by an attempt to organize the world to promote a universal political and social model. In this respect it clearly distinguished itself from the internationalism and UN multilateralism of the decades following World War II.

The NIEO was introduced within the forum of the UN General Assembly and relayed by the ILO, UNESCO, and the WHO. Yet it was within international arenas dominated by Western countries—the World Bank, the IMF, GATT, and the Organisation for Economic Co-operation and Development—that neoliberals mobilized against the NIEO.[21] The NIEO did not call into question the logic of free enterprise and the free movement of goods that served as the foundation of the capitalist economic order, but in the name of defending the sovereignty of newly independent countries, its supporters deemed it legitimate and necessary to oversee and limit them. It was in this respect that representatives of the neoliberal movement perceived it as a threat. This threat assumed concrete form when the International Law Commission was tasked with providing a legal basis for the requests formulated by the 1974 declaration, especially with regard to the right of nationalization. The threat was all the more real as the NIEO appeared to have the support of part of the Social Democrat movement: in addition to the Brandt Report mentioned earlier, the Club of Rome appointed a commission under the direction of the Keynesian economist Jan Tinbergen to study the possibility of implementing reforms. In 1976 the economist Wassily Leontief, the winner of the Nobel Prize for Economics in 1973, submitted a report to the UN that called for a reorganization of the global economic order in which the Global South would have a say.

Various economists from the neoliberal movement, who were often also members of the Mont Pelerin Society, such as Gottfried Haberler, Karl Brunner, and Peter Tamas Bauer, clearly came out against the NIEO; they attacked these reform proposals in the name of economic efficiency and the defense of liberties.[22] During late 1970s they issued numerous pamphlets and articles to denounce the NIEO as a major threat to the values of the West and the free world, and they even stressed that its triumph would pave the way for spreading totalitarianism on the Soviet model. Once again, Cold War discourse disqualified the reform proposals that can hardly be reduced to the Communist discourse. The neoliberal critique of the NIEO also targeted development economics—which had been institutionalized at the Institute of Development Studies at the University of Sussex, founded in 1966 by the UN economist Dudley Seers—and more broadly the entire Third Worldist movement, which asserted itself as an alternative on the left to Communist dirigisme.

Neoliberal economists, Bauer in particular, rejected the moral and political argument underpinning aid to the Third World and refuted the idea that it promoted economic development. This criticism met with that of supporters of a humanitarian approach, including the French intellectual Pascal Bruckner, a member of the Board of Directors for Action Against Hunger. In his *Le Sanglot de l'homme blanc* (The tears of the white man) from 1983, he suggested that the misery of the Global South was less due to the poor distribution of wealth between former colonial powers and newly independent countries than to the corruption of the elites of these very same countries, who under the cover of dirigisme secured their own resources. This pillaging was made possible by a failure to respect democracy and human rights. In the same vein, the political branch of Doctors Without Borders, which was founded in 1985 and known as Liberty Without Borders, came out against Third Worldism and demands for a right to development. For the founders of Liberty Without Borders as well as for Bruckner, human rights and democracy should serve as both the pillars of and the conditions for development. This approach did not garner unanimous support at Doctors Without Borders, and Liberty Without Borders was shut down in 1989. It nevertheless illustrates a decisive evolution in perceptions.[23]

For representatives of the economic neoliberal movement and supporters of a humanitarian approach to the problems of the Third World, international economic regulations were not effective tools for reducing global inequality. They challenged the very idea that it could serve as an objective. They believed the solution to poverty resided in democratizing the countries themselves and giving more power to private economic actors. In lieu of structural development aid, neoliberal economists promoted the state's disengagement from the economy, and supporters of humanitarian solutions called for occasional interventions to relieve the misery of populations.

While the Brandt Report was discussed during the North-South Summit held in Cancun, Mexico, in 1981, the NIEO was definitively put to rest there in the face of Thatcher's and Reagan's intransigence.[24] Its opponents relied on the economic success of the Asian Tigers—Hong Kong, Singapore, Taiwan, and Korea—which seemed to offer proof that emerging from underdevelopment was chiefly connected to the responsibility of elites from the Global South. Little did it matter that the governments in question had established regimes that were economically liberal but also politically authoritarian.[25]

Some economists, such as Deepak Lal, a World Bank researcher in the 1980s, deduced from the economic success of the Asian Tigers that development could play a positive role only if backed by—and was even conditional on—economic restructuring. This served as justification for the structural adjustment measures recommended by the IMF and the World Bank, which in the 1980s offered loans that were conditional on structural economic reforms and sought to have these countries join the orthodoxy of market capitalism. These measures, often referred to as the Washington Consensus, can be divided into three large groups: strict budgetary discipline and a reduction in public spending; protection of private property and the reprivatization of state monopolies; and the liberalization of interest rates and foreign trade.[26] These solutions, generally referred to as neoliberal, were driven by a new generation of economists from the Chicago school of economics, or, in the case of GATT, by international jurists, some of whom were from the Graduate Institute of International Studies in Geneva.[27] At the same time, some Communist cadres were also won over to the ideas of state disengagement and deregulation.

Economic Failures and the Neoliberal Conversion of Communist Cadres

While they offered an alternative model of economic development to those of capitalist countries, with high growth rates until the 1970s, state socialist countries fell into crisis at the same time as those from the capitalist West. What's more, like those in the Global South, in the late 1970s they fell under the dependency of lenders from Western banks. Finally, with the increasing openness of their economies, beginning in the late 1970s socialist countries were deeply affected by the repercussions of the deregulation brought about by capitalist economic globalization.[28] In the 1980s Comecon countries experienced a strong slowdown in growth; it neared zero in Hungary, which was nevertheless one of the bloc's most prosperous countries. Before this period of sluggishness, Eastern European leaders were confident in the growth of their economies and had begun to borrow from Western banks. This allowed them to procure in the West the technologies they needed, and to purchase the consumer products they provided their populations at subsidized prices in order to secure their loyalty. At the time they were optimistic regarding their capacity to repay, but the period of recession that succeeded the crisis plunged them into a vicious cycle of debt.

In 1980 the GDR's debts to Western banks reached $25 billion, most of it to West German banks. In 1974 Poland's debt was already $4 billion, rising to $20 billion in 1980, while Hungary's debt was $18 billion. Taken as a whole, in 1989 Comecon countries had accumulated $90 billion in debt, a considerable sum when compared to their ability to repay; just paying interest emptied their coffers of needed currency. In the 1980s these countries had de facto lost their economic sovereignty to Western banks.[29]

The debt was all the more concerning given that trade between Comecon countries and the capitalist world shrank in the 1980s: 27 percent of exports and 37 percent of imports in 1975 decreased to 21 percent and 23 percent, respectively, in 1986. Leaders of Western countries complained about the bureaucratic difficulties connected to centralized planning, and especially about the low quality of products manufactured in Comecon countries, with a few limited exceptions, such as Zeiss lenses in Jena.

In 1978 the Carter administration reduced exports to the USSR of cutting-edge equipment for the petroleum industry. In 1979 in response to the Soviet invasion of Afghanistan, this policy was extended to other technological sectors and agricultural products: of the twenty-five million tons of grain that were supposed to be delivered by U.S. producers to Soviet consumers, seventeen million were embargoed in 1980, an embargo that was also imposed on French suppliers.[30] While this policy did not endanger the Soviet population's food supply, with Argentina picking up the slack, it struck a major blow to French grain exports. With Reagan's rise to power, U.S. authorities pressured their allies within CoCom to expand the list of embargoed products in 1984, and once again in 1988.[31]

As was the case in the 1950s, this policy met with resistance from European allies, who were the primary trading partners of Eastern European countries by a large margin. Comecon countries conducted 60 percent of their trade with countries from the European Economic Community in 1985, 19 percent with the FRG alone. This penetration of West German interests in the East was of course encouraged by political leaders in connection with their *Ostpolitik*, but it resulted primarily from the dynamism of German capitalism.[32] In all countries, European associations representing European industry exerted pressure on the EEC to resist the U.S. embargo policy. They were supported by staff from the United Nations Economic Commission for Europe, which continued to serve as a space for economic leaders from the two parts of Europe to meet and discuss.[33]

There were two thousand economic agreements between OECD and Comecon countries in 1986, as opposed to just six hundred in 1973. Poland, Hungary, and the USSR were the primary countries involved. There were approximately four hundred joint production companies in 1983, including sixty-three in the FRG. As part of agreements, Eastern European countries were home to production and assembly units and played more the role of disadvantaged subcontractors than full-fledged economic partners. Often limited to older economic sectors such as mechanics and chemistry, these agreements contributed little to modernizing the means of production of socialist countries and increased their dependence on Western technology and standards. Finally, joint production companies required adapting the legal framework, and even creating special zones (in Hungary and Poland) where Western prices were introduced, sometimes even in convertible currency. In general, there was a kind of rampant recolonization of the economies of Eastern European countries by Western actors, German ones in particular, a phenomenon that increased rapidly after the end of communism.[34] What Gunnar Myrdal described in 1947 as a "semicolonial" situation, from which he hoped to free Eastern Europe thanks to UNECE, was an enduring reality forty years later. Socialism did not succeed in freeing Eastern European countries from their dependence on the West. This dependence was incidentally encouraged by Comecon itself, which in a final attempt at reform in 1986, and upon the order of Mikhail Gorbachev, set itself the goal of intensified "cooperation" with capitalist countries.[35]

The new secretary-general of the Soviet Communist Party wanted to develop economic relations with the West, as well as to pursue a large series of economic reforms giving greater autonomy to socialist enterprises, in keeping with those proposed throughout the Eastern bloc in the early 1960s. To promote the greater economic integration of Eastern European countries, the reformist economist Oleg Bogomolov, who was the director of the Institute for the Socialist World Economic System at the Academy of Sciences and an advisor to Gorbachev in 1989, wanted to imitate EEC policies. He proposed "transitioning from an administrative model of socialist economic management to a regulated market model" by accepting a policy of "real prices."[36] He also expressed support for transforming Comecon into a genuine single market for the East by introducing the convertibility of currencies and eliminating customs tariffs between countries.[37]

FROM INTERNATIONALISMS TO GLOBALISM

This dual "conversion" to the market economy and economic integration was part of a longer history. Marxist economists such as Oskar Lange formulated the idea of market socialism during the interwar period.[38] Members of Bogomolov's institute positively evaluated the experience of a single market and economic integration in the early 1960s in the context of economic reforms in the East.[39] These reforms were fostered by the arrival within enterprises and administrations of a new generation of cadres, who were keenly aware of the statist economy's difficulties, and even of its impasses. Thanks to management training as part of UN and Ford Foundation development programs, they were gradually acclimated to Western corporate cultures.[40] In Czechoslovakia, during the period of "normalization" that followed the suppression of the Prague Spring, they were obliged to renounce their goals of reform but remained within the state apparatus and played an important role during the shift to a market economy during the transition.[41] A roughly equivalent situation unfolded in Hungary, where economic managers, some of whom had been trained by the Ford Foundation's management programs, carried out the transition with the capitalist economy.[42] CEPECA in Romania, which was established under the Communist regime with the help of experts from the United Nations Development Programme, became a school for training new economic elites in capitalist Romania after the fall of the Berlin Wall.[43]

These evolutions had their roots in the economic difficulties of socialist countries, which were familiar to the socialist cadres who were in regular contact with their colleagues in the West. International organizations played an important role in this respect. What's more, in a context where socialism gradually stopped serving as a credible economic and political alternative, international civil servants and experts promoted the gradual abandonment of socialism as a reference among the economist or reformist cadres of these countries by depoliticizing the very idea of economic development. With the triumph of neoliberal thought, this evolution contributed to the decline of socialism as a competing internationalism.

THE LONG DECLINE OF A COMPETING INTERNATIONALISM

The Eastern bloc collapsed in 1989 to the surprise of contemporaries, but historians have since unearthed various elements pertaining to the economic and political fragility that help explain it.[44] This collapse was

FROM INTERNATIONALISMS TO GLOBALISM

accompanied by the gradual disappearance of the three pillars on which Communist internationalism was based: the existence of a "bloc," solidarity with the Global South, and the international Communist movement.[45]

The Disintegration of the Bloc

The bloc was more of a reaction than a concerted program and was marked from the beginning by structural weakness.[46] In spite of—or perhaps because of—the armed interventions in Hungary in 1956 and Czechoslovakia in 1968, its collapse ineluctably continued and accelerated with the controversies relating to the Czechoslovak reform experience of 1968. While Władysław Gomułka and Erich Honecker argued for conformity in 1968, in the name of the Polish and East German Communist Parties, the Yugoslavs supported the reformist Prague Communists led by Alexander Dubček, and Romanian leaders refused to join Warsaw Pact troops in August 1968. The degradation and subsequent break in Sino-Soviet relations between 1959 and 1965, in addition to competition between the two states with respect to the elite of Third World countries, led to the defection of Albania, whose leaders left Comecon in 1962 and the Warsaw Pact in 1968. During the same decade, Romanian leaders affirmed their difference and scuttled the economic integration program that Comecon proposed in 1964. Neighborly relations among Poland, the GDR, and Czechoslovakia were disturbed in the late 1970s. The Communist leaders of the latter two countries were suspicious of their Polish counterparts, whom they deemed incapable of "holding" their population. The borders between the GDR and Poland were closed in 1980. This defiance extended to all sectors, including security, which had been the subject of a genuine policy of uniformization during the first decade of the bloc's existence. Cooperation was admittedly never excellent, but there was a trend toward reinforcing the defense of national interests. In the late 1980s, when the directors of the Polish political police thought they could find their place within the democratic regime under discussion at roundtables, Stasi leaders believed they were betraying the socialist order.[47] This divergence grew and came into the open when the new secretary-general of the Communist Party of the Soviet Union, Mikhail Gorbachev, announced perestroika in 1985. This reform policy was rejected by the nomenklatura of the Bulgarian, Czechoslovak,

FROM INTERNATIONALISMS TO GLOBALISM

and East German Communist Parties, without being genuinely supported by the others.

Disunion became obvious within international organizations, where, from the 1980s onward, the bloc stopped speaking as a single voice. For instance, in 1983, when the ILO implemented a commission of inquiry that condemned the failure to respect union freedom in Poland, the Polish government threatened to leave the organization, but after considering a group departure, the leaders of other countries from the bloc opted to stay in the organization.[48] Nationalist positions gradually won out over socialist solidarity; at the UN in 1989, the Hungarian representative voted for a Swedish resolution that condemned the territorial reorganization of Romania, in addition to the grouping of the rural population into new semiurban units, which also affected the Hungarian-speaking minorities of Transylvania.[49]

Hungary precociously embarked on a solitary path within international organizations. At the ICC, Odön Kallos, the president of the Hungarian Chamber of Commerce, emphasized that the approach based on blocs was no longer appropriate, and that Hungary would pursue a highly liberal and open policy.[50] Since the 1970s it had developed relations with the EEC to the detriment of its privileged relations with Comecon countries.[51] In 1982 it became the second Comecon country after Romania to join the IMF. Its leaders hoped to borrow more easily, all while accepting to liberalize their economy in exchange. Aside from access to credit, some reformist economic leaders from Comecon countries saw joining the IMF and GATT as a way to promote the reforms needed for the economic survival of their country, against the views of more conservative factions within the state apparatus and Communist Party in power.[52]

International organizations thus became invaluable resources for the reformist Communist leaders seeking inspiration and support. This is reflected in a report by a Stasi informant at the ILO, who was upset by the uncritical attitude of the Soviet delegation at the International Labour Conference in 1988. The head of the Soviet delegation affirmed to him that it was important to accept aid from capitalist countries in order to emerge from underdevelopment and apparently insisted that the ILO could help reorganize society.[53] While GDR leaders were offended by the abandoned belief in the advantages of socialism and maintained an intransigent position, at least in their discourse, they themselves already had one foot in capitalism via the FRG, from which they could borrow interest free.

In reality, most economic and technical cadres of these countries—but not necessarily political leaders—were convinced that state socialism, in the rigid forms it had adopted, was incapable of addressing the economic difficulties they faced. In the 1980s Comecon ceased being attractive for its members, starting with the Soviets themselves, who exported raw materials to countries in the bloc at below-market rates and received in return manufactured products of mediocre quality, whereas to modernize their means of production they especially needed access to the cutting-edge technology they could acquire only by selling these raw materials on currency markets. Hungarian leaders, who were oriented toward the global market, expressed support for the convertibility of their currency and seriously considered leaving Comecon in the late 1980s to ensure this convertibility. In 1985 Tamás Bácskai, the director of the National Bank of Hungary, who was known for his reform positions, stressed that economic relations primarily had to be practiced bilaterally, and not between blocs. Socialism thus ceased to serve as a basis for a common belonging, while for the Global South it gradually stopped representing an alternative to the capitalist world.[54]

What Remained of the Communist World-System?

At UNCTAD, the division in charge of trade relations between countries in the East and the Global South was denounced or ignored on multiple occasions by other divisions, and the General Secretariat no longer asked it for reports. This marginalization reflected the real decline in influence and attractiveness within the Third World of the European socialist model and countries in the bloc. It also experienced new tension, especially of a religious nature. In 1969 twenty-five conservative or progressive Muslim countries joined together in the Organisation of the Islamic Conference, which grew to forty-two members in 1978. The organization, based in Saudi Arabia, soon presented itself as an alternative to the Non-Aligned Movement and Third Worldism.[55] While an Islamist regime denouncing Western materialism was established in Iran, it was in the name of a common religious identity and against Communist atheism that the Organisation of the Islamic Conference unanimously condemned the Soviet invasion of Afghanistan and later secured its condemnation at the UN in

FROM INTERNATIONALISMS TO GLOBALISM

November 1980. A new internationalism based on religion had thus emerged and enjoyed active support from the U.S. government.

The socialist camp was deeply divided between pro-Soviets and pro-Chinese. It is true that strictly Maoist parties and guerrilla fighters, who had broad support from the Chinese government, remained in the minority. Maoists were especially powerful in India with the Naxalite movement, and with the Shining Path in Peru, but they eroded the legitimacy of the Communist movement organized around the USSR. On the other side, the crimes of the Maoist revolution in Cambodia during the late 1970s heightened the condemnation of Communist revolutions. Finally, with Gorbachev's rise to power in the USSR in 1985, priority was henceforth given to accelerated integration within the capitalist global economy, in an effort to pull the country out of its economic backwardness and crisis; the project of the Communist world-system lost its vigor.[56]

There were, of course, numerous countries that laid claim to socialism, or that were considered to be friendly regimes. Comecon welcomed in its midst Mongolia, Cuba, and Vietnam; it had privileged relations with countries on all continents, particularly Algeria, Mozambique, Angola, India, Iraq, Syria, South Yemen, and Nicaragua, which obtained observer status. In certain domains, such as women's rights, socialist countries served as an inspiration until the late 1970s. This is demonstrated by the alliance between representatives from socialist and Third World countries during the first UN World Conference on Women held in Mexico in 1975 and the extensive discussions during the World Congress for International Women's Year held in Berlin the same year.[57] Similarly, until the late 1970s, socialist countries could still serve as a model for preventive social medicine, and until the Cold War they could even offer their allies the expertise of well-trained medical staff.[58]

Comecon countries, however, renounced gathering Third World countries around them with a view to constituting a Communist world-system. While affirming solidarity with G77 countries at the UN, they did not embark on the NIEO project and turned away from UNCTAD when it became clear that it had not succeeded in replacing GATT as a platform for organizing global trade, as they had hoped. In addition, Comecon evaded the requests expressed in 1976 by the Global South, which wanted socialist countries to dedicate a fixed percentage of their GDP to development aid, in the same manner as developed capitalist ones. Communist leaders claimed to offer an alternative conception of economic aid based on political and economic solidarity, although the export of the socialist development model encountered major difficulties in the 1980s, and the countries that had adopted it, such as Tanzania, Ethiopia, and Angola, fell into deep poverty.[59] Economic aid weighed disproportionately on Comecon countries and the USSR in particular, just as they were facing major domestic difficulties. Communist leaders reduced their already low contributions to the UNDP and were accused by various actors from Western countries of benefiting from international aid much more than they contributed to it.[60]

Cooperation projects continued nevertheless. In 1987 there were approximately five thousand economic projects between Comecon countries and those in the Global South, which increasingly had a multilateral dimension by involving multiple Comecon countries, as in the case of the construction of a slaughterhouse in Iraq in the 1970s, for which the Romanians erected the building and the East Germans provided machines. This division of labor led to great difficulties in coordination, reflecting the rifts in solidarity of the socialist world.[61] Despite a discourse of "solidarity" toward poor countries, the projects distinguished themselves less and less from the forms of aid implemented by the capitalist West. The solidarity of the East was no more gratuitous than that of the West, but it took the form of compensatory barter agreements. In the 1980s the Bulgarian government sent technical staff to help the Syrians and Algerians extract phosphate and in return received some of this phosphate. In reality, the large majority of what Communist elites referred to as solidarity, or what they labeled as "cooperation agreements," actually fell under trade relations, including the arms trade when it involved "coming to the aid" of liberation movements or friendly countries. Czechoslovakia played a major role in this respect in the 1980s, with its involvement in the arms trade being clearly motivated by the goal of obtaining hard currency.[62]

These economic relations remained modest, however, and tended even to regress: during the 1980s they represented no more than 1 percent of the global market. This decline can be explained by the industrialization of some countries in the Global South, which imported poor-quality end products from socialist Europe on a less frequent basis. The nature of economic relations between the USSR and India tended to inverse itself, with the USSR increasingly providing raw materials, oil in particular, in exchange for

FROM INTERNATIONALISMS TO GLOBALISM

industrial goods, and even more advanced technology such as computers.[63] Finally, trade relations were more and more dependent on the rule of global trade imposed by the powers of the capitalist West. Capitalist enterprises served as financial intermediaries for payment in currency or for clearing agreements, and cooperation between enterprises increasingly involved private Western partners; in 1985 there were approximately three hundred examples of tripartite West-East-South cooperation.[64]

What remained of the discourse of solidarity and the Communist world-system in the actual relations between Comecon countries and those in the Global South? It was still embodied in the warm human relations established in the field, for what socialist countries provided freely were first and foremost engineers, technical staff, and doctors who were well-trained and less demanding than their Western counterparts. In the field these experts personified a solidarity of the poorest against the West, which was perceived as arrogant and dominating. They developed friendly and warm relations, which have been clearly presented in the case of Romanian architects in Iraq, and East German ones in Vietnam.[65] Nevertheless, while this proximity and the forms of friendship it created were deployed as part of socialist solidarity, they were not specific to the socialist project, which struggled to redefine itself.

The Dissolution of the International Communist Movement

In general, the Communist project lost its attractiveness in Western countries in the late 1970s. This was primarily marked by decreasing membership in Communist Parties in countries where they were powerful, such as France and Italy. The French Communist Party had substantial electoral setbacks in the late 1970s, which was also the case in Italy ten years later.[66] This ebb was also marked by the unavoidable decline of Communist mass organizations such as youth organizations, women's organizations, and sports movements, which represented spaces for an alternative culture as well as the crucible for Communist sociability. In Europe, this ebb was concurrent with the development of new forms of dissenting expression, as well as the apparent decline of laborers in large industry, the traditional social base for Communist Parties.

The split with China offered an alternative on the left to the Soviet model, with small Maoist parties organizing in all Western countries in the late

1960s. Their attractiveness with some youth was connected to the value ascribed to the revolutionary "experience." The *établi* movement—those who decided to leave everything to experience life in a factory—represented an extreme form. The influence of these movements was ephemeral, with a sharp decrease in the late 1970s, although they formulated and diffused a severe criticism of bureaucratic communism, which fed into the disillusionment already underway.[67]

Finally, Communist Parties and movements demanded, in diverse forms, the possibility of paths specific to socialism and took part in the weakening of Communist internationalism from within. This slow disintegration actually began in the 1950s but accelerated quickly with the intervention of Warsaw Pact armies in Prague in August 1968.[68] In Europe, the Italians were the first to formulate a highly developed criticism of the Soviet model. Unlike the French, they could rely on the original and specific doctrinal corpus of Antonio Gramsci, who, like other thinkers of Marxist inspiration that were independent of Leninist orthodoxy (Rosa Luxemburg was another figure), offered an alternative Communist program.

Italian women had challenged, early on, the alignment of the Women's International Democratic Federation with the objectives of Soviet international policy, and this dissent was affirmed at the time of the Prague Spring.[69] The same independence characterized the trade union movement and the Italian General Confederation of Labor. It was led until his death in 1957 by the Communist Giuseppe Di Vittorio, who had simultaneously served as president of the pro-Communist World Federation of Trade Unions since 1953. In 1956 Di Vittorio came out against the Soviet intervention in Budapest, and in 1957 the CGIL leadership supported a reformist position on unionism, emphasizing demands that promoted the increased purchasing power of workers in capitalism; they took a favorable view of the Single Market, which they saw as an opportunity for the social advancement of Italian laborers. With divisions deepening, the CGIL left the management of the WFTU in 1968, adopted associate status in 1973, and withdrew from the organization in 1978 to join the European Trade Union Confederation.[70]

Condemnation of the Prague intervention from Waldeck Rochet and Luigi Longo, the general secretaries of the French and Italian Communist Parties, marked the disintegration of solidarity between Communist Parties in the West and elsewhere. While they conserved the common language of class struggle, as well as the rejection of imperialism and capitalism—and adopted a single model of organization, namely, democratic centralism—Communist Parties developed strategies and programs that increasingly stood out from one another and sought primarily to respond to the social and political problems they were facing nationally. The Popular Front in Chile in the early 1970s was far removed from the armed struggle in Vietnam, while in the Arab world, Communists supported nationalist regimes in Egypt, Syria, and Iraq.

In Western Europe, Communist Parties, which were still dependent on Soviet financing, nevertheless distanced themselves from real socialism. The years 1975–1976 were marked by meetings among the Italian, French, and Spanish Communist Parties, with support from the Japanese Communist Party. In February 1976 the secretary-general of the Italian Communist Party, Enrico Berlinguer, argued for a diverse Communist movement at the Twenty-Fifth Congress of the Communist Party of the Soviet Union in Moscow; during the meeting of European Communist Parties in Berlin in June 1976, he used the term *Eurocommunist* for the first time. During its Twenty-Second Congress in February of the same year, the French Communist Party, which had embarked on a *Programme commun* (Common Program) with the socialists, renounced—against the wishes of Soviet Communist leaders—the idea that a dictatorship of the proletariat was a necessary phase in the march toward communism and the decline of the state. Leaving behind the notion of a "dictatorship of the proletariat" was in keeping with a more long-term reform movement within the international Communist movement, which advocated for a democratic socialism that was more respectful toward liberties and individual rights.

This reformist language emerged during the period of de-Stalinization and formulated more precise objectives in Hungary in 1956, and especially during the Prague Spring in 1968. The armed intervention in August 1968, and the repression suffered by Czechoslovak Communist leaders, drove a strong sense of disillusionment, which was followed by a hemorrhaging of members from Western Communist Parties. In the East, reformist Communists asked for greater liberty and rebelled against the enduring confusion between the proletariat and the Communist Party apparatus. Most did not yet challenge the socialist project itself, but these critical positions condemned them in the eyes of Communist leaders, who considered them to be dissidents, pushed them into marginality, sent them to prison, or exiled them.[71] This was the case in the 1970s for Rudolf Bahro and Wolf Biermann in the GDR.

In the West, reform Communists adopted strategies of alliance with socialists, such as in Chile or France as part of the Common Program of government between 1972 and 1977, and even with Christian Democrats, as in Italy in 1977, but they did not succeed in developing a common reformist political platform. The difficulties of such an attempt were amplified by Cold War oppositions. The U.S. government, as well as Soviet Communist leaders, fought Eurocommunism. The U.S. government saw it as a dangerous influence in Western Europe, while the Soviet leadership succeeded in dividing the movement. The Italian, Spanish, British, and Japanese Communist Parties condemned the Soviet invasion of Afghanistan, while the French and Portuguese ones provided support during a conference in Paris in May 1980.

Eurocommunism ceased to exist, but the reformist ideas that it championed continued to flourish; calls for reform and greater autonomy were highly influential in Yugoslavia, Hungary, and Poland and were amplified by Gorbachev's program, which called for the end of censorship and the separation of the party and the state. Meanwhile, dissidents were released from prison. These reforms bore the mark of socialism "with a human face," a program promoted by various reformist efforts. However, Italian Communist leaders were the only ones to officially rally to Gorbachev's program in the late 1980s. In reality, Communist internationalism had ceased to exist, with new demands and utopias being formulated and affirmed without—and even counter to—the Communist project.[72]

NEW UTOPIAS

Pacifism and Disarmament Between the East and the West

During the Cold War period, it is estimated that the United States built approximately seventy thousand nuclear warhead missiles and the USSR approximately forty-five thousand, not counting the few hundred rockets produced by smaller nuclear powers such as China, France, and Great Britain. This arsenal, largely sufficient to destroy the planet, was behind a mobilization for peace. It was also based on a scientific internationale, whose structuring around the Pugwash movement in the 1950s was discussed in chapter 4. Deteriorating relations between the two major powers, as demonstrated by the U.S. Senate not ratifying the SALT II agreement concluded in June 1979, reactivated networks that had been on standby since the SALT I agreement in 1972. Soviet scientists organized in 1983 as part of a disarmament association, which had various Western counterparts. Together, the scientists involved in these associations explored the possibility of limiting the arms race.

This scientific internationale that transcended global divisions was accompanied by mobilizations for peace, which grew in scope in the 1980s, all while changing in nature. The International Peace Movement developed in the 1940s and 1950s, often in the wake of the Communist movement. Less virulent during the 1960s and 1970s, a period of arms limitation, it gained renewed energy in the 1980s with the announcement that U.S. Pershing II missiles were being installed in European countries.[73] Presented as a response to the deployment of Soviet SS-20 missiles, the installation of Pershing II was decided during a meeting of the NATO integrated command in 1979 and was in keeping with the renewed arms race that marked the 1980s.[74] As in the 1950s, Soviet leaders, governments of the Eastern bloc, and the international Communist movement tried to transform the peace movement into a condemnation of Western militarism. Communist Parties were highly involved in the protests, with Soviet authorities providing financial support. The East German Stasi infiltrated various movements in Great Britain and Holland. It was precisely this alignment with positions of the Warsaw Pact, however, that weakened the movement in Great Britain and France, while in Holland the largest peace organization, the Interconfessional Council for Peace, which campaigned for the nuclear disarmament of both blocs, enjoyed great success.[75] For geopolitical and historical reasons, and the shadow cast by Nazism, the movement was the most powerful in the FRG. In the fall of 1983 more than a million people across the country demonstrated against the installation of Pershing missiles: a human chain 800 kilometers long connected Ulm with Stuttgart.

The Dutch and German movements shared a number of characteristics: the aggregation of various political forces, from the Communists to the center left, the youth of the participants, the inventive forms of protest inspired by the movements of 1968, and finally the important role played by Protestant churches as spiritual authorities and spaces for gathering and networking. The World Council of Churches played a driving role in the internationalization of this pacifism. Founded in Geneva in 1948, it supported peace and disarmament early on, especially through the intermediary of the Commission of the Churches on International Affairs.

Protestant Churches promoted the coordination of protests: the Dutch peace movement was in contact with dissidents in Eastern Europe, especially with Charter 77 in Czechoslovakia, and East German dissidents organized within the Lutheran Church. In the GDR, Protestant churches launched large protests in 1979 against the introduction of military instruction at school, while the peace movement developed and culminated in September 1987 with the Olof Palme Peace March, in reference to the former Swedish prime minister, who was assassinated in 1986. In 1982 the Independent Commission on Disarmament and Security, presided over by the Social Democrat Palme, had issued a report that recommended concrete measures supporting disarmament. This march for a denuclearized Europe set out from the GDR but brought together peace movements in both Germanies and Czechoslovakia, thereby transcending the geographical and ideological divisions of the Cold War.[76]

Feminisms and the Environment: New Social Movements and Dissent

The new social movements that emerged during and after the events of 1968 promoted forms of organization and formulated demands that moved away from Communist discourse, including in areas where it had represent an international inspiration.[77]

This was true of the woman question, for which Communist leaders, backed by the foundational Engels text, *The Origin of the Family, Private Property and the State*, formulated a favorable discourse of equality early on. Since the interwar period, Soviet representatives in international organizations had emphasized that by including women within the means of production and in politics, socialism provided them with an equal role in society. Aside from the position taken by the Women's International Democratic Federation, representatives from Eastern bloc countries began to work within ECOSOC to pass as broad an interpretation as possible for the Declaration on the Elimination of Discrimination Against Women, especially with respect to equal pay.[78] The issue of collective social and economic rights remained central in the Communist rhetoric of the World Congress of the International Women's Year held in Berlin in 1975. Nevertheless, the

FROM INTERNATIONALISMS TO GLOBALISM

permanence and forms of male domination, especially in private life, were explored little or not at all, nor was the essentialization of women as mothers.[79] In the 1960s this view was challenged and competed against by demands that insisted—in the wake of second wave feminism—more on the individual emancipation of women, especially their liberty to dispose of their body and to control their sexuality. In addition to demands for civic equality and equal pay, second wave feminism worked to legalize contraception and abortion, and for better distribution of family responsibilities.[80] Socialist countries precociously guaranteed the right to reproductive choice, beginning with the Russian Soviet Federative Socialist Republic, which was the first state to legalize abortion in 1920. In Romania and Poland, abortion was legalized in 1956. In the GDR, contraception was freely available since 1965, and abortion was legalized in 1972 (while it remained very difficult in the FRG). For all that, these policies were not primarily guided by feminist concerns and could be revisited in the name of natalist arguments, as was the case in the USSR in the 1930s and Romania in 1966. These same hesitations were present in Western Communist Parties. In Italy, to mark its opposition to a powerful Catholicism, the Communist Party early on adopted a program supporting abortion, and the French Communist Party submitted a bill in 1932 calling for the legalization of abortion. Natalist rhetoric, however, clearly won out in the French Communist Party in the1950s. Second wave feminists criticized Communists for not exploring specific forms of domination linked to the patriarchical organization of society. They emphasized that this domination was not—or was not exclusively— due to the organization of relations of production, and that the advent of socialism would not automatically make it disappear.

Similarly, the environmental issue presented Communist elites in power with a contradiction. On the one hand, the socialist economy did not pursue the objective of indefinite growth in consumption. The socialist consumer society discussed by Communist elites in the 1960s sought to meet the needs of populations without artificially creating them. Yet in reality, the dysfunction of centralized planning led to shortages and encouraged practices of recycling and reuse that echo contemporary concerns. On the other hand, Communists in power often adopted a predatory stance toward nature that contradicted the letter of Marxism but was in keeping with the productivist ideology dominant in both the West and the East.[81] During the Cold War, the biosphere—access to natural resources—was clearly an area

FROM INTERNATIONALISMS TO GLOBALISM

of competition between the two blocs. The first environmental demands were formulated against this predatory and productivist approach and organized internationally in reaction to major accidents such as black tides. The establishment of Greenpeace, initially in Canada in 1971, was a first step. In 1972 the UN held the Conference on the Human Environment in Stockholm, which led to the creation of the UN Environment Programme and the signing of a series of international conventions to protect specific natural settings. In 1983, at the request of the UN General Assembly, the secretary-general established the World Commission on Environment and Development, under the presidency of Norwegian prime minister Gro Harlem Brundtland, the former minister for the environment. The commission organized public meetings in various regions of the world and met with representatives of environmental associations, to whom it offered a megaphone of sorts.[82]

Communist leaders were little involved in these initiatives, even though they agreed to sign the Helsinki Final Act—which provided for trans-European cooperation to combat pollution of the air, fresh water, seawater, and soil—and continued participating in UNECE initiatives in this area.[83] The environmental movement therefore proceeded on various international stages without the Communists. While not directed against them, it nevertheless helped weaken Communist regimes, for at least two reasons. First, due to the absence of an opposing power and organized public opinion, the leaders of socialist countries had engaged in the intensive use of their resources with no regard for the population, from whom they tried to hide the consequences. This policy of secrecy was a correlate of the nationalization of the economy, which transformed any critical discourse on the environment into a challenge of the socialist state and the economic development model it promoted. The environmental groups that developed in the East during the 1980s were immediately considered as being dissident and even oppositional, all the more so if they interacted with groups and associations active in the West. This was the case in the GDR, where, according to Cold War logic, the Communists in power saw them as subversive groups "directed" by the West.

The demands formulated by these groups were perceived as being even more dangerous for the stability of the socialist regimes because in both the East and the West they were accompanied by a critique of nuclear technology and its dangers: in 1971 Greenpeace was created in response to nuclear tests in Alaska.[84] This antinuclear movement, which was transnational and trans-European from its beginnings, nevertheless assumed a particular dimension in the East after the explosion of the Chernobyl reactor in 1986, and especially the secrecy in which Soviet authorities shrouded the disaster. The absence of information prompted sharp criticism from Western governments and public opinion, but it especially fed into the defiance of citizens in the East toward the authorities in place.[85]

Even though Communist Parties and regimes were not necessarily "behind" in relation to Western elites on certain issues such as new feminist demands, the renewed forms they adopted—in addition to their presence in a new ideological landscape more focused on satisfying individual demands—helped weaken the scope of the Communist discourse of collective emancipation. Mobilizations connected to human rights in the 1970s clearly illustrate this phenomenon.

Human Rights and International Mobilizations in Support of Solidarność

The return of human rights on the international stage was not connected primarily to the Cold War and, contrary to what is often claimed, was not a distinctive feature of the West.

Since the 1960s the leaders of countries in the Global South, with support from those in socialist countries, formulated demands at the UN for economic and political sovereignty through the rhetoric of human rights.[86] In the early 1970s demands for individual political liberties were primarily directed against Latin American dictatorships supported or installed by the leaders of the United States.[87] The internationalization of the human rights discourse by dissidents from socialist countries helped transform it into a key aspect of the Cold War, with Western political leaders seizing on the issue. Once again, however, the discourse was not "invented" by the West. In the 1960s the first Soviet dissidents founded the Group for the Defense of Human Rights, taking inspiration from the letter of socialism. In December 1965 the first demonstrations for the respect of political rights in Moscow relied on the text of the Soviet constitution, and not on international treaties. Faced with indifference and repression, these activists sent letters to the UN Commission on Human Rights; they were the first actors in the internationalization of their cause. In November 1970 a group of scientists, under the direction of the physicist Andrei Sakharov, formed the

Committee on Human Rights, which encouraged sending letters of support to political prisoners. In 1971 they became affiliated with the International League for Human Rights, and in 1973 an Amnesty International office was established in Moscow.[88]

The internationalization of demands for human rights could take a tortuous path, as demonstrated by the repercussions of the Helsinki Accords. Dissidents in the East, who were already mobilized, seized on the agreement to formulate demands from their governments, appealed to public opinion, and used international legal instruments.[89] In 1976 Andrei Sakharov and Yuri Orlov created the Moscow Helsinki Group, which was imitated in people's democracies; Charter 77 in Czechoslovakia also claimed to adhere to the commitments made in Helsinki. Immediately afterward, Western governments used the follow-up conferences in Belgrade (1977–1978), Madrid (1980–1983), and Vienna (1986–1989) to exert pressure on Communist authorities. Finally, in 1979 the Ford Foundation, which played a role as an unofficial arm of U.S. Department of State policy, created a Helsinki Committee to aid dissidents. While anticommunist objectives were not concealed, mobilizations supporting human rights went beyond this Cold War strategy and were based on a fertile ground of associations and networks of solidarity with dissidents in the East. Their activity developed beginning in the late 1960s within the reconfiguration of both the landscape and political practices. These mobilizations could rely on long-standing and enduring relations between the two parts of Europe, especially but not exclusively within Social Democratic circles.[90] Czechoslovak intellectuals known in the West and with connections there launched Charter 77. This was one of the keys to its success. The movement drafted thousands of communiqués, declarations, analyses, and *samizdats*, many of which were sent abroad through political and friendship networks, and through Czechoslovak émigrés; these links were behind the creation of the support committees established in all Western countries.[91] These committees provided material support and offered a platform for various dissident groups, with the Soviet *Refuzniki*, who were forbidden from emigrating, being the most familiar. The "second left" movement played a decisive role in organizing solidarity with dissidents; it drove an antitotalitarian movement on the left, one that was critical of Communist regimes and quite different from traditional anticommunism.

FROM INTERNATIONALISMS TO GLOBALISM

The diversity of actors involved in these movements is clearly illustrated by the international support campaign for the Polish trade union Solidarność. Around a nucleus of traditional anticommunist actors, there quickly arose a broad movement of international solidarity including unionists of Social Democratic and Christian inspiration, as well as a movement emerging from the "second left" attracted by the affirmation of a union practice of self-management.[92] Everything began in 1979 with a coal mine strike in Poland, which continued with the dockyards of Gdansk. There were many strikes in the East, but this movement was different from preceding ones because it gave rise to an independent union under the direction of the electrical worker Lech Wałęsa. Communist authorities first recognized Solidarność in August 1979 at the signing of the Gdansk Agreement, before it was banned in October 1982. Support for the new union transformed into an international cause thanks to the intervention of major union federations, especially the American Federation of Labor-Congress of Industrial Organizations (AFL-CIO) in the United States, which as we saw earlier was a crucial actor in the Cold War.

At the time the AFL-CIO was led by Lane Kirkland, a staunch anticommunist, who saw the Gdansk strikes as proof that it was the man in the street and not diplomats who would overthrow Communist regimes. He established contact with the leaders of Solidarność on August 19, 1980, and launched a fundraising campaign in support of the new union.[93] The campaign intensified after the declaration of martial law in December 1981; the AFL-CIO took the initiative of creating a Committee in Support of Solidarność in New York, which led in July 1982 to the creation of the Brussels-based Coordinating Office Abroad. The AFL-CIO and the U.S. government were the office's primary sources of financial support but were not the only ones. At the request of the AFL-CIO, the International Confederation of Free Trade Unions quickly became involved in the solidarity movement. It was tasked with sending funds to Poland, in order to avoid accusations of subversion from the United States.[94]

The support movement broadened via the ICFTU. It especially received support from the ILO, where the ICFTU wielded decisive influence. The French director-general of the International Labour Office, Francis Blanchard, visited Poland in 1981, and following negotiations Lech Wałęsa was included in the delegation of Polish workers at the International Labor

Conference in May 1981.[95] He spoke "amid a religious silence" and drew "intense and sustained applause."[96] In addition to the unconditional support of the ICFTU, Wałęsa could also count on that of representatives from social Christianity and the World Confederation of Labor. Wałęsa, who was a fervent Catholic, had the support of the Polish Pope John Paul II, who met with him at the Vatican. In 1986, in a notable exception, Solidarność joined two international trade union confederations: the ICFTU and the World Confederation of Labor, of Christian allegiance.

At the ILO, the Committee on Freedom of Association examined the Polish situation, after which the Polish government was accused at the International Labor Conference in 1983 of violating Conventions 87 (freedom of association) and 98 (collective bargaining), both of which it had ratified. That same year, the organization's Administration Committee established a commission of inquiry whose June 1984 report led to the condemnation of Poland. In addition to union internationalism and the ILO, the defense of Solidarność mobilized actors from a broad movement defending human rights. Major international associations such as Amnesty International, Human Rights Watch International, and the International League for Human Rights intervened and helped adopt resolutions at the UN Commission on Human Rights in 1982 and 1983 condemning the Polish government. Finally, during its meeting in Madrid, the Coordinating Office of the CSCE produced a long document on human rights in Poland. In addition to the involvement of associations and international organizations, Solidarność enjoyed support from a host of local committees that raised funds and demonstrated in Western countries, especially in France and Italy, where the movement was led by an antiauthoritarian and self-management left. The campaign supporting Solidarność clearly illustrates the reconfigurations of international discourse at work in the 1980s, in which the language of human rights won out over that of social rights. Around this rhetoric of human rights coalesced the traditional anticommunist movement, as well as representatives of a democratic and antitotalitarian left that was very active locally, and also powerfully connected internationally.

The reaction of Communist elites to these mobilizations attests to the exhaustion of Communist regimes and discourse. For instance, the Polish government threatened to leave the ILO in 1984 but ultimately retracted, while Solidarność, which had not yet been made official, was tolerated and

FROM INTERNATIONALISMS TO GLOBALISM

later became an important actor in organizing roundtables in 1988. This roundtable movement that spread in Eastern European countries fostered the peaceful emergence from state socialism.

The example of the GDR, whose very existence depended on the permanence of the Communist project, is particularly interesting in this respect. As in other countries, the citizens of the GDR expressed criticism, which assumed a new and organized form in the 1970s by relying on the letter of socialism. As in the USSR and Poland, the 1980s were marked by the internationalization of these demands, which were promoted by the signing of the Helsinki Accords. The government of the GDR had committed to not curtail the freedom of movement, especially for families separated by the division of Germany. This international commitment was followed by a significant increase in the number of travel requests submitted to authorities. These requests exposed those who made them to repressive measures, ranging from loss of employment to imprisonment. To achieve their ends, those targeted by these measures made recourse to the UN Commission on Human Rights in Geneva. In 1988 an informant mentioned thousands of complaint letters, which had been encouraged by Brigitte Klump with the help of the UN civil servant Meike Noll-Wagenfeld.[97] Klump, who grew up in the GDR and studied journalism in Leipzig, settled in the West in 1957 and in 1979 sought to help her nephew Klaus Klump leave the GDR. To this end, she led a movement that centralized files on GDR citizens seeking to emigrate to the West and collectively submitted them to the UN Commission in Geneva with a view to using the 1503 Procedure, which allowed for examining human rights situations within specific countries, and led to the condemnation of the GDR. The government, forced to justify itself, ultimately committed to easing its policy.[98]

Aside from demands for the freedom of movement, which were directly inspired by the Helsinki Accords, East German citizens engaged international authorities to assert their workplace rights. In 1987 the East German representative to the ILO had to contend with a commission of inquiry in which his government was accused of practicing a discriminatory policy toward certain professional groups, which were subject to an obligation of loyalty toward the party in power.[99] In 1988 a scientific collaborator of the major IT firm Robotron in Dresden sued for discrimination based on Convention 111 of the ILO, which the government of the GDR had ratified. After submitting a request to travel abroad, he was relieved of his duties.

Measures put in place by the president of the GDR Council of Ministers provided for such requests to be punished with dismissals. Deprived of their jobs, the victims of these dismissals were transformed into "asocials" and risked being sent to labor camps. The authorities were thus guilty of major infringements to two international conventions they had ratified—against forced labor and discrimination. The Stasi officer who followed this affair was incidentally very concerned.[100]

These examples call for three remarks: First, the citizens of countries in the bloc produced, quite early on, a language of human rights by drawing inspiration from the letter of socialism, as well as the commitments made by the governments of their countries. Second, their demands were transformed into an international cause through a confluence of movements and initiatives that attest to the eclectic diffusion of human rights rhetoric. This rhetoric was appropriated by the usual actors of Cold War anticommunism—the Ford Foundation, the AFL-CIO, the CIA, and the Catholic Church—but it was also mobilized by new groups structured around demands for self-management and the protection of individual rights. These movements, which often organized locally, were supported, relayed, and overseen by major international associations. These mobilizations led to condemnations within various official international arenas. Third, the governments of socialist countries were defenseless before these procedures, for they were ensnared in the contradictions among the discourse on rights that Communist elites produced, the international commitments they had made, and the reality of repressive policies that these same elites put in place to remain in power.

While it contributed, it was not the Reagan administration's war on communism that brought an end to the Cold War. This end had multiple roots. The first was the exhaustion of the Communist model itself: primarily economic, as demonstrated by the enormous debt that various countries contracted with the West; secondly ideological, which was marked by the dissolution of the Communist world-system and ideal. The gradual abandonment of human rights rhetoric to anticommunist actors and the fact that they did not reaffirm the social dimension of human rights were signs of this exhaustion.

This was also the case within the new ideological and economic context. Instead of an internationalist and universalist discourse driven by the movements that emerged from antifascism, new international solidarities centered on novel subjects, such as the environment, and assumed various forms, as with second wave feminism or the reformulation of human rights. Values of social equality, whose authoritarian excesses were emphasized, were gradually disqualified. Multiple networks led the discourse on liberty and individual emancipation, which was amplified within different international spaces. Among these were the UN Commission on Human Rights, various follow-on institutions to the Helsinki Accords, and major NGOs such as Amnesty International or Greenpeace, as well as Protestant and Catholic churches, which gradually served as spaces for the First and the Second World of the Cold War to meet.

This evolution of the form and content of political mobilizations developed in parallel to the triumph of economic neoliberalism, which replaced the internationalists' objective of organizing the world with a globalist project, one that saw the world as a space for free trade and promoted competition among people and nations.

The decline of internationalisms did not exclusively affect the Communist movement, whose failure was the death knell for the Cold War. In reality, it also deeply challenged the very goal of international regulation driven by the Keynesians, Social Democrats, and social liberals who dominated the international organizations of the UN system. This loss of reference points bears witness to the advent within Western European countries of a liberal socialist (rather than social liberal) movement, embodied by Tony Blair of Great Britain and Gerhard Schroeder of Germany. The governments they led challenged the programs for economic regulation and social redistribution that had served as the foundation for a peaceful society, which had nevertheless been promoted by reform-minded socialists.

CONCLUSION

Beyond the Cold War

The goal of this book has been to explore the period called the Cold War through the lens of international organizations, seen as global actors and vantage points. The task was not easy. On the one hand, there was the power of Cold War discourse, binary and simplifying, which tends to ossify shifting and unstable realities, to conceal other issues—economic and social ones in particular—and to cover over older divisions. On the other, there was the thick tangle of documents and literature, the infinite diversity of actors involved across my multiple fields of exploration, the abundant knowledge they mobilized, and the opinions they expressed. Whom to heed? What direction to take? What path would be the surest one? I often went astray. When I finally came to the end of this long and perilous journey, I was able to formulate another account of the period, one that denies neither the divisions nor the powerful rhetoric that marked it, but that also unearths other aspects, giving voice to actors neglected or marginalized in traditional accounts. Following this long and intimate study of the sources of international organizations, I also became convinced of the need to reevaluate their importance, and more generally the forms of internationalism they promoted and deployed within them—an internationalism that is cruelly lacking in today's world.

Far be it for me to exalt the regulatory power of international organizations, or to excessively praise the advantages of UN multilateralism and the

CONCLUSION

forms of international intervention promoted by various international NGOs. All these organizations were—and still are—subject to power relations and reproduced—or reinforced—the global inequalities that gave rise to them, even when claiming to combat them. However, they were also spaces for challenging these inequalities, and sometimes even for subverting these power relations. They were places where issues were formulated, solutions developed, and other possible worlds invented, ones that were more solidary and even more equitable. That these other worlds did not come to be does not condemn the internationalist projects that gave rise to them.

The worlds of the Cold War did not set out on equal footing within international arenas. Western political, intellectual, and economic elites had a more long-standing experience of internationalism, developing powerful associations during the course of the nineteenth century. After World War I the governments of Western European countries, with support from U.S. actors, built the League of Nations, from which Bolshevik Russia was excluded in 1919. While relations developed between some Soviet actors and the League secretariat, and the USSR was a member of the organization between 1934 and 1939, it nevertheless remained on the margins of liberal internationalism. After 1945 the Western internationalists of the interwar period joined the UN system and became the architects of powerful Western regional organizations. The "Second World" did not have the same experience; socialist and Communist internationalism was established as a response to the liberal model and always remained fragile. Its practice required linguistic, financial, and cultural resources that the leaders of the nineteenth-century labor movement did not necessarily possess. Beginning in the 1960s, however, UN General Assemblies served as important occasions for developing a common discourse for Communist countries, and it was in Geneva—in the wings of UNECE meetings rather than in Moscow— that Comecon became a reality in the 1960s and 1970s. Similarly, it was at the UN that decolonized countries formed a "Third World" in 1964, via UNCTAD and the G77.

The emergence of this Third World at the UN can be seen as an ironic reversal, for major colonial powers intended to use the organization to preserve their domination over these very same countries. The gradual failure of the initiatives following the vote for the Declaration for a New International Economic Order reflects the powerlessness of this third internationalism in the face of opposition from the most powerful actors.

CONCLUSION

Nevertheless, the general assemblies of UN agencies and major international conferences served as spaces where the First and Second—and later Third—Worlds of the Cold War presented themselves, developing and deploying their rhetoric. Ideological oppositions and divergences drove these internationalisms; they led to the creation of competing networks and organizations, along with international causes demonstrating the mobilization capacity of various camps, often beyond their own forces. These mobilizations were in turn behind a blossoming of NGOs, commissions, and agencies within or on the margins of the UN system. The civil servants and experts who worked there cultivated an international practice based on the exchange of information and know-how. Spaces such as the United Nations Economic Commission for Europe, the International Atomic Energy Agency, UNESCO's Centre for Social Science Research, the International Institute for Applied Systems Analysis, and many others bear witness to efforts to organize the world around jointly developed projects, and solutions conceived for application everywhere. The notion that there could be universal models—which the civil servants and experts of international organizations believed they were promoting—resisted the binary discourse of the Cold War. While the direct confrontations of the Cold War seemingly dominated UN arenas, it was only slowly and imperfectly that they replaced antifascist internationalism within the secretariats of UN agencies. Many of the first civil servants had been part of the United Nations Relief and Rehabilitation Administration and believed it was important to maintain the wartime alliance in order to anticipate crises and the return of conflicts. They were often from Social Democratic or New Deal networks and, inspired by Keynesianism, believed in the virtues of planning and organization. Gunnar Myrdal of Sweden, the first UNECE secretary, is a good example. Like other nationals from Northern European countries, during the war he joined the Group of Democratic Socialists, where he mixed with numerous leaders from Central European countries. Exiled or forced to join Communist Parties after 1947–1948, these Social Democrats of Central Europe—the Poles and Czechoslovaks in particular—maintained ties with Western Social Democrats, including via the international organizations of which their countries had been members since the interwar period. The longevity of these pan-European networks and this international know-how distinguished Central European countries from the USSR and affords a better grasp of the specific role they played within the

CONCLUSION

UN system. As a result, beyond the propagandistic discourses of plenary assemblies and the various conflicts that marked their functioning, the Cold War never became a hegemonic reality within international organizations. It rather appears as a veil, one that imperfectly conceals other forms of divisions, while interwar networks—along with the issues discussed and solutions formulated at the time—silently endure. This was particularly true with respect to the issue of global inequality.

As early as 1943, future international civil servants stressed that in order to avoid the return of wars, it was important to end the persistent inequalities between the two parts of Europe. This objective came up against the U.S. policy of economic embargo. Central and Eastern European countries led by Communists were established as a Second World on the periphery of the First, a position that continued their economic and cultural marginality from the interwar period. After 1955, when the group of Communist states was strengthened and recently decolonized countries joined international organizations, the Western world developed its own spaces of prosperity. The Single Market in 1957, the OECD in 1961, and the G7 in 1975 were responses to the demands of G77 countries and represented the well-guarded spaces of this exclusive club. Wherever Europeans came together in international organizations—at UNECE or in the International Labour Office—the European margins, especially Central and Eastern Europe, were seen as less-developed or underdeveloped peripheries and were established as a space of experimentation for international development policies, such as in the 1930s.

This position conferred on the Communist leaders of these countries a legitimacy to openly formulate demands for justice and global equality, and to propose an alternative vision of development. It was in this respect that Communist representatives supported the demands formulated in the 1950s by leaders from recently decolonized countries, which culminated in the declaration of the New International Economic Order in 1974. Since the Russian Revolution, Communist leaders were well aware that economic independence was a condition for their political sovereignty and ideological independence, and on this issue they agreed with the demands made by leaders from Third World countries. Beyond the Cold War, solidarity between the East and the South was rooted in shared experiences of marginality and relative underdevelopment. These experiences had already given rise during the interwar period to convergence, as well as to the

CONCLUSION

exchange of know-how and models between the Balkans and Latin America. The Romanian economist Mihail Manoilescu can be considered, during the 1930s, as a precursor to dependency theory, which made its way to the United Nations Conference on Trade and Development via the Argentinian economist Raùl Prebisch. This solidarity was also rooted in geographical proximities and long-standing (trans-) imperial circulations: this was especially true of the enduring ties between the Balkans and the Middle East, which emerged from the same Ottoman mold and were driven by the presence of strong Muslim communities in the Balkans and the USSR. International organizations conserved and encouraged such proximities within. During the 1960s and 1970s some Central European countries were established as models of development for Middle Eastern countries by international civil servants, who did not approach the world through the interpretive framework of the Cold War, but rather through that of global inequalities and the development policies tasked with combatting them.

These examples are a reminder that divisions, oppositions, and rapprochements too hastily interpreted as expressions of the "Cold War"—as is the case once again today—were quite often in keeping with longer histories. These continuities, veiled and even obscured by Cold War discourse, continued through networks developed within international organizations. Civil servants and experts relied on these networks to give life to internationalism, to circulate knowledge and know-how, and to establish or encourage connections. For the same reasons, marginal actors or countries within the bipolar world of the Cold War played a prominent role in the secretariats of international organizations, especially those within the UN system. This was true for nationals from neutral countries such as Austria, Finland, Yugoslavia, and the Nordic countries, who often sustained Social Democrat and reformist networks. As spaces for ordering into blocs, international organizations were thus also instruments for subverting this order. Regional organizations played an ambiguous role in this respect. They clearly served as spaces for meeting, working together, and building a shared culture for a particular bloc, although disagreements were forcefully expressed. There was not always harmony within the regional organizations of the Western world, as illustrated by the difficulties encountered by U.S. actors in validating their lists of embargoed products within CoCom. In appearance more closely knit, and more strongly

CONCLUSION

dominated by the USSR, the Eastern bloc experienced intense political and economic tension. The leaders of developed countries in Central Europe, especially Czechoslovakia and the GDR, pursued objectives within Comecon that were quite different from those of their Balkan allies. These disagreements could be in keeping with the long history of rivalries between the major Eastern European empires: the Habsburgs and the Ottomans. They can also be explained by the persistence of economic nationalism, which was powerful during the interwar period, and reinforced by the central planning that strengthened the nation-state in real socialism. In certain international arenas such as UNECE, GATT, and UNESCO, representatives from governments in Central Europe and international civil servants from these same countries exhibited a relative autonomy, which cuts against the monolithic representation of the bloc developed by anticommunist actors.

These inter- and intrabloc fluidities made it possible to work within the secretariats and their numerous commissions. For this reason, the civil servants and experts working there were often considered as representatives of a depoliticized technocracy. What I wanted to show was that these secretariats were above all places where a different conception of politics prevailed, one that was not cut off from "the learned (*savants*)." Civil servants and experts used the figures and texts they compiled from a wide range of national spaces, allowing them to produce international knowledge, based on which they developed and proposed solutions to the issues presented by their constituencies. These solutions at least partially escaped power relations, as well as immediate national and international considerations. They nevertheless involved policy choices and often had an indirect influence on orientations and policy decision within national spaces.

Just as Cold War discourse ossified the blocs, it also distorted and simplified certain major international causes, such as women's rights, access to health care, and children's rights. Contrary to what is often suggested, the fixed and binary presentation of these issues, structured according to Cold War divisions, did not necessarily paralyze discussions but instead often allowed for opening the debate. This is demonstrated by the issue of forced labor. Initiated as a Cold War debate and led by the highly anticommunist AFL against labor camps in the Eastern bloc, the international investigation that it prompted at the initiative of the ILO/UN commission helped to open the debate and to broaden the notion of forced labor itself.

Similarly, beginning in the 1970s, the rhetoric of human rights became an international cause because leaders in the Global South seized on it in the 1950s to defend their sovereignty, with support from Communist leaders, while dissidents and critics in the East used international forums to assert the rights that were formally granted to them by the constitution of their country but denied in reality. The context of ideological opposition produced by the Cold War fostered the internationalization of these causes. International organizations, and their civil servants and experts, were the conveyors and facilitators of this internationalization.

Finally, seen from international spaces, the end of communism and the Cold War seemed to result from a slow evolution, as well as the gradual dissolution of the Eastern bloc and Communist internationalism. The recourse some Central European governments made to development programs—and their joining GATT and the World Bank—bears witness to their heightened economic and technological dependence on Western resources. Starting in 1985 it was in the West that Gorbachev and his team sought solutions to the economic crisis of state socialism, including the use of resources offered by international organizations. In reality, Western expertise and economic interests had penetrated the countries of Central and Eastern Europe since the 1960s. We saw earlier the role played by development programs, especially in the field of professional training, and how Communist cadres were converted to Western management early on. The crisis of the socialist model of development was reinforced by the oil shocks that clearly struck these countries more than those in the West.

This weakening fostered the affirmation of a "new spirit of capitalism," which was initially formulated in response to the demands for an NIEO announced by leaders from the Global South.[1] Recourse to traditional Cold War arguments, according to which regulating the activity of multinationals posed a threat to private property, served to delegitimize the project. In this dual context—the crisis of state socialism and mobilization against the NIEO—neoliberal discourse and solutions progressively replaced the Keynesian model as a dominant international paradigm. This replacement was promoted by the gradual disappearance of the antifascist generation and the Social Democratic networks in which it had organized.[2] At the same time, new forms of mobilization and organization formulated and gave voice to demands for individual emancipation, which gradually prevailed

CONCLUSION

over the promotion of major collective projects. They, somewhat paradoxically, accompanied the triumph of the neoliberal paradigm.

The logic of instilling competition between individuals and praising the "self-employed," which was characteristic of the "new spirit of capitalism," spread in the 1980s. This was marked internationally by the declining influence of the actors and organizations most involved in long-term planning, to the benefit of those promoting the logic of competition. In all international organizations, greater recourse to funding from private foundations encouraged the implementation of occasional, short-term projects, with an expectation of immediately measurable results.

The crisis of the Social Democratic model of regulation and UN multilateralism in the early twenty-first century are delayed consequences of the end of this period, which is wrongly reduced to the "Cold War." On the national level, this crisis of the Social Democratic model has translated into growing social inequality, paving the way for populist discourses that offer false solutions of withdrawal into the nation, seen as the final protective cocoon, even as economically and politically weakened states increasingly struggle to resist the growing power of major multinational enterprises. On the international level, these narrow nationalisms have translated into serious challenges to multilateralism, to the benefit of the power politics for which the world is today a stage. Yet yesterday as well as today, projects for organizing and regulating the world to combat global inequality remain essential to ensuring world peace. Human societies and their natural environment need them now more than ever.

NOTES

ABBREVIATIONS FOR ARCHIVES CONSULTED

Arch-Hoover   Archives of the Hoover Library at Stanford University, California

Arch-IFZ   Archiv des Instituts für Zeitgeschichte (Archives of the Institute for Contemporary History), Munich

Arch-IISH (ICFTU)   Archives of the International Institute for Social History, Amsterdam, International Confederation of Free Trade Unions

Arch-ILO   Archives of the International Labour Office, Geneva

Arch-MfS   Archiv des Ministeriums für Staatssicherheit (Stasi Records Archive), Berlin

Arch-SAPMO   Stiftung Archiv der Parteien und Massenorganisationen der DDR im Bundesarchiv (Foundation Archives of the Political Parties and Mass Organisations of the GDR at the Federal Archives), Berlin

Arch-UN-NYC   United Nations Archives, New York

Arch-UNESCO   UNESCO Archives, Paris

Arch-UNIDO   Archives of the United Nations Industrial Development Organization, Vienna

Arch-UNOG   United Nations Archives, Geneva

Arch-UNOG-UNECE   Archives of the United Nations Economic Commission for Europe, Geneva

Arch-WFTU   Archives of the World Federation of Trade Unions, Prague

RArchC   Rockefeller Archives, Sleepy Hollow, New York

INTRODUCTION

1. Arch-ILOILO Z 3/1/7, "Records of official visits by the director general 1948–1961: two subfiles Poland Czechoslovakia."

2. Odd Arne Westad, *The Global Cold War: Third World Interventions and the Making of Our Times* (Cambridge: Cambridge University Press, 2005), 3. For a history of the notion and its evolution among historians, see also Westad, "The Cold War and the International History of the Twentieth Century," in *The Cambridge History of the Cold War*, Vol. 1: *Origins, 1945–1962*, ed. Melvyn P. Leffler and Odd Arne Westad (Cambridge: Cambridge University Press, 2010), 3–8.

3. See especially György Péteri, *Nylon Curtain: Transnational and Transsystemic Tendencies in the Cultural Life of State-Socialist Russia and East-Central Europe* (Trondheim: Trondheim Studies on East European Cultures & Societies, 2006); Sophie Coeuré and Sabine Dullin, eds., *Frontières du communisme: mythologies et réalités de la division de l'Europe de la Révolution d'octobre au mur de Berlin* (Paris: La Découverte, 2007); Sari Autio-Sarasmo and Katalin Miklóssy, eds., *Reassessing Cold War Europe* (New York: Routledge, 2011); and Angela Romano and Federico Romero, eds., *European Socialist Regimes' Fateful Engagement with the West: National Strategies in the Long 1970s* (London: Routledge, 2020), https://doi.org/10.4324/9780429340703.

4. For a recent and complete account in French, see Georges-Henri Soutou, *La Guerre froide: 1943–1990* (Paris: Pluriel, 2011). In English, see the most recent work by Odd Arne Westad, *The Cold War: A World History* (New York: Basic Books, 2017). The various books devoted to the history of international organizations provide an account: Guillaume Devin and Marie-Claude Smouts, *Les Organisations internationales* (Paris: A. Colin, 2011); in English, see Bob Reinalda, *Routledge History of International Organizations: From 1815 to the Present Day* (London: Routledge, 2009); and Madeleine Herren, *Geschichte der internationalen Organisation* (Darmstadt, Ger.: Wissenschaftliche Buchgesellschaft, 2009).

5. See Akira Iriye, *Global Community: The Role of International Organizations in the Making of the Contemporary World* (Berkeley: University of California Press, 2002); and Glenda Sluga, *Internationalism in the Age of Nationalism* (Philadelphia: University of Pennsylvania Press, 2013).

6. Akira Iriye, "Historicizing the Cold War," in *The Oxford Handbook of the Cold War*, ed. Richard H. Immerman and Petra Goedde (Oxford: Oxford University Press, 2013), 15–32.

7. Sunil Amrith and Glenda Sluga, "New Histories of the United Nations," *Journal of World History* 19, no. 3 (2008): 251–74.

8. Grosser, *Les Temps*, 19–69; Westad, *The Global Cold War*, 8–72.

9. On this approach, see Margaret E. Keck and Kathryn Sikkink, eds., *Activists Beyond Borders: Advocacy Networks in International Politics* (Ithaca, N.Y.: Cornell University Press, 1998).

10. On proxy wars, see especially Westad, *The Global Cold War*.

11. This is the objective established and not entirely met by Samantha Christiansen and Zachary A. Scarlett, eds., *The Third World in the Global 1960s* (New York: Berghahn Books, 2015).

INTRODUCTION

12. Saull, Richard, "Locating the Global South in the Theorisation of the Cold War: Capitalist Development, Social Revolution and Geopolitical Conflict," *Third World Quarterly* 26, no. 2 (2005): 253–80; Steven L. B. Jensen, "Inequality and Post-War International Organization: Discrimination, the World Social Situation and the United Nations, 1948–1957," in *Histories of Global Inequality: New Perspectives*, ed. Christian Olaf Christiansen and Steven L. B. Jensen (London: Palgrave Macmillan, 2019), 131–55.

13. On the importance of ideology in understanding the Cold War, see Pierre Grosser, *Les Temps de la guerre froide: réflexions sur l'histoire de la guerre froide et sur les causes de sa fin* (Brussels: Complexe, 1995); and Mark Kramer, "Ideology and the Cold War," *Review of International Studies* 25, no. 4 (1999): 539–76. See also David Engerman, "Ideology and the Origins of the Cold War 1917–1962," in Leffler and Westad, *The Cambridge History of the Cold War*, 20–43.

14. See Jessica Gienow-Hecht, "Culture and the Cold War in Europe," in Leffler and Westad, *The Cambridge History of the Cold War*, 398–420; Ioana Popa, "La circulation transnationale du livre: un instrument de la guerre froide culturelle," *Histoire@Politique* 15, no. 3 (2011): 25; Peter Romijn, Giles Scott-Smith, and Joes Segal, eds., *Divided Dreamworlds? The Cultural Cold War in East and West* (Amsterdam: Amsterdam University Press, 2012); and Pierre Grémion, *Intelligence de l'anticommunisme. Le congrès pour la liberté de la culture à Paris 1950–1975* (Paris: Fayard, 1995).

15. For a stimulating reflection on these questions, see Richard Saull, *The Cold War and After: Capitalism, Revolution and Superpower Politics* (London: Pluto Press, 2007).

16. Bob Reinalda and Madeleine Herren have both emphasized that the emergence of intergovernmental organizations was closely connected to the existence of prior international associations and networks.

17. As demonstrated by the sustained debates surrounding them, especially among political scientists. An overview citing the relevant literature appeared in three dedicated issues of *Critique internationale*: "Une autre approche de la globalisation: socio-histoire des organisations internationales (1900–1940)," 52, no. 3 (2011); "Le changement dans les organisations internationales," 53, no. 4 (2011); and "L'anthropologie des organisations internationales," 54, no. 1 (2012). Also see the more recent issue, "La (dé)politisation des organisations internationale," 76, no. 3 (2017), or the complete collection of the journal *International Organizations*, which has published numerous theoretical and methodological articles on international organizations since 1947.

18. On the notion of epistemic communities, see Peter Haas, "Introduction: Epistemic Communities and International Policy Coordination," *International Organization* 46, no. 1 (1992): 1–35. See also Annabelle Littoz-Monnet, ed., *The Politics of Expertise in International Organizations* (London: Routledge, 2017); and Michel Christian, Sandrine Kott, and Ondrej Matejka, "International Organizations in the Cold War: The Circulation of Experts Beyond the East-West Divide," *Studia Territorialia* 1 (2017): 35–60. On secretariats, see Bob Reinalda, *International Secretariats: Two Centuries of International Civil Servants and Secretariats* (London: Routledge, 2020).

19. On this approach, see Sandrine Kott, "Les organisations internationales, terrains d'étude de la globalisation. Jalons pour une approche socio-historique," *Critique internationale* 52, no. 3 (2011): 9–16.
20. I have borrowed this expression from the first director of the International Labour Office, Albert Thomas, who used it during his speech opening the conference of the International Union of Health Insurance Funds, held in Vienna September 10–14, 1925. Arch-ILO SI/1000/11/2.

1. THE TWO PARTS OF EUROPE DURING THE POSTWAR PERIOD

1. For France, see, for example, Serge Berstein and Pierre Milza, eds., *L'Année 1947* (Paris: Presses de Sciences Po, 1999).
2. On this point see, among others, Georges-Henri Soutou, *La Guerre froide: 1943–1990* (Paris: Pluriel, 2011), 227–66.
3. Jan de Graaf, *Socialism Across the Iron Curtain: Socialist Parties in East and West and the Reconstruction of Europe After 1945* (Cambridge: Cambridge University Press, 2019), 13–41.
4. See the reports from the three roundtables held in connection with the Balzan project: Flora Tsilage, "Relief and Rehabilitation in the Immediate Aftermath of War," *History Workshop Journal* 61, no. 1 (2006): 299–304; 63, no. 1 (2006): 371–74; and 65, no. 1 (2008): 279–84.
5. Daniel Plesch and Thomas Weiss, eds., *Wartime Origins and the Future United Nations* (New York: Routledge, 2015); Daniel Plesch, *America, Hitler and the UN: How the Allies Won World War II and Forged a Peace* (London: Tauris, 2015).
6. This is a corrective to Mark Mazower's overly unilateral interpretation in *No Enchanted Palace: The End of Empire and the Ideological Origins of the United Nations* (Princeton, N.J.: Princeton University Press, 2009).
7. Arch-UNOG ECE-ARR 14/1360 80, "Gunnar Myrdal, The challenge of European reconstruction based on a survey of the economic situation and prospects of Europe, first draft for Rostow."
8. Atina Grossmann, "A Question of Silence: The Rape of German Women by Occupation Soldiers," in *West Germany Under Reconstruction: Politics, Society and Culture in the Adenauer Era*, ed. Robert G. Moeller (Ann Arbor: University of Michigan Press, 1997); Olivier Wieviorka, *Normandy: The Landings to the Liberation of Paris* (Cambridge, Mass.: Belknap Press of Harvard University Press, 2008), chap. 13.
9. Fabrice Virgili, *La France virile: des femmes tondues à la Libération* (Paris: Payot, 2000).
10. Thérèse Brosse, *L'Enfance victime de la guerre. Une étude de la situation européenne* (Paris: UNESCO, 1949), 29.
11. Tara Zahra, *The Lost Children: Reconstructing Europe's Families After World War II* (Cambridge, Mass.: Harvard University Press, 2015).
12. For a precise description of the situation of these countries, see George Woodbridge, *UNRRA: The History of the United Nations Relief and Rehabilitation Administration* (New York: Columbia University Press, 1950), 2:81–361.

1. THE TWO PARTS OF POSTWAR EUROPE

13. Ivan Berend, *Central and Eastern Europe, 1944–1993: Detour from the Periphery to the Periphery* (Cambridge: Cambridge University Press, 2010), 4–6.
14. See the introduction in Stefan-Ludwig Hoffmann, Sandrine Kott, Peter Romijn, and Olivier Wieviorka, eds., *Seeking Peace in the Wake of War: Europe, 1943–1947* (Amsterdam: Amsterdam University Press, 2015).
15. Arch-UN-NYC-S 0441-0078-03.
16. Jan T. Gross, "Social Consequences of War: Preliminaries to the Study of Imposition of Communist Regimes in East Central Europe," *East European Politics and Societies* 3, no. 2 (1989): 198–214.
17. Arch-UNOG ECE ARR 14/1360 80, "The Challenge of European Reconstruction," 1947.
18. See Jessica Reinisch, "'Auntie UNRRA' at the Crossroads," *Past & Present* 218, no. suppl. 8 (2013): 70–97.
19. Bruno Cabanes, *The Great War and the Origins of Humanitarianism, 1918–1924* (Cambridge: Cambridge University Press, 2014), 189–247.
20. Woodbridge, *UNRRA*, 1:7.
21. On the attitude of Soviet leaders, see Andrew Harder, "The Politics of Impartiality: The United Nations Relief and Rehabilitation Administration in the Soviet Union, 1946–7," *Journal of Contemporary History* 2 (2012): 347–69.
22. On Hot Springs and its ambiguities, see Ruth Jachertz, "Stable Agricultural Markets and World Order: FAO and ITO, 1943–1949," in Plesch and Weiss, *Wartime Origins*, 179–98; Bryan McDonald, *Food Security: Dimensions of Security* (Cambridge: Polity, 2010), 16–18.
23. National Planning Association, "UNRRA: Gateway to Recovery," *Planning Pamphlets*, no. 30–31 (1944): 62. See also Jessica Reinisch, "Internationalism in Relief: The Birth (and Death) of UNRRA," *Past & Present* 210 (2011): 258–89.
24. See the brief treatment of this topic in William I. Hitchcock, *The Bitter Road to Freedom: A New History of the Liberation of Europe* (New York: Free Press, 2008), 215–49.
25. Iris Borowy, *Coming to Terms with World Health: The League of Nations Health Organisation, 1921–1946* (Frankfurt: Peter Lang, 2009), 436; Marta Aleksandra Balińska, *Une vie pour l'humanitaire: Ludwik Rajchman (1881–1965)* (Paris: La Découverte, 2015), 310–20.
26. Reinisch, "'Auntie UNRRA.'"
27. *Economic Recovery in the Countries Assisted by UNRRA* (Washington, D.C., 1946), 15, http://hdl.handle.net/2027/coo.31924013708890.
28. Melvyn P. Leffler, *The Specter of Communism: The United States and the Origins of the Cold War, 1917–1953* (New York: Hill and Wang, 1994), esp. 50–64.
29. Arch-Hoover, Stanford, "Arthur Kemp Papers," 1: 2–3.
30. Harder, "The Politics of Impartiality," 347–69.
31. UN-NY-Arch-UNRRA S-0527-1107.
32. This criticism also came from within UNRRA. See especially, with respect to Yugoslavia, D. W., "Success of a Mission: U.N.R.R.A. in Yugoslavia," *The World Today* 2, no. 8 (1946): 376–83.
33. Vaclav Kostelecky, *The United Nations Economic Commission for Europe: The Beginning of a History* (Göteborg, Ger.: Graphic Systems, 1989), 16.

1. THE TWO PARTS OF POSTWAR EUROPE

34. Arch-UNOG, Economic and Social Council, E/245/Rev.1/Corr.1, 11 August 1947.
35. Paul Weindling, "Public Health and Political Stability: The Rockefeller Foundation in Central and Eastern Europe Between the Two World Wars," *Minerva* 31, no. 3 (1993), 253; Benjamin B. Page, "The Rockefeller Foundation and Central Europe: A Reconsideration," *Minerva* 40 (2002): 265–87.
36. RArchC Cox-Reece FA 418 21 448, memo from 25 April 1952.
37. RArchC RG.1.1 789–1, 24 July 1947, Thomas Appleget.
38. RArchC RG. 1.1 710–5, correspondence 1946–1947.
39. RArchC RG. 1.1 789–4.
40. RArchC RG.1.1 789–1. On the National Institute of Hygiene in the context of Central Europe, see Katrin Steffen, "Experts and the Modernization of the Nation: The Arena of Public Health in Poland in the First Half of the Twentieth Century," *Jahrbücher für Geschichte Osteuropas* 61, no. 4 (2013): 574–90.
41. RArchC RG. 1.1 750–1.
42. RArchC RG. 1.1 750–1, letter from John Grant to George Storke, 12 July 1948.
43. Ondřej Matějka, "Social Engineering and Alienation Between East and West: Czech Christian-Marxist Dialogue in the 1960s from the National Level to the Global Arena," in *Planning in Cold War Europe: Competition, Cooperation, Circulations (1950s–1970s)*, ed. Michel Christian, Sandrine Kott, and Ondřej Matějka (Berlin: De Gruyter, 2018), 165–86.
44. Albania, Bulgaria, Hungary, and Romania joined in 1955, and the GDR in 1973.
45. UNICEF archives are not available, but the organization has posted documents online. See especially "First Report of the First Executive Board of the United Nations International Children's Emergency Fund, 11 December 1946–31 December 1950," ECOSOC, 12, supplement 3, https://digitallibrary.un.org /record/67581.
46. On Morse, see especially his "Oral History Interview" with James R. Fuchs for the Harry S. Truman Presidential Library and Museum, Washington, D.C., August 3, 1977, https://www.trumanlibrary.org/oralhist/morse3.htm#132.
47. Arch-ILO Z 3/64/2, "Director-General's Mission to Austria and Eastern Europe, March-April 1958."
48. Arch-ILO P 2765, P 14/11/41.
49. Arch-ILO P1289, Oswald Stein personal file; Arch-ILO P3926, Emil Schönbaum personal file. On the role of Stein and Schönbaum within the International Labour Office, see Sandrine Kott, "Un modèle international de protection sociale est-il possible? L'organisation internationale du travail entre assurance et sécurité sociale (1919–1952)," *Revue d'histoire de la protection sociale* 10, "Experts internationaux et politiques sociales" (2017): 62–84.
50. On Czechoslovak Social Democrats during these years, see de Graaf, *Socialism Across the Iron Curtain.*
51. See the correspondence on social security: Arch-ILO SI-0-17.
52. Unsigned article, "Social Security in Czechoslovakia," *International Labour Review* 58, no. 2 (1948): 151–86.
53. Maurice Milhaud, "Social Commission," *World Affairs* 110, no. 4 (Winter 1947): 247–51.

1. THE TWO PARTS OF POSTWAR EUROPE

54. Arch-UN-NYC S-0441-0075-4, letter from Roland Berger to Raphael Cilento, 9 September 1949.
55. Arch-UN-NYC S-0441-75-1.
56. "Report of the FAO Mission for Poland, Food and Agriculture Organization of the United Nations," Washington, D.C., 1948.
57. Elizabeth Borgwardt, *A New Deal for the World: America's Vision for Human Rights* (Cambridge, Mass.: Harvard University Press, 2005), 14–44.
58. Geneva organizations had to face budget cuts. Under the leadership of its interim director, Sean Lester of Ireland, the League of Nations budget shrank by one-third compared to prewar amounts. The ILO conserved 63 of the 316 civil servants who held positions in 1939. The United States, Great Britain, and the Commonwealth of Nations contributed two-thirds of the ILO's budget during the war. See Victor-Yves Ghebali, *Organisation internationale et guerre mondiale. Le cas de la Société des Nations et de l'Organisation internationale du travail pendant la Seconde Guerre mondiale* (Grenoble: Institut d'études politiques, 1975).
59. Peter J. Beck, "The League of Nations and the Great Powers, 1936–1940," *World Affairs* 157, no. 4 (1995): 175–89; Ludovic Tournès, "The Rockefeller Foundation and the Transition from the League of Nations to the UN (1939–1946)," *Journal of Modern European History* 12 (2014): 323–41.
60. One emissary was from the Free French Forces, which presented itself as the only true representative of France. For a report on the conference, see "Conference of the International Labor Organisation," ILO, Montreal, 1941.
61. "Conference of the International Labor Organisation," 5.
62. "Conference of the International Labor Organisation," especially appendix 1: "Resolution on Post-War Emergency and Reconstruction Measures," quote on 163.
63. Arch-ILO PWR 1/17, PWR 1/31.
64. See the inventory of the board's archives preserved at the New York Public Library, http://archives.nypl.org/mss/501.
65. Paul N. Rosenstein-Rodan, "Problems of Industrialisation of Eastern and South-Eastern Europe," *Economic Journal* 53, no. 210–211 (1943): 202–11; Rosenstein-Rodan, "The International Development of Economically Backward Areas," *International Affairs* 20, no. 2 (1944): 157–65. See also the interview he gave in 1961 as part of the World Bank Oral History Project: https://oralhistory.worldbank .org/transcripts/transcript-oral-history-interview-paul-rosenstein-rodan-held -august-14-1961.
66. Eric Helleiner, *Forgotten Foundations of Bretton Woods: International Development and the Making of the Postwar Order* (Ithaca, N.Y.: Cornell University Press, 2014), 234–45.
67. Arch-ILO Z1/61/1/3, correspondence between Phelan and Perkins in December 1941.–
68. See Arch-ILO CAT 6B-7-4 and L1/14/3; Denis Guerin, *Albert Thomas au BIT 1920–1932. De l'internationalisme à l'Europe* (Geneva: EURYOPA-Institut européen Genève, 1996), 90. On the failure of these projects, see Sylvain Schirmann, *Crise, coopération économique et financière entre États européens, 1929–1933*, Histoire économique et financière de la France XIXe–XXe siècles (Vincennes: Institut de la gestion publique et du développement économique, 2011), 122–23, 252–68.

69. Kenneth Bertrams, "Une inspiration tout en contrastes," *Genèses. Sciences sociales et Histoire* 71, no. 2 (2008): 64–83; Kiran Klaus Patel, *The New Deal: A Global History* (Princeton, N.J.: Princeton University Press, 2016), 261–78.
70. Brian Waddell, "Economic Mobilization for World War II and the Transformation of the State," *Politics & Society* 22, no. 2 (1994): 165–94.
71. See the publications of the Economic and Financial Section and its director Alexander Loveday, "The Economics of Transition," *Proceedings of the American Philosophical Society* 87, no. 2 (1943): 189–93.
72. Helleiner, *Forgotten Foundations,* 266. Patricia Clavin, *Securing the World Economy: The Reinvention of the League of Nations, 1920–1946* (Oxford: Oxford University Press, 2013).
73. Michele Alacevich, *The Political Economy of the World Bank: The Early Years* (Stanford, Calif.: Stanford University Press, 2009); Sarah Babb, "Embeddedness, Inflation, and International Regimes: The IMF in the Early Postwar Period," *American Journal of Sociology* 113 (2007): 128–64; and especially Helleiner, *Forgotten Foundations.*
74. Sheldon R. Anderson, *A Dollar to Poland Is a Dollar to Russia: US Economic Policy Toward Poland, 1945–1952* (New York: Garland, 1993), 116–24.
75. On UNECE, see Yves Berthelot and Paul Rayment, "Economic Commission for Europe," in *Unity and Diversity in Development Ideas Perspectives from the UN Regional Commissions,* ed. Yves Berthelot (Bloomington: Indiana University Press, 2004), 46–70.
76. Arch-UNOG ECE ARR 14/1360/67, letter to Gunnar Myrdal, April 1947.
77. Daniel Stinsky, *International Cooperation in Cold War Europe: The United Nations Economic Commission for Europe, 1947–64* (n.p.: Bloomsbury, 2022), 47–51; Stinsky, "A Bridge Between East and West? Gunnar Myrdal and the UN Economic Commission for Europe, 1947–1957," in Christian, Kott, and Matějka, *Planning in Cold War Europe,* 45–68.
78. Örjan Appelqvist, "Rediscovering Uncertainty: Early Attempts at a Pan-European Post-War Recovery," *Cold War History* 8, no. 3 (2008): 327–52. On the International Group of Democratic Socialists, see Klaus Misgeld, *Die "Internationale Gruppe demokratischer Sozialisten" in Stockholm 1942–1945. Zur sozialistischen Friedensdiskussion während des Zweiten Weltkrieges* (Uppsala, Sweden: Acta Universitatis Upsaliensis, 1976); and Elisabeth Röhrlich, *Kreiskys Außenpolitik: zwischen österreichischer Identität und internationalem Programm* (Vienna: Vienna University Press, 2011), 74–84.
79. Wolfram Kaiser and Johan Schot, *Writing the Rules for Europe: Experts, Cartels, and International Organizations* (Basingstoke, U.K.: Palgrave Macmillan, 2014), 83–85, for UNECE.
80. Gunnar Myrdal, "Twenty Years of the United Nations Economic Commission for Europe," *International Organization* 22 (1968): 617–28.
81. Arch-UNOG-ECE ARR14/1360/80, "Walt Rostow: The ECE First Year."
82. Arch-UNOG-ECE E/EMP/SUB.1/39/Add. 2, "Temporary Sub-committee on the Economic Reconstruction of Devastated Areas. Proposal for the Establishment of an Economic Commission for Europe," 10 September 1946.
83. Arch-UNOG-ECE ARR 14/1360/80. Notes of Walter Rostow regarding a discussion, 5 May 1948.

2. THE EMERGENCE OF A "SECOND WORLD"

84. On these two points, see the contributions of Vincent Lagendijk, *Electrifying Europe: the Power of Europe in the Construction of Electricity Networks* (Amsterdam: Aksant, 2008); and Frank Schipper, *Driving Europe: Building Europe on Roads in the Twentieth Century* (Amsterdam: Amsterdam University Press, 2009).

85. See Myrdal's interview with Ernest O. Hauser, n.d. (but probably February–March 1949), in Arch-UNOG-ECE ARR 14/1360/80.

86. Arch-UNOG-ECE ARR 14/1360/80, letter/report to Gunnar Myrdal, 20 August 1948.

87. Arch-UNOG-ECE ARR 14/1360/80, Myrdal 1948.

88. Arch-UNOG-ECE ARR 14/1360/80, Myrdal 1948.

89. Arch-UNOG-E/ECE/ID/2, 14 August 1948, Special Committee for Industrial Development and Foreign Trade.

90. On the U.S. position, see the telegram "The Deputy United States Representative of the Economic Commission for Europe (Porter) to the Secretary of State," in *Foreign Relations of the United States*, 1948, Eastern Europe; The Soviet Union, Vol. IV (Washington, D.C.: Government Printing Office, 1979), Document 362, p. 571: https://history.state.gov/historicaldocuments/frus1948v04/d362.

91. See the explicit position of the U.S. representative in the telegram "The Secretary of State to the Consulate in Geneva," in *Foreign Relations of the United States*, 1948, Eastern Europe; The Soviet Union, Vol. IV, Document 355, p. 561: https://history.state.gov/historicaldocuments/frus1948v04/d355.

92. Mazower, *No Enchanted Palace*.

93. For a precise account of these negotiations based on Soviet, U.S., and British diplomatic archives, see Ilya V. Gaiduk, *Divided Together: The United States and the Soviet Union in the United Nations, 1945–1965* (Stanford, Calif.: Stanford University Press, 2012), 9–42.

2. THE EMERGENCE OF A "SECOND WORLD"

1. For a complete presentation of Asia-related issues, see Odd Arne Westad, *The Cold War: A World History* (New York: Basic Books, 2017), 129–82.

2. For a precise description, see Mario Bettati, "L'admission des deux Allemagnes à l'O.N.U.," *Annuaire français de droit international* 19, no. 1 (1973): 211–31.

3. This is conveyed well by Ilya V. Gaiduk, *Divided Together: The United States and the Soviet Union in the United Nations, 1945–1965*, 195–202; and Evan Luard, *A History of the United Nations*, vol. 1, *The Years of Western Domination, 1945–1955* (London: Palgrave Macmillan, 1982).

4. See the critical position of Albert O. Hirschman, "Grandeur et décadence de l'économie du développement," *Annales* 36, no. 5 (1981): 725–44; and Gilbert Rist, *Le Développement: histoire d'une croyance occidentale* (Paris: Presses de Sciences Po, 2015), 199–222. I will revisit this topic in greater detail in chapter 5.

5. For such an interpretation for the interwar and post–Cold war periods, see Ivan Berend, *Central and Eastern Europe, 1944–1993: Detour from the Periphery to the Periphery* (Cambridge: Cambridge University Press, 2010).

6. On this contradiction, see Régine Perron, *Histoire du multilatéralisme: l'utopie du siècle américain de 1918 à nos jours* (Paris: PUPS, 2014), 195–205.

2. THE EMERGENCE OF A "SECOND WORLD"

7. Simon Godard, *Le Laboratoire de l'internationalisme: le CAEM et la construction du bloc socialiste (1949–1991)* (Paris: Sciences Po, 2021).

8. See especially Edward H. Buehrig, "The United States, the United Nations and Bi-Polar Politics," *International Organization* 4, no. 4 (1950): 573–84. For a more nuanced point of view, see Gaiduk, *Divided Together*.

9. On the presence of U.S. actors in the League of Nations system, see Ludovic Tournès, *Les États-Unis et la Société des Nations: 1914–1946. Le système international face à l'émergence d'une superpuissance* (Bern: Peter Lang, 2016).

10. Vladislav M. Zubok, *A Failed Empire: The Soviet Union in the Cold War from Stalin to Gorbachev*, New Cold War History (Chapel Hill: University of North Carolina Press, 2007), 51–61.

11. Serge Wolikow, *L'Internationale communiste (1919–1943): le Komintern ou le rêve déchu du parti mondial de la révolution* (Paris: Les Éditions de l'Atelier/Éditions ouvrières, 2010); Brigitte Studer, *Reisende der Weltrevolution eine Globalgeschichte der Kommunistischen Internationale* (Berlin: Suhrkamp, 2021); and Silvio Pons, *The Global Revolution: A History of International Communism 1917–1991* (Oxford: Oxford University Press, 2014), 144–68.

12. Vladislav M. Zubok, "The Soviet Union and European Integration from Stalin to Gorbachev," *Journal of European Integration History* 2, no. 1 (1996): 85–98.

13. Natalia Egorova, "La formation du bloc de l'Est comme frontière occidentale du système communiste (1947–1955)," in *Frontières du communisme*, Recherches, ed. Sophie Coeuré and Sabine Dullin (Paris: La Découverte, 2007), 248–71.

14. Sabine Dullin, *La Frontière épaisse: aux origines des politiques soviétiques (1920–1940)* (Paris: Éd. de l'EHESS, 2014).

15. Konstantin Azadovskii and Boris Egorov, "From Anti-Westernism to Anti-Semitism," *Journal of Cold War Studies* 4, no. 1 (2002): 66–80.

16. Vladislav M. Zubok and Constantine Pleshakov, *Inside the Kremlin's Cold War: From Stalin to Khrushchev* (Cambridge, Mass.: Harvard University Press, 1996), 37–77. The two authors, whose study focuses on leaders, consider Stalin's diplomacy as being "poor."

17. Sabine Dullin, "Une diplomatie plébéienne? Profils et compétences des diplomates soviétiques 1936–1945," *Cahiers du monde russe. Russie-Empire russe-Union soviétique et États indépendants* 44, no. 2–3 (2003): 437–64. The role of those with language skills (especially written) increased after 1953 (22).

18. See especially Arch-ILO Z 1/64/1/1 (J3), meeting between Thomson and Yelden (ILO) with a Russian, Belorussian, and Ukrainian delegation, 31 January 1955.

19. Arch-UN-NYC S 0441-0075-4, letter from Roland Berger, manager of the Eastern European sector, to Raphael Cilento.

20. Arch-UN-NYC S 0441-0086-12, letter from Henri Laugier, 21 May 1948.

21. Lars Haga, "Imaginer la démocratie populaire: l'institut d'économie mondiale et la carte mentale soviétique de l'Europe de l'Est (1944–1948)," *Vingtième Siècle. Revue d'histoire* 109 (2011): 12–30.

22. Arch-UNOG-ECE ARR 14/1360 Box 95, letter from Gunnar Myrdal 16 July 1953 to Adrian Pelt, director of the UN office in Geneva.

23. Arch-UNOG-ECE GX 18/9/1/47.

24. David Caute, *The Great Fear: The Anti-Communist Purge Under Truman and Eisenhower* (New York: Simon and Schuster, 1978).

2. THE EMERGENCE OF A "SECOND WORLD"

25. Éric Toussaint, *Banque mondiale, le coup d'État permanent. L'agenda caché du consensus de Washington* (Paris: CADTM, 2006), 35.
26. Luard, *A History*, 354–56.
27. Chloé Maurel, "L'UNESCO de 1945 à 1974," Ph.D. diss., Université Panthéon-Sorbonne, Paris, 2006, https://tel.archives-ouvertes.fr/tel-00848712, 241–42.
28. E. K. Abel, E. Fee, and T. M. Brown, "Milton I. Roemer Advocate of Social Medicine, International Health, and National Health Insurance," *American Journal of Public Health* 98, no. 9 (2008): 1596–97. On the general context of suspicion toward internationalist physicians in the United States, see Jane Pacht Brickman, "Medical McCarthyism and the Punishment of Internationalist Physicians in the United States," in *Comrades in Health, U.S. Health Internationalists, Abroad and at Home*, ed. Anne-Emanuelle Birn and Theodore M. Brown (New Brunswick, N.J.: Rutgers University Press, 2013), 82–100.
29. See Aurélien Zaragori, "L'Organisation internationale du travail et les milieux chrétiens (1919–1969)," Ph.D. diss., université Lyon 3, 2018, 555–65.
30. RArchC Cox. Reece RG 3.2 21, 447–48.
31. RArchC RG1.1 789 C, 4, "Letter Elizabeth Brackett," 2 November 1949.
32. RArchC RG1 789.1.
33. RArchC, RG2 712 E 465 3120, letter from Dagmar Eisnerova to Charles Fahs, 16 January 1949.
34. On Štampar, see Sara Silverstein, "The Periphery Is the Centre: Some Macedonian Origins of Social Medicine and Internationalism," *Contemporary European History* 28, no. 2 (May 2019): 220–33.
35. RArchC RG 1.1-710-5, letter from Chas. N. Leach to G. K. Strode, 30 May 1946.
36. RArchC FA418 1 21 451; see the letter from Edward F. D'Arms to Elenerova, 28 January 1949.
37. Marc J. Selverstone, *Constructing the Monolith: The United States, Great Britain, and International Communism, 1945–1950* (Cambridge, Mass.: Harvard University Press, 2009).
38. Arch-UN-NYC S 0441-0075-4, letter of 28 December 1949 from Maurice Milhaud, head of the Department of Social Activities in Geneva, to Raphael Cilento, director of the Division of Social Activities, Lake Success.
39. On UNICEF, see Marta Aleksandra Balińska, *Une vie pour l'humanitaire: Ludwik Rajchman (1881–1965)* (Paris: La Découverte, 2015), 349–50. For all that, after receiving a visit from a team of experts in 1950, Polish authorities continued to request equipment from UNICEF and also applied for fellowships. See Arch-UN-NYC S 0441 0078-03, letter of 8 May 1950.
40. For Czechoslovakia, see especially Archives of the Central Committee of the Communist Party of Czechoslovakia (international office) KSČ ÚV–100/3 (Mezinárodní oddělení ÚV), file 12, unit 31.
41. Arch-ILO SI 2-0-17.
42. Alexander W. Rudzinski, "The Influence of the United Nations on Soviet Policy," *International Organization* 5 (1951): 282–99.
43. Jane Degras, ed., *The Communist International 1919–1943: Documents*, vol. 1 (London: Royal Institute of International Affairs, 1955), 89. More generally on this point, see Mark Mazower, *Governing the World: The History of an Idea* (London: Penguin Press, 2012), 126–28.

2. THE EMERGENCE OF A "SECOND WORLD"

44. Gaiduk, *Divided Together*, 195–202.

45. See Oscar Sanchez-Sibony, *Red Globalization: The Political Economy of the Soviet Cold War from Stalin to Khrushchev* (Cambridge: Cambridge University Press, 2016), 65–80; Sanchez-Sibony, "Capitalism's Fellow Traveler: The Soviet Union, Bretton Woods, and the Cold War, 1944–1958," *Comparative Studies in Society and History* 56, no. 2 (2014): 290–319.

46. Francis Snyder, "The Origins of the 'Nonmarket Economy': Ideas, Pluralism and Power in EC Anti-Dumping Law About China," *European Law Journal* 7 (2001): 377–79.

47. Michel Kostecki, *East-West Trade and the GATT System* (London: Palgrave, 1979), 2–4.

48. See Sandrine Kott, "OIT, justice sociale et mondes communistes. Concurrences, émulations, convergences," *Le Mouvement social* (April–June 2018): 139–51.

49. Anthony Alcock, *History of the International Labour Organization* (New York: Octagon Books, 1971), 130–33.

50. See the debate that also opposed Christian workers and socialists in *International Labour Conference. Record of Proceedings* (Geneva: ILO, 1937): 297–303.

51. For an account of this episode, see Alcock, *History*, 290–311; Victor-Yves Ghebali, *The International Labour Organization: A Case Study on the Evolution of U.N. Specialised Agencies* (Dordrecht, Neth.: Martinus Nijhoff, 1989), 164–75.

52. Minutes from the Board of Directors session A 131, 6–10 March 1956, "Report of the Committee on Freedom of Employers' and Workers' Organizations." See also *International Labour Conference. Record of Proceedings* (Geneva, 1956), 133–61.

53. Arch-ILO Z 1/1/1/25 (J1). The documents regarding employer relations demonstrate their opposition to the International Labour Office from 1952 onward (the date of Convention 102 on social security, which they saw as socialism). They used the issue of employer representation from the East to attack the ILO as an international social agency.

54. "Memorandum Prepared in the Department of State for the White House," 29 May 1953, in *Foreign Relations of the United States, 1952–1954*: Vol. 3, *United Nations Affairs*, ed. William Z. Slany and Ralph R. Goodwin (Washington, D.C.: Government Printing Office, 1979), Document 23, https://history.state.gov /historicaldocuments/frus1952-54v03/d23. On the context, see Kenneth Alan Osgood, *Total Cold War: Eisenhower's Secret Propaganda Battle at Home and Abroad* (Lawrence: University of Kansas, 2008), 52–53.

55. See Ian Jackson, *The Economic Cold War: America, Britain and East-West Trade, 1948–63* (Basingstoke, UK: St. Martin's Press, 2001).

56. For an economic analysis of the plan, see Alan Milward, *The Reconstruction of Western Europe, 1945–1951* (London: Methuen, 1987).

57. For an overview, see John Agnew and J. Nicholas Entrikin, *The Marshall Plan Today: Model and Metaphor* (London: Routledge, 2004).

58. For example, see Diane B. Kunz, "The Marshall Plan Reconsidered: A Complex of Motives," *Foreign Affairs* 76 (1997): 162–70; Anthony Carew, *Labour Under the Marshall Plan: The Politics of Productivity and the Marketing of Management Science* (Manchester, UK: Manchester University Press, 1987), 92–110.

59. Werner Abelshauser, *Deutsche Wirtschaftsgeschichte seit 1945* (Munich: Beck, 2004), Lizenz BZpB (distributed by the Bundeszentrale für politische Bildung),

2. THE EMERGENCE OF A "SECOND WORLD"

130–54; Dominique Barjot, "Introduction," in *La Reconstruction économique de l'Europe (1945–1953). Histoire, économie & société* 18 (1999): 227–43.

60. For two somewhat different visions, see Luc Boltanski, "America, America . . . le plan Marshall et l'importation du management américain," *Actes de la recherche en sciences sociales* 38 (1981): 19–41; Bent Boel, *The European Productivity Agency and Transatlantic Relations, 1953–1961* (Copenhagen: Museum Tusculanum Press/ University of Copenhagen, 2003).

61. Gérard Bossuat, *L'Europe occidentale à l'heure américaine: le Plan Marshall et l'unité européenne (1945–1952)* (Brussels: Éditions Complexe, 1992), 93–120.

62. See the exception in Anderson, *A Dollar to Poland Is a Dollar to Russia: US Economic Policy Toward Poland, 1945–1952* (New York: Garland, 1993), 109–209.

63. On this and the ensuing points, see Scott D. Parrish and Mikhail M. Narinsky, "New Evidence on the Soviet Rejection of the Marshall Plan, 1947: Two Reports," Cold War International History Project Working Papers Series, no. 9 (1994), https://www.wilsoncenter.org/sites/default/files/ACFB73.pdf.

64. See especially Oleg Timofeevich Bogomolov, *Socialisme et compétitivité: les pays de l'Est dans l'économie mondiale* (Paris: Presses de la Fondation nationale des sciences politiques, 1989), 69–144; Marie Lavigne, *Les Économies socialistes soviétique et européennes*, 3rd ed., rev. and updated (Paris: Colin, 1979), 345–82; Uwe Müller and Dagmara Jajesniak-Quast, eds., "Comecon Revisited: Integration in the Eastern Bloc and Entanglements with the Global Economy," *Comparativ* 27 (2018); and Godard, *Le Laboratoire de l'internationalisme*, 19–76.

65. See Thomas David, *Nationalisme économique et industrialisation: l'expérience des pays d'Europe de l'Est (1789–1939)* (Geneva: Droz, 2009), 199–233.

66. On this topic, see the observations of William Diebold, Jr., "East-West Trade and the Marshall Plan," *Foreign Affairs* 26 (1948): 709–22.

67. Laurien Crump and Simon Godard, "Reassessing Communist International Organisations: A Comparative Analysis of COMECON and the Warsaw Pact in Relation to Their Cold War Competitors," *Contemporary European History* 27, no. 1 (2017): 1–25; Godard, "Another Europe, Rather than the Other Europe? COMECON's Ambiguous Shaping of Europe (from 1962 to the Helsinki Process)," *Politique européenne* 76, no. 2 (2022).

68. Diane B. Kunz, *Butter and Guns: America's Cold War Economic Diplomacy* (New York: Free Press, 1997); Jackson, *The Economic Cold War*.

69. Carew, *Labour Under the Marshall Plan*. For a moderate but realist assessment, see Jack Kantrowitz, "L'influence américaine sur Force ouvrière: mythe ou réalité?," *Revue française de science politique* 28 (1978): 717–39.

70. Milward, *The Reconstruction of Western Europe*, 77–79.

71. Arch-UNOG-ECE GX/10/2/1/12CzECE; see letter from E. V. Rostow to Ludwik Frejke, 7 February 1950.

72. Arch-UNOG-ECE/COAL/AWP/19, 7–8.

73. The commission was already aware of the problem relating to the balance of payments deficit, as well as the dependence of the concerned countries on the dollar zone: Yves Berthelot and Paul Rayment, *Looking Back and Peering Forward: A Short History of the United Nations Economic Commission for Europe, 1947–2007* (New York: UN, 2007), 25–27.

74. Diebold, Jr., "East-West Trade," 709–722.

2. THE EMERGENCE OF A "SECOND WORLD"

75. Arch-UNOG-ECE GX 10/2/1/12/CZ, letter from Walt Rostow to his brother.
76. Arch-UNOG-ECE/COAL/SR.8/1, 26.
77. Jackson, *Economic Cold War*, 17–25.
78. Anderson, *A Dollar to Poland*, 140–47.
79. Michael Mastanduno, "Trade as a Strategic Weapon: American and Alliance Export Control Policy in the Early Postwar Period," *International Organization* 42, no. 1 (1988): 121–50; Anderson, *A Dollar to Poland*, 146.
80. Arch-UNOG-ECE ARR 14/1360/80, letter from Walter Rostow during a trip to Prague in August 1948.
81. Vincent Lagendijk, "The Structure of Powers: the UNECE and East-West Electricity Connections, 1947–1975," *Comparativ. Zeitschrift für Globalgeschichte und vergleichende Gesellschaftsforschung* 24, no. 1 (2014): 50–65.
82. Michael Mastanduno, *Economic Containment: CoCom and the Politics of East-West Trade* (Ithaca, N.Y.: Cornell University Press, 1992); Tor Egil Førland, "'Economic Warfare' and 'Strategic Goods': A Conceptual Framework for Analyzing COCOM," *Journal of Peace Research* 28, no. 2 (1991): 191–204. Mastanduno believes that this economic war transformed into an embargo in 1954, while for Førland economic war continued even after the easing of 1954.
83. Robert Mark Spaulding, *Osthandel and Ostpolitik: German Trade Policies in Eastern Europe from Bismarck to Adenauer* (Providence: Berghahn Books, 1997), 296–349. See also the archives of the German chamber of commerce, Institut für Zeitgeschichte (IFZ), Munich, ED 347/37, Nachlass Riedberg Gerhard, Minutes of German ICC National Committee, Niederschrift über die Präsidialsitzung am 18 September in Frankfurt a. M, 18 September 1956, 4.
84. See Klaus Ammann, "Swiss Trade with the East in the Early Cold War," in *East-West Trade and the Cold War*, ed. Jari Eloranta and Jari Ojala (Jyväskylä, Fin.: University of Jyväskylä, 2005), 114–31.
85. Jacqueline McGlade, "Cocom and the Containment of Western Trade and Relations," in Eloranta and Ojala, *East-West Trade*, 47–61.
86. This delegation of power was especially clear during Morse's trip to Czechoslovakia in April 1958. On a number of occasions, Morse told Czech officials that the issue had to be resolved by a discussion between U.S. and Soviet leaders. Arch-ILO Z 3/64/2.
87. Arch-ILO P 7594, 7594, and P 8891. Koudriatzev had pursued a career in international textile unionism. He spoke only Russian and French (not English, which he learned during his time at the International Labour Office). Unlike Koudriatzev, Orlov came from the diplomatic service. He spoke Russian, German, and English (but not French).
88. Arch-ILO, "Director General Mission to Czechoslovakia (September 1964)," Z 3/31/1, "Director General Mission to Hungary," 1965; Z 8/3/66, "Mr. P. D. Orlov," 1960–1966.
89. See Gaiduk, *Divided Together*, 238–40; Godard, "Construire le 'bloc' par l'économie: configuration des territoires et des identités socialistes au Conseil d'aide économique mutuelle (CAEM), 1949–1989," Ph.D. diss., University of Geneva, 2014, 10.13097/archive-ouverte/unige: 45004.
90. See the clarification provided in Grosser, *Les Temps*, 19–49.

2. THE EMERGENCE OF A "SECOND WORLD"

91. For the numbers, see Thérèse Brosse, *L'Enfance victime de la guerre. Une étude de la situation européenne* (Paris: UNESCO, 1949).
92. Celia Donert, "Women's Rights in Cold War Europe: Disentangling Feminist Histories," *Past & Present* 218 (2013): 180–202.
93. Friedrich Engels, *The Origin of the Family, Private Property and the State*, trans. Alick West, rev. Mark Harris and Martin Swayne, https://www.marxists.org /archive/marx/works/1884/origin-family/index.htm.
94. Catriona Kelly, "Defending Children's Rights, 'In Defense of Peace': Children and Soviet Cultural Diplomacy," in *Imagining the West in Eastern Europe and the Soviet Union*, ed. Gyorgy Peteri (Pittsburgh: Pittsburgh University Press, 2010), 59.
95. "Comptes rendus de la Conférence internationale du travail," Geneva, 1937, 137.
96. On this discussion in relation to the UN Commission, see Eileen Boris, "Equality's Cold War: The ILO and the UN Commission on the Status of Women, 1946-1970s"; and Silke Neunsinger, "The Unobtainable Magic of Numbers: Equal Remuneration, the ILO and the International Trade Union Movement 1950s–1980s," in *Women's ILO: Transnational Networks, Global Labour Standards and Gender Equity, 1919 to Present*, ed. Eileen Boris, Dorothea Hoehtker, and Susan Zimmermann (Leiden: Brill, 2018), 97–120 and 121–49, respectively.
97. For an analysis of this discourse, see Kristen Ghodsee, "Revisiting the United Nations Decade for Women: Brief Reflections on Feminism, Capitalism and Cold War Politics in the Early Years of the International Women's Movement," *Women's Studies International Forum* 32, no. 6 (December 2009): 3–12.
98. "Report of the FAO Mission for Poland, Food and Agriculture Organization of the United Nations," Washington, D.C., 1948, 8. See chapter 1 of this volume for the context in which this report was developed.
99. On this discussion, see Sandrine Kott and Françoise Thébaud, eds., "Le 'socialisme réel' à l'épreuve du genre," *CLIO. Femmes, Genre, Histoire* 41 (2015).
100. The full text of the convention is available at https://www.unhcr.org/protect /PROTECTION/3b66c2aa10.pdf.
101. Marga Vicedo, "The Social Nature of the Mother's Tie to Her Child: John Bowlby's Theory of Attachment in Post-War America," *British Journal for the History of Science* 44 (2011): 401–26.
102. See Tara Zahra, *The Lost Children: Reconstructing Europe's Families After World War II* (Cambridge, Mass.: Harvard University Press, 2015), 222–40.
103. Sandrine Kott, "Die Kinderkrippe," in *Erinnerungsorte der DDR*, ed. Martin Sabrow (Munich: Beck, 2009), 281–91.
104. See the grant requests in Arch-UN NY S 0441 0078-03.
105. Gabriele Arndt, *Das wissenschaftliche Werk Eva Schmidt-Kolmers unter besonderer Berücksichtigung ihrer Beiträge zum Kinder- und Jugendgesundheitsschutz in der DDR*, Diss. med., Greifswald, 2001; Michel Christian, "Un autre printemps des crèches? Le développement des crèches est-allemandes des années 1950 aux années 1980," *Annales de démographie historique* 137, no. 1 (2019): 185–215.
106. Robert Colin, "Création d'un centre international de l'enfance à Paris," *Population* 5 (1950): 199–200; Balińska, *Une vie*, 359–61; Yves Denéchère and Patrice Marcilloux, eds., *Le Centre international de l'enfance (1949–1997). Des archives à l'histoire* (Rennes: Presses universitaires de Rennes, 2016).

2. THE EMERGENCE OF A "SECOND WORLD"

107. Cited in Denéchère and Marcilloux, *Le Centre international*, 59.
108. Catherine Bouve, *Les Crèches collectives: usagers et représentations sociales. Contribution à une sociologie de la petite enfance* (Paris: L'Harmattan, 2005), S. 63–64. See also the website for the Pikler Lóczy Association in France, http://www.pikler.fr/.
109. Myriam David and Geneviève Appell, *Lóczy ou le maternage insolite* (Paris: Éditions du Scarabée, 1973).
110. Education could also be added to this list, for which see Charles Dorn and Kristen Ghodsee, "The Cold War Politicization of Literacy: Communism, UNESCO, and the World Bank," *Diplomatic History* 36, no. 2 (April 2012): 373–98.
111. Kott, "OIT, justice sociale et mondes communistes," 139–51.
112. *International Labour Conference. Record of Proceedings* (Geneva), 1935, 225–31; 1936, 141–45; and 1937, 136–38.
113. Archives of the Central Committee of the Communist Party of Czechoslovakia (International Bureau) KSČ ÚV—100/3 (Mezinárodní oddělení ÚV), file 12, unit 31. I thank Ondrej Matejka for this information.
114. Reformist trade unionism (the TUC in Great Britain, the DGB in Germany, and the CIO in the United States), along with the new union confederations supported by the CIA (FO-CGT in France), joined the new global union federation. Geert van Goethem, "Labor's Second Front: The Foreign Policy of the American and British Trade Union Movements During the Second World War," *Diplomatic History* 34, no. 4 (2010): 663–80; Jean-François Michel, "La scission de la Fédération syndicale mondiale (1947–1949)," *Le Mouvement social* 117 (1981): 33–52.
115. See Arch-IISH, ICFTU-1895, "International board meeting 25–27 May 1950, item 15 machinery as a counter-mechanism to the attacks of the WFTU."
116. See the WFTU archives in Prague, SOF, LIRO 108, 1956, 590a, press kit and correspondence on being expelled from Vienna.
117. Harold Karan Jacobson, *The USSR and the UN's Economic and Social Activities* (Notre Dame, Ind.: University of Notre Dame Press, 1963); and Jacobson Karan, "Labor, The UN and the Cold War," *International Organization* 11, no. 1 (1957): 55–67.
118. Arch-IISH, ICFTU-1895, contains various files regarding these relations with the WFTU between 1950 and 1955.
119. Arch-ILO Z 8/1/15 (J3), "Meetings of the Directorate: Reports, 1948–1964."
120. The convention is available at https://www.ilo.org/dyn/normlex/fr/f?p=NORMLEXPUB:12100:0::NO::P12100_ILO_CODE:C087.
121. See the numerous cases in the files Arch-ILO TUR (fifty-year embargo), especially for Czechoslovakia, Arch-ILO TUR 1-17-1, and for the GDR after 17 June 1953, Arch-ILO TUR 1-24-B 123 1955.
122. Arch-ILO TUR 1-61-D.

3. INTERNATIONALISMS DURING THE COLD WAR

1. Frederick H. Gareau, "The Soviet Bloc and the United Nations System: The Quantitative Record," *Western Political Quarterly* 25, no. 2 (1972): 268–94; Kazimierz Grzybowski, "International Organizations from the Soviet Point of View," *Law and*

3. INTERNATIONALISMS DURING THE COLD WAR

Contemporary Problems 29, no. 4 (1964): 882–95; Harold Karan Jacobson, *The USSR and the UN's Economic and Social Activities* (Notre Dame, Ind.: University of Notre Dame Press, 1963); and Alvin Z. Rubinstein, *The Soviets in International Organizations: Changing Policy Toward Developing Countries, 1953–1963* (Princeton, N.J.: Princeton University Press, 1964).

2. Louis Porter, "Cold War Internationalisms: The USSR in UNESCO, 1945–1967," PhD diss., University of North Carolina, 2018, 75–133.

3. Cited by Diane B. Kunz, *Butter and Guns: America's Cold War Economic Diplomacy* (New York: Free Press, 1997), 95. See also Marshall E. Dimock, "Management in the USSR—Comparisons to the United States," *Public Administration Review* 20, no. 3 (1960): 139–47.

4. The title of this section was inspired by that of Ilya V. Gaiduk's book, *Divided Together: The United States and the Soviet Union in the United Nations, 1945–1965* (Stanford, Calif.: Stanford University Press, 2012).

5. András Nagy, "Shattered Hopes Amid Violent Repression: The Hungarian Revolution and the United Nations (Part 1)," *Journal of Cold War Studies* 19, no. 4 (2017): 42–73; Evan Luard, *A History of the United Nations*, vol. 2: *The Age of Decolonization, 1955–1965*, 2nd ed. (London: Palgrave Macmillan, 2016), 58–75.

6. A detailed account of these crises can be found in Georges-Henri Soutou, *La Guerre froide: 1943–1990* (Paris: Pluriel, 2011), 445–98. On the UN's role, see Luard, *A History of the United Nations*, 2:18–74, 377–407.

7. Eva-Maria Muschik, *Building States: The United Nations, Development, and Decolonization, 1945–1965* (New York: Columbia University Press, 2022).

8. Oscar Sanchez-Sibony, *Red Globalization: The Political Economy of the Soviet Cold War from Stalin to Khrushchev* (Cambridge: Cambridge University Press, 2016), 92.

9. Arch-IFZ ED 347–37.

10. Francine McKenzie, "GATT and the Cold War: Accession Debates, Institutional Development, and the Western Alliance, 1947–1959," *Journal of Cold War Studies* 10, no. 3 (2008): 78–109.

11. See especially, for the FRG, Karsten Rudolph, *Wirtschaftsdiplomatie im Kalten Krieg: die Ostpolitik der westdeutschen Großindustrie 1945–1991* (Frankfurt: Campus-Verlag, 2004); Sven Jüngerkes, *Diplomaten der Wirtschaft: die Geschichte des Ost-Ausschusses der Deutschen Wirtschaft* (Osnabrück, Ger.: Fibre, 2012), esp. 26–29. For the British case, see Ian Jackson, *The Economic Cold War: America, Britain and East-West Trade, 1948–63* (Basingstoke, U.K.: St. Martin's Press, 2001), 110–15.

12. Daniel Stinsky, *International Cooperation in Cold War Europe: The United Nations Economic Commission for Europe, 1947–64* (London: Bloomsbury, 2022), 130–220.

13. Arch-UNOG, ECE-ARR 2100, Box 34, message from president of the commission Oskar Lange, published in the book *ECE. The First Ten Years. 1947–1957*, June 19, 1957.

14. Arch-UNOG ARR 14/1360/8 and United Nations Press Release ECE/GEN/337, 21 April 1956.

15. For instance, for 1956, see Arch-UNOG-ECE GX 18/12/1/33.

16. See Stinsky, *International Cooperation*.

17. See Yves Berthelot and Paul Rayment, *Looking Back and Peering Forward: A Short History of the United Nations Economic Commission for Europe, 1947–2007* (New

York: UN, 2007), 64–74; and especially Frank Schipper, *Driving Europe: Building Europe on Roads in the Twentieth Century* (Amsterdam: Amsterdam University Press, 2009), 220–57.

18. Arch-ILO Z 3/64/2. See the role played in Poland by Jan Rosner, who submitted the first requests to the ILO in 1957.

19. Arch-UN NYC S-0175-1729-08.

20. Arch-UN NYC S-0175-1729-04.

21. Arch-ILO, OTA 50–1 (A) Fs.

22. Arch-UNOG ECE/GX/10/2/1/15, letters from 16 May 1958 and 30 March 1962.

23. See the excellent examples involving UNESCO in Porter, *Cold War*, 151–355.

24. Gaiduk, *Divided Together*, 255–58.

25. See Annie Kriegel, *Le Système communiste mondial* (Paris: PUF, 1984).

26. Frits L. van Holthoon and Marcel van der Linden, eds., *Internationalism in the Labour Movement: 1830–1940* (Leiden: Brill, 1988); Serge Wolikow, "Les interprétations du mouvement communiste international," in *Le Siècle des communismes*, ed. Michel Dreyfus et al. (Paris: Éditions de l'Atelier, 2000), 83–93.

27. Patrizia Dogliani, "The Fate of Socialist Internationalism," in *Internationalisms: A Twentieth-Century History*, ed. Glenda Sluga and Patricia Clavin (Cambridge: Cambridge University Press, 2016), 38–61. On the International Workingmen's Association more specifically, see Fabrice Bensimon, Quentin Deluermoz, and Jeanne Moisand, eds., *"Arise Ye Wretched of the Earth": The First International in a Global Perspective* (Leiden: Brill, 2019).

28. For this and what followed, see the issue of *Monde(s), communisme transnational* 2 (2016), especially the introduction by Sabine Dullin and Brigitte Studer, "L'équation retrouvée de l'internationalisme au premier xxe siècle"; see also Holger Weiss, ed., *International Communism and Transnational Solidarity: Radical Networks, Mass Movements and Global Politics, 1919–1939* (Leiden: Brill, 2017); Silvio Pons, *The Global Revolution: A History of International Communism, 1917–1991* (Oxford: Oxford University Press, 2014), 7–35; Serge Wolikow, "The Comintern as a World Network," in *The Cambridge History of Communism*, ed. Silvio Pons and Stephen Smith (Cambridge: Cambridge University Press, 2017), 232–55; and Wolikow, *Le Komintern ou le rêve déchu du parti mondial de la révolution* (Paris: Éditions ouvrières, 2011).

29. Stephen White, "Colonial Revolution and the Communist International, 1919–1924," *Science & Society* 40, no. 2 (July 1976): 173–93; Stephan Scheuzger, "Reading of Cosmopolitanism: Revolutionaries' Biographies in the Intersections of Marxism and Anti-colonialism in the Interwar Years," *Monde(s)* 10, no. 2 (2016): 151–66.

30. See David Mayer, "À la fois influente et marginale: l'Internationale communiste et l'Amérique latine," *Monde(s)* 10, no. 2 (2016): 109–28.

31. See Jean-François Fayet, *Karl Radek (1885–1939): biographie politique* (Bern: Peter Lang, 2004).

32. Lilly Marcou, *Le Kominform: le communisme de guerre froide* (Paris: Presses de la Fondation nationale des sciences politiques, 1977).

33. Arch-WFTU, box with no call number for 1968–1969.

34. Arch-IISH ICFTU 1889 and 1896

35. Arch-IISH ICFTU 1888 and 1893.

3. INTERNATIONALISMS DURING THE COLD WAR

36. Francisca de Haan, "Continuing Cold War Paradigms in Western Historiography of Transnational Women's Organisations: The Case of the Women's International Democratic Federation (WIDF)," *Women's History Review* 19, no. 4 (September 2010): 547–73; Celia Donert, "Femmes, communisme et internationalisme: La Fédération démocratique internationale des femmes en Europe centrale (1945–1979)," *Vingtième Siècle. Revue d'histoire* 126, vol. 7 (2015): 119–31; Kristen Ghodsee, "Internationalisme socialiste et féminisme d'État pendant la guerre froide. Les relations entre Bulgarie et Zambie," *Clio* 41 (2015): 115–38. A different approach can be found in Yulia Gradskova, "Women's international Democratic Federation, the 'Third World' and the Global Cold War from the Late-1950s to the Mid-1960s," *Women's History Review* (August 2019): 270–88.
37. See Lilly Marcou, *Le Mouvement communiste international depuis 1945* (Paris: PUF, 1990), 289–310.
38. Nick Rutter, "The Western Wall: The Iron Curtain Recast in Midsummer 1951," in *Cold War Crossings: International Travel and Exchange Across the Soviet Bloc, 1940s–1960s*, ed. Patryk Babiracki and Kenyon Zimmer (Arlington: Texas University Press, 2014), 78–107.
39. See Justine Faure and Sandrine Kott, eds., "Le bloc de l'Est en question," *Vingtième Siècle. Revue d'histoire* 109 (2011): 2–10.
40. E. A. Rees, "The Sovietization of Eastern Europe," in *The Sovietization of Eastern Europe: New Perspectives on the Postwar Period*, ed. Balázs Apor, Péter Apor, and E. A. Rees (Washington, D.C.: New Academia, 2008), 1–29.
41. Emmanuel Droit, *Les Polices politiques du bloc de l'Est. À la recherche de l'Internationale tchékiste 1955–1989* (Paris: Gallimard, 2019), 50–75.
42. Michel Christian, "Les partis communistes du bloc de l'Est: un objet transnational. L'exemple des écoles supérieures du parti," *Vingtième Siècle. Revue d'histoire* 109 (2011): 31–43; Christian, *Camarades ou apparatchiks? Les communistes en RDA et en Tchécoslovaquie: 1945–1989* (Paris: PUF, 2016).
43. Godard, *Le laboratoire de l'internationalisme*. For a good description of Comecon and other economic organizations of the bloc, see Marie Lavigne, *Les Économies socialistes, soviétique et européennes*, 3rd ed. rev. and updated (Paris: Armand Colin, 1979), 345–80.
44. Lucia Dragomir, "L'Union des écrivains. Un modèle institutionnel et ses limites," *Vingtième Siècle. Revue d'histoire* 109 (2011): 59–70.
45. Lars Haga, "Imaginer la démocratie populaire: The Institute of World Economics et la carte mentale soviétique de l'Europe de l'Est (1944–1948)," *Vingtième Siècle. Revue d'histoire* 109 (2011): 12–30.
46. On Romania, see Irina Gridan, "Du communisme national au national-communisme, réactions roumaines à la soviétisation dans les années 1960," *Vingtième Siècle. Revue d'histoire* 109 (2011): 113–27. On Hungary, see Aniko Macher, "La Hongrie entre tutelle soviétique et intérêt national au cours des années 1960," *Relations internationales* 148 (2011): 81–94.
47. Jacques Lévesque, "Essai sur la spécificité des relations entre l'URSS et l'Europe de l'Est de 1945 à 1989," *Relations internationales* 148 (2011): 7–16.
48. Jérôme Bazin, Pascal Dubourg Glatigny, and Piotr Piotrowski, eds., *Art Beyond Borders: Artistic Exchange in Communist Europe (1945–1989)* (Budapest: Central European University Press, 2016).

3. INTERNATIONALISMS DURING THE COLD WAR

49. Laurien Crump and Simon Godard, "Reassessing Communist International Organisations: A Comparative Analysis of COMECON and the Warsaw Pact in Relation to Their Cold War Competitors," *Contemporary European History* 27, no. 1 (2017): 1–25.

50. For example, see Elidor Mëhilli, "Socialist Encounters: Albania and the Transnational Eastern Bloc in the 1950s," in *Cold War Crossings: International Travel and Exchange Across the Soviet Bloc, 1940s–1960s*, ed. Patryk Babiracki and Kenyon Zimmer (Arlington: University of Texas Press, 2014), 40–78.

51. Caroline Moine, *Cinéma et guerre froide. Histoire du festival de films documentaires de Leipzig (1955–1990)* (Paris: Publications de la Sorbonne, 2014).

52. Bundeszenrale für politische Bildung, Weltfestspiele 1973, http://www.bpb.de /geschichte/deutsche-geschichte/weltfestspiele-73/.

53. Numerous works have recently documented this internationalism toward Third World countries. See especially Artemy Kalinovsky, Steffi Marung, and James Mark, eds., *Alternative Globalisations: Eastern Europe and the Postcolonial World* (Bloomington: Indiana University Press, 2020); James Mark and Paul Betts, eds., *Socialism Goes Global: The Soviet Union and Eastern Europe in the Age of Decolonization* (Oxford: Oxford University Press, 2022).

54. On these commissions and economic regionalism within the UN in general, see Yves Berthelot, *Unity and Diversity in Development Ideas Perspectives from the UN Regional Commissions* (Bloomington: Indiana University Press, 2004).

55. Abigail Judge Kret, "'We Unite with Knowledge': The Peoples' Friendship University and Soviet Education for the Third World," *Comparative Studies of South Asia, Africa and the Middle East* 33, no. 2 (2013): 239–56.

56. On GDR-Egypt relations, see Amélie Regnauld, "La RDA en Égypte, 1969–1989: la construction d'une politique étrangère. De la solidarité anti-impérialiste aux avantages réciproques," Ph.D. diss., université Paris 1, 2016.

57. Constantin Katsakioris, "Leçons soviétiques: la formation des étudiants africains et arabes en URSS pendant la guerre froide," Ph.D. diss., EHESS, 2015; "Soviet Lessons for Arab Modernization: Soviet Educational Aid Towards Arab Countries After 1956," *Journal of Modern European History* 8, no. 1 (2010): 85–106; and "L'Union soviétique et les intellectuels africains. Internationalisme, panafricanisme et négritude pendant les années de la décolonisation, 1954–1964," *Cahiers du monde russe. Russie-Empire russe-Union soviétique et États indépendants* 47, no. 1–2 (2006): 15–32.

58. Sandrine Kott and Cyrus Schayegh, "Eastern European-Middle Eastern Relations: Continuities and Changes from the Time of Empires to the Cold War," *Contemporary European History* 30, no. 4 (2021): 1–15.

59. Taline Ter Minassian, *Colporteurs du Komintern: l'Union soviétique et les minorités au Moyen-Orient* (Paris: Presses de Sciences Po, 1997); Hanna E. Jansen, "Peoples' Internationalism: Central Asian Modernisers Soviet Oriental Studies and Cultural Revolution in the East (1936–1977)," Ph.D. diss., University of Amsterdam, 2020.

60. See especially Katsakioris, "Soviet Lessons for Arab Modernization," 85–105; Constantin Katsakioris, "Les étudiants de pays arabes formés en Union soviétique pendant la guerre froide, 1956–1991," *Revue européenne des migrations internationales* 32, no. 2 (2016): 13–38.

3. INTERNATIONALISMS DURING THE COLD WAR

61. See Eric Burton, James Mark, and Steffi Marung, "Development," in *Socialism Goes Global: The Soviet Union and Eastern Europe in the Age of Decolonization*, ed. James Mark and Paul Betts (Oxford: Oxford University Press, 2022), 75–114. For the Bulgarian example, see Theodora Dragostinova, "The 'Natural Ally' of the 'Developing World': Bulgarian Culture in India and Mexico," *Slavic Review* 77, no. 3 (2018): 661–84.

62. Joseph L. Love, *Crafting the Third World: Theorizing Underdevelopment in Rumania and Brazil* (Stanford, Calif.: Stanford University Press, 1996); Love, "Theorizing Underdevelopment: Latin America and Romania, 1860–1950," *Estudos Avançados* 4, no. 8 (1990): 62–95.

63. Paul N. Rosenstein-Rodan, "Problems of Industrialisation of Eastern and South-Eastern Europe," *Economic Journal* 53, no. 210–11 (June–September 1943): 202–11; Rosenstein-Rodan, "The International Development of Economically Backward Areas," *International Affairs* 20, no. 2 (1944): 157–65.

64. Michele Alacevich, "Planning Peace: The European Roots of the Post-War Global Development Challenge," *Past & Present* 239, no. 1 (2018): 219–64. For a specific example, see also Małgorzata Mazurek, "Measuring Development: An Intellectual and Political History of Ludwik Landau's Scale of World Inequality," *Contemporary European History* 28, no. 2 (2019): 156–71.

65. See Georges-Henri Abtour, "L'URSS et l'Amérique latine pendant la guerre froide," *Outre-Mers. Revue d'histoire* 94, no. 354 (2007): 9–22; Tobias Ruprecht, *Soviet Internationalism After Stalin: Interaction and Exchange Between the USSR and Latin America During the Cold War* (Cambridge: Cambridge University Press, 2016).

66. Rubinstein, *The Soviets in International Organizations*, 162.

67. For a complete and partial presentation see Hanumanthu Lajipathi Rai, *Indo-Soviet Trade Relations* (New Delhi: Mittal Publications, 1991), 21–53. For a discussion on the significance of this aid in the context of the Cold War, see David C. Engerman, *The Price of Aid: The Economic Cold War in India* (Cambridge, Mass.: Harvard University Press, 2018), 121–34.

68. Arch-UN E/CN.11/SR. 150, p. 236–238, "Records of meeting 11. Session, 1955."

69. Sara Lorenzini, "Comecon and the South in the Years of *Détente*: A Study on East-South Economic Relations," *European Review of History. Revue européenne d'histoire* 21, no. 2 (2014): 183–99.

70. Rubinstein, *The Soviets in International Organizations*, 78–80.

71. Alessandro Iandolo, "The Rise and Fall of the 'Soviet Model of Development' in West Africa, 1957–64," *Cold War History* 12, no. 4 (2012): 683–704.

72. Monique de Saint Martin and Patrice Yengo, eds., "Élites de retour de l'Est. Quelles contributions des élites 'rouges' au façonnement des États post-coloniaux?," *Cahiers d'Études africaines* 226, no. 2 (2017): 231–58. For the specific case of the GDR and Egypt, see Amélie Regnauld, "Les limites du 'remodelage socialiste:' les Égyptiens formés en RDA (1969–1989)," *Revue européenne des migrations internationales* 32, no. 2 (2016): 57–76.

73. "Report of the Committee on Freedom of Employers' and Workers' Organizations," board of directors meeting minutes, 131st session, 6–10 March 1956. See also the discussion in *International Labour Conference. Record of Proceedings*, Geneva, 1956, 133–61.

3. INTERNATIONALISMS DURING THE COLD WAR

74. M. Bhaktavatsalam (Indian government representative), *International Labour Conference. Records of Proceedings*, Geneva, 1956, 136–37.
75. See Bernd Faulenbach, *Antikommunismus*, Docupedia Zeitgeschichte, 3 May 2017, http://docupedia.de/zg/faulenbach_antikommunismus_v1_de_2017.
76. See Michel Caillat, "L'Entente internationale anticommuniste de Theodore Aubert. Organisation interne, réseaux et action d'une internationale anti-marxiste," Ph.D. diss., University of Geneva, 2013. See also Caillat et al., "Une source inédite de l'histoire de l'anticommunisme: les archives de l'Entente internationale anticommuniste (EIA) de Théodore Aubert (1924–1950)," *Matériaux pour l'histoire de notre temps* 73 (2004): 25–31.
77. Stéphanie Roulin, *Un credo anticommuniste. La commission Pro Deo de l'Entente Internationale Anticommuniste ou la dimension religieuse d'un combat politique (1924–1945)* (Lausanne: Antipodes, 2010).
78. For an overview, see Luc Van Dongen, Stéphanie Roulin, and Giles Scott-Smith, eds., *Transnational Anti-Communism and the Cold War Agents, Activities, and Networks* (Basingstoke, UK: Palgrave Macmillan, 2014).
79. Markku Ruotsila, "Transnational Anti-Communism and the Cold War: Agents, Activities, and Networks," in Van Dongen, Roulin, and Scott-Smith, *Transnational Anti-Communism*, 235–50.
80. Johannes Grossmann, "The Comité international de défense de la civilisaton chrétienne and the Transnationalisation of Anti-Communist Propaganda After the Second World War," in Van Dongen, Roulin, and Scott-Smith, *Transnational Anti-Communism*, 251–62.
81. On the Congress for Cultural Freedom, see Pierre Grémion, *Intelligence de l'anticommunisme. Le Congrès pour la liberté de la culture à Paris (1950–1975)* (Paris: Fayard, 1995). For an apologetic vision on the International Commission of Jurists, see Howard B. Tolley, *The International Commission of Jurists: Global Advocates for Human Rights* (Philadelphia: University of Pennsylvania Press, 1994). For a more critical view, see Yves Dezalay and Bryant Garth, "Droits de l'homme et philanthropie hégémonique," *Actes de la recherche en sciences sociales* 121 (1998): 23–41, esp. 25–26.
82. Nicolas Guilhot, "A Network of Influential Friendships: The Fondation pour une entraide intellectuelle européenne and East-West Cultural Dialogue, 1957–1991," *Minerva* 44, no. 4 (2006): 379–409.
83. Bernard Ludwig, "La paix et l'Europe dans la propagande anticommuniste du réseau Paix et Liberté," *Matériaux pour l'histoire de notre temps* 108 (2012): 39–45; Ludwig, "La propagande anticommuniste en Allemagne fédérale," *Vingtième Siècle. Revue d'histoire* 80, no. 4 (2003): 33–42.
84. Arch-IFZ-ED347-37, "Über die Präsidialsitzung am 18. September (1956) in Frankfurt a. M." In addition to the collaboration of major German employers in the Nazi project, recent research focusing on the various ministries under Nazism and during the first years of the FRG has shown that the senior civil service was not denazified. For a quick overview, see Christian Mentel et al., *Die zentralen deutschen Behörden und der Nationalsozialismus: Stand und Perspektiven der Forschung* (Munich: IFZ, ZZF, 2016).
85. For France, see the "Socialism or Barbarism" movement active between 1948 and 1967, and the importance of the book by the philosopher and former director of an industrial combine, Rudolf Bahro, *L'Alternative* (Paris: Stock, 1979).

3. INTERNATIONALISMS DURING THE COLD WAR

86. On the specific role of the FBI in this anticommunist wave, see, for the preceding period, Regin Schmid, *Red Scare: FBI and the Origins of Anticommunism in the United States, 1919–1943* (Copenhagen: Copenhagen Museum Tusculanum Press, University of Copenhagen, 2000).

87. Friederike Kind-Kovács, "Voices, Letters, and Literature Through the Iron Curtain: Exiles and the (Trans)mission of Radio in the Cold War," *Cold War History* 13, no. 2 (2013): 193–219; Volker Rolf Berghahn, *America and the Intellectual Cold Wars in Europe: Shepard Stone Between Philanthropy, Academy, and Diplomacy* (Princeton, N.J.: Princeton University Press, 2001), esp. 143–276.

88. See also Igor Czernecki, "An Intellectual Offensive: The Ford Foundation and the Destalinization of the Polish Social Sciences," *Cold War History* 13, no. 3 (2013): 289–310.

89. RArchC FF FA 748, series V, Box 7.

90. RArchC FF FA 748, series V, Box 7, Shepard Stone report from September 1957.

91. RArchC FA 748, series V, Box 7, "Dickey's report," 27 February 1961.

92. The IUCTG's archives are located at Indiana University. A description of the collection is available at http://webapp1.dlib.indiana.edu/findingaids/view?doc.view =entire_text&docId=InU-Ar-VAB8814.

93. RArchC FFFA 748, series V, Box 7, letter of 26 January 1968, "Prospect to the East European Program CE Black."

94. P. Angoulevent, "Nouvelle orientation de la politique commerciale en Yougoslavie," *Économie et statistique* 5, no. 4 (1950): 86–95.

95. Marc J. Selverstone, *Constructing the Monolith: The United States, Great Britain, and International Communism, 1945–1950* (Cambridge, Mass.: Harvard University Press, 2009), 117–94.

96. John R. Lampe, Russell O. Prickett, and Ljubiša S. Adamović, *Yugoslav-American Economic Relations Since World War II* (Durham, N.C.: Duke University Press, 1990); Lorraine M. Lees, *Keeping Tito Afloat: The United States, Yugoslavia, and the Cold War* (University Park: Pennsylvania State University Press, 1997).

97. Arch-UN-NYC, S-0175-2197-03 and 04.

98. Andrej Markovič and Ivan Obadić, "A Socialist Developing Country in a Western Capitalist Club: Yugoslavia and the OEEC/OECD, 1955–1980," in *The OECD and the International Political Economy Since 1948*, ed. Matthieu Leimgruber and Matthias Schmelzer (London: Palgrave MacMillan, 2017), 89–113.

99. See Johanna Bockman, *Markets in the Name of Socialism: The Left-Wing Origins of Neoliberalism* (Stanford, Calif.: Stanford University Press, 2011), 83–93.

100. Benedetto Zacharia, "Learning from Yugoslavia? Western Europe and the Myth of Self-Management (1968–1975)," in *Planning in Cold War Europe: Competition, Cooperation, Circulations (1950s–1970s)*, ed. Michel Christian, Sandrine Kott, and Ondrej Matejka (Berlin: De Gruyter, 2018), 213–37.

101. See Bockman, *Markets in the Name of Socialism*, 100–104.

102. Radivoj Uvalić, "The Management of Undertakings by the Workers in Yugoslavia," *International Labour Review* 69, no. 3 (1954) 235–54; Leon Gešković, "The System of Producers' Councils in Yugoslavia," *International Labour Review* 71, no.1 (1955): 34–59, *Workers Management in Yugoslavia*, Studies and Reports, 64, ILO, 1962.

103. Ivan Obadić, "A Troubled Relationship: Yugoslavia and the European Economic Community in *détente*," *European Review of History* 21, no. 2 (2014): 329.

104. Godard, *Le laboratoire de l'internationalisme*, 281.
105. Arch-UN-NY S-0175-2197-04.
106. See Rinna Kullaa, *Non-Alignment and Its Origins in Cold War Europe: Yugoslavia, Finland and the Soviet Challenge* (London: Tauris, 2012).
107. Alvin Z. Rubinstein, *Yugoslavia and the Non-Aligned World* (Princeton, N.J.: Princeton University Press, 1970), 155–56.
108. Lagendijk, *Electrifying Europe*, 175.
109. Rubinstein, *Yugoslavia and the Non-Aligned World*, 73–114.
110. Muschik, *Building States*.
111. See the well-argued examples in Luard, *A History of the United Nations*.

4. THE EUROPE OF CONVERGENCES

1. RArchC, "Ford records," FA 748, Box 7.
2. See Wilfried Loth and Georges-Henri Soutou, eds., *The Making of Détente: Eastern and Western Europe in the Cold War, 1965–75* (London: Routledge, 2008).
3. See Michel Christian, Sandrine Kott, and Ondrej Matejka, "International Organizations in the Cold War: The Circulation of Experts Beyond the East-West Divide," *Studia Territorialia* 1 (2017): 35–60.
4. For a discussion of the emergence and formulation of this vision, see Nils Gilman, *Mandarins of the Future: Modernization Theory in Cold War America* (Baltimore: Johns Hopkins University Press, 2003), 24–72.
5. See chapter 3.
6. See the two reference works on this subject: Alain Tourraine, *La Société post-industrielle. Naissance d'une société* (Paris: Denoël, 1969); and Daniel Bell, *The Coming of Post-Industrial Society* (New York: Harper Colophon Books, 1974).
7. Théofil Kis, "État des travaux sur la problématique de la convergence: théories et hypothèses," *Études internationales* 2, no. 3 (1971): 443–87.
8. In his *Dix-huit leçons sur la société industrielle* published in 1962, Aron admitted that there were similarities between the industrial societies of Eastern and Western Europe, but he contested the idea of convergence. He believed that political divergence between the socialist and capitalist worlds rendered economic and social convergence impossible. On this topic and the French debate in general, see Georges Henri Soutou, "Convergence Theories in France During the 1960s and the 1970s," in Loth and Soutou, *The Making of Détente*, 25–48.
9. See Donald R. Kelley, "The Soviet Debate on the Convergence of the American & Soviet Systems," *Polity* 2 (1973): 174–95.
10. See Marie Lavigne, *Les Économies socialistes soviétique et européennes*, 3rd ed. rev. and updated (Paris: Armand Colin, 1979), 78–143. See also the more recent symposium, "Managing Communist Enterprises: Poland, Hungary and Czechoslovakia, 1945–1970," *Enterprise and Society* 19, no. 3 (2018), especially Philip Scranton, "Managing Communist Enterprises: Poland, Hungary and Czechoslovakia, 1945–1970," 492–537; and Pál Germuska, "What Can We Learn from the Business History of Communist Enterprises?," 538–45.

4. THE EUROPE OF CONVERGENCES

11. On Tinbergen, see Aad Blok, "Socialist Intellectual as Social Engineer: Jan Tinbergen Ideas on Economic Policy and the Optimal Economic Order (1930–1960)," *Socialist History* 27 (2005): 43–60.

12. RArchC FF, "Records FA748 V Exchanges Box 7 Eastern European Programs. Communist Controlled Countries. Exchange with the USSR," November 1959.

13. RArchC FF FA 021, 2, 2, 1.

14. Suvi Kansikas, *Socialist Countries Face the European Community Soviet-Bloc Controversies Over East-West Trade* (Bern: Peter Lang, 2014); Kansikas, "Acknowledging Economic Realities: The CMEA Policy Change *vis-à-vis* the European Community, 1970–3," *European Review of History: Revue européenne d'histoire* 21, no. 2 (March 4, 2014): 311–28.

15. RArchC FA748 Box 7.

16. On CESES, see Johanna Bockman, *Markets in the Name of Socialism: The Left-Wing Origins of Neoliberalism* (Stanford, Calif.: Stanford University Press, 2011), 133–56.

17. On Kreisky's foreign policy as minister and later chancellor, see Elisabeth Röhrlich, *Kreiskys Aussenpolitik: zwischen österreichicher Identität und internationalem Programm* (Vienna: Vienna University Press, 2011), esp. 276–86 for multilateral orientations.

18. See also Christian Bailey, "Socialist Visions of European Unity in Germany: *Ostpolitik* Since the 1920s," *Contemporary European History* 26, no. 2 (2017): 243–60.

19. Dominique Pestre, "Repenser les variantes du complexe militaire-industriel-universitaire," in *Les Sciences pour la guerre, 1940–1960*, ed. Dominique Pestre and Amy Dahan (Paris: Éd. de l'EHESS, 2004), 195–221; Pestre, "La recherche opérationnelle pendant la dernière guerre et ses suites, la pensée des systèmes," *Revue scientifique et technique de la défense* 54 (2001): 63–69; and Jenny Andersson, *The Future of the World: Futurology, Futurists, and the Struggle for the Post Cold War Imagination* (Oxford: Oxford University Press, 2018), 75–97.

20. Leena Riska-Campbell, *Bridging East and West: The Establishment of the International Institute for Applied Systems Analysis (IIASA) in the United States Foreign Policy of Bridge Building, 1964–1972* (Helsinki: Finnish Society of Science and Letters, 2011); Riska-Campbell, "Managing Systemic Convergence. American Multilateral Bridge Building in Europe During the 1960s and Early 1970s," *Valahian Journal of Historical Studies* 20 (Winter 2013): 135–68; and Egle Rindzeviciute, *The Power of Systems: How Policy Sciences Opened Up the Cold War World* (Ithaca, N.Y.: Cornell University Press, 2016), 52–73.

21. On CoCom's effect on the development of computer science in the USSR, see Frank Cain, "Computers and the Cold War: United States Restrictions on the Export of Computers to the Soviet Union and Communist China," *Journal of Contemporary History* 40, no. 1 (2005): 131–47.

22. Elisabeth Roehrlich, *Inspectors for Peace: A History of the International Atomic Energy Agency* (Baltimore: John Hopkins University Press, 2022).

23. Elisabeth Roehrlich, "The Cold War, the Developing World, and the Creation of the International Atomic Energy Agency (IAEA), 1953–1957," *Cold War History* 16, no. 2 (April 2016): 195–212.

4. THE EUROPE OF CONVERGENCES

24. Arch-MfS HA II 41856, "UNIDO Trainingskurs, und der Hochschule für Ökonomie Bruno Leuschner in Berlin 19/4-8/5 1976."
25. Arch-UNOG-ECE GX 10/2/2/109.
26. Arch-UNESCO, SHC.76/Conf.807/6, "United Nations Scientific and Cultural Organization, Meeting on Inter-regional Co-operation in Social Sciences, Paris, 23–27 August 1976, Social Science Co-operation in Europe by Adam Schaff"; and Arch-UNOG JIU/Rep/13 Ge.72-1890, "European Coordination Centre for Research and Documentation in Social Sciences by Lucio Garcia del Solar Joint Inspection Unit, December 1971."
27. Gilman, *Mandarins of the Future*; Andersson, *The Future of the World*.
28. Rindzeviciute, *The Power of Systems*.
29. See an example in Michael Hutter, "Ecosystems Research and Policy Planning: Revisiting the Budworm Project (1972–1980)," in *Planning in Cold War Europe: Competition, Cooperation, Circulations (1950s–1970s)*, ed. Michel Christian, Sandrine Kott, and Ondrej Matejka (Berlin: De Gruyter, 2018), 261–84.
30. Alexander Szalai, Riccardo Petrella, and Stein Rokkan, *Cross-National Comparative Survey Research: Theory and Practice* (Oxford: Pergamon Press, 1977). For the role played by certain Eastern European countries in research, see Katja Naumann, "International Research Planning Across the Iron Curtain: East-Central European Social Scientists in the ISSC and Vienna Center," in Christian, Kott, and Matejka, *Planning in Cold War Europe*, 97–122.
31. The CSCE has recently been the subject of a rich literature based essentially on Western archives. See especially Angela Romano, *From Détente in Europe to European Détente: How the West Shaped the Helsinki CSCE* (Brussels: P.I.E., 2009); Loth and Soutou, *The Making of Détente*, esp. 153–220; and Matthias Peter and Hermann Wentker, *Die KSZE im Ost-West-Konflikt, Internationale Politik und gesellschaftliche Transformation 1975–1990* (Berlin: De Gruyter, 2015). For the French point of view, see Nicolas Badalassi, "Adieu Yalta? La France, la détente et les origines de la Conférence sur la Sécurité et la Coopération en Europe, 1965–1975," Ph.D. diss., université de la Sorbonne, 2011, https://tel.archives-ouvertes.fr/tel-00713652; Badalassi, "'Neither Too Much nor Too Little': France, the USSR and the Helsinki CSCE," *Cold War History* 18, no. 1 (2018): 1–17.
32. See Romano, *From Détente in Europe to European Détente*, 55–89.
33. See Steven L. B. Jensen, *The Making of International Human Right: The 1960s, Decolonization, and the Reconstruction of Global Values* (Cambridge: Cambridge University Press, 2016), 210–19. For a reappraisal of the role of the UN General Assembly, see Guillaume Devin, Franck Petiteville, and Simon Tordjman, *L'Assemblée générale des Nations unies* (Paris: Presses de Sciences Po, 2020).
34. Arch-UNESCO 008 (4) A 06 "72" Part 1 and DG/74/2.
35. On UNESCO, see Chloé Maurel, "L'UNESCO de 1945 à 1974," Ph.D. diss., université Panthéon-Sorbonne, Paris, 2006, https://tel.archives-ouvertes.fr/tel-00848712.
36. UNESCO, "Actes de la Conférence générale, treizième session, Paris, 1964. Résolutions," 1965, 30–31.
37. Mircea Malitza, "L'enseignement supérieur: son rôle et sa contribution à notre progrès commun. Réflexion sur la création et le fonctionnement de l'UNESCO-CEPES: l'avis personnel de l'un de ses fondateurs," *L'Enseignement supérieur en Europe* 1–2 (2002): 11–31.

4. THE EUROPE OF CONVERGENCES

38. Arch-UNESCO 008 (4) A 06 "72" /19.
39. For cultural relations between the United States and the USSR, see Richmond Yale, *Cultural Exchange and the Cold War: Raising the Iron Curtain* (University Park: Pennsylvania State University Press, 2004). For an example of film coproductions, see Marsha Siefert, "Coproducing Cold War Culture: East-West Film-Making and Cultural Diplomacy," in *Divided Dreamworlds? The Cultural Cold War in East and West*, ed. Peter Romijn, Giles Scott-Smith, and Joel Segal (Amsterdam: University of Amsterdam Press, 2012), 73–95; or Moine, *Cinéma et guerre froide*.
40. Arch-UNESCO 008 (4) A 06 "72" Part 1 and DG/74/2.
41. Arch-ILO RC 156-2-100; Arch-ILO, "Jenks papers."
42. See the WFTU's point of view in the archives of the GDR, especially Arch-SAPMO DY 34/11522-1 ILO "Industrieausschüsse 1963–1975."
43. Arch-ILO, RC 156-2-0, 3.
44. Arch-IISHS, ICFTU 1888 and 1889. Anthony Carew, "Conflict Within the ICFTU: Anti-communism and Anti-colonialism in the 1950s," *International Review of Social History* 41 (1996): 147–81; Victor Devinatz, "A Cold War Thaw in the International Working Class Movement? The World Federation of Trade Unions and the International Confederation of Free Trade Unions, 1967–1977," *Science & Society* 77, no. 3 (2013): 342–71.
45. Arch-IISHS ICFTU 1891, declaration of November 23, 1973.
46. Arch-ILO RC 156-2-100. See also, for the German case, Stefan Müller, *Die Ostkontakte der westdeutschen Gewerkschaften. Entspannungspolitik zwischen Zivilgesellschaft und internationaler Politik 1969 bis 1989* (Bonn: Dietz, 2020).
47. Arch-ILO RC 156-2-1307-1. Francesco Petrini, "Capital Hits the Road: Regulating Multinational Corporations During the Long 1970s," in *Contesting Deregulation: Debates, Practices and Developments in the West Since the 1970s*, ed. Knud Andresen and Stefan Müller (New York: Berghahn Books, 2017), 185–98.
48. Arch-ILO, RC-156-2-402, report from 7 November 1972. See also "L'emploi en Europe. Quelques problèmes d'importance croissante," in "Deuxième conférence régionale européenne, Genève janvier 1974," report 2, International Labour Office, 1974.
49. Some of these movements appear in Simo Mikkonen and Pia Koivunen, *Beyond the Divide: Entangled Histories of Cold War Europe* (New York: Berghahn Books, 2015).
50. Arch-UNOG-ECE GX 2/2/108, "Assemblée des représentants de l'opinion publique pour la sécurité et la coopération européennes," Brussels, 1972.
51. Giles Scott-Smith, "Opening up Political Space. Informal Diplomacy, East-West Exchanges, and the Helsinki Process," in Mikkonen and Koivunen, *Beyond the Divide*, 31.
52. Soutou, *La Guerre froide*, 414.
53. "Conférence sur la sécurité et la coopération en Europe. Acte final," Helsinki, 1975, 14.
54. See the detailed account in Soutou, *La Guerre froide*, 600–602, 643–48, 679–82, and 743–73.
55. Guy Gosselin, "L'ONU et la paix internationale depuis 1945," *Études internationales* 16, no. 4 (1985): 741–56; John Simpson, "The UN's Role in Disarmament: Retrospect and Prospect," *Contemporary Security Policy* 15, no. 1 (1994): 55–67;

4. THE EUROPE OF CONVERGENCES

Bertrand G. Ramcharan, *Preventive Diplomacy at the UN* (Bloomington: Indiana University Press, 2008), 105–25.

56. See Astrid Mignon Kirchhof and Jan-Henrik Meyer, "Global Protest Against Nuclear Power: Transfer and Transnational Exchange in the 1970s and 1980s," *Historical Social Research* 39, no. 1 (2014): 165–90; Holger Nehring, "National Internationalists: British and West German Protests Against Nuclear Weapons, the Politics of Transnational Communications and the Social History of the Cold War, 1957–1964," *Contemporary European History* 14, no. 4 (2005): 559–82.

57. For the United States, see Paul Rubinson, *Redefining Science, Scientists, the National Security State, and Nuclear Weapons in Cold War America* (Amherst: University of Massachusetts Press, 2016).

58. The negotiations surrounding the second economic basket from Helsinki unfolded within five subcommissions: trade, industrial cooperation and projects of common interest, science and technology, environment, and cooperation in other sectors, transport in particular.

59. On the close relation between UNECE and the Helsinki negotiations, see Paul J. Bailey and Ilka Bailey-Wiebecke, "All-European Co-operation: The CSCE's Basket Two and the ECE," *International Journal* 32, no. 2 (1977): 386–407.

60. On the integration of the USSR in the global market during the 1950s, see Oscar Sanchez-Sibony, *Red Globalization: The Political Economy of the Soviet Cold War from Stalin to Khrushchev* (Cambridge, Mass.: Cambridge University Press, 2016).

61. Tapani Paavonen, "Special Arrangements for the Soviet Trade in Finland's Integration Solutions—a Consequence of Finland's International Position or Pursuit of Profit?," in *East-West Trade and the Cold War*, ed. Jari Eloranta and Jari Ojala (Jyväskylä, Fin.: University of Jyväskylä, 2005), 153–65.

62. See Margarita Maximova, "Industrial Cooperation Between Socialist and Capitalist Countries: Forms, Trends, Problems," in *East-West Cooperation in Business: Inter-firm Studies*, ed. Christopher Thomas Saunders (New York: Springer, 1977), 15–27; and Lavigne, *Les Économies socialistes*, 384–94.

63. Karl-Heinz Schlarp, "Das Dilema des westdeutschen Osthandels und die Entstehung des Ost-Auschusses der deutschen Wirtschaft, 1950–1952," *Vierteljahrshefte für Zeitgeschichte* 41, no. 2 (1993): 223–76.

64. Studies on the automobile industry based on Eastern European archives tend to revise the highly Western-centric vision of the literature, emphasizing the reciprocal contributions that governed these exchanges; see Valentina Fava and Luminita Gatejel, "East-West Cooperation in the Automobile Industry: Enterprises, Mobility, Production," *Journal of the Transport History* 38 (2017): 11–19.

65. Arch-IFZ ED 708–1 1499, "Special meeting Monday 4th December 1978."

66. Robert Mark Spaulding, Jr., *Osthandel and Ospolitik: German Foreign Trade Policies in Eastern Europe from Bismarck to Adenauer* (Oxford: Berghahn, 1997). For the preceding period, see Stephen Gross, *Export Empire: German Soft Power in Southeastern Europe, 1890–1945* (Cambridge: Cambridge University Press, 2017).

67. On the twists and turns of U.S. trade policy, see Marie-Hélène Labbé, "Y a-t-il une politique américaine de commerce avec l'URSS?," *Politique étrangère* 4 (1988): 899–906.

68. Arch-Hoover-Stanford Atlantic Council-136.

4. THE EUROPE OF CONVERGENCES

69. Jacqueline McGlade, "Cocom and the Containment of Western Trade and Relations," in Eloranta and Ojala, *East-West Trade and the Cold War*, 47–61; Kazimierz Grzybowski, "United States-Soviet Union Trade Agreement of 1972," *Law and Contemporary Problems* 37, no. 3 (1972): 395–428; and Grzybowski, "East-West Trade Regulations in the United States," *Journal of World Trade* 11, no. 6 (January 1, 1977): 501–13.
70. Badalassi, "Adieu Yalta," 618–41.
71. Sari Autio-Sarasmo, "Knowledge Through the Iron Curtain: Soviet Scientific-Technical Cooperation with Finland and West Germany," in *Reassessing Cold War Europe*, ed. Autio-Sarasmo and Katalin Miklóssy (New York: Routledge, 2011), 66–83; and Christopher Thomas Saunders, ed., *Industrial Policies and Technology Transfers Between East and West* (New York: Springer, 1978).
72. Agota Gueulette, *Politique économique extérieure dans un modèle marxiste: le cas soviétique (1917–1947)* (Paris: Publisud, 1997), 140–50; Georges Sokoloff, *L'Économie de la détente: l'U.R.S.S. et le capital occidental* (Paris: Fondation nationale des sciences politiques, 1983); Friedrich Leivk and Jan Stankovsky, "East-West Economic Relations in the 1970s and 1980s," in *East-West Trade and Finance in the World Economy: A New Look for the 1980s*, ed. Christopher Thomas Saunders (New York: St. Martin's Press, 1985), 77–124. For the Hungarian example, see Csaba Békés, "Hungary, the Soviet Bloc, the German Question, and the CSCE Process, 1965–1975," *Journal of Cold War Studies* 18, no. 3 (July 1, 2016): 95–138.
73. Kansikas, "Acknowledging Economic Realities," 311–28.
74. Kansikas, *Socialist Countries Face the European Community*; Angela Romano, "Untying Cold War Knots: The EEC and Eastern Europe in the Long 1970s," *Cold War History* 14, no. 2 (2014): 153–73.
75. Juhana Aunesluoma, "Finlandisation in Reverse: The CSCE and the Rise and Fall of Economic Détente 1968–1975," in *Helsinki 1975 and the Transformation of Europe*, ed. Oliver Bange and Gottfried Niedhart (New York: Berghahn Books, 2008), 98–113.
76. See, for example, Lucia Coppolaro, "East-West Trade and the General Agreement on Tariffs and Trade (GATT) and the Cold War: Poland's Accession to the GATT, 1957–1967," in Eloranta and Ojala, *East-West Trade and the Cold War*, 77–93.
77. The historiography on human rights has developed considerably in the last two decades. For a history of the "liberal" origins of human rights, see Lynn Avery Hunt, *Inventing Human Rights: A History* (New York: Norton, 2007). See also Stefan-Ludwig Hoffmann, "Human Rights and History," *Past & Present* 232, no. 1 (2016): 279–310.
78. Daniel Charles Thomas, *The Helsinki Effect: International Norms, Human Rights, and the Demise of Communism* (Princeton, N.J.: Princeton University Press, 2001); Sarah B. Snyder, *Human Rights Activism and the End of the Cold War: A Transnational History of the Helsinki Network* (Leiden: Cambridge University Press, 2011).
79. Samuel Moyn, *The Last Utopia: Human Rights in History* (Cambridge, Mass.: Harvard University Press, 2012); Jan Eckel, "Humanitarisierung der internationalen Beziehungen? Menschenrechtspolitik in den 1970er Jahren," *Geschichte und Gesellschaft* 38, no. 4 (2012): 603–35; and Moyn, *Not Enough: Human Rights in an Unequal World* (Cambridge, Mass.: Harvard University Press, 2018).
80. Jensen, *The Making of International Human Rights*.

4. THE EUROPE OF CONVERGENCES

81. For a longue durée perspective on the centrality of social rights, see Steven L. B. Jensen and Charles Walton, eds., *Social Rights and the Politics of Obligation in History* (Cambridge: Cambridge University Press, 2022), especially their introduction, "Not 'Second-Generation Rights:' Rethinking the History of Social Rights," 1–25.

82. On this evolution, see Mark Mazower, "The Strange Triumph of Human Rights, 1933–1950," *Historical Journal* 47, no. 2 (2004): 379–98; Eric D. Weitz, "From the Vienna to the Paris System: International Politics and the Entangled Histories of Human Rights, Forced Deportations, and Civilizing Missions," *American Historical Review* 5 (2008): 1313–43.

83. See Sandrine Kott, "Fighting the War or Preparing for Peace? The ILO During the Second World War," *Journal of Modern European History* 12, no. 3 (2014): 359–76.

84. Alain Supiot, *L'Esprit de Philadelphie: la justice sociale face au marché total* (Paris: Seuil, 2010).

85. Roger Normand and Sarah Zaidi, *Human Rights at the UN: The Political History of Universal Justice*, United Nations Intellectual History Project (Bloomington: Indiana University Press, 2008), 107–138.

86. Daniel J. Whelan, *Indivisible Human Rights: A History* (Philadelphia: University of Pennsylvania Press, 2010), esp. 136–56.

87. Valentina Vardabasso, "La Convention européenne des droits de l'homme," *Relations internationales* 131 (2007): 73–90.

88. Marco Duranti, "Curbing Labour's Totalitarian Temptation: European Human Rights Law and British Postwar Politics," *Humanity: An International Journal of Human Rights, Humanitarianism, and Development* 3, no. 3 (October 31, 2012): 361–83; Anne Deighton, "The British in Strasbourg: Negotiating the European Convention on Human Rights, 1950," in *Human Rights in Europe During the Cold War*, ed. Rasmus Mariager, Karl Molin, and Kjersti Brathagen (London: Routledge, 2014), 27–42.

89. For a general presentation, see Antony Alcock, *History of the International Labour Organization* (New York: Octagon Books, 1971), 270–83; Daniel Maul, *The International Labour Organization: 100 Years of Global Social Policy* (Berlin: De Gruyter, 2019), 200–204.

90. "Governing Body Report," no. 128 (March 1955): 52; and no. 129 (May–June 1955): 35.

91. On Czechoslovakia, see Peter Heumos, "Stalinismus in der Tschechoslowakei. Forschungslage und sozialgeschichtliche Anmerkungen am Beispiel der Industriearbeiterschaft," *Journal of Modern European History* 2, no. 1 (2004): 82–109. On the Soviet Union, see Marcel van der Linden, "Forced Labour and Non-capitalist Industrialization: The Case of Stalinism (1929–1956)," in *Free and Unfree Labour: The Debate Continues*, ed. Tom Brass and Marcel van der Linden (New York: Peter Lang, 1997), 351–63; Robert William Davies, "Forced Labour Under Stalin: The Archive Revelations," *New Left Review* 214 (1995): 62–89.

92. See Sandrine Kott, "The Forced Labor Issue Between Human and Social Rights, 1947–1957," *Humanity: An International Journal of Human Rights, Humanitarianism, and Development* 3, no. 3 (2012): 321–35.

93. Arch-ILO FLC 2-1-4, letter from Zwahlen to Salkin, 29 January 1952. On this practice and the different forms of forced labor that accompanied the establishment

of a free labor market on the American continent, see especially the articles by Larian Angelo, "Old Ways in the New South: The Implication of the Recreation of an Unfree Labor Force"; and David McCreery, "Wage Labor, Free Labor and Vagrancy Laws: The Transition to Capitalism in Guatemala, 1920–1945," in Brass and van der Linden, *Free and Unfree Labour*, 173–201 and 281–303, respectively.

94. See the Soviet allegation, formulated against the United States, seeking to demonstrate that forced labor "is the basis of the capitalist economy": "PV, Conseil économique et social," 8th session, sitting 237, 12th session, sitting 469.

95. For a summary of these allegations, see "Report of Ad Hoc," appendix 3, especially those concerning the United States (255–60). In addition to the Soviet allegations were those made by Stetson Kennedy (1919–2011), a folklore expert and human rights activist, who conducted numerous investigations during the interwar period on political and economic discrimination in the southern United States.

96. Steven L. B. Jensen, "Inequality and Post-War International Organization: Discrimination, the World Social Situation and the United Nations, 1948–1957," in *Histories of Global Inequality: New Perspectives*, ed. Christian Olaf Christiansen and Steven L. B. Jensen (London: Palgrave Macmillan, 2019), 136–39.

97. For an approach from a critical sociological perspective, see Yves Dezalay and Bryant Garth, "Droits de l'homme et philanthropie hégémonique," *Actes de la recherche en sciences sociales* 121, no. 1 (1998): 23–41. See also Jessica Whyte, *The Morals of the Market: Human Rights and the Rise of Neoliberalism* (London: Verso, 2019), especially 60–97.

98. On this important discussion, see Olav Stokke, *The UN and Development: From Aid to Cooperation*, United Nations Intellectual History Project (Bloomington: Indiana University Press, 2009), 289–315.

99. See Jonas Brendebach, "A New Global Media Order: Debates and Policies on Media and Mass Communication at UNESCO," Ph.D. diss., European University Institute, 2019.

5. THE THIRD WORLD AND THE NEW INTERNATIONAL ECONOMIC ORDER

1. United Nations, Office of the High Commissioner for Human Rights, "Declaration on the Granting of Independence to Colonial Countries and Peoples," General Assembly resolution 1514 (XV), December 14, 1960, https://www.ohchr.org/en/instruments-mechanisms/instruments/declaration-granting-independence-colonial-countries-and-peoples.

2. For a nuanced view of the relation between the United Nations and decolonization, see Nicole Eggers, Jessica L. Pearson, and Aurora Almada e Santos, eds., *The United Nations and Decolonization* (New York: Routledge, 2020); Eva-Maria Muschik, "Special Issue Introduction: Towards a Global History of International Organizations and Decolonization," *Journal of Global History* 17, no. 2 (July 2022): 173–90; and Muschik, *Building States: The United Nations, Development, and Decolonization, 1945–1965* (New York: Columbia University Press, 2022). On the General Assembly's role in formulating alternative discourses regarding development and the New International Economic Order, see Adrien Fauve and

5. THE THIRD WORLD

Mathilde Leloup, "Le temps du développement à l'Assemblée," in *L'Assemblée générale des Nations unies*, ed. Guillaume Devin, Franck Petiteville, and Simon Tordjman (Paris: Presses de Sciences Po, 2020), 161–80.

3. Cited by Chloé Maurel, "L'UNESCO de 1945 à 1974," Ph.D. diss., Université Panthéon-Sorbonne, 2006, 165–69, https://tel.archives-ouvertes.fr/tel-00848712.

4. For an overview of the debate surrounding development, see, among many others, the *Journal of Modern European History* 8, no. 1 (April 15, 2010), especially Frederick Cooper, "Writing the History of Development," 5–23. See also Nick Cullather, "Development? It's History," *Diplomatic History* 24, no. 4 (2000): 641–53; Corinna Unger, "Histories of Development and Modernization: Findings, Reflections, Future Research," 2010, H-Soz-u-Kult/Forum/Forschungsberichte: http://hsozkult.geschichte.hu-berlin.de/forum/2010-12-001; and Marc Frey and Sönke Kunkel, "Writing the History of Development: A Review of the Recent Literature," *Contemporary European History* 20, no. 2 (2011): 215–32.

5. General Assembly, 3rd Session, Official Records, 2nd Committee, Summary Records of the 69th Meeting, held at Palais De Chaillot, Paris, Tuesday, 2 November 1948, A/C.2/SR.69 p. 164, https://documents-dds-ny.un.org/doc/UNDOC/GEN/NL3/254/85/pdf/NL325485.pdf?OpenElement.

6. See Véronique Plata-Stenger and Matthias Schulz, eds., *Décolonisation et développement: genèses, pratiques et interdépendances, Relations internationales* 177, no. 1 (2019).

7. On this relation between development and the Cold War, see Sara Lorenzini, *Global Development: A Cold War History* (Princeton, N.J.: Princeton University Press, 2019).

8. On this critique of development, see especially Gilbert Rist, *The History of Development: From Western Origins to Global Faith* (London: Zed Books, 2019); Arturo Escobar, *Encountering Development: The Making and Unmaking of the Third World* (Princeton, N.J.: Princeton University Press, 1995).

9. For India, see especially David C. Engerman, "The Romance of Economic Development and New Histories of the Cold War," *Diplomatic History* 28, no. 1 (2004): 23–54. For the training of elites, see the contributions of Corinna Unger, "The United States, Decolonization, and the Education of Third World Elites," and Andreas Hilger, "Building a Socialist Elite? Khruschev's Soviet Union and Elite Formation in India," both in *Elites and Decolonization in the Twentieth Century*, ed. Jost Dülffer and Marc Frey (Basingstoke, UK: Palgrave Macmillan, 2011), 241–61 and 262–86, respectively.

10. Massimiliano Trentin, "Modernization as State Building: The Two Germanies in Syria, 1963–1972," *Diplomatic History* 33, no. 3 (2009): 487–505; Trentin, "La République démocratique allemande et la Syrie du parti Baas," *Les Cahiers Sirice* 10 (2013): 55–67.

11. For growth indicators and their genealogy, see Daniel Speich Chassé, *Die Erfindung des Bruttosozialprodukts: Globale Ungleichheit in der Wissensgeschichte der Ökonomie*, Kritische Studien zur Geschichtswissenschaft (Göttingen, Ger.: Vandenhock & Ruprecht, 2013).

12. Margherita Zanasi, "Exporting Development: The League of Nations and Republican China," *Comparative Studies in Society and History* 49, no. 1 (2007): 143–69.

5. THE THIRD WORLD

13. Susan Pedersen, "The Meaning of the Mandates System: An Argument," *Geschichte und Gesellschaft* 32, no. 4 (2006): 560–82; Pedersen, *The Guardians: The League of Nations and the Crisis of Empire* (Oxford: Oxford University Press, 2015).

14. Michele Alacevich, "Planning Peace: The European Roots of the Post-War Global Development Challenge," *Past & Present* 239, no. 1 (2018): 219–64.

15. On the Bruce Report, see Victor-Yves Ghebali, *La Société des Nations et le rapport Bruce*, Cinquante ans de la Société des Nations (Centre européen de la dotation Carnegie, 1970); Martin D. Dubin, "Toward the Bruce Report: The Economic and Social Programs of the League of Nations in the Avenol Era," in *The League of Nations in Retrospect / La Société des Nations: Rétrospective*, Proceedings of the Symposium Organized by the United Nations Library and the Graduate Institute of International Studies, Geneva, November 6–9, 1980 (Berlin: De Gruyter, 1983), 42–72; and Patricia Clavin, *Securing the World Economy: The Reinvention of the League of Nations, 1920–1946* (Cambridge: Cambridge University Press, 2013), 240–51.

16. Arch-ILO, Cat 1/30/1/3. On this notion, see the speech by Albert Thomas at "l'Alliance française de Sofia," 26 February 1930.

17. See the work of Véronique Plata-Stenger, *Social Reform, Modernization and Technical Diplomacy: The ILO Contribution to Development (1930–1946)* (Berlin: De Gruyter, 2020); Plata-Stenger, "L'OIT et le problème du sous-développement en Asie dans l'entre-deux-guerres," *Le Mouvement social* 263, no. 2 (2018): 109–122; and Plata-Stenger, "L'OIT et l'assurance sociale en Amérique latine dans les années 30 et 40: enjeux et limites de l'expertise internationale," *Revue d'histoire de la protection sociale* 10, no. 1 (2017): 42–61.

18. On the World War II period, see Kott, "Fighting the War or Preparing for Peace?," 359–76.

19. See Department of State, *The Point Four Program*, December 1949, and an analysis of the program in Rist, *The History of Development*, 70–79.

20. In June 1949 Henryk Altman, the Polish delegate to the ILO Governing Body, voted against this program on the pretext that "it is firstly an attempt to reinforce the capitalist expansion of the United States": International Labour Office, *Compte rendu du Conseil d'administration* (Geneva: ILO, 1949), vol. 109, 61; Harald Karan Jacobson, *The USSR and the UN's Economic and Social Activities* (South Bend, Ind.: University of Notre Dame Press, 1963), 6–7; and Lorenzini, *Global Development*, 26–29.

21. Craig Murphy, *The United Nations Development Programme: A Better Way?* (Cambridge: Cambridge University Press, 2006), esp. 41–42, for the influence of the United States during the founding of the program.

22. On UN development programs, see Amy L. S. Staples, *The Birth of Development: How the World Bank, Food and Agriculture Organization and World Health Organization Have Changed the World 1945–1965* (Kent, Ohio: Kent State University Press, 2006); Olav Stokke, *The UN and Development: From Aid to Cooperation*, United Nations Intellectual History Project (Bloomington: Indiana University Press, 2009). See also Marc Frey, Sönke Kunkel, and Corinna Unger, eds., *International Organizations and Development, 1945–1990* (London: Palgrave Macmillan, 2014).

5. THE THIRD WORLD

23. See Matthias Schmelzer, "A Club of the Rich to Help the Poor? The OECD 'Development' and the Hegemony of Donor Countries," in Frey, Kunkel, and Unger, *International Organizations and Development*, 171–96.

24. For an analysis, see Nils Gilman, *Mandarins of the Future: Modernization Theory in Cold War America* (Baltimore: Johns Hopkins University Press, 2003).

25. Walt. W. Rostow, *The Stages of Economic Growth: A Non-Communist Manifesto*, 3rd ed. (Cambridge: Cambridge University Press, 1990 [1960]), especially his engaging chapter 10, "Marxism, Communism and the Stages of Growth," 147–67.

26. David Ekbladh, *The Great American Mission: Modernization and the Construction of an American World Order* (Princeton, N.J.: Princeton University Press, 2010).

27. See the classic book by Thomas P. Hughes, *American Genesis: A Century of Invention and Technological Enthusiasm 1870–1970* (Chicago: University of Chicago Press, 1989), 249–95.

28. Gilman, *Mandarins of the Future*, 42–45.

29. See Murphy, *The United Nations Development Programme*, which was written in response to a call from the UN Development Programme and provides a promotional—if not official—history of the program that is highly U.S.-centric.

30. See the hagiographic but useful book by Gerald M. Meier and Dudley Seers, *Pioneers in Development*, World Bank Publication (New York: Oxford University Press, 1984). See also, in general, Régine Perron, *Histoire du multilatéralisme. L'utopie du siècle américain de 1918 à nos jours* (Paris: PUPS, 2014), 88–92.

31. David Owen, "The United Nations Expanded Program of Technical Assistance: A Multilateral Approach," *Annals of the American Academy of Political and Social Science* 323 (1959): 25–32.

32. See chapter 4.

33. *Yearbook of the United Nations*, 1969.

34. Arch-UNOG-E/CN.14/UAP/2 27 August 1962. Commission économique pour l'Afrique. Cycle d'étude sur les problèmes administratifs urgents des gouvernements africains; Muschik, *Building States*, 166–97; and Eva-Marie Muschik, "Managing the World: The United Nations, Decolonization, and the Strange Triumph of State Sovereignty in the 1950s and 1960s," *Journal of Global History* 13, no. 1 (2018): 121–44.

35. Joseph M. Hodge, "British Colonial Expertise, Post-Colonial Careering and the Early History of International Development," *Journal of Modern European History* 8, no. 1 (April 15, 2010): 24–46. For the role of French colonial administrators within the European Community Directorate-General for Development, see Véronique Dimier, "Institutionnalisation et bureaucratisation de la Commission européenne: l'exemple de la DG développement," *Politique européenne* 11, no. 3 (December 1, 2003): 99–121.

36. See chapter 1.

37. See chapter 4.

38. See Michel Christian's work at the UNIDO archives in Vienna as part of the research project funded by the Fonds national de la recherche suisse: "Shared Modernities or Competing Modernities? Europe Between West and East (1920s–1970s)."

39. Arch-ILO Z 11–5.

5. THE THIRD WORLD

40. Arch-ILO WEP 2–34-1, "Employment policies and manpower planning in several European socialist countries: agro-industrial integration and its impact on employment, 1978–1979."
41. Arch-ILO WEP 86-3-14-3, for the résumés of the first generation of experts in the Colombian project.
42. *A Programme for Colombia Prepared by an Inter-agency Team Organized by the International Labour Office* (Geneva: ILO, 1970).
43. International Labor Office, *Employment, Growth and Basic Needs: A One-World Problem: The International "Basic-Needs" Strategy Against Chronic Poverty* (New York: Praeger, 1977).
44. Mireille Calame et al., eds., *Il faut manger pour vivre. Controverses sur les besoins fondamentaux et le développement* (Geneva: Cahiers de l'Institut universitaires d'étude du développement, 1980).
45. Martin Gorsky and Christopher Sirrs, "The Rise and Fall of 'Universal Health Coverage' as a Goal of International Health Politics, 1925-1952," *American Journal of Public Health* 108, no. 3 (2018): 334–42.
46. Thomas Zimmer has since defended this point of view in *Welt ohne Krankheit. Geschichte der internationalen Gesundheitspolitik 1940–1970* (Göttingen, Ger.: Wallstein, 2017). See the contribution by Dora Vargha at http://historyofmedicineinireland.blogspot.co.uk/2017/03/a-forgotten-episode-of-international.html.
47. Randall M. Packard, "Malaria Dreams: Postwar Visions of Health and Development in the Third World," *Medical Anthropology* 17 (1997): 279–96.
48. Elizabeth Fee, Marcos Cueto, and Theodor M. Brown, "At the Roots of The World Health Organization's Challenges: Politics and Regionalization," *American Journal for Public Health* 106 (2016): 1912–17.
49. See Bogdan C. Iacob, "Malariology and Decolonization: Eastern European Experts from the League of Nations to the World Health Organization," *Journal of Global History* 17, no. 2 (July 2022): 233–53.
50. Marcos Cueto, "The Origins of Primary Health Care and Selective Primary Health Care," *American Journal of Public Health* 94 (2004): 1864–74.
51. See Zhou Xun, "From China's 'Barefoot Doctor' to Alma Ata: The Primary Health Care Movement in the Long 1970s," in *China, Hong Kong, and the Long 1970s: Global Perspectives*, ed. Priscilla Roberts and Odd Arne Westad (Cham: Springer International, 2017), 135–57.
52. See, for example, Dóra Vargha, *Polio across the Iron Curtain: Hungary's Cold War with an Epidemic* (Cambridge: Cambridge University Press, 2018).
53. For a critical interpretation of the "basic needs" approach, see Rist, *The History*, 162–69.
54. Daniel J. Whelan, "'Under the Aegis of Man:' The Right to Development and the Origins of the New International Economic Order," *Humanity: An International Journal of Human Rights, Humanitarianism, and Development* 6, no. 1 (2015): 93–108.
55. Stephen J. Kobrin, "Expropriation as an Attempt to Control Foreign Firms in LDCs: Trends from 1960 to 1979," *International Studies Quarterly* 28, no. 3 (1984): 329–48. Here I focus on the economic aspect of the phenomenon, although international jurists such as Bedjaoui of Algeria and Röling of Holland were also active in formulating the NIEO. See especially Umut Özsu, "Neoliberalism and the New

5. THE THIRD WORLD

International Economic Order: A History of Contemporary Legal Thought," in *Searching for Contemporary Legal Thought*, ed. Justin Desautels-Stein and Christopher L. Tomlins (Cambridge: Cambridge University Press, 2017), 330–47.

56. The declaration is available at https://en.unesco.org/about-us/legal-affairs/declaration-fundamental-principles-concerning-contribution-mass-media. For the context and a precise analysis, see Jonas Brendebach, "A New Global Media Order: Debates and Policies on Media and Mass Communication at UNESCO," Ph.D. diss., European University Institute, 2019, 353–485.

57. Alfred Sauvy, "Trois mondes, une planète," *L'Observateur*, August 14, 1952, http://www.homme-moderne.org/societe/demo/sauvy/3mondes.html.

58. Jürgen Dinkel, *The Non-aligned Movement: Genesis, Organization and Politics (1927–1992)* (Leiden: Brill, 2019), 42–225.

59. "Final Communiqué of the Asian-African Conference of Bandung (24 April 1955), https://www.cvce.eu/obj/communique_final_de_la_conference_afro_asiatique_de_bandung_24_avril_1955-fr-676237bd-72f7-471f-949a-88b6ae513585.html

60. See Dinkel, *The Non-aligned Movement*, 88–103.

61. For an already critical view, see Catherine Coquery-Vidrovitch, *Connaissance du tiers-monde* (Paris: Cahiers Jussieu 4, UGE, 1977); Maxime Szczepanski-Huillery, "L'idéologie tiers-mondiste. Constructions et usages d'une catégorie intellectuelle en 'crise,'" *Raisons politiques* 18, no. 2 (2005): 27–48.

62. Eric Helleiner, *Forgotten Foundations of Bretton Woods: International Development and the Making of the Postwar Order* (Ithaca, N.Y.: Cornell University Press, 2014), 266.

63. Francine McKenzie, "GATT and the Cold War: Accession Debates, Institutional Development, and the Western Alliance, 1947–1959," *Journal of Cold War Studies* 10, no. 3 (2008): 78–109; McKenzie, "Free Trade and Freedom to Trade: The Development Challenge to GATT, 1947–1968," in Frey, Kunkel and Unger, *International Organizations and Development*, 150–70.

64. On UNCTAD, see Hans W. Singer, "La création de la CNUCED et l'évolution de la pensée contemporaine sur le développement," *Revue Tiers-monde* 35, no. 139 (1994): 489–98; Johanna Bockman, "Socialist Globalization Against Capitalist Neocolonialism: The Economic Ideas Behind the New International Economic Order," *Humanity: An International Journal of Human Rights, Humanitarianism & Development* 6, no. 1 (2015): 109–28. See also Sönke Kunkel, "Contesting Globalization: The United Nations Conference on Trade and Development and the Transnationalization of Sovereignty," in Frey, Kunkel, and Unger, *International Organizations and Development*, 240–52; Michel Christian, "'It Is Not a Question of Rigidly Planning Trade': UNCTAD and the Regulation of the International Trade in the 1970s," in *Planning in Cold War Europe: Competition, Cooperation, Circulations (1950s–1970s)*, ed. Michel Christian, Sandrine Kott, and Ondrej Matejka et al. (Berlin: De Gruyter, 2018), 285–314.

65. Edgar Dosman, *The Life and Times of Raúl Prebisch, 1901–1986* (Montreal: McGill-Queen's University Press, 2008), 378–409.

66. Arch-UNOG ARR 40/1842 72 TDO 300.

67. Arch-UNOG ARR 40/1842 TDO 430 and GX 18/12/1/51.

68. Arch-UNOG GX 18/12/1/51.

5. THE THIRD WORLD

69. The organization into four groups—developing countries, developed countries with a market economy (OECD countries), Latin American countries, and socialist countries—nevertheless combined differences in development and economic systems. Some NATO countries that saw themselves as underdeveloped, such as Greece and Turkey, were included in the group of developed countries with a market economy, while Romania, which considered itself to be "developing," joined the camp of socialist countries. On the other hand, socialist countries—such as Mongolia, Cuba, and Vietnam, which were Comecon members since 1962, 1972, and 1978 respectively—were part of the underdeveloped group. See Michel Christian, "UNCTAD," in *Den kalten Krieg vermessen: über Reichweite und Alternative einer binären Ordnungsvorstellung*, ed. Frank Reichherzer, Emmanuel Droit, and Jan Jansen, (Berlin: De Gruyter, 2018), 297–313.

70. Lubjica Spaskovska, "Building a Better World? Construction, Labour Mobility and the Pursuit of Collective Self-Reliance in the 'Global South,' 1950–1990," *Labor History* 59, no. 3 (2018): 331–51; Alvin Z. Rubinstein, *The Soviets in International Organizations: Changing Policy Toward Developing Countries, 1953–1963* (Princeton, N.J.: Princeton University Press, 1964), 165–77.

71. For a report on these international discussions, see Laurent Warlouzet, *Governing Europe in a Globalizing World: Neoliberalism and Its Alternatives Gollowing the 1973 Oil Crisis* (London: Routledge, 2018), 57–77. See also Francesco Petrini, "Capital Hits the Road: Regulating Multinational Corporations During the Long 1970s," in *Contesting Deregulation: Debates, Practices and Developments in the West Since the 1970s*, ed. Knud Andresen and Stefan Müller (New York: Berghahn Books, 2017), 185–98.

72. Jennifer Bair, "Taking Aim at the New International Economic Order," in *The Road from Mont Pèlerin: The Making of the Neoliberal Thought*, ed. Philip Mirowski and Dieter Plehwe (Cambridge, Mass.: Harvard University Press, 2015), 367–74.

73. For the highly emblematic case of Switzerland, see Sabine Pitteloud, "Les invisibles deviennent visibles. Le rôle politique des multinationales et les débats sur l'internationalisation en Suisse (1942–1993)," Ph.D. diss., University of Geneva, 2019, esp. 288–326, https://archive-ouverte.unige.ch/unige:121457.

74. Samuel Beroud and Thomas Hajduk, "L'OCDE et les bonnes pratiques. Une histoire inséparable," in *Les Bonnes Pratiques des relations internationales*, ed. Camille Laporte, Asmara Klein, and Marie Saiget (Paris: Presses de Sciences Po, 2015), 61–77; Hajduk, "An 'Instrument of Moral Persuasion'—Multinational Enterprises and International Codes of Conduct in the 1970s," in *Code of Conduct on Transnational Corporations: Challenges and Opportunities*, ed. Mia Mahmudur Rahim (New York: Springer International, 2019), 23–43.

75. The ILO gathered "the messages and statements, World Symposium on the Social Implications of a New International Economic Order, Geneva 19-23 January 1976." Numerous documents regarding this forum were created by the International Institute of Social Studies of the International Labour Office, especially Mario Bettati (general rapporteur); Robert Cox, "Labor and the Multinationals," ILO-Arch NOEI/D.24; or the Soviet point of view in T. Timofeev, "The Role and Place of the Social Factors in Formation of a New International Economic Order," ILO-Arch NOEI/D.16/A.

5. THE THIRD WORLD

76. https://www.ilo.org/empent/areas/mne-declaration/lang--en/index.htm. See Chloé Maurel, "OIT et responsabilité sociale des entreprises transnationales depuis les années 1970," in *L'Organisation internationale du travail. Origine. Développement. Avenir*, ed. Isabelle Lespinet-Moret and Vincent Viet (Rennes: Presses universitaires de Rennes, 2011), 179–92; Hajduk, *An Instrument*.

77. Khalil Hamdani and Lorraine Ruffing, *United Nations Centre on Transnational Corporations: Corporate Conduct and the Public Interest*, Global Institutions 98 (London: Routledge, 2015).

78. Daniel J. Sargent, "North/South: The United States Responds to the New International Economic Order," *Humanity: An International Journal of Human Rights, Humanitarianism, and Development* 6, no. 1 (2015): 201–16.

79. On the more ambiguous position of the Social Democrats within the European Commission, see the failure of the Vederling directive explored by Warlouzet, *Governing Europe*, 67–77.

80. Gunnar Myrdal, Nobel Prize Lecture, https://www.nobelprize.org/prizes/economic-sciences/1974/myrdal/lecture/.

81. Willy Brandt and Independent Commission on International Development Issues, *North-South: a Programme for Survival* (London: PanBooks, 1980). For a more critical view of the Brandt Report, see Umut Özsu, "Neoliberalism and Human Rights: The Brandt Commission and the Struggle for a New World," *Law & Contemporary Problems* 81, no. 4 (2018): 139–65.

82. Guia Migani, "Lomé and the North-South Relations (1975–1984): From the 'New International Economic Order' to a New Conditionality," in *Europe in a Globalizing World. Global Challenges and European Responses in the "Long" 1970s*, ed. Claudia Hiepel (Baden-Baden, Ger.: Nomos, 2014), 123–46.

83. Patrick Sharma, "Between North and South: The World Bank and the New International Economic Order," *Humanity: An International Journal of Human Rights, Humanitarianism, and Development* 6, no. 1 (2015): 189–200.

84. Victor McFarland, "The New International Economic Order, Interdependence, and Globalization," *Humanity: An International Journal of Human Rights, Humanitarianism, and Development* 6, no. 1 (2015): 217–33.

85. See Ludivine Bantigny, Boris Gobille, and Eugénia Palerki, eds., "Les années 1968: circulations révolutionnaires," *Monde(s)* 11, no. 1 (2017).

86. William D. Graaf, "The Theory of the Non-Capitalist Road," in *The Soviet Bloc and the Third World*, ed. Brigitte Schulz and William W. Hansen (Boulder, Colo.: Westview Press, 1989), 27–52.

87. On the position of Comecon countries with respect to the NIEO, see in general Oleg Bogomolov, "The CMEA Countries and the New International Economic Order," in *East, West, South: Economic Interactions Between Three Worlds*, ed. Christopher Thomas Saunders (New York: St. Martin's Press, 1981), 246–56; or Robert Bosc, "L'URSS face aux revendications du Tiers-monde: soutien de principe et intérêt mutuel," *Revue française de science politique* 26, no. 4 (1976): 696–708.

88. Jeremy Friedman, "Soviet Policy in the Developing World and the Chinese Challenge in the 1960s," *Cold War History* 10, no. 2 (2010): 247–72.

89. See the ongoing work of Yi-Tang Lin; and Sigrid Schmalzer, *Red Revolution, Green Revolution: Scientific Farming in Socialist China* (Chicago: University of Chicago Press, 2016), 66.

5. THE THIRD WORLD

90. See Agotta Gueulette, *Politique économique extérieure dans un modèle marxiste: le cas soviétique (1917–1947)* (Paris: Publisud, 1997), 109–50.
91. Marian Paszynski, "The Economic Interest of the CMEA Countries in Relation with the Developing Countries," and Izván Dobosi and András Inotoi, "Prospects of Economic Cooperation Between CMEA Countries and Developing Countries," both in *Economic Interactions Between Three Worlds*, ed. Christopher Thomas Saunders (New York: St. Martin's Press, 1981), 33–47 and 48–65, respectively. See the detailed numbers in Yves Berthelot, "The Interest of the Industrial West in Relations with Developing Countries," in Saunders, *East, West, South*, 19–32.
92. On the discussion surrounding the international socialist division of labor, see Simon Godard, *Le laboratoire de l'internationalisme: le CAEM et la construction du bloc socialiste (1949–1991)* (Paris: Sciences Po, 2021), 110–24. On its origins, see Gueulette, *Politique économique extérieure*, 162–72; Oleg Timofeevich Bogomolov, *Socialisme et compétitivité: les pays de l'Est dans l'économie mondiale* (Paris: Presses de la Fondation nationale des sciences politiques, 1989), 69–88.
93. Leonid Sergeevich Yagodovsky, *The World Socialist System: Its Role in the World Today* (Moscow: Novosti Press Agency Publishing House, 1975), 16.
94. For example, see Jan C. Behrends, Thomas Lindenberger, and Patrice G. Poutrus, eds., *Fremde und Fremd-Sein in der DDR: zu historischen Ursachen der Fremdenfeindlichkeit in Ostdeutschland* (Berlin: Metropol, 2003).
95. Michel Christian, "UNCTAD," in Reichherzer, Droit, and Jansen, *Den kalten Krieg vermessen: über Reichweite und Alternative einer binären Ordnungsvorstellung*, 297–313.
96. See the interesting reports from the informant Koch in 1977–1989 in the Stasi archives: Arch-MfS Ingrid Koch 11045/91.
97. On China as a Third World country, see Paul Bairoch, "Du Tiers-Monde aux Tiers-Mondes. Convergences et clivages," *Population* 47, no. 6 (1992): 1485–1503.
98. Arch-UNOG GA-OR A/10015/Rev.1, "Report of the Trade and Development Board (10 March–2 October 1975)."
99. RArchC FA748 V Exchanges Box 7, "Eastern European Programs. Communist Controlled Countries."
100. Arch-UNIDO OR 212/2 (1), mission letter from the Socialist Republic of Romania, Vienna, 1971. For the position of Romania in the global economic space, see Madeleine Balussou, "Les échanges de la Roumanie avec l'OCDE (1970–1980)," *Revue d'études comparatives Est-Ouest* 12, no. 4 (1981): 91–114. See also the rapprochement with the EEC in Elena Dragomir, "Romania Turns West: National and International Rationales," in *European Socialist Regimes Fateful Engagement with the West: National Strategies in the Long 1970s*, ed. Angela Romano and Federico Romero (London: Routledge, 2020), 191–220.
101. Arch-UN-NYC S-139/1/22, "Draft letter of endorsement of final report POL /68/509 16 July 1973."
102. Arch-UNIDO ID/OR 340 GDR, ID/OA 321 BUL 1–33 ID/OA 321 POL 1–28 ID/OA 321 HUN ID/OA 321 ROM 1–71 ID/OA CZE 1–3. I thank Michel Christian for making these documents available to me.
103. Arch-UNIDO ID/OA BUL 14, 1971.

5. THE THIRD WORLD

104. See the work of Victor Petrov and his essay "Communist Robot Dreams," April 26, 2018, https://aeon.co/essays/how-communist-bulgaria-became-a-leader-in-tech -and-sci-fi.
105. Arch-UNIDO ID/OA 321 BUL 11, 12, 14, 28, 30. DP/BUL/81/002.
106. Arch-ILO Z 11/1/2 ILO, "Activities in the Field of Productivity, 1952–1956."
107. "Productivity Missions to Underdeveloped Countries," *International Labour Review* 76, no. 1 (1957): 2–29.
108. ILO, "The Effectiveness of ILO Management Development and Productivity Projects. Report and Conclusions," *Management Development Series* 3, Geneva, 1965, 6.
109. Arch-ILO OTA/Poland/R.1, "Report to the government of Poland on a survey mission in connection with management, productivity, supervisory of vocational training." For a complete account, see Sandrine Kott, "The Social Engineering Project: Exportation of Capitalist Management Culture to Eastern Europe (1950–1980)," in Christian, Kott, and Matejka, *Planning in Cold War Europe*, 123–43.
110. "National Management Development Centre Poland, Report for the Government of Poland. Report Prepared for the Government of Poland by the International Labour Organisation Acting as Executing Agency for the Special Fund Sector of the United Nations Development Programme" (Geneva: ILO, 1966); Arch-ILO UNDP 7/B09/256.
111. Zdeněk Mošna, "The New Economic System and Management Development in Czechoslovakia," *International Labour Review* 3 (1967): 61–81.
112. Anna-Maria Catanus, "Official and Unofficial Futures of the Communism System Romanian: Futures Studies between Control and Dissidence," in *The Struggle for the Long-Term in Transnational Science and Politics: Forging the Future*, ed. Jenny Andersson and Egle Rindzevičiūtė (New York: Routledge, 2015), 173.
113. See "National Management Development Centre Poland. Report prepared for the Government of Poland by the International Labour Organization acting as executing agency for the Special Fund Sector of the United Nations Development Programme," Geneva, 1966.
114. Arch-ILO UNDP, 52-2-B-1-1, "Review mission, Schiefelbusch," 18 April 1975.
115. Arch-ILO UNDP, 10-2-B-2-1-1, "Technical report 2," November 1971.
116. Arch-SAPMO DY 3023-802 Bl. 204, "Information der Botschaft der DDR in der UVR. Wirtschaftspolitische Abteilung. Budapest, den 7.3.1968"; Arch-ILO-A Z 1/17/1.
117. RArchC, Ford, FA 538, 1971–72.
118. Arch-SAPMO DY 34 / 12515, "ILO. Information über die Konferenz der Vertreter der Ministerien für Arbeit der RGWStaaten am 19.4.1973 in Bukarest zum Tagesordnungpunkt Fragen der ILO."
119. Arch-UN NYC S-139/1/22, "Draft letter of endorsement of final report POL /68/509," 16 July 1973. For the Vistula Basin, "Water Resource Engineers Inc Walnut Creek Cal/USA and Hydraulics Research Station," Wallingdorf (GB).
120. Arch-ILO MI 221, "Missions—Cecil Rhys Wynne-Roberts Report on mission to Bulgaria," 10–17 October 1970.
121. Arch-ILO TAP 14–57, letter from Rens to Morse, 24 July 1957. Arch-ILO Z 11/10/3. In 1953, when the Burmese government asked Czechoslovak experts to provide

6. FROM INTERNATIONALISMS TO GLOBALISM

training in social security, David Morse responded that it was out of the question to recruit Eastern European experts.

122. Arch-ILO SI 2-0-17, "Social security Cz 1943_1960 et TAP 14–57."
123. Arch-ILO TAP 14–130, "Report, 1968."
124. For Poland, Arch-UNIDO ID/OA 332/(3) 1, 13, 26, 101, 111; for Czechoslovakia, ID/OA 332/3, 3, 23, 104.
125. Romanian and Bulgarian leaders within Comecon also used this argument: John Michael Montias, "Background and Origins of the Rumanian Dispute with Comecon," *Soviet Studies* 16, no. 2 (1964): 125–51.
126. Arch-ILO MI 221, "Letter Jean Fauchon," 23 September 1965.
127. Arch-ILO MI 221, "Jean Ozet to Blanchard," 11 October 1970.
128. International Labour Organization, *An Introduction of Cooperative Practice*, Geneva, 1952, text largely developed during a conference held by W.K.H. Campbell, an active promoter of developing cooperatives in the League of Nations development program in the 1930s.
129. Arch-ILO UNDP 52-2-b-1-1, "Rabenold to Stig Andersen (UNDP Regional Bureau)."

6. FROM INTERNATIONALISMS TO GLOBALISM

1. For such an analysis, see Georges-Henri Soutou, *La Guerre froide: 1943–1990* (Paris: Pluriel, 2011), 983–1039. For a critical analysis of this point of view, see Pierre Grosser, *Les Temps de la guerre froide: réflexions sur l'histoire de la guerre froide et sur les causes de sa fin* (Brussels: Complexe, 1995), 263–304.
2. A number of historians have stressed the importance of the 1970s for understanding the arrival within a new world: Niall Ferguson et al., eds., *The Shock of the Global: The 1970s in Perspective* (Cambridge, Mass.: Harvard University Press, 2011); Frank Bösch, *Zeitenwechsel 1979. Als die Welt von heute begann* (Munich: Verlag C.H. Beck, 2019).
3. For a brief summary, see Odd Arne Westad, *The Cold War: A World History* (New York: Basic Books, 2017), 531–34.
4. The literature on this point is vast. For a synthesis, see Ivan Berend, *Central and Eastern Europe, 1944–1993: Detour from the Periphery to the Periphery* (Cambridge: Cambridge University Press, 2010) 222–301, as well as various insights in Juliane Fürst, Silvio Pons, and Mark Selden, eds., *Endgames? Late Communism in Global Perspective, 1968 to the Present* (Cambridge: Cambridge University Press, 2017).
5. For the WHO, see especially Theodore M. Brown, Marcos Cueto, and Elizabeth Fee, "The World Health Organization and the Transition from 'International' to 'Global' Public Health," *American Journal of Public Health* 96, no. 1 (2006): 62–72.
6. On this and the following, see Eric Helleiner, *States and the Reemergence of Global Finance: From Bretton Woods to the 1990s* (Ithaca, N.Y.: Cornell University Press, 1996 [1994]).
7. See Bob Reinalda, *Routledge History of International Organizations: From 1815 to the Present Day* (London: Routledge, 2009), 521–37.
8. See chapter 3.
9. See chapter 4.

6. FROM INTERNATIONALISMS TO GLOBALISM

10. See the stimulating analysis of Luc Boltanski and Ève Chiapello in *The New Spirit of Capitalism*, trans. Gregory Elliott (New York: Verso, 2007) (published in French in 1999).

11. On this temporary concordance and the difficulty in establishing causality, see Umut Özsu, "Neoliberalism and Human Rights: The Brandt Commission and the Struggle for a New World," *Law & Contemporary Problems* 81, no. 4 (2018): 139–65. For the establishment of more direct relations via the study of works by neoliberal economists, see Jessica Whyte, *The Morals of the Market: Human Rights and the Rise of Neoliberalism* (London: Verso, 2019).

12. See chapter 5.

13. The term *crisis* can be disputed. See Boltanski and Chiapello, *The New Spirit*, 17–28.

14. On the origins of neoliberalism, see especially François Denord, "Aux origines du néo-libéralisme en France," *Le Mouvement social* 195, no. 2 (2001): 9–34.

15. Ralf Ptak, "Revisiting the Ordoliberal Foundations of the Social Market Economy," in *The Road from Mont Pèlerin: The Making of the Neoliberal Thought*, ed. Philip Mirowski and Dieter Plehwe (Cambridge, Mass.: Harvard University Press, 2015), 98–138.

16. Matthias Schmelzer, *Freiheit für Wechselkurse und Kapital: die Ursprünge neoliberaler Währungspolitik und die Mont Pèlerin Society* (Marburg, Ger.: Metropolis-Verlag, 2010); Jean Solchany, *Wilhelm Röpke, l'autre Hayek: aux origines du néolibéralisme* (Paris: Publications de la Sorbonne, 2015); and Patricia Commun, *Les Ordolibéraux: histoire d'un libéralisme à l'allemande* (Paris: Les Belles Lettres, 2016).

17. François Denord, "Le prophète, le pèlerin et le missionnaire : la circulation internationale du néo-libéralisme et ses acteurs," *Actes de la recherche en sciences sociales* 145, no. 5 (2002): 9–34.

18. For the Swiss example, see Yves Steiner, "Les riches amis suisses du néolibéralisme," *Traverse. Revue d'histoire* 14, no. 1 (2007): 114–26.

19. On this and the following, see Quinn Slobodian, *Globalists: The End of Empire and the Birth of Neoliberalism* (Cambridge, Mass.: Harvard University Press, 2018).

20. Jean Solchany, "Le problème plus que la solution: la démocratie dans la vision du monde néolibérale," *Revue de philosophie économique* 17, no. 1 (2016): 135–69.

21. John Toye and Richard Toye, *The UN and Global Political Economy: Trade, Finance and Development* (Bloomington: Indiana University Press, 2004), 254–75.

22. Jennifer Bair, "Taking Aim at the New International Economic Order," in Mirowski and Plehwe, *The Road from Mont Pèlerin*, 347–85.

23. On Doctors Without Borders, from Third Worldism to humanitarianism, see Eleanor Davey, *Idealism Beyond Borders: The French Revolutionary Left and the Rise of Humanitarianism, 1954–1988* (Cambridge: Cambridge University Press, 2015).

24. Toye and Toye, *The UN and Global Political Economy*, 257.

25. Gilbert Rist, *History of Development: From Western Origins to Global Faith* (London: Zed Books, 2019), 240–60. See also Davey, *Idealism Beyond Borders*, 215–47.

26. See Olivier Lafourcade and Michèle Guerard, "Banque mondiale et ajustement structurel," *Revue d'économie financière* 4, no. 1 (1994): 355–67. For a sociohistorical analysis of this consensus, see Yves Dezalay and Bryant Garth, "Le 'Washington consensus,' " *Actes de la recherche en sciences sociales* 121, no. 1 (1998): 3–22.

6. FROM INTERNATIONALISMS TO GLOBALISM

27. Slobodian, *Globalists*, 244.
28. For a fine treatment of this topic, see Federico Romero, "Socialism Between Détente and Globalisation," in *European Socialist Regimes: Fateful Engagement with the West: National Strategies in the Long 1970s*, ed. Angela Romano and Federico Romero (London: Routledge, 2020), 11–30.
29. Kotkin, "The Kiss of Debt," in Ferguson et al., *The Shock of the Global*, 80–101.
30. Marie-Hélène Labbé, "L'embargo céréalier de 1980 ou les limites de l'"arme verte,'" *Politique étrangère* 51, no. 3 (1986): 771–83; Labbé, "Y a-t-il une politique américaine de commerce avec l'URSS?," 899–906.
31. See Timofeevich Bogomolov, *Socialisme et compétitivité*, and the highly insightful introduction by Marie Lavigne, 9–17; Lavigne, *Les Économies socialistes: les pays de l'Est dans l'économie mondiale* (Paris: Presses de la Fondation nationale des sciences politiques, 1989), 384–97; and Lavigne, *Économie internationale des pays socialistes* (Paris: Armand Colin, 1985), 214–21.
32. See in particular the role of the Ost-Ausschuss der deutschen Wirtschaft (German Eastern Business Association), in Sven Jüngerkes, *Diplomaten der Wirtschaft: die Geschichte des Ost-Ausschusses der Deutschen Wirtschaft* (Osnabrück, Ger.: Fibre, 2012).
33. See André Steiner, "The Globalisation Process and the Eastern Bloc Countries in the 1970s and 1980s," *European Review of History* 21, no. 2 (2014): 165–81.
34. Bogomolov, *Socialisme et compétitivité*, 203.
35. Kazimierz Grzybowski, "La communauté socialiste et les projets de Gorbatchev," *Revue d'études comparatives Est-Ouest* 19, no. 2 (1988): 131–44.
36. Bogomolov, *Socialisme et compétitivité*, 87.
37. Bogomolov, 27–37.
38. Johanna Bockman, *Markets in the Name of Socialism: The Left-Wing Origins of Neoliberalism* (Stanford, Calif.: Stanford University Press, 2011; Johanna Bockman and Gil Eyal, "Eastern Europe as a Laboratory for Economic Knowledge: The Transnational Roots of Neoliberalism," *American Journal of Sociology* 108, no. 2 (2002): 310–52; and Bockman, "The Origins of Neoliberalism Between Soviet Socialism and Western Capitalism: 'A Galaxy without Borders,'" *Theory and Society* 36 (2007): 343–71.
39. See Angela Romano, "Pan-Europe: A Continental Space for Cooperation," in Romano and Romero, *European Socialist Regimes*, 38–40.
40. On these programs, see chapter 5.
41. Pavel Szobi, "Czechoslovakia's Pan-European Relations During the 'Long 1970s,'" in Romano and Romero, *European Socialist Regimes*, 138–40.
42. Gil Eyal, Iván Szelényi, and Eleanor R. Townsley, *Making Capitalism Without Capitalists: Class Formation and Elite Struggles in Post-Communist Central Europe* (London: Verso, 1998).
43. Tudor Ciumara, "Contributions to the History of Management Consulting in Communist Romania," *Procedia Economics and Finance* 8 (2014): 175–81.
44. For economic rigidity, see the still-relevant analysis of Janos Kornai, *Economics of Shortage: Contributions to Economic Analysis* (Amsterdam: North-Holland, 1980); and Kornai, *Le Système socialiste. L'économie politique du communisme* (Grenoble: PUG, 1996).
45. See chapter 3.

6. FROM INTERNATIONALISMS TO GLOBALISM

46. See chapter 2.
47. Emmanuel Droit, *Les Polices politiques du bloc de l'Est. À la recherche de l'Internationale tchékiste 1955–1989* (Paris: Gallimard, 2019), 216–44.
48. Arch-SAPMO DY 34 / 13371, "Information über die Teilnahme an der Abschlusssitzung der ständigen Arbeitsgruppe des RGW zu ILO-Fragen," 15 March 1985. See also the Stasi's point of view in Arch-MFS ZAIG 13156, "Wocheneinschätzung aktueller Vorgänge in der VRP," 25 November 1986.
49. Arch-MfS XVIII Ka/100 (CD).
50. Arch-IFZ 708-1-1489, "Exploratory Meeting with the Chambers of Commerce of the Socialist Countries," 22 September 1967.
51. Pal Germuska, "Balancing Between the COMECON and the EEC: Hungarian Elite Debates on European Integration During the Long 1970s," *Cold War History* 19, no. 3 (2019): 401–20.
52. Harold James, *International Monetary Cooperation Since Bretton Woods* (New York: Oxford University Press, 1996), 559–61.
53. Arch-MfS XVIII Ka/100 (Aufnahme 1989, 2ᵉ piste).
54. See Tamás Bácskai, "East-West Financial Problems and Their Solution in a World-Wide Context," in *East-West Trade and Finance in the World Economy: A New Look for the 1980s*, ed. Christopher Thomas Saunders (New York: St. Martin's Press, 1985), 137–46.
55. Mark Zimdars, "L'Organisation de la conférence islamique," *Verfassung und Recht in Übersee/Law and Politics in Africa, Asia and Latin America* 24, no. 4 (1991): 406–48.
56. Edward Kolodziej and Roger E. Kanet, "L'Union soviétique et le monde en développement: Thermidor dans la lutte révolutionnaire," *Revue d'études comparatives Est-Ouest* 19, no. 2 (1988): 5–22.
57. See, for example, Chiara Bonfiglioli, "The First UN World Conference on Women (1975) as a Cold War Encounter: Recovering Anti-Imperialist Non-Aligned and Socialist Genealogies," *Filozofija i Društvo* 27, no. 3 (2016): 521–41; Kristen Ghodsee, "Rethinking State Socialist Mass Women's Organizations: The Committee of the Bulgarian Women's Movement and the United Nations Decade for Women. 1975–1985," *Journal of Women's History* 24, no. 4 (2012): 49–73; and Ghodsee, "Internationalisme socialiste et féminisme d'État pendant la guerre froide. Les relations entre Bulgarie et Zambie," *Clio* 41, no. 25 (2015): 115–38.
58. Bogdan C. Iacob, "Health," in *Socialism Goes Global: The Soviet Union and Eastern Europe in the Age of Decolonization*, ed. James Mark and Paul Betts (Oxford: Oxford University Press, 2022), 255–89.
59. Alessandro Iandolo, "The Rise and Fall of the 'Soviet Model of Development' in West Africa, 1957–64," *Cold War History* 12, no. 4 (2012): 683–704.
60. For an example, see Simon Godard, "Les calculs intéressés de la Guerre froide: l'Economic Commission for Europe et le monde socialiste face à la révision de la quantification du développement," *Revue d'histoire moderne contemporaine* 65, no. 4 (2018): 33–58.
61. Lukasz Stanek, "Buildings for Dollars and Oil: East German and Romanian Construction Companies in Cold War Iraq," *Journal of Contemporary European History*, forthcoming.

6. FROM INTERNATIONALISMS TO GLOBALISM

62. Jan Adamec, "Czechoslovakia and Arms Deliveries to Syria 1955–1989," *Les Cahiers Sirice* 10 (2013): 69–81.
63. On this and the following, see Marie Lavigne, ed., *Les Relations Est-Sud dans l'économie mondiale* (Paris : Economica, 1986).
64. Bogomolov, *Socialisme et compétitivité*, 201.
65. Christina Schwenkel, "Affective Solidarities and East German Reconstruction of Postwar Vietnam," in *Comrades of Color: East Germany in the Cold War World*, ed. Quinn Slobodian (New York: Berghahn Books, 2015), 267–93.
66. For an analysis of this ebb for France, see Bernard Pudal, "La beauté de la mort communiste," *Revue française de science politique* 52, no. 5 (2002): 545–59.
67. Robert J. Alexander, *Maoism in the Developed World* (Westport, Conn.: Praeger, 2001).
68. On this and the following, see Silvio Pons, *The Global Revolution: A History of International Communism, 1917–1991* (Oxford: Oxford University Press, 2014), 255; Fürst, Pons, and Selden, *Endgames?*
69. See chapter 3.
70. Jean-Marie Pernot, "Dedans, dehors, la dimension internationale dans le syndicalisme français," Ph.D. diss., Université de Nanterre, 2001, 338–61, https://tel.archives-ouvertes.fr/tel-00927161/document.
71. On the difficulty of such a position, see Sonia Combe, *La Loyauté à tout prix. Les floués du "socialisme réel"* (Bordeaux: Éditions du Bord de l'eau, 2019).
72. See Silvio Pons and Michele Donato, "What Was Reform Communism?," in Fürst, Pons, and Selden, *Endgames?*, 178–202.
73. Pierre Milza, "Les mouvements pacifistes et les guerres froides depuis 1947," *Publications de l'École française de Rome* 95, no. 1 (1987): 265–83.
74. For an in-depth and nuanced discussion of this question of responsibility, see Oliver Bange, "SS-20 and Pershing II: Weapon Systems and the Dynamization of East-West Relations," in *The Nuclear Crisis: The Arms Race, Cold War Anxiety, and the German Peace Movement of the 1980s*, ed. Christoph Becker-Schaum et al. (New York: Berghahn Books, 2016), 70–86.
75. Matthew Evangelista, "Transnational Organizations and the Cold War," *Cambridge History of the Cold War*, vol. 3: *Endings* (Cambridge: Cambridge University Press, 2012), 415; Beatrice de Graaf, "Détente from Below: The Stasi and the Dutch Peace Movement," *Journal of Intelligence History* 3, no. 2 (2003): 9–20.
76. Sebastian Stude, "Frieden als Demokratieforderung. Evangelische Kirche in den 1980er Jahren in der DDR," *Deutschland Archiv*, June 26, 2014, http://www.bpb.de/1866931.
77. Robert Gildea, "The Global 1968 and International Communism," in Fürst, Pons, and Selden *Endgames?*, 23–49.
78. On the Women's International Democratic Federation, see chapter 2.
79. Celia Donnert, "Feminism, Communism and Global Socialism: Encounters and Entanglements," in Fürst, Pons, and Selden, *Endgames?*, 399–421.
80. See, among many others, Michelle Zancarini-Fournel, "Genre et politique : les années 1968," *Vingtième Siècle. Revue d'histoire* 75, no. 3 (2002): 133–43; and Brigitte Studer, *1968 und die Formung des feministischen Subjekts* (Vienna: Picus Verlag, 2011).

81. Douglas Weiner, "Communism and Environment," in Fürst, Pons, and Selden, *Endgames?*, 529–54.
82. World Commission on Environment and Development, *Our Common Future* (1987), https://sustainabledevelopment.un.org/content/documents/5987our-common -future.pdf.
83. Yannick Mahrane and Christophe Bonneuil, "Gouverner la biosphère. De l'environnement de la guerre froide à l'environnement néolibéral," in Dominique Pestre, ed., *Le Gouvernement des technosciences* (Paris: La Découverte, 2014), 133–69.
84. On this relation between the environmental and peace movements, see the example of Germany (East and West) in Becker-Schaum, *The Nuclear Crisis*.
85. Mélanie Arndt, ed., *Politik und Gesellschaft nach Tschernobyl. (Ost)Europäische Perspektiven* (Berlin: Christoph Links, 2015).
86. See Jensen, *The Making of International Human Rights: The 1960s, Decolonization, and the Reconstruction of Global Values* (Cambridge: Cambridge University Press, 2016), on the support of representatives from socialist countries at the UN. Also see Paul Betts, "Rights," in *Socialism Goes Global: The Soviet Union and Eastern Europe in the Age of Decolonisation*, ed. James Mark and Paul Betts (Oxford: Oxford University Press, 2022), 180–220.
87. Rosemary Foot, "The Cold War and Human Rights," in Leffler and Westad, *The Cambridge History of the Cold War*, vol. 3: *Endings*, 445–66; Jan Eckel, "The Rebirth of Politics from the Spirit of Morality: Explaining the Human Rights Revolution of the 1970s," in *The Breakthrough: Human Rights in the 1970s*, ed. Jan Eckel and Samuel Moyn (Philadelphia: University of Pennsylvania Press, 2013), 226–57.
88. On demands for rights by actors and dissidents in the East, see Benjamin Nathans, "The Disenchantment of Socialism: Soviet Dissidents, Human Rights and the New Global Morality," in Eckel and Moyn, *The Breakthrough*, 33–48; Philip Bradley, "Human Rights and Communism," in Fürst, Pons, and Selden, *Endgames?*, 151–77; and Eric Weitz, *A World Divided. The Global Struggle for Human Rights in the Age of Nation-States* (Princeton, N.J.: Princeton University Press, 2019), 302–16.
89. See Daniel Charles Thomas, *The Helsinki Effect: International Norms, Human Rights, and the Demise of Communism* (Princeton, N.J.: Princeton University Press, 2001); and Sarah B. Snyder, *Human Rights Activism and the End of the Cold War: A Transnational History of the Helsinki Network* (Cambridge: Cambridge University Press, 2011).
90. Bent Boel, "Transnationalisme social-démocrate et dissidents de l'Est pendant la guerre froide," *Vingtième Siècle. Revue d'histoire* 109, no. 1 (2011): 169–81.
91. Benjamin Gutmann, "Relais et réseaux de la Charte 77 en France, entre 1977 et 1989," *Bulletin de l'Institut Pierre Renouvin* 33, no. 1 (2011): 49–64.
92. See Jean-Yves Potel, "La revendication autogestionnaire dans la Pologne de Solidarité," *Sociologie du travail* 24, no. 3 (1982): 262–78.
93. Gregory F. Domber, "The AFL-CIO, the Reagan Administration and Solidarność," *Polish Review* 52, no. 3 (2007): 277–304.
94. Arch-IISH Ac 392, 393, 394 files ICFTU 4000.6, Poland, for the role of the ICFTU.
95. On the role of the ILO in the internationalization of support, see Isdebald Goddeeris, "The Limits of Lobbying: ILO and Solidarność," in *ILO Histories: Essays*

on the International Labour Organization and Its Impact on the World During the Twentieth Century, ed. Jasmien Van Daele et al. (Bern: Peter Lang, 2010), 423–41.

96. "Compte rendu des débats de la 67e Conférence internationale du travail," ILO, Geneva, 1981, 310.

97. Arch-MfS HA XVIII20180, Bericht 2 March 1988.

98. Arch-MfS HA IX 18487.

99. Arch-MfS HA XVIII20180 and MfS XVIII Ka/100 (CD).

100. Arch-MfS HA XVIII20180.

CONCLUSION

1. Luc Boltanski and Ève Chiapello, *The New Spirit of Capitalism*, trans. Gregory Elliott (New York: Verso, 2007).

2. See the research emphasizing the importance of the socialist internationalism inherited from the interwar period in understanding Brandt's *Ostpolitik*: Talbot Imlay, " 'The Policy of Social Democracy Is Self-Consciously Internationalist': The SPD's Internationalism After 1945," *Journal of Modern History* 86 (2014): 81–123; and Christian Bailey, "Socialist Vision of European Unity in Germany: *Ostpolitik* Since the 1920s?," *Contemporary European History* 25, no. 2 (2017): 243–60.

BIBLIOGRAPHY

Abel, E. K., E. Fee, and T. M. Brown. "Milton I. Roemer Advocate of Social Medicine, International Health, and National Health Insurance." *American Journal of Public Health* 98, no. 9 (2008): 1596–97.

Abtour, Georges-Henri. "L'URSS et l'Amérique latine pendant la guerre froide." *Outre-Mers. Revue d'histoire* 94, no. 354 (2007): 9–22.

Adamec, Jan. "Czechoslovakia and Arms Deliveries to Syria 1955–1989." *Les Cahiers Sirice* 10 (2013): 69–81.

Agnew, John, and J. Nicholas Entrikin. *The Marshall Plan Today: Model and Metaphor*. London: Routledge, 2004.

Alacevich, Michele. "Planning Peace: The European Roots of the Post-War Global Development Challenge." *Past & Present* 239, no. 1 (2018): 219–64.

——. *The Political Economy of the World Bank: The Early Years*. Stanford, Calif.: Stanford University Press, 2009.

Alcock, Antony. *History of the International Labour Organization*. New York: Octagon Books, 1971.

Alexander, Robert J. *Maoism in the Developed World*. Westport, Conn.: Praeger, 2001.

Ammann, Klaus. "Swiss Trade with the East in the Early Cold War." In *East-West Trade and the Cold War*, ed. Jari Eloranta and Jari Ojala, 114–31. Jyväskylä, Fin.: University of Jyväskylä, 2005.

Amrith, Sunil, and Glenda Sluga. "New Histories of the United Nations." *Journal of World History* 19, no. 3 (2008): 251–74.

Anderson, Sheldon R. *A Dollar to Poland Is a Dollar to Russia: US Economic Policy Toward Poland, 1945–1952*. New York: Garland, 1993.

Andersson, Jenny. *The Future of the World: Futurology, Futurists, and the Struggle for the Post Cold War Imagination*. Oxford: Oxford University Press, 2018.

Angoulevent, P. "Nouvelle orientation de la politique commerciale en Yougoslavie." *Économie et statistique* 5, no. 4 (1950): 86–95.

Appelqvist, Örjan. "Rediscovering Uncertainty: Early Attempts at a Pan-European Post-War Recovery." *Cold War History* 8, no. 3 (2008): 327–52.

Arndt, Gabriele. "Das wissenschaftliche Werk Eva Schmidt-Kolmers unter besonderer Berücksichtigung ihrer Beiträge zum Kinder- und Jugendgesundheitsschutz in der DDR." Diss. med., Greifswald, 2001.

Arndt, Mélanie, ed. *Politik und Gesellschaft nach Tschernobyl. (Ost)Europäische Perspektiven.* Berlin: Christoph Links, 2015.

Aunesluoma, Juhana. "Finlandisation in Reverse: The CSCE and the Rise and Fall of Economic Détente 1968–1975." In *Helsinki 1975 and the Transformation of Europe*, ed. Oliver Bange and Gottfried Niedhart, 98–113. New York: Berghahn Books.

Aute, David. *The Great Fear: The Anti-Communist Purge under Truman and Eisenhower.* New York: Simon and Schuster, 1978.

Autio-Sarasmo, Sari. "Knowledge Through the Iron Curtain: Soviet Scientific-Technical Cooperation with Finland and West Germany." In *Reassessing Cold War Europe*, ed. Sari Autio-Sarasmo and Katalin Miklóssy, 66–83. New York: Routledge, 2011.

Autio-Sarasmo, Sari, and Katalin Miklóssy, eds. *Reassessing Cold War Europe.* New York: Routledge, 2011.

Azadovskii, Konstantin, and Boris Egorov. "From Anti-Westernism to Anti-Semitism." *Journal of Cold War Studies* 4, no. 1 (2002): 66–80.

Babb, Sarah. "Embeddedness, Inflation, and International Regimes: The IMF in the Early Postwar Period." *American Journal of Sociology* 113 (2007): 128–64.

Bácskai, Tamás. "East-West Financial Problems and Their Solution in a World-Wide Context." In *East-West Trade and Finance in the World Economy: A New Look for the 1980s*, ed. Christopher Thomas Saunders, 137–46. New York: St. Martin's Press, 1985.

Badalassi, Nicolas. "Adieu Yalta? La France, la détente et les origines de la Conférence sur la Sécurité et la Coopération en Europe, 1965–1975." Ph.D. diss., université de la Sorbonne, 2011. https://tel.archives-ouvertes.fr/tel-00713652.

——. "'Neither Too Much nor Too Little': France, the USSR and the Helsinki CSCE." *Cold War History* 18, no. 1 (2018): 1–17.

Bailey, Christian. "Socialist Visions of European Unity in Germany: *Ostpolitik* Since the 1920s." *Contemporary European History* 26, no. 2 (2017): 243–60.

Bailey, Paul J., and Ilka Bailey-Wiebecke. "All-European Co-operation: The CSCE's Basket Two and the ECE." *International Journal* 32, no. 2 (1977): 386–407.

Bair, Jennifer. "Taking Aim at the New International Economic Order." In *The Road from Mont Pèlerin: The Making of the Neoliberal Thought*, ed. Philip Mirowski and Dieter Plehwe, 347–85. Cambridge, Mass.: Harvard University Press, 2015.

Bairoch, Paul. "Du Tiers-Monde aux Tiers-Mondes. Convergences et clivages." *Population* 47, no. 6 (1992): 1485–1503.

Balińska, Marta Aleksandra. *Une vie pour l'humanitaire: Ludwik Rajchman (1881–1965).* Paris: La Découverte, 2015.

Balussou, Madeleine. "Les échanges de la Roumanie avec l'OCDE (1970–1980)." *Revue d'études comparatives Est-Ouest* 12, no. 4 (1981): 91–114.

Bange, Oliver. "SS-20 and Pershing II: Weapon Systems and the Dynamization of East-West Relations." In *The Nuclear Crisis: The Arms Race, Cold War Anxiety, and the*

BIBLIOGRAPHY

German Peace Movement of the 1980s, ed. Christoph Becker-Schaum et al., 70–86. New York: Berghahn Books, 2016.

Bantigny, Ludivine, Boris Gobille, and Eugénia Palieraki, eds. "Les années 1968: circulations révolutionnaires." *Monde(s)* 11, no. 1 (2017).

Barjot, Dominique. "Introduction." In *La Reconstruction économique de l'Europe (1945 1953). Histoire, économie & société* 18 (1999): 227–43.

Bazin, Jérôme, Pascal Dubourg Glatigny, and Piotr Piotrowski, eds. *Art Beyond Borders: Artistic Exchange in Communist Europe (1945–1989)*. Budapest: Central European University Press, 2016.

Beck, Peter J., "The League of Nations and the Great Powers, 1936–1940." *World Affairs* 157, no. 4 (1995): 175–89.

Becker-Schaum, Christoph, et al., eds. *The Nuclear Crisis: The Arms Race, Cold War Anxiety, and the German Peace Movement of the 1980s*. New York: Berghahn Books, 2016.

Behrends, Jan C., Thomas Lindenberger, and Patrice G. Poutrus, eds. *Fremde und Fremd-Sein in der DDR: zu historischen Ursachen der Fremdenfeindlichkeit in Ostdeutschland*. Berlin: Metropol, 2003.

Békés, Csaba. "Hungary, the Soviet Bloc, the German Question, and the CSCE Process, 1965–1975." *Journal of Cold War Studies* 18, no. 3 (July 1, 2016): 95–138.

Bensimon, Fabrice, Quentin Deleurmoz, and Jeanne Moisand, eds. *"Arise Ye Wretched of the Earth." The First International in a Global Perspective*. Leiden: Brill, 2019.

Berend, Ivan. *Central and Eastern Europe, 1944–1993: Detour from the Periphery to the Periphery*. Cambridge: Cambridge University Press, 2010.

Berghahn, Volker Rolf. *America and the Intellectual Cold Wars in Europe: Shepard Stone Between Philanthropy, Academy, and Diplomacy*. Princeton, N.J.: Princeton University Press, 2001.

Beroud, Samuel, and Thomas Hajduk. "L'OCDE et les bonnes pratiques. Une histoire inséparable." In *Les Bonnes Pratiques des relations internationales*, ed. C. Laporte, A. Klein, and M. Saiget, 61–77. Paris: Presses de Sciences Po, 2015.

Berstein, Serge, and Pierre Milza, eds. *L'Année 1947*. Paris: Presses de Sciences Po, 1999.

Berthelot, Yves. "The Interest of the Industrial West in Relations with Developing Countries." In *East, West, South: Economic Interactions Between Three Worlds*, ed. Christopher Thomas Saunders, 19–32. New York: St. Martin's Press, 1981.

——. *Unity and Diversity in Development Ideas Perspectives from the UN Regional Commissions*. Bloomington: Indiana University Press, 2004.

Berthelot, Yves, and Paul Rayment. "Economic Commission for Europe." In *Unity and Diversity in Development Ideas Perspectives from the UN Regional Commissions*, ed. Yves Berthelot, 46–70. Bloomington: Indiana University Press, 2004.

——. *Looking Back and Peering Forward: A Short History of the United Nations Economic Commission for Europe, 1947-2007*. New York: UN, 2007.

Bertrams, Kenneth. "Une inspiration tout en contrastes." *Genèses. Sciences sociales et Histoire* 71, no. 2 (2008): 64–83.

Bettati, Mario. "L'admission des deux Allemagnes à l'O.N.U." *Annuaire français de droit international* 19, no. 1 (1973): 211–31.

Betts, Paul. "Rights." In *Socialism Goes Global: The Soviet Union and Eastern Europe in the Age of Decolonisation*, ed. James Mark and Paul Betts, 180–220. Oxford: Oxford University Press, 2022.

BIBLIOGRAPHY

Blok, Aad. "Socialist Intellectual as Social Engineer. Jan Tinbergen Ideas on Economic Policy and the Optimal Economic Order (1930–1960)." *Socialist History* 27 (2005): 43–60.

Bockman, Johanna. *Markets in the Name of Socialism: The Left-Wing Origins of Neoliberalism*. Stanford, Calif.: Stanford University Press, 2011.

——. "The Origins of Neoliberalism Between Soviet Socialism and Western Capitalism: 'A Galaxy Without Borders.'" *Theory and Society* 36 (2007): 343–71.

——. "Socialist Globalization Against Capitalist Neocolonialism: The Economic Ideas Behind the New International Economic Order." *Humanity: An International Journal of Human Rights, Humanitarianism & Development* 6, no. 1 (2015): 109–28.

Bockman, Johanna, and Gil Eyal. "Eastern Europe as a Laboratory for Economic Knowledge: The Transnational Roots of Neoliberalism." *American Journal of Sociology* 108, no. 2 (2002): 310–52.

Boel, Bent. *The European Productivity Agency and Transatlantic Relations, 1953–1961*. Copenhagen: Museum Tusculanum Press/University of Copenhagen, 2003.

——. "Transnationalisme social-démocrate et dissidents de l'Est pendant la guerre froide." *Vingtième Siècle. Revue d'histoire* 109, no. 1 (2011): 169–81.

Bogomolov, Oleg. "The CMEA Countries and the New International Economic Order." In *East, West, South: Economic Interactions Between Three Worlds*, ed. Christopher Thomas Saunders, 246–56. New York: St. Martin's Press, 1981.

Bogomolov, Timofeevich. *Socialisme et compétitivité: les pays de l'Est dans l'économie mondiale*. Paris: Presses de la Fondation nationale des sciences politiques, 1989.

Boltanski, Luc. "America, America . . . Le plan Marshall et l'importation du management américain." *Actes de la recherche en sciences sociales* 38 (1981): 19–41.

Boltanski, Luc, and Ève Chiapello. *The New Spirit of Capitalism*, trans. Gregory Elliott. New York: Verso, 2007 (first published in French in 1999, last edition in English in 2018).

Bonfiglioli, Chiara. "The First UN World Conference on Women (1975) as a Cold War Encounter: Recovering Anti-Imperialist Non-Aligned and Socialist Genealogies." *Filozofija i Društvo* 27, no. 3 (2016): 521–41.

Borgwardt, Elizabeth. *A New Deal for the World: America's Vision for Human Rights*. Cambridge, Mass.: Harvard University Press, 2005.

Boris, Eileen. "Equality's Cold War: The ILO and the UN Commission on the Status of Women, 1946–1970s." In *Women's ILO: Transnational Networks, Global Labour Standards and Gender Equity, 1919 to Present*, ed. Eileen Boris, Dorothea Hoehtker, and Susan Zimmermann, 97–120. Leiden: Brill, 2018.

Borowy, Iris. *Coming to Terms with World Health: The League of Nations Health Organisation, 1921–1946*. Frankfurt: Peter Lang, 2009.

Bosc, Robert. "L'URSS face aux revendications du Tiers-monde: soutien de principe et intérêt mutuel." *Revue française de science politique* 26, no. 4 (1976): 696–708.

Bossuat, Gérard. *L'Europe occidentale à l'heure américaine: le Plan Marshall et l'unité européenne (1945–1952)*. Brussels: Éditions Complexe, 1992.

Bradley, Philip. "Human Rights and Communism." In *Endgames? Late Communism in Global Perspective, 1968 to the Present*, ed. Juliane Fürst, Silvio Pons, and Mark Selden, 151–77. Cambridge: Cambridge University Press, 2017.

Brendebach, Jonas. "A New Global Media Order: Debates and Policies on Media and Mass Communication at UNESCO." Ph.D. diss., European University Institute, 2019.

BIBLIOGRAPHY

Brosse, Thérèse. *L'Enfance victime de la guerre. Une étude de la situation européenne.* Paris: UNESCO, 1949.

Brown, Theodore M., Marcos Cueto, and Elizabeth Fee. "The World Health Organization and the Transition from 'International' to 'Global' Public Health." *American Journal of Public Health* 96, no. 1 (2006): 62–72.

Buehrig, Edward H. "The United States, the United Nations and Bi-Polar Politics." *International Organization* 4, no. 4 (1950): 573–84.

Burton, Eric, James Mark, and Steffi Marung. "Development." In *Socialism Goes Global: The Soviet Union and Eastern Europe in the Age of Decolonization*, ed. James Mark and Paul Betts, 75–114. Oxford: Oxford University Press, 2022.

Cabanes, Bruno. *The Great War and the Origins of Humanitarianism, 1918–1924.* Cambridge: Cambridge University Press, 2014.

Caillat, Michel. "L'Entente internationale anticommuniste de Theodore Aubert. Organisation interne, réseaux et action d'une internationale anti-marxiste." Ph.D. diss., University of Geneva, 2013.

Caillat, Michel, et al. "Une source inédite de l'histoire de l'anticommunisme: les archives de l'Entente internationale anticommuniste (EIA) de Théodore Aubert (1924–1950)." *Matériaux pour l'histoire de notre temps* 73 (2004): 25–31.

Cain, Frank. "Computers and the Cold War: United States Restrictions on the Export of Computers to the Soviet Union and Communist China." *Journal of Contemporary History* 40, no. 1 (2005): 131–47.

Calame, Mireille, Christine Dabat, Juliette Michaëlis, Dominique Perrot, Yvonne Preiswerk, Roy Preiswerk, Gilbert Rist, and Jacques Vallet, eds. *Il faut manger pour vivre. Controverses sur les besoins fondamentaux et le développement*. Geneva: Cahiers de l'Institut universitaires d'étude du développement, 1980.

Carew, Anthony. "Conflict Within the ICFTU: Anti-communism and Anti-colonialism in the 1950s." *International Review of Social History* 41 (1996): 147–81.

——. *Labour Under the Marshall Plan: The Politics of Productivity and the Marketing of Management Science*. Manchester, UK: Manchester University Press, 1987.

Catanus, Anna-Maria. "Official and Unofficial Futures of the Communism System: Romanian Futures Studies Between Control and Dissidence." In *The Struggle for the Long-Term in Transnational Science and Politics: Forging the Future*, ed. Jenny Andersson and Egle Rindzeviĉiūtė, 169–94. New York: Routledge, 2015.

Christian, Michel. "Un autre printemps des crèches ? Le développement des crèches est allemandes des années 1950 aux années 1980." *Annales de démographie historique* 137, no. 1 (2019): 185–215.

——. *Camarades ou apparatchiks? Les communistes en RDA et en Tchécoslovaquie: 1945 1989.* Paris: PUF, 2016.

——. "'It Is Not a Question of Rigidly Planning Trade.' UNCTAD and the Regulation of the International Trade in the 1970s." In *Planning in Cold War Europe: Competition, Cooperation, Circulations (1950s–1970s)*, ed. Michel Christian, Sandrine Kott, and Ondrej Matejka, 285–313. Berlin: De Gruyter, 2018.

——. "Les partis communistes du bloc de l'Est : un objet transnational. L'exemple des écoles supérieures du parti." *Vingtième Siècle. Revue d'histoire* 109 (2011): 31–43.

——. "UNCTAD." In *Den kalten Krieg vermessen: über Reichweite und Alternative einer binären Ordnungsvorstellung*, ed. Frank Reichherzer, Emmanuel Droit, and Jan Jansen, 297–313. Berlin: De Gruyter, 2018.

BIBLIOGRAPHY

Christian, Michel, Sandrine Kott, and Ondrej Matejka. "International Organizations in the Cold War: The Circulation of Experts Beyond the East-West Divide." *Studia Territorialia* 1 (2017): 35–60.

Christiansen, Samantha, and Zachary A. Scarlett, eds. *The Third World in the Global 1960s*. New York: Berghahn Books, 2015.

Ciumara, Tudor. "Contributions to the History of Management Consulting in Communist Romania." *Procedia Economics and Finance* 8 (2014): 175–81.

Clavin, Patricia. *Securing the World Economy: The Reinvention of the League of Nations, 1920–1946*. Oxford: Oxford University Press, 2013.

Coeuré, Sophie, and Sabine Dullin, eds. *Frontières du communisme: mythologies et réalités de la division de l'Europe de la Révolution d'octobre au mur de Berlin*. Paris: La Découverte, 2007.

Colin, Robert. "Création d'un centre international de l'enfance à Paris." *Population* 5 (1950): 199–200.

Combe, Sonia. *La Loyauté à tout prix. Les floués du "socialisme réel."* Bordeaux: Éditions du Bord de l'eau, 2019.

Commun, Patricia. *Les Ordolibéraux : histoire d'un libéralisme à l'allemande*. Paris: Les Belles Lettres, 2016.

Cooper, Frederick. "Writing the History of Development." *Journal of Modern European History* 8, no. 1 (April 2010): 5–23.

Coppolaro, Lucia. "East-West Trade and the General Agreement on Tariffs and Trade (GATT) and the Cold War: Poland's Accession to the GATT, 1957–1967." In *East-West Trade and the Cold War*, ed. Jari Eloranta and Jari Ojala, 77–92. Jyväskylä, Fin.: University of Jyväskylä, 2005.

Coquery-Vidrovitch, Catherine. *Connaissance du tiers-monde*. Paris: Cahiers Jussieu 4, UGE, 1977.

Crump, Laurien, and Simon Godard. "Reassessing Communist International Organisations: A Comparative Analysis of COMECON and the Warsaw Pact in Relation to Their Cold War Competitors." *Contemporary European History* 27, no. 1 (2017): 1–25.

Cueto, Marcos. "The Origins of Primary Health Care and Selective Primary Health Care." *American Journal of Public Health* 94, no. 11 (2004): 1864–74.

Cullather, Nick. "Development? It's History." *Diplomatic History* 24, no. 4 (2000): 641–53.

Czernecki, Igor. "An Intellectual Offensive: The Ford Foundation and the Destalinization of the Polish Social Sciences." *Cold War History* 13 (2013): 289–310.

Dagmara, Jajesniak-Quast, and Uwe Müller, eds. "Comecon Revisited: Integration in the Eastern Bloc and Entanglements with the Global Economy." *Comparativ* 27 (2018).

Davey, Eleanor. *Idealism Beyond Borders: The French Revolutionary Left and the Rise of Humanitarianism, 1954–1988*. Cambridge: Cambridge University Press, 2015.

David, Myriam, and Geneviève Appell. *Lóczy ou le maternage insolite*. Paris: Éditions du Scarabée, 1973.

David, Thomas. *Nationalisme économique et industrialisation: l'expérience des pays d'Europe de l'Est (1789–1939)*. Geneva: Droz, 2009.

Davies, Robert William. "Forced Labour Under Stalin: The Archive Revelations." *New Left Review* 214 (1995): 62–89.

BIBLIOGRAPHY

Degras, Jane. *The Communist International 1919–1943: Documents*. Vol 1. London: Royal Institute of International Affairs, 1955.

Deighton, Anne. "The British in Strasbourg. Negotiating the European Convention on Human Rights, 1950." In *Human Rights in Europe During the Cold War*, ed. Rasmus Mariager, Karl Molin, and Kjersti Brathagen, 27–42. London: Routledge, 2014.

Denéchère, Yves, and Patrice Marcilloux, eds. *Le Centre international de l'enfance (1949 1997). Des archives à l'histoire*. Rennes: Presses universitaires de Rennes, 2016.

Denord, François. "Aux origines du néo-libéralisme en France." *Le Mouvement social* 195, no. 2 (2001): 9–34.

——. "Le prophète, le pèlerin et le missionnaire: la circulation internationale du néo-libéralisme et ses acteurs." *Actes de la recherche en sciences sociales* 145, no. 5 (2002): 9–34.

Devin, Guillaume, and Marie-Claude Smouts. *Les Organisations internationales*. Paris: Armand Colin, 2011.

Devinatz, Victor. "A Cold War Thaw in the International Working-Class Movement? The World Federation of Trade Unions and the International Confederation of Free Trade Unions, 1967–1977." *Science & Society* 77, no. 3 (2013): 342–71.

Dezalay, Yves, and Bryant Garth. "Droits de l'homme et philanthropie hégémonique." *Actes de la recherche en sciences sociales* 121 (1998): 23–41.

——. "Le 'Washington consensus.'" *Actes de la recherche en sciences sociales* 121, no. 1 (1998): 3–22.

Diebold, William Jr. "East-West Trade and the Marshall Plan." *Foreign Affairs* 26 (1948): 709–22.

Dimier, Véronique. "Institutionnalisation et bureaucratisation de la Commission européenne: l'exemple de la DG développement." *Politique européenne* 11, no. 3 (December 1, 2003): 99–121.

Dimock, Marshall E. "Management in the USSR—Comparisons to the United States." *Public Administration Review* 20, no. 3 (1960): 139–47.

Dinkel, Jürgen. *The Non-aligned Movement: Genesis, Organization and Politics (1927–1992)*. Leiden: Brill, 2019.

Dobosi, Izván, and András Inotoi. "Prospects of Economic Cooperation Between CMEA Countries and Developing Countries." In *East, West, South: Economic Interactions Between Three Worlds*, ed. Christopher Thomas Saunders, 48–65. New York: St. Martin's Press, 1981.

Dogliani, Patrizia. "The Fate of Socialist Internationalism." In *Internationalisms. A Twentieth-Century History*, ed. Glenda Sluga and Patricia Clavin, 38–61. Cambridge: Cambridge University Press, 2016.

Domber, Gregory F. L. "The AFL-CIO, the Reagan Administration and Solidarność." *Polish Review* 52, no. 3 (2007): 277–304.

Donert, Celia. "Feminism, Communism and Global Socialism: Encounters and Entanglements." In *Endgames? Late Communism in Global Perspective, 1968 to the Present*, ed. Juliane Fürst, Silvio Pons, and Mark Selden, 399–421. Cambridge: Cambridge University Press, 2017.

——. "Femmes, communisme et internationalisme: La Fédération démocratique internationale des femmes en Europe centrale (1945–1979)." *Vingtième Siècle. Revue d'histoire* 126, no. 7 (2015): 119–31.

——. "Women's Rights in Cold War Europe: Disentangling Feminist Histories." *Past & Present* 218 (2013): 180–202.

Dorn, Charles, and Kristen Ghodsee. "The Cold War Politicization of Literacy: Communism, UNESCO, and the World Bank." *Diplomatic History* 36, no. 2 (April 2012): 373–98.

Dosman, Edgar. "The Life and Times of Raúl Prebisch, 1901–1986." Montreal: McGill Queen's University Press, 2010.

Dragomir, Lucia. "L'Union des écrivains. Un modèle institutionnel et ses limites." *Vingtième Siècle. Revue d'histoire* 109 (2011): 59–70.

Dragostinova, Theodora. "The 'Natural Ally' of the 'Developing World': Bulgarian Culture in India and Mexico." *Slavic Review* 77, no. 3 (2018): 661–84.

Droit, Emmanuel. *Les Polices politiques du bloc de l'Est. À la recherche de l'Internationale tchékiste 1955–1989*. Paris: Gallimard, 2019.

Dubin, Martin D. "Toward the Bruce Report: The Economic and Social Programs of the League of Nations in the Avenol Era." In *The League of Nations in Retrospect / La Société des Nations: Rétrospective*. Proceedings of the Symposium Organized by the United Nations Library and the Graduate Institute of International Studies, Geneva, November 6–9, 1980. Berlin: de Gruyter, 1983.

Dullin, Sabine. "Une diplomatie plébéienne? Profils et compétences des diplomates soviétiques 1936–1945." *Cahiers du monde russe. Russie-Empire russe-Union soviétique et États indépendants* 44, no. 2–3 (2003): 437–64.

——. *La Frontière épaisse: aux origines des politiques soviétiques (1920–1940)*. Paris: Éd. de l'EHESS, 2014.

Dullin, Sabine, and Brigitte Studer, eds. "Communisme transnational." *Monde(s)* 2 (2016).

Duranti, Marco. "Curbing Labour's Totalitarian Temptation: European Human Rights Law and British Postwar Politics." *Humanity: An International Journal of Human Rights, Humanitarianism, and Development* 3, no. 3 (October 31, 2012): 361–83.

Eckel, Jan. "Humanitarisierung der internationalen Beziehungen? Menschenrechtspolitik in den 1970er Jahren." *Geschichte und Gesellschaft* 38, no. 4 (2012): 603–35.

——. "The Rebirth of Politics from the Spirit of Morality: Explaining the Human Rights Revolution of the 1970s." In *The Breakthrough: Human Rights in the 1970s*, ed. Jan Eckel and Samuel Moyn, 226–57. Philadelphia: University of Pennsylvania Press, 2013.

Eggers Nicole, Jessica L. Pearson, and Almada e Santos Aurora, eds. *The United Nations and Decolonization*. New York: Routledge, 2020.

Egorova, Natalia. "La formation du bloc de l'Est comme frontière occidentale du système communiste (1947–1955)." In *Frontières du communisme*, ed. Sophie Coeuré and Sabine Dullin, 248–71. Paris: La Découverte, "Recherches," 2007.

Ekbladh, David. *The Great American Mission: Modernization and the Construction of an American World Order*. Princeton, N.J.: Princeton University Press, 2010.

Engerman, David C. "Ideology and the Origins of the Cold War 1917–1962." In *The Cambridge History of the Cold War*. Vol. 1: *Origins, 1945–1962*, ed. Melvyn P. Leffler and Odd Arne Westad, 20–43. Cambridge: Cambridge University Press, 2010.

——. *The Price of Aid: The Economic Cold War in India*. Cambridge, Mass.: Harvard University Press, 2018.

———. "The Romance of Economic Development and New Histories of the Cold War." *Diplomatic History* 28, no. 1 (2004): 23–54.

Escobar, Arturo. *Encountering Development: The Making and Unmaking of the Third World*. Princeton, N.J.: Princeton University Press, 1995.

Evangelista, Matthew. "Transnational Organizations and the Cold War." In *The Cambridge History of the Cold War*. Vol. 3, *Endings*, ed. Melvyn P. Leffler and Odd Arne Westad, 400–21. Cambridge: Cambridge University Press, 2010.

Eyal, Gil, Iván Szelényi, and Eleanor R. Townsley, eds. *Making Capitalism Without Capitalists: Class Formation and Elite Struggles in Post-Communist Central Europe*. London: Verso, 1998.

Faure, Justine, and Sandrine Kott, eds. "Le bloc de l'Est en question." *Vingtième Siècle. Revue d'histoire* 109 (2011): 2–10.

Fauve, Adrien, and Mathilde Leloup. "Le temps du développement à l'Assemblée." In *L'Assemblée générale des Nations unies*, ed. Guillaume Devin, Franck Petiteville, and Simon Tordjman, 161–80. Paris: Presses de Sciences Po, 2020.

Fava, Valentina, and Luminita Gatejel. "East-West Cooperation in the Automobile Industry. Enterprises, Mobility, Production." *Journal of the Transport History* 38 (2017): 11–19.

Fayet, Jean-François. *Karl Radek (1885–1939): biographie politique*. Bern: Peter Lang, 2004.

Fee, Elizabeth, Marcos Cueto, and Theodor M. Brown. "At the Roots of the World Health Organization's Challenges: Politics and Regionalization." *American Journal for Public Health* 106 (2016): 1912–17.

Ferguson, Niall, Charles S. Maier, Erez Manela, and Daniel J. Sargent, eds. *The Shock of the Global: The 1970s in Perspective*. Cambridge, Mass.: Harvard University Press, 2011.

Foot, Rosemary. "The Cold War and Human Rights." In *The Cambridge History of the Cold War*. Vol. 3: *Endings*, ed. Melvyn P. Leffler and Odd Arne Westad, 445–66. Cambridge: Cambridge University Press, 2010.

Frey, Marc, and Sönke Kunkel. "Writing the History of Development: A Review of the Recent Literature." *Contemporary European History* 20, no. 2 (2011): 215–32.

Frey, Marc, Sönke Kunkel, and Corinna Unger, eds. *International Organizations and Development, 1945–1990*. London: Palgrave Macmillan, 2014.

Friedman, Jeremy. "Soviet Policy in the Developing World and the Chinese Challenge in the 1960s." *Cold War History* 10, no. 2 (2010): 247–72.

Fürst, Juliane, Silvio Pons, and Mark Selden, eds. *Endgames? Late Communism in Global Perspective, 1968 to the Present*. Cambridge: Cambridge University Press, 2017.

Gaiduk, Ilya V. *Divided Together: The United States and the Soviet Union in the United Nations, 1945–1965*. Stanford, Calif.: Stanford University Press, 2012.

Gareau, Frederick H. "The Soviet Bloc and the United Nations System: The Quantitative Record." *Western Political Quarterly* 25, no. 2 (1972): 268–94.

Germuska, Pál. "Balancing Between the COMECON and the EEC: Hungarian Elite Debates on European Integration During the Long 1970s." *Cold War Review* 19, no. 3 (2019): 401–20.

———. "What Can We Learn from the Business History of Communist Enterprises?" *Enterprise and Society* 19, no. 3 (2018): 538–45.

BIBLIOGRAPHY

Getachew, Adom. *Worldmaking After Empire: The Rise and Fall of Self-Determination.* Princeton, N.J.: Princeton University Press, 2019.

Ghebali, Victor-Yves. *The International Labour Organization: A Case Study on the Evolution of U.N. Specialised Agencies.* Dordrecht, Neth.: Martinus Nijhoff, 1989.

——. *Organisation internationale et guerre mondiale. Le cas de la Société des Nations et de l'Organisation internationale du travail pendant la Seconde Guerre mondiale.* Grenoble, Fr.: Institut d'études politiques, 1975.

——. *La Société des Nations et le rapport Bruce.* Cinquante ans de la Société des Nations. (Paris: Centre européen de la dotation Carnegie, 1970).

Ghodsee, Kristen. "Internationalisme socialiste et féminisme d'État pendant la guerre froide. Les relations entre Bulgarie et Zambie." *Clio* 41 (2015): 115–138.

——. "Rethinking State Socialist Mass Women's Organizations: The Committee of the Bulgarian Women's Movement and the United Nations Decade for Women, 1975 1985." *Journal of Women's History* 24, no. 4 (2012): 49–73.

——. "Revisiting the United Nations Decade for Women: Brief Reflections on Feminism, Capitalism and Cold War Politics in the Early Years of the International Women's Movement." In *Women's Studies International Forum* (December 2009): 3–12.

Gienow-Hecht, Jessica. "Culture and the Cold War in Europe." In *The Cambridge History of the Cold War.* Vol. 1: *Origins, 1945–1962*, ed. Melvyn P. Leffler and Odd Arne Westad, 398–420. Cambridge: Cambridge University Press, 2010.

Gildea, Robert. "The Global 1968 and International Communism." In *Endgames? Late Communism in Global Perspective, 1968 to the Present*, ed. Juliane Fürst, Silvio Pons, and Mark Selden, 23–49. Cambridge: Cambridge University Press, 2017.

Gilman, Nils. *Mandarins of the Future: Modernization Theory in Cold War America.* Baltimore: Johns Hopkins University Press, 2003.

——. "The New International Economic Order: A Reintroduction." *Humanity: An International Journal of Human Rights, Humanitarianism, and Development* 6, no. 1 (2015): 1–16.

Godard, Simon. "Another Europe, Rather than the Other Europe? COMECON's Ambiguous Shaping of Europe (from 1962 to the Helsinki Process)." *Politique européenne* 76, no. 2 (2022): 68–94.

——. "Les calculs intéressés de la Guerre froide : l'Economic Commission for Europe et le monde socialiste face à la révision de la quantification du développement." *Revue d'histoire moderne contemporaine* 65, no. 4 (2018): 33–58.

——. "Construire le 'bloc' par l'économie: configuration des territoires et des identités socialistes au Conseil d'aide économique mutuelle (CAEM), 1949–1989." Ph.D. diss., University of Geneva, 2014.

——. *Le Laboratoire de l'internationalisme: le CAEM et la construction du bloc socialiste (1949–1991).* Paris: Sciences Po, 2021.

Goddeeris, Isdebald. "The Limits of Lobbying: ILO and Solidarność." In *ILO Histories: Essays on the International Labour Organization and Its Impact on the World During the Twentieth Century*, ed. Jasmien Van Daele et al., 423–41. New York: Peter Lang, 2010.

Goethem, Geert van. "Labor's Second Front: The Foreign Policy of the American and British Trade Union Movements During the Second World War." *Diplomatic History* 34, no. 4 (2010): 663–80.

BIBLIOGRAPHY

Gorsky, Martin, and Christopher Sirrs. "The Rise and Fall of 'Universal Health Coverage' as a Goal of International Health Politics, 1925–1952." *American Journal of Public Health* 108, no. 3 (2018): 334–42.

Gosselin, Guy. "L'ONU et la paix internationale depuis 1945." *Études internationales* 16, no. 4 (1985): 741–56.

Graaf, Beatrice de. "Détente from Below: The Stasi and the Dutch Peace Movement." *Journal of Intelligence History* 3, no. 2 (2003): 9–20.

Graaf, Jan de. *Socialism Across the Iron Curtain: Socialist Parties in East and West and the Reconstruction of Europe After 1945*. Cambridge: Cambridge University Press, 2019.

Graaf, William D. "The Theory of the Non-Capitalist Road." In *The Soviet Bloc and the Third World*, ed. Brigitte Schulz and William W. Hansen, 27–52. Boulder, Colo.: Westview Press, 1989.

Gradskova, Yulia. "Women's International Democratic Federation, the 'Third World' and the Global Cold War from the Late-1950s to the Mid-1960s." *Women's History Review* 29, no. 2 (August 2019): 270–88.

Grémion, Pierre. *Intelligence de l'anticommunisme: le Congrès pour la liberté de la culture à Paris 1950–1975*. Paris: Fayard, 1995.

Gridan, Irina. "Du communisme national au national-communisme, réactions roumaines à la soviétisation dans les années 1960." *Vingtième Siècle. Revue d'histoire* 109 (2011): 113–27.

Gross, Jan T. "Social Consequences of War: Preliminaries to the Study of Imposition of Communist Regimes in East Central Europe." *East European Politics and Societies* 3, no. 2 (1989): 198–214.

Gross, Stephen. *Export Empire: German Soft Power in Southeastern Europe, 1890–1945*. New York: Cambridge University Press, 2017.

Grosser, Pierre. *Les Temps de la guerre froide : réflexions sur l'histoire de la guerre froide et sur les causes de sa fin*. Brussels: Complexe, 1995.

Grossmann, Atina. "A Question of Silence: The Rape of German Women by Occupation Soldiers." In *West Germany Under Reconstruction: Politics, Society and Culture in the Adenauer Era*, ed. Robert G. Moeller. Ann Arbor: University of Michigan Press, 1997.

Grossmann, Johannes. "The Comité international de défense de la civilisation chrétienne and the Transnationalisation of Anti-Communist Propaganda After the Second World War." In *Transnational Anti-Communism and the Cold War Agents, Activities, and Networks*, ed. Luc Van Dongen, Stéphanie Roulin, and Giles Scott-Smith, 251–62. Basingstoke, UK: Palgrave Macmillan, 2014.

Grzybowski, Kazimierz. "East-West Trade Regulations in the United States." *Journal of World Trade* 11, no. 6 (January 1, 1977): 501–13.

——. "International Organizations from the Soviet Point of View." *Law and Contemporary Problems* 29, no. 4 (1964): 882–95.

——. "La communauté socialiste et les projets de Gorbatchev." *Revue d'études comparatives Est-Ouest* 19, no. 2 (1988): 131–44.

——. "United States-Soviet Union Trade Agreement of 1972." *Law and Contemporary Problems* 37, no. 3 (1972): 395–428.

Guerin, Denis. *Albert Thomas au BIT 1920–1932. De l'internationalisme à l'Europe*. Geneva: EURYOPA-Institut européen Genève, 1996.

BIBLIOGRAPHY

Gueulette, Agota. *Politique économique extérieure dans un modèle marxiste: le cas soviétique (1917–1947)*. Paris: Publisud, 1997.

Guilhot, Nicolas. "A Network of Influential Friendships: The Fondation Pour Une Entraide Intellectuelle Européenne and East-West Cultural Dialogue, 1957–1991." *Minerva* 44, no. 4 (2006): 379–409.

Gutmann, Benjamin. "Relais et réseaux de la Charte 77 en France, entre 1977 et 1989." *Bulletin de l'Institut Pierre Renouvin* 33, no. 1 (2011): 49–64.

Haan, Francisca de. "Continuing Cold War Paradigms in Western Historiography of Transnational Women's Organisations: The Case of the Women's International Democratic Federation (WIDF)." *Women's History Review* 19, no. 4 (September 2010): 547–73.

Haas, Peter. "Introduction: Epistemic Communities and International Policy Coordination." *International Organization* 46, no. 1 (1992): 1–35.

Haga, Lars. "Imaginer la démocratie populaire: The Institute of World Economics et la carte mentale soviétique de l'Europe de l'Est (1944–1948)." *Vingtième Siècle. Revue d'histoire* 109 (2011): 12–30.

Hajduk, Thomas. "An 'Instrument of Moral Persuasion'—Multinational Enterprises and International Codes of Conduct in the 1970s." In *Code of Conduct on Transnational Corporations: Challenges and Opportunities*, ed. Rahim M. Mahmudur, 23–43. New York: Springer, 2019.

Harder, Andrew. "The Politics of Impartiality: The United Nations Relief and Rehabilitation Administration in the Soviet Union, 1946–7." *Journal of Contemporary History* 2 (2012): 347–69.

Helleiner, Eric. *Forgotten Foundations of Bretton Woods: International Development and the Making of the Postwar Order*. Ithaca, N.Y.: Cornell University Press, 2014.

——. *States and the Reemergence of Global Finance: From Bretton Woods to the 1990s*. Ithaca, N.Y.: Cornell University Press, 1996 [1994].

Herren, Madeleine. *Geschichte der internationalen Organisation*. Darmstadt, Ger.: Wissenschaftliche Buchgesellschaft, 2009.

Heumos, Peter. "Stalinismus in der Tschechoslowakei. Forschungslage und sozialgeschichtliche Anmerkungen am Beispiel der Industriearbeiterschaft." *Journal of Modern European History* 2, no. 1 (2004): 82–109.

Hilger, Andreas. "Building a Socialist Elite? Khruschev's Soviet Union and Elite Formation in India." In *Elites and Decolonization in the Twentieth Century*, 262–86. Basingstoke, UK: Palgrave Macmillan, 2011.

Hirschman, Albert O. "Grandeur et décadence de l'économie du développement." *Annales* 36, no. 5 (1981): 725–44.

Hitchcock, William I. *The Bitter Road to Freedom: A New History of the Liberation of Europe*. New York: Free Press, 2008.

Hodge, Joseph M. "British Colonial Expertise, Post-Colonial Careering and the Early History of International Development." *Journal of Modern European History* 8, no. 1 (April 15, 2010): 24–46.

Hoffmann, Stefan-Ludwig. "Human Rights and History." *Past & Present* 232, no. 1 (2016): 279–310.

Hoffmann, Stefan-Ludwig, Sandrine Kott, Peter Romijn, and Olivier Wievorka, eds. *Seeking Peace in the Wake of War. Europe, 1943–1947*. Amsterdam: University of Amsterdam Press, 2015.

BIBLIOGRAPHY

Holthoon, Frits L. van, and Marcel van der Linden, eds. *Internationalism in the Labour Movement: 1830–1940*. Leiden: Brill, 1988.

Hunt, Lynn Avery. *Inventing Human Rights: A History*. New York: Norton, 2007.

Hutter, Michael. "Ecosystems Research and Policy Planning: Revisiting the Budworm Project (1972–1980)." In *Planning in Cold War Europe: Competition, Cooperation, Circulations (1950s–1970s)*, ed. Michel Christian, Sandrine Kott, and Ondrej Matejka, 261–84. Berlin: De Gruyter, 2018.

Iacob, Bogdan C. "Health." In *Socialism Goes Global: The Soviet Union and Eastern Europe in the Age of Decolonization*, ed. James Mark and Paul Betts, 255–89. Oxford: Oxford University Press, 2022.

——. "Malariology and Decolonization: Eastern European Experts from the League of Nations to the World Health Organization." *Journal of Global History* 17, no. 2 (July 2022): 233–53.

Iandolo, Alessandro. "The Rise and Fall of the 'Soviet Model of Development' in West Africa, 1957–64." *Cold War History* 12, no. 4 (2012): 683–704.

Imlay, Talbot. "'The Policy of Social Democracy Is Self-Consciously Internationalist': The SPD's Internationalism After 1945." *Journal of Modern History* 86 (2014): 81–123.

Iriye, Akira. *Global Community: The Role of International Organizations in the Making of The Contemporary World*. Berkeley: University of California Press, 2002.

——. "Historicizing the Cold War." In *The Oxford Handbook of the Cold War*, ed. Richard H. Immerman and Petra Goedde, 15–32. Oxford: Oxford University Press, 2013.

Jachertz, Ruth. "Stable Agricultural Markets and World Order. FAO and ITO, 1943–1949." In *Wartime Origins and the Future United Nations*, ed. Daniel Plesch and Thomas Weiss, 179–98. London: Routledge, 2015.

Jackson, Ian. *The Economic Cold War: America, Britain and East-West Trade, 1948–63*. Basingstoke, UK: St. Martin's Press, 2001.

Jacobson, Harold Karan. "Labor, the UN and the Cold War." *International Organization* 11, no. 1 (1957): 55–67.

——. *The USSR and the UN's Economic and Social Activities*. Notre Dame, Ind.: University of Notre Dame Press, 1963.

James, Harold. *International Monetary Cooperation Since Bretton Woods*. New York: Oxford University Press, 1996.

Jansen, Hanna E. "Peoples' Internationalism: Central Asian Modernisers Soviet Oriental Studies and Cultural Revolution in the East (1936–1977)." Ph.D. diss., University of Amsterdam, 2020.

Jensen, Steven L. B.. "Inequality and Post-War International Organization: Discrimination, the World Social Situation and the United Nations, 1948–1957." In *Histories of Global Inequality: New Perspectives*, ed. Christian Olaf Christiansen and Steven L. B. Jensen, 131–55. London: Palgrave Macmillan, 2019.

——. *The Making of International Human Rights: The 1960s, Decolonization, and the Reconstruction of Global Values*. Cambridge: Cambridge University Press, 2016.

Jensen, Steven L. B., and Charles Walton, eds. *Social Rights and the Politics of Obligation in History*. Cambridge: Cambridge University Press, 2022.

Judge Kret, Abigail. "'We Unite with Knowledge': The Peoples' Friendship University and Soviet Education for the Third World." *Comparative Studies of South Asia, Africa and the Middle East* 33, no. 2 (2013): 239–56.

BIBLIOGRAPHY

Jüngerkes, Sven. *Diplomaten der Wirtschaft: die Geschichte des Ost-Ausschusses der Deutschen Wirtschaft*. Osnabrück, Ger.: Fibre, 2012.

Kaiser, Wolfram, and Johan Schot. *Writing the Rules for Europe: Experts, Cartels, and International Organizations*. Basingstoke, UK: Palgrave Macmillan, 2014.

Kalinovsky, Artemy, Steffi Marung, and James Mark, eds. *Alternative Globalisations: Eastern Europe and the Postcolonial World*. Bloomington: Indiana University Press, 2020.

Kansikas, Suvi. "Acknowledging Economic Realities. The CMEA Policy Change *vis-à-vis* the European Community, 1970–3." *European Review of History: Revue européenne d'histoire* 21, no. 2 (March 4, 2014): 311–28.

——. *Socialist Countries Face the European Community. Soviet-bloc Controversies Over East West Trade*. New York: Peter Lang, 2014.

Kantrowitz, Jack. "L'influence américaine sur Force ouvrière: mythe ou réalité?" *Revue française de science politique* 28 (1978): 717–39.

Katsakioris, Constantin. "Les étudiants de pays arabes formés en Union soviétique pendant la guerre froide, 1956–1991." *Revue européenne des migrations internationales* 32, no. 2 (2016): 13–38.

——. "Leçons soviétiques: la formation des étudiants africains et arabes en URSS pendant la guerre froide." Ph.D. diss., EHESS, 2015.

——. "Les limites du 'remodelage socialiste': les Égyptiens formés en RDA (1969–1989)." *Revue européenne des migrations internationales* 32 (2016): 57–76.

——. "Soviet Lessons for Arab Modernization: Soviet Educational Aid Towards Arab Countries After 1956." *Journal of Modern European History* 8, no. 1 (2010): 85–106.

——. "L'Union soviétique et les intellectuels africains. Internationalisme, panafricanisme et négritude pendant les années de la décolonisation, 1954–1964." *Cahiers du monde russe. Russie-Empire russe-Union soviétique et États indépendants* 47, no. 1–2 (2006): 15–32.

Keck, Margaret E., and Kathryn Sikkink, eds. *Activists Beyond Borders: Advocacy Networks in International Politics*. Ithaca, N.Y.: Cornell University Press, 1998.

Kelley, Donald R. "The Soviet Debate on the Convergence of the American & Soviet Systems." *Polity* 2 (1973): 174–95.

Kelly, Catriona. "Defending Children's Rights, 'in Defense of Peace': Children and Soviet Cultural Diplomacy." In *Imagining the West in Eastern Europe and the Soviet Union*, ed. Gyorgy Peteri, 59–86. Pittsburgh, Penn.: Pittsburgh University Press, 2010.

Kind-Kovács, Friederike. "Voices, Letters, and Literature Through the Iron Curtain: Exiles and the (Trans)mission of Radio in the Cold War." *Cold War History* 13, no. 2 (2013): 193–219.

Kirchhof, Astrid Mignon, and Jan-Henrik Meyer. "Global Protest Against Nuclear Power: Transfer and Transnational Exchange in the 1970s and 1980s." *Historical Social Research* 39, no. 1 (2014): 165–90.

Kis, Théofil. "État des travaux sur la problématique de la convergence: théories et hypothèses." *Études internationales* 2, no. 3 (1971): 443–87.

Kobrin, Stephen J. "Expropriation as an Attempt to Control Foreign Firms in LDCs: Trends from 1960 to 1979." *International Studies Quarterly* 28, no. 3 (1984): 329–48.

BIBLIOGRAPHY

Kolodziej, Edward, and Roger E. Kanet. "L'Union soviétique et le monde en développement: Thermidor dans la lutte révolutionnaire." *Revue d'études comparatives Est-Ouest* 19, no. 2 (1988): 5–22.

Kornai, Janos. *Economics of Shortage. Contributions to Economic Analysis.* Amsterdam: North-Holland, 1980.

——. *Le Système socialiste. L'économie politique du communisme.* Grenoble, Fr.: PUG, 1996.

Kostecki, Michel. *East-West Trade and the GATT System.* London: Palgrave, 1979.

Kostelecky, Vaclav. *The United Nations Economic Commission for Europe: The Beginning of a History.* Gothenburg. Sweden: Graphic Systems, 1989.

Kotkin, Stephen. "The Kiss of Debt." In *The Shock of the Global: The 1970s in Perspective*, ed. Niall Ferguson et al., 80–101. Cambridge, Mass.: Harvard University Press, 2011.

Kott, Sandrine. "Die Kinderkrippe." In *Erinnerungsorte der DDR*, ed. Martin Sabrow, 281–91. Munich: Beck, 2009.

——. "Fighting the War or Preparing for Peace? The ILO During the Second World War." *Journal of Modern European History* 12, no. 3 (2014): 359–76.

——. "The Forced Labor Issue Between Human and Social Rights, 1947–1957." *Humanity: An International Journal of Human Rights, Humanitarianism, and Development* 3, no. 3 (2012): 321–35.

——. "Les organisations internationales, terrains d'étude de la globalisation. Jalons pour une approche socio-historique." *Critique internationale* 52, no. 3 (2011): 9–16.

——. "OIT, justice sociale et mondes communistes. Concurrences, émulations, convergences." *Le Mouvement social* (April–June 2018): 139–51.

——. "The Social Engineering Project: Exportation of Capitalist Management Culture to Eastern Europe (1950–1980)." In *Planning in Cold War Europe: Competition, Cooperation, Circulations (1950s–1970s)*, ed. Michel Christian, Sandrine Kott, and Ondrej Matejka, 123–43. Berlin: De Gruyter, 2018.

——. "Un modèle international de protection sociale est-il possible ? L'Organisation internationale du travail entre assurance et sécurité sociale (1919–1952)." *Revue d'histoire de la protection sociale* 10, "Experts internationaux et politiques sociales" (2017): 62–84.

Kott, Sandrine, and Martine Mespoulet, eds. *Le Postcommunisme dans l'histoire.* Brussels: Presses universitaires de Bruxelles, 2006.

Kott, Sandrine, and Cyrus Schayegh. "Eastern European-Middle Eastern Relations: Continuities and Changes from the Time of Empires to the Cold War." *Contemporary European History* 30, no. 4 (2021): 1–15.

Kott, Sandrine, and Françoise Thébaud, eds. "Le 'socialisme réel' à l'épreuve du genre." *CLIO. Femmes, Genre, Histoire* 41 (2015).

Kramer, Mark. "Ideology and the Cold War." *Review of International Studies* 25, no. 4 (1999): 539–76.

Kriegel, Annie. *Le Système communiste mondial.* Paris: PUF, 1984.

Kullaa, Rinna. *Non-Alignment and Its Origins in Cold War Europe: Yugoslavia, Finland and the Soviet Challenge.* London: Tauris, 2012.

Kunkel, Sönke. "Contesting Globalization: The United Nations Conference on Trade and Development and the Transnationalization of Sovereignty." In *International*

Organizations and Development, 1945–1990, ed. Marc Frey, Sönke Kunkel, and Corinna Unger, 240–52. London: Palgrave Macmillan, 2014.

Kunz, Diane B. *Butter and Guns: America's Cold War Economic Diplomacy*. New York: Free Press, 1997.

——. "The Marshall Plan Reconsidered: A Complex of Motives." *Foreign Affairs* 76 (1997): 162–70.

Labbé, Marie-Hélène. "L'embargo céréalier de 1980 ou les limites de l''arme verte.'" *Politique étrangère* 51, no. 3 (1986): 771–83.

——. "Y a-t-il une politique américaine de commerce avec l'URSS?" *Politique étrangère* 4 (1988): 899–906.

Lafourcade, Olivier, and Michèle Guerard. "Banque mondiale et ajustement structurel." *Revue d'économie financière* 4, no. 1 (1994): 355–67.

Lagendijk, Vincent. "The Structure of Powers: The UNECE and East-West Electricity Connections, 1947–1975." *Comparativ. Zeitschrift für Globalgeschichte und vergleichende Gesellschaftsforschung* 24, no. 1 (2014): 50–65.

Lajipathi Rai, Hanumanthu. *Indo-Soviet Trade Relations*. New Delhi: Mittal, 1991.

Lampe, John R., Russell O. Prickett, and Ljubiša S. Adamović. *Yugoslav-American Economic Relations Since World War II*. Durham, N.C.: Duke University Press, 1990.

Larian, Angelo. "Old Ways in the New South: The Implication of the Recreation of an Unfree Labor Force." In *Free and Unfree Labour: The Debate Continues*, ed. Tom Brass and Marcel van der Linden, 173–201. New York: Peter Lang AG, 1997.

Lavigne, Marie. *Économie internationale des pays socialistes*. Paris: Armand Colin, 1985.

——. *Les Économies socialistes soviétique et européennes*. 3rd ed. rev. and updated. Paris: Armand Colin, 1979.

——, ed. *Les Relations Est-Sud dans l'économie mondiale*. Paris: Economica, 1986.

Lees, Lorraine M. *Keeping Tito Afloat: The United States, Yugoslavia, and the Cold War*. University Park: Pennsylvania State University Press, 1997.

Leffler, Melvyn P. *The Specter of Communism: The United States and the Origins of the Cold War, 1917–1953*. New York: Hill and Wang, 1994.

Leivk, Friedrich, and Jan Stankovsky. "East-West Economic Relations in the 1970s and 1980s." In *East-West Trade and Finance in the World Economy: A New Look for the 1980s*, ed. Christopher Thomas Saunders (Wiener Institut für Internationale Wirtschaftsvergleiche), 77–124. New York: St. Martin's Press, 1985.

Lévesque, Jacques. "Essai sur la spécificité des relations entre l'URSS et l'Europe de l'Est de 1945 à 1989." *Relations internationales* 148 (2011): 7–16.

Linden, Marcel van der. "Forced Labour and Non-capitalist Industrialization: The Case of Stalinism (1929–1956)." In *Free and Unfree Labour: The Debate Continues*, ed. Tom Brass and Marcel van der Linden, 351–63. New York: Peter Lang AG, 1997.

Littoz-Monnet, Annabelle. *The Politics of Expertise in International Organizations*. London: Routledge, 2017.

Lorenzini, Sara. "Comecon and the South in the Years of *détente*: A Study on East-South Economic Relations." *European Review of History. Revue européenne d'histoire* 21, no. 2 (2014): 183–99.

——. *Global Development: A Cold War History*. Princeton, N.J.: Princeton University Press, 2019.

Loth, Wilfried, and Georges-Henri Soutou, eds. *The Making of Détente: Eastern and Western Europe in the Cold War, 1965–75*. London: Routledge, 2008.

BIBLIOGRAPHY

Love, Joseph L. *Crafting the Third World: Theorizing Underdevelopment in Rumania and Brazil.* Stanford, Calif.: Stanford University Press, 1996.

——. "Theorizing Underdevelopment: Latin America and Romania, 1860–1950." *Estudos Avançados* 4, no. 8 (1990): 62–95.

Luard, Evan. *A History of the United Nations.* Vol. 1: *The Years of Western Domination, 1945–1955.* London: Palgrave Macmillan, 1982.

——. *A History of the United Nations.* Vol. 2: *The Age of Decolonization, 1955–1965.* 2nd ed. London: Palgrave Macmillan, 2016.

Ludwig, Bernard. "La paix et l'Europe dans la propagande anticommuniste du réseau Paix et Liberté." *Matériaux pour l'histoire de notre temps* 108 (2012): 39–45.

——. "La propagande anticommuniste en Allemagne fédérale." *Vingtième Siècle. Revue d'histoire* 80, no. 4 (2003): 33–42.

Macher, Aniko. "La Hongrie entre tutelle soviétique et intérêt national au cours des années 1960." *Relations internationales* 148 (2011): 81–94.

Mahrane, Yannick, and Christophe Bonneuil. "Gouverner la biosphère. De l'environnement de la guerre froide à l'environnement néolibéral." In *Le Gouvernement des technosciences,* ed. Dominique Pestre, 133–69. Paris: La Découverte, 2014.

Malitza, Mircea. "L'enseignement supérieur: son rôle et sa contribution à notre progrès commun. Réflexion sur la création et le fonctionnement de l'UNESCO-CEPES: l'avis personnel de l'un de ses fondateurs." *L'Enseignement supérieur en Europe* 1–2 (2002): 11–31.

Marcou, Lilly. *Le Kominform : le communisme de guerre froide.* Paris: Presses de la Fondation nationale des sciences politiques, 1977.

——. *Le Mouvement communiste international depuis 1945.* Paris: PUF, 1990.

Marieke, Louis. "La diplomatie sociale des multinationales." In *Le Pouvoir des multinationales,* ed. Christian Chavagneux and Marieke Louis. Paris: PUF, 2018. https://laviedesidees.fr/La-diplomatie-sociale-des-multinationales.html.

Mark, James, and Paul Betts, eds. *Socialism Goes Global: The Soviet Union and Eastern Europe in the Age of Decolonization.* Oxford: Oxford University Press, 2022.

Mark, James, Bogdan C. Iacob, Tobias Rupprecht, and Ljubica Spaskovska. *1989: A Global History of Eastern Europe.* Cambridge: Cambridge University Press, 2019.

Marković, Andrej, and Ivan Obadić. "A Socialist Developing Country in a Western Capitalist Club: Yugoslavia and the OEEC/OECD, 1955–1980." In *The OECD and the International Political Economy Since 1948,* ed. Matthieu Leimgruber and Matthias Schmelzer, 89–113. London: Palgrave MacMillan, 2017.

Mastanduno, Michael. *Economic Containment: CoCom and the Politics of East-West Trade.* Ithaca, N.Y.: Cornell University Press, 1992.

——. "Trade as a Strategic Weapon: American and Alliance Export Control Policy in the Early Postwar Period." *International Organization* 42, no. 1 (1988): 121–50.

Matějka, Ondřej. "Social Engineering and Alienation Between East and West: Czech Christian-Marxist Dialogue in the 1960s from the National Level to the Global Arena." In *Planning in Cold War Europe: Competition, Cooperation, Circulations (1950s–1970s),* ed. Michel Christian, Sandrine Kott, and Ondrej Matejka, 165–86. Berlin: De Gruyter, 2018.

Maul, Daniel. *The International Labour Organization: 100 Years of Global Social Policy.* Berlin: De Gruyter, 2019.

BIBLIOGRAPHY

Maurel, Chloé. "L'UNESCO de 1945 à 1974." Ph.D. diss., Université Panthéon-Sorbonne, 2006. https://tel.archives-ouvertes.fr/tel-00848712.

——. "OIT et responsabilité sociale des entreprises transnationales depuis les années 1970." In *L'Organisation internationale du travail. Origine. Développement. Avenir*, ed. Isabelle Lespinet-Moret and Vincent Viet, 179–92. Rennes, Fr. Presses universitaires de Rennes, 2011.

Maximova, Margarita. "Industrial Cooperation Between Socialist and Capitalist Countries: Forms, Trends, Problems." In *East-West Cooperation in Business: Inter-firm Studies*, ed. Christopher Thomas Saunders, 15–27. New York: Springer, 1977.

Mayer, David. "À la fois influente et marginale : l'Internationale communiste et l'Amérique latine." *Monde(s)* 10, no. 2 (2016): 109–28.

Mazower, Mark. *Governing the World: The History of an Idea*. London: Penguin Press, 2012.

——. *No Enchanted Palace: The End of Empire and the Ideological Origins of the United Nations*. Princeton, N.J.: Princeton University Press, 2009.

——. "The Strange Triumph of Human Rights, 1933–1950." *Historical Journal* 47, no. 2 (2004): 379–98.

Mazurek, Małgorzata. "Measuring Development: An Intellectual and Political History of Ludwik Landau's Scale of World Inequality." *Contemporary European History* 28, no. 2 (2019): 156–71.

McCreery, David. "Wage Labor, Free Labor and Vagrancy Laws: The Transition to Capitalism in Guatemala, 1920–1945." In *Free and Unfree Labour: The Debate Continues*, ed. Tom Brass and Marcel van der Linden, 281–303. New York: Peter Lang AG, 1997.

McDonald, Bryan. *Food Security: Dimensions of Security*. Cambridge: Polity, 2010.

McFarland, Victor. "The New International Economic Order, Interdependence, and Globalization." *Humanity: An International Journal of Human Rights, Humanitarianism, and Development* 6, no. 1 (2015): 217–33.

McGlade, Jacqueline. "Cocom and the Containment of Western Trade and Relations." In *East-West Trade and the Cold War*, ed. Jari Eloranta and Jari Ojala, 47–61. Jyväskylä, Fin.: University of Jyväskylä, 2005.

McKenzie, Francine. "Free Trade and Freedom to Trade: The Development Challenge to GATT, 1947–1968." In *International Organizations and Development, 1945–1990*, ed. Marc Frey, Sönke Kunkel, and Corinna Unger, 150–70. London: Palgrave Macmillan, 2014.

——. "GATT and the Cold War: Accession Debates, Institutional Development, and the Western Alliance, 1947–1959." *Journal of Cold War Studies* 10, no. 3 (2008): 78–109.

Mëhilli, Elidor. "Socialist Encounters: Albania and the Transnational Eastern Bloc in the 1950s." In *Cold War Crossings: International Travel and Exchange Across the Soviet Bloc, 1940s–1960s*, ed. Patryk Babiracki and Kenyon Zimmer, 40–78. Arlington: University of Texas Press, 2014.

Meier, Gerald M., and Dudley Seers. *Pioneers in Development*. World Bank Publication. Oxford: Oxford University Press, 1984.

Mentel, Christian, et al. *Die zentralen deutschen Behörden und der Nationalsozialismus: Stand und Perspektiven der Forschung*. Munich: IFZ, Potsdam ZZF, 2016.

Michel, Jean-François. "La scission de la Fédération syndicale mondiale (1947–1949)." *Le Mouvement social* 117 (1981): 33–52.

BIBLIOGRAPHY

Migani, Guia. "Lomé and the North-South Relations (1975–1984): From the 'New International Economic Order' to a New Conditionality." In *Europe in a Globalizing World. Global Challenges and European Responses in the "Long" 1970s*, ed. Claudia Hiepel, 123–46. Baden-Baden, Ger.: Nomos, 2014.

Mikkonen, Simo, and Pia Koivunen. *Beyond the Divide: Entangled Histories of Cold War Europe*. New York: Berghahn Books, 2015.

Milward, Alan. *The Reconstruction of Western Europe, 1945–1951*. London: Methuen, 1987.

Milza, Pierre. "Les mouvements pacifistes et les guerres froides depuis 1947." *Publications de l'École française de Rome* 95, no. 1 (1987): 265–83.

Misgeld, Klaus. *Die "Internationale Gruppe demokratischer Sozialisten" in Stockholm 1942–1945. Zur sozialistischen Friedensdiskussion während des Zweiten Weltkrieges.* Uppsala, Sweden: Acta Universitatis Upsaliensis, 1976.

Moine, Caroline. *Cinéma et guerre froide. Histoire du festival de films documentaires de Leipzig (1955–1990)*. Paris: Publications de la Sorbonne, 2014.

Montias, John Michael. "Background and Origins of the Rumanian Dispute with Comecon." *Soviet Studies* 16, no. 2 (1964): 125–51.

Mošna, Zdeněk. "The New Economic System and Management Development in Czechoslovakia." *International Labour Review* 3 (1967): 61–81.

Moyn, Samuel. *The Last Utopia: Human Rights in History*. Cambridge, Mass.: Harvard University Press, 2012.

——. *Not Enough: Human Rights in an Unequal World*. Cambridge, Mass.: Harvard University Press, 2018.

Müller, Birgit, ed. "L'anthropologie des organisations internationales." *Critique internationale* 54, no. 1 (2012).

Müller, Stefan. *Die Ostkontakte der westdeutschen Gewerkschaften. Entspannungspolitik zwischen Zivilgesellschaft und internationaler Politik 1969 bis 1989*. Bonn: Dietz, 2020.

Murphy, Craig. *The United Nations Development Programme: A Better Way?* Cambridge: Cambridge University Press, 2006.

Muschik, Eva-Maria. *Building States: The United Nations, Development, and Decolonization, 1945–1965*. New York: Columbia University Press, 2022.

——. "Managing the World: The United Nations, Decolonization, and the Strange Triumph of State Sovereignty in the 1950s and 1960s." *Journal of Global History* 13, no. 1 (2018): 121–44.

——. "Special Issue Introduction: Towards a Global History of International Organizations and Decolonization." *Journal of Global History* 17, no. 2 (July 2022): 173–90.

Myrdal, Gunnar. "Twenty Years of the United Nations Economic Commission for Europe." *International Organization* 22 (1968): 617–28.

Nagy, András. "Shattered Hopes amid Violent Repression: The Hungarian Revolution and the United Nations (Part 1)." *Journal of Cold War Studies* 19, no. 4 (2017): 42–73.

Nathans, Benjamin. "The Disenchantment of Socialism: Soviet Dissidents, Human Rights and the New Global Morality." In *The Breakthrough: Human Rights in the 1970s*, ed. Jan Eckel and Samuel Moyn, 33–48. Philadelphia: University of Pennsylvania Press, 2013.

Naumann, Katja. "International Research Planning Across the Iron Curtain: East-Central European Social Scientists in the ISSC and Vienna Center." In *Planning in*

Cold War Europe: Competition, Cooperation, Circulations (1950s–1970s), ed. Michel Christian, Sandrine Kott, and Ondrej Matejka, 97–122. Berlin: De Gruyter, 2018.

Nehring, Holger. "National Internationalists: British and West German Protests Against Nuclear Weapons, the Politics of Transnational Communications and the Social History of the Cold War, 1957–1964." *Contemporary European History* 14, no. 4 (2005): 559–82.

Neunsinger, Silke. "The Unobtainable Magic of Numbers: Equal Remuneration, the ILO and the International Trade Union Movement 1950s–1980s." In *Women's ILO: Transnational Networks, Global Labour Standards and Gender Equity, 1919 to Present*, ed. Eileen Boris, Dorothea Hoehtker, and Susan Zimmermann, 121–49. Leiden: Brill, 2018.

Normand, Roger, and Sarah Zaidi. *Human Rights at the UN: The Political History of Universal Justice*. United Nations Intellectual History Project Series. Bloomington: Indiana University Press, 2008.

Obadič, Ivan. "A Troubled Relationship: Yugoslavia and the European Economic Community in *Détente.*" *European Review of History* 21, no. 2 (2014): 329–48.

Osgood, Kenneth Alan. *Total Cold War: Eisenhower's Secret Propaganda Battle at Home and Abroad*. Lawrence: University Press of Kansas, 2008.

Owen, David. "The United Nations Expanded Program of Technical Assistance: A Multilateral Approach." *Annals of the American Academy of Political and Social Science* 323 (1959): 25–32.

Özsu, Umut. "Neoliberalism and Human Rights: The Brandt Commission and the Struggle for a New World." *Law & Contemporary Problems* 81, no. 4 (2018): 139–65.

——. "Neoliberalism and the New International Economic Order: A History of Contemporary Legal Thought." In *Searching for Contemporary Legal Thought*, ed. Justin Desautels Stein and Christopher L. Tomlins, 330–47. New York: Cambridge University Press, 2017.

Paavonen, Tapani. "Special Arrangements for the Soviet Trade in Finland's Integration Solutions—A Consequence of Finland's International Position or Pursuit of Profit?" In *East-West Trade and the Cold War*, ed. Jari Eloranta and Jari Ojala, 153–68. Jyväskylä, Fin.: University of Jyväskylä, 2005.

Pacht Brickman, Jane. "Medical McCarthyism and the Punishment of Internationalist Physicians in the United States." In *Comrades in Health, U.S. Health Internationalists, Abroad and at Home*, ed. Anne-Emanuelle Birn and Theodore M. Brown, 82–100. New Brunswick, N.J.: Rutgers University Press, 2013.

Packard, Randall M. "Malaria Dreams: Postwar Visions of Health and Development in the Third World." *Medical Anthropology* 17 (1997): 279–96.

Page, Benjamin B. "The Rockefeller Foundation and Central Europe: A Reconsideration." *Minerva* 40 (2002): 265–87.

Parrish, Scott D., and Mikhail M. Narinsky. "New Evidence on the Soviet Rejection of the Marshall Plan, 1947: Two Reports." Cold War International History Project Working Papers Series, no. 9, 1994.

Paszynski, Marian. "The Economic Interest of the CMEA Countries in Relation with the Developing Countries." In *East, West, South: Economic Interactions Between Three Worlds*, ed. Christopher Thomas Saunders, 33–47. New York: St. Martin's Press, 1981.

BIBLIOGRAPHY

Patel, Kiran Klaus. *The New Deal: A Global History.* Princeton, N.J.: Princeton University Press, 2016.

Pedersen, Susan. *The Guardians: The League of Nations and the Crisis of Empire.* Oxford: Oxford University Press, 2015.

——. "The Meaning of the Mandates System: An Argument." *Geschichte und Gesellschaft* 32, no. 4 (2006): 560–82.

Pernot, Jean-Marie. "Dedans, dehors, la dimension internationale dans le syndicalisme français." Ph.D. diss., Université Paris Nanterre, 2001. https://tel.archives ouvertes .fr/tel-00927161/document.

Perron, Régine. *Histoire du multilatéralisme : l'utopie du siècle américain de 1918 à nos jours.* Paris: PU Paris-Sorbonne, 2014.

Pestre, Dominique. "La recherche opérationnelle pendant la dernière guerre et ses suites, la pensée des systèmes." *Revue scientifique et technique de la défense* 54 (2001): 63–69.

——. "Repenser les variantes du complexe militaire-industriel-universitaire." In *Les Sciences pour la guerre, 1940–1960,* ed. Dominique Pestre and Amy Dahan, 195–221. Paris: Éd. de l'EHESS, 2004.

Peter, Matthias, and Hermann Wentker, eds. *Die KSZE im Ost-West-Konflikt, Internationale Politik und gesellschaftliche Transformation 1975–1990.* Berlin: De Gruyter, 2015.

Péteri, György. *Nylon Curtain: Transnational and Transsystemic Tendencies in the Cultural Life of State-Socialist Russia and East-Central Europe.* Trondheim, Nor.: Trondheim Studies on East European Cultures & Societies, 2006.

Petiteville, Franck, ed. "La politisation résiliente des organisations internationales." *Critique internationale* 76, no. 3 (2017).

Petiteville, Franck, and Simon Tordjman, eds. *L'Assemblée générale des Nations unies.* Paris: Presses de Sciences Po, 2020.

Petrini, Francesco. "Capital Hits the Road: Regulating Multinational Corporations During the Long 1970s." In *Contesting Deregulation: Debates, Practices and Developments in the West Since the 1970s,* ed. Knud Andresen and Stefan Müller, 185–98. New York: Berghahn Books, 2017.

Petrov, Victor. "Communist Robot Dreams." Aeon.co, April 26, 2018. https://aeon.co /essays/how-communist-bulgaria-became-a-leader-in-tech-and-sci-fi.

Pitteloud, Sabine. "Les invisibles deviennent visibles. Le rôle politique des multinationales et les débats sur l'internationalisation en Suisse (1942–1993)." Ph.D. diss., University of Geneva, 2019. https://archive-ouverte.unige.ch/unige:121457.

——. *Les multinationales suisses dans l'arène politique (1942–1993).* Geneva: Droz, 2022.

Plata-Stenger, Véronique. "L'OIT et l'assurance sociale en Amérique latine dans les années 30 et 40: enjeux et limites de l'expertise internationale." *Revue d'histoire de la protection sociale* 10, no. 1 (2017): 42–61.

——. "L'OIT et le problème du sous-développement en Asie dans l'entre-deux-guerres." *Le Mouvement social* 263, no. 2 (2018): 109–22.

——. *Social Reform, Modernization and Technical Diplomacy: The ILO Contribution to Development (1930–1946).* Berlin: de Gruyter, 2020.

Plata-Stenger, Véronique, and Matthias Schulz, eds. "Décolonisation et développement: genèses, pratiques et interdépendances." *Relations internationales* 177, no. 1 (2019).

BIBLIOGRAPHY

Plesch, Daniel. *America, Hitler and the UN: How the Allies Won World War II and Forged a Peace*. London: Tauris, 2015.

Plesch, Daniel, and Thomas Weiss, eds. *Wartime Origins and the Future United Nations*. New York: Routledge, 2015.

Pons, Silvio. *The Global Revolution: A History of International Communism, 1917–1991*. Oxford: Oxford University Press, 2014.

Pons, Silvio, and Michele Donato. "What Was Reform Communism?" In *Endgames? Late Communism in Global Perspective, 1968 to the Present*, ed. Juliane Fürst, Silvio Pons, and Mark Selden, 178–202. Cambridge: Cambridge University Press, 2017.

Popa, Ioana. "La circulation transnationale du livre : un instrument de la guerre froide culturelle." *Histoire@Politique* 15, no. 3 (2011): 25–41.

Porter, Louis. "Cold War Internationalisms: The USSR in UNESCO, 1945–1967." Ph.D. diss., University of North Carolina Chapel Hill, 2018.

Potel, Jean-Yves. "La revendication autogestionnaire dans la Pologne de Solidarité." *Sociologie du travail* 24, no. 3 (1982): 262–78.

Ptak, Ralf. "Revisiting the Ordoliberal Foundations of the Social Market Economy." In *The Road from Mont Pèlerin: The Making of the Neoliberal Thought*, ed. Philip Mirowski and Dieter Plehwe, 98–138. Cambridge, Mass.: Harvard University Press, 2015.

Pudal, Bernard. "La beauté de la mort communiste." *Revue française de science politique* 52, no. 5 (2002): 545–59.

Ramcharan, Bertrand G. *Preventive Diplomacy at the UN*. Bloomington: Indiana University Press, 2008.

Rees, E. A. "The Sovietization of Eastern Europe." In *The Sovietization of Eastern Europe: New Perspectives on the Postwar Period*, ed. Balázs Apor, Péter Apor, and E. A. Rees, 1–29. Washington, D.C.: New Academia, 2008.

Regnauld, Amélie. "La RDA en Égypte, 1969–1989: la construction d'une politique étrangère. De la solidarité anti-impérialiste aux avantages réciproques." Ph.D. diss., université Paris 1, 2016.

Reinalda, Bob. *International Secretariats. Two Centuries of International Civil Servants and Secretariats*. London: Routledge, 2020

——. *Routledge History of International Organizations: From 1815 to the Present Day*. London: Routledge, 2009.

Reinisch, Jessica. "'Auntie UNRRA' at the Crossroads." *Past & Present* 218, no. 8 (2013): 70–97.

——. "Comparing Europe's Post-War Reconstructions: First Balzan Workshop, Birkbeck College, London, 28 October 2005." *History Workshop Journal* 61, no. 1 (2006): 299–304.

——. "Internationalism in Relief: The Birth (and Death) of UNRRA." *Past & Present* 210 (2011): 258–89.

Rindzeviciute, Egle. *The Power of Systems: How Policy Sciences Opened Up the Cold War World*. Ithaca, N.Y.: Cornell University Press, 2016.

Riska-Campbell, Leena. *Bridging East and West: The Establishment of the International Institute for Applied Systems Analysis (IIASA) in the United States Foreign Policy of Bridge Building, 1964–1972*. Helsinki: Finnish Society of Science and Letters, 2011.

BIBLIOGRAPHY

——. "Managing Systemic Convergence: American Multilateral Bridge Building in Europe During the 1960s and Early 1970s." *Valahian Journal of Historical Studies* 20 (Winter 2013): 135–68.

Rist, Gilbert. *The History of Development: From Western Origins to Global Faith*. London: Zed Books, 2019 (first published in French 1996).

Roehrlich, Elisabeth. "The Cold War, the Developing World, and the Creation of the International Atomic Energy Agency (IAEA), 1953–1957." *Cold War History* 16, no. 2 (April 2016): 195–212.

——. *Inspectors for Peace: A History of the International Atomic Energy Agency*. Baltimore: John Hopkins University Press, 2022.

——. *Kreiskys Aussenpolitik: zwischen österreichicher Identität und internationalem Programm*. Vienna: Vienna University Press, 2011

Romano, Angela. *From Détente in Europe to European Détente: How the West Shaped the Helsinki CSCE*. Brussels: P.I.E., 2009.

——. "Untying Cold War Knots: The EEC and Eastern Europe in the Long 1970s." *Cold War History* 14, no. 2 (2014): 153–73.

Romano, Angela, and Federico Romero, eds. *European Socialist Regimes Fateful Engagement with the West: National Strategies in the Long 1970s*. London: Routledge, 2020.

Romijn, Peter, Giles Scott-Smith, and Joes Segal, eds. *Divided Dreamworlds? The Cultural Cold War in East and West*. Amsterdam: University of Amsterdam Press, 2012.

Rosenstein-Rodan, Paul N. "The International Development of Economically Backward Areas." *International Affairs* 20, no. 2 (1944): 157–65.

——. "Problems of Industrialisation of Eastern and South-Eastern Europe." *Economic Journal* 53, no. 210–211 (June–September 1943): 202–11.

Roulin, Stéphanie. *Un credo anticommuniste. La commission Pro Deo de l'Entente Internationale Anticommuniste ou la dimension religieuse d'un combat politique (1924–1945)*. Lausanne, Switz.: Antipodes, 2010.

Rubinson, Paul. *Redefining Science, Scientists, the National Security State, and Nuclear Weapons in Cold War America*. Boston: University of Massachusetts Press, 2016.

Rubinstein, Alvin Z. *The Soviets in International Organizations: Changing Policy Toward Developing Countries, 1953–1963*. Princeton, N.J.: Princeton University Press, 1964.

——. *Yugoslavia and the Non-Aligned World*. Princeton, N.J.: Princeton University Press, 1970.

Rudolph, Karsten. *Wirtschaftsdiplomatie im Kalten Krieg: die Ostpolitik der westdeutschen Großindustrie 1945–1991*. Frankfurt: Campus-Verlag, 2004.

Rudzinski, Alexander W. "The Influence of the United Nations on Soviet Policy." *International Organization* 5 (1951): 282–299.

Ruotsila, Markku. "Transnational Anti-Communism and the Cold War: Agents, Activities, and Networks." In *Transnational Anti-Communism and the Cold War Agents, Activities, and Networks*, ed. Luc Van Dongen, Stéphanie Roulin, and Giles Scott-Smith, 235–50. Basingstoke, UK: Palgrave Macmillan, 2014.

Rupprecht, Tobias. "Die sowjetische Gesellschaft in der Welt des Kalten Kriegs: Neue Forschungsperspektiven." *Jahrbücher für Geschichte Osteuropas* 58 (2010): 381–99.

——. *Soviet Internationalism After Stalin: Interaction and Exchange Between the USSR and Latin America During the Cold War*. Cambridge: Cambridge University Press, 2016.

BIBLIOGRAPHY

Ruter, Nick. "The Western Wall: The Iron Curtain Recast in Midsummer 1951." In *Cold War Crossings: International Travel and Exchange Across the Soviet Bloc, 1940s–1960s*, ed. Patryk Babiracki and Kenyon Zimmer, 78–107. Arlington: University of Texas Press, 2014.

Sagafi-nejad, Tagi, and John Dunning. *The UN and Transnational Corporations: From Code of Conduct to Global Compact.* Bloomington: Indiana University Press, 2008.

Saint Martin, Monique de, and Patrice Yengo, eds. "Élites de retour de l'Est. Quelles contributions des élites 'rouges' au façonnement des États post-coloniaux?" *Cahiers d'Études africaines* 226, no. 2 (2017): 231–58.

Sanchez-Sibony, Oscar. *Red Globalization: The Political Economy of the Soviet Cold War from Stalin to Khrushchev.* Cambridge, Mass.: Cambridge University Press, 2016.

Silverstein, Sara. "The Periphery Is the Centre: Some Macedonian Origins of Social Medicine and Internationalism." *Contemporary European History* 28, no. 2 (May 2019): 220–33.

Sargent, Daniel J. "North/South: The United States Responds to the New International Economic Order." *Humanity: An International Journal of Human Rights, Humanitarianism, and Development* 6, no. 1 (2015): 201–16.

Saull, Richard. *The Cold War and After: Capitalism, Revolution and Superpower Politics.* London: Pluto Press, 2007.

——. "Locating the Global South in the Theorisation of the Cold War: Capitalist Development, Social Revolution and Geopolitical Conflict." *Third World Quarterly* 26, no. 2 (2005): 253–80.

Saunders, Christopher Thomas, ed. *Industrial Policies and Technology Transfers Between East and West.* New York: Springer, 1978.

Sauvant, Karl. "The Negotiations of the United Nations Code of Conduct on Transnational Corporations: Experience and Lessons Learned." *Journal of World Investment & Trade* 16, no. 1 (2015): 11–87.

Sauvy, Alfred. "Trois mondes, une planète." *L'Observateur*, August 14, 1952. http://www.homme-moderne.org/societe/demo/sauvy/3mondes.html.

Scheuzger, Stephan. "Reading of Cosmopolitanism: Revolutionaries' Biographies in the Intersections of Marxism and Anti-colonialism in the Interwar Years." *Monde(s)* 10, no. 2 (2016): 151–66.

Schipper, Frank. *Driving Europe: Building Europe on Roads in the Twentieth Century.* Amsterdam: University of Amsterdam Press, 2009.

Schirmann, Sylvain. *Crise, coopération économique et financière entre États européens, 1929–1933.* Vincennes: Institut de la gestion publique et du développement économique, 2011.

Schlarp, Karl-Heinz. "Das Dilema des westdeutschen Osthandels und die Entstehung des Ost Auschusses der deutschen Wirtschaft, 1950–1952." *Vierteljahrshefte für Zeitgeschichte* 41, no. 2 (1993): 223–76.

Schmalzer, Sigrid. *Red Revolution, Green Revolution: Scientific Farming in Socialist China.* Chicago: University of Chicago Press, 2016.

Schmelzer, Matthias. "A Club of the Rich to Help the Poor? The OECD 'Development' and the Hegemony of Donor Countries." In *International Organizations and Development, 1945–1990*, ed. Marc Frey, Sönke Kunkel, and Corinna Unger, 171–96. London: Palgrave Macmillan, 2014.

BIBLIOGRAPHY

——. *Freiheit für Wechselkurse und Kapital: die Ursprünge neoliberaler Währungspolitik und die Mont Pèlerin Society.* Marbourg: Metropolis-Verlag, 2010.

Schmid, Regin. *Red Scare: FBI and the Origins of Anticommunism in the United States, 1919–1943.* Museum Tusculanum Press, University of Copenhagen, 2000.

Schwenkel, Christina. "Affective Solidarities and East German Reconstruction of Postwar Vietnam." In *Comrades of Color: East Germany in the Cold War World,* ed. Quinn Slobodian, 267–93. New York: Berghahn Books, 2015.

Scott-Smith, Giles. "Opening Up Political Space. Informal Diplomacy, East-West Exchanges, and the Helsinki Process." In *Beyond the Divide: Entangled Histories of Cold War Europe,* ed. Simo Mikkonen and Pia Koivunen, 23–43. New York: Berghahn Books, 2015.

Scranton, Philip. "Managing Communist Enterprises: Poland, Hungary and Czechoslovakia, 1945–1970." In *Enterprise and Society* 19, no. 3 (2018): 492–537.

Selverstone, Marc J. *Constructing the Monolith: The United States, Great Britain, and International Communism, 1945–1950.* Cambridge, Mass.: Harvard University Press, 2009.

Sharma, Patrick. "Between North and South: The World Bank and the New International Economic Order." *Humanity: An International Journal of Human Rights, Humanitarianism, and Development* 6, no. 1 (2015): 189–200.

Siefert, Marsha. "Coproducing Cold War Culture. East-West Film-Making and Cultural Diplomacy." In *Divided Dreamworlds? The Cultural Cold War in East and West,* ed. Peter Romijn, Giles Scott-Smith, and Joel Segal, 73–95. Amsterdam: University of Amsterdam Press, 2012.

Simpson, John. "The UN's Role in Disarmament: Retrospect and Prospect." *Contemporary Security Policy* 15, no. 1 (1994): 55–67.

Singer, Hans W. "La création de la CNUCED et l'évolution de la pensée contemporaine sur le développement." *Revue Tiers-monde* 35, no. 139 (1994): 489–98.

Slany, William Z., and Ralph R. Goodwin, eds. *Foreign Relations of the United States, 1952–1954: Vol. 3, United Nations Affairs.* Washington, D.C.: Government Printing Office, 1979, Document 23.

Slobodian, Quinn, *Globalists: The End of Empire and the Birth of Neoliberalism.* Cambridge, Mass.: Harvard University Press, 2018.

Sluga, Glenda. *Internationalism in the Age of Nationalism.* Philadelphia: University of Pennsylvania Press, 2013.

Snyder, Sarah B. *Human Rights Activism and the End of the Cold War: A Transnational History of the Helsinki Network.* Cambridge: Cambridge University Press, 2011.

Sokoloff, Georges. *L'Économie de la détente : l'U.R.S.S. et le capital occidental.* Paris: Fondation nationale des sciences politiques, 1983.

Solchany, Jean. "Le problème plus que la solution: la démocratie dans la vision du monde néolibérale." *Revue de philosophie économique* 17, no. 1 (2016): 135–69.

——. *Wilhelm Röpke, l'autre Hayek : aux origines du néolibéralisme.* Paris: Publications de la Sorbonne, 2015.

Soutou, Georges-Henri. "Convergence Theories in France during the 1960s and the 1970s." In *The Making of Détente: Eastern and Western Europe in the Cold War, 1965–75,* ed. Wilfried Loth and Georges-Henri Soutou, 25–48. London: Routledge, 2008.

——. *La Guerre froide: 1943–1990.* Paris: Pluriel, 2011.

BIBLIOGRAPHY

Spaskovska, Lubjica. "Building a Better World? Construction, Labour Mobility and the Pursuit of Collective Self-Reliance in the 'Global South,' 1950–1990." *Labor History* 59, no. 3 (2018): 331–51.

Spaulding, Robert Mark. *Osthandel and Ostpolitik: German Trade Policies in Eastern Europe from Bismarck to Adenauer.* Providence, R.I.: Berghahn Books, 1997.

Speich Chassé, Daniel. *Die Erfindung des Bruttosozialprodukts: Globale Ungleichheit in der Wissensgeschichte der Ökonomie.* Göttingen, Ger.: Vandenhock & Ruprecht, 2013.

Staples, Amy L. S. *The Birth of Development: How the World Bank, Food and Agriculture Organization and World Health Organization Have Changed the World 1945–1965.* Kent, Ohio: Kent State University Press, 2006.

Steffen, Katrin. "Experts and the Modernization of the Nation: The Arena of Public Health in Poland in the First Half of the Twentieth Century." *Jahrbücher für Geschichte Osteuropas* 61, no. 4 (2013): 574–90.

Steiner, André. "The Globalisation Process and the Eastern Bloc Countries in the 1970s and 1980s." *European Review of History* 21, no. 2 (2014): 165–81.

Steiner, Yves. "Les riches amis suisses du néolibéralisme." *Traverse. Revue d'histoire* 14, no. 1 (2007): 114–26.

Stinsky, Daniel. "A Bridge Between East and West? Gunnar Myrdal and the UN Economic Commission for Europe, 1947–1957." In *Planning in Cold War Europe: Competition, Cooperation, Circulations (1950s–1970s),* ed. Michel Christian, Sandrine Kott, and Ondřej Matějka, 45–68. Berlin: De Gruyter, 2018.

——. *International Cooperation in Cold War Europe: The United Nations Economic Commission for Europe, 1947–1964.* India: Bloomsbury, 2022.

——. "'Sisyphus' Palace" The United Nations Economic Commission for Europe, 1947–1960." Ph.D. diss., Maastricht University, 2019.

Stokke, Olav. *The UN and Development: From Aid to Cooperation.* United Nations Intellectual History Project Series. Bloomington: Indiana University Press, 2009.

Stude, Sebastian. "Frieden als Demokratieforderung. Evangelische Kirche in den 1980er Jahren in der DDR." *Deutschland Archiv,* June 26, 2014. http://www.bpb.de/1866931.

Studer, Brigitte. *1968 und die Formung des feministischen Subjekts.* Vienna: Picus Verlag, 2011.

——. *Reisende der Weltrevolution eine Globalgeschichte der Kommunistischen Internationale.* Berlin: Suhrkamp, 2021.

Supiot, Alain. *L'Esprit de Philadelphie : la justice sociale face au marché total.* Paris: Seuil, 2010.

Szalai, Alexander, Riccardo Petrella, and Stein Rokkan. *Cross-National Comparative Survey Research: Theory and Practice.* Oxford: Pergamon Press, 1977.

Szczepanski-Huillery, Maxime. "L'idéologie tiers-mondiste. Constructions et usages d'une catégorie intellectuelle en 'crise.'" *Raisons politiques* 18, no. 2 (2005): 27–48.

Ter Minassian, Taline. *Colporteurs du Komintern: l'Union soviétique et les minorités au Moyen-Orient.* Paris: Presses de Sciences Po, 1997.

Thomas, Daniel Charles. *The Helsinki Effect: International Norms, Human Rights, and the Demise of Communism.* Princeton, N.J.: Princeton University Press, 2001.

Tolley, Howard B. *The International Commission of Jurists: Global Advocates for Human Rights.* Philadelphia: University of Pennsylvania Press, 1994.

BIBLIOGRAPHY

Tor Egil, Førland. "'Economic Warfare' and 'Strategic Goods': A Conceptual Framework for Analyzing COCOM." *Journal of Peace Research* 28, no. 2 (1991): 191–204.

Tournès, Ludovic. *Les États-Unis et la Société des Nations: 1914–1946. Le système international face à l'émergence d'une superpuissance.* Bern, Switz.: Peter Lang, 2016.

——. "The Rockefeller Foundation and the Transition from the League of Nations to the UN (1939–1946)." *Journal of Modern European History* 12 (2014): 323–41.

Tourraine, Alain. *La Société post-industrielle. Naissance d'une société.* Paris: Denoël, 1969.

Toussaint, Éric. *Banque mondiale, le coup d'État permanent. L'agenda caché du consensus de Washington.* Paris: CADTM, 2006.

Toye, John, and Richard Toye. *The UN and Global Political Economy: Trade, Finance and Development.* Bloomington: Indiana University Press, 2004.

Trentin, Massimiliano. "La République démocratique allemande et la Syrie du parti Baas." *Les Cahiers Sirice* 10 (2013): 55–67.

——. "Modernization as State Building: The Two Germanies in Syria, 1963–1972." *Diplomatic History* 33, no. 3 (2009): 487–505.

Tsilage, Flora. "Relief and Rehabilitation in the Immediate Aftermath of War." *History Workshop Journal* 61, no. 1 (2006): 299–304; 63, no. 1 (2007): 371–74; 65, no. 1 (2008): 279–84.

Unger, Corinna. "Histories of Development and Modernization: Findings, Reflections, Future Research." 2010. H-Soz-u-Kult/Forum/Forschungsberichte. http://hsozkult .geschichte.hu-berlin.de/forum/2010-12-001.

——. "The United States, Decolonization, and the Education of Third World Elites." In *Elites and Decolonization in the Twentieth Century*, ed. Jost Dülffer and Marc Frey, 241–61. Basingstoke, UK: Palgrave Macmillan, 2011.

Van Dongen, Luc, Stéphanie Roulin, and Giles Scott-Smith, eds. *Transnational Anti-Communism and the Cold War Agents, Activities, and Networks.* Basingstoke, UK: Palgrave Macmillan, 2014.

Vardabasso, Valentina. "La Convention européenne des droits de l'homme." *Relations internationales* 131 (2007): 73–90.

Vargha, Dora. "A Forgotten Episode of International Health." *History of Medicine* (blog), March 13, 2017. http://historyofmedicineinireland.blogspot.com/2017/03/a -forgotten-episode-of-international.html.

——. *Polio across the Iron Curtain: Hungary's Cold War with an Epidemic.* Cambridge: Cambridge University Press, 2018.

Vicedo, Marga. "The Social Nature of the Mother's Tie to Her Child: John Bowlby's Theory of Attachment in Post-War America." *British Journal for the History of Science* 44 (2011): 401–26.

Virgili, Fabrice. *La France virile: des femmes tondues à la Libération.* Paris: Payot, 2000.

Waddell, Brian. "Economic Mobilization for World War II and the Transformation of the State." *Politics & Society* 22, no. 2 (1994): 165–94.

Warlouzet, Laurent. *Governing Europe in a Globalizing World: Neoliberalism and Its Alternatives Following the 1973 Oil Crisis.* London: Routledge, 2018.

Weindling, Paul. "Public Health and Political Stability: The Rockefeller Foundation in Central and Eastern Europe Between the Two World Wars." *Minerva* 31, no. 3 (1993): 253–67.

Weiner, Douglas. "Communism and Environment." In *Endgames? Late Communism in Global Perspective, 1968 to the Present*, ed. Juliane Fürst, Silvio Pons, and Mark Selden, 529–54. Cambridge: Cambridge University Press, 2017.

Weiss, Holger, ed. *International Communism and Transnational Solidarity: Radical Networks, Mass Movements and Global Politics, 1919–1939*. Leiden: Brill, 2017.

Weitz, Eric D. "From the Vienna to the Paris System: International Politics and the Entangled Histories of Human Rights, Forced Deportations, and Civilizing Missions." *American Historical Review* 5 (2008): 1313–43.

——. *A World Divided. The Global Struggle for Human Rights in the Age of Nation-States*. Princeton, N.J.: Princeton University Press, 2019.

Westad, Odd Arne. *The Cold War: A World History*. New York: Basic Books, 2017.

——. "The Cold War and the International History of the Twentieth Century." In *The Cambridge History of the Cold War*. Vol. 1: *Origins, 1945–1962*, ed. Melvyn P. Leffler and Odd Arne Westad, 1–19. Cambridge: Cambridge University Press, 2010.

——. *The Global Cold War: Third World Interventions and the Making of Our Times*. Cambridge: Cambridge University Press, 2005.

Whelan, Daniel J. *Indivisible Human Rights: A History*. Philadelphia: University of Pennsylvania Press, 2010.

——. "'Under the Aegis of Man': The Right to Development and the Origins of the New International Economic Order." *Humanity: An International Journal of Human Rights, Humanitarianism, and Development* 6, no. 1 (2015): 93–108.

White, Stephen. "Colonial Revolution and the Communist International, 1919–1924." *Science & Society* 40, no. 2 (July 1976): 173–93.

Whyte, Jessica. *The Morals of the Market: Human Rights and the Rise of Neoliberalism*. London: Verso, 2019.

Wieviorka, Olivier. *Normandy: The Landings to the Liberation of Paris*. Cambridge, Mass.: Belknap Press of Harvard University Press, 2008.

Wolikow, Serge. "The Comintern as a World Network." In *The Cambridge History of Communism*, ed. Silvio Pons and Stephen Smith, 232–55. Cambridge: Cambridge University Press, 2017.

——. *L'Internationale communiste (1919–1943): le Komintern ou le rêve déchu du parti mondial de la révolution*. Paris: Les Éditions de l'Atelier/Éditions ouvrières, 2010.

——. "Les interprétations du mouvement communiste international." In *Le Siècle des communismes*, ed. Michel Dreyfus et al., 83–93. Paris: Éditions de l'Atelier, 2000.

Woodbridge, George (United Nations Relief and Rehabilitation Administration). *UNRRA: The History of the United Nations Relief and Rehabilitation Administration*. 3 vols. New York: Columbia University Press, 1950.

Xun, Zhou. "From China's 'Barefoot Doctor' to Alma Ata: The Primary Health Care Movement in the Long 1970s." In *China, Hong Kong, and the Long 1970s: Global Perspectives*, ed. Priscilla Roberts and Odd Arne Westad, 135–57. Cham, Switz.: Palgrave Macmillan, 2017.

Yagodovsky, Leonid Sergeevich. *The World Socialist System: Its Role in the World Today*. Moscow: Novosti Press Agency Publishing House, 1975.

Yale, Richmond. *Cultural Exchange and the Cold War: Raising the Iron Curtain*. Philadelphia: University of Pennsylvania Press, 2004.

Zacharia, Benedetto. "Learning from Yugoslavia? Western Europe and the Myth of Self Management (1968–1975)." In *Planning in Cold War Europe: Competition,*

Cooperation, Circulations (1950s–1970s), ed. Michel Christian, Sandrine Kott, and Ondrej Matejka, 213–37. Berlin: De Gruyter, 2018.

Zahra, Tara. *The Lost Children: Reconstructing Europe's Families After World War II.* Cambridge, Mass.: Harvard University Press, 2015.

Zaidi, Waqar. "Planning, Production and Reconstruction in Postwar Europe. Fourth Balzan Workshop, Birkbeck College, London, 26 June 2007." *History Workshop Journal* 65, no. 1 (2008): 279–84.

Zanasi, Margherita. "Exporting Development: The League of Nations and Republican China." *Comparative Studies in Society and History* 49, no. 1 (2007): 143–69.

Zancarini-Fournel, Michelle. "Genre et politique: les années 1968." *Vingtième Siècle. Revue d'histoire* 75, no. 3 (2002): 133–43.

Zaragori, Aurélien. "L'Organisation internationale du travail et les milieux chrétiens (1919 1969)." Ph.D. diss., université Lyon 3, 2018.

Zimdars, Mark. "L'Organisation de la conférence islamique." *Verfassung und Recht in Übersee / Law and Politics in Africa, Asia and Latin America* 24, no. 4 (1991): 406–48.

Zimmer, Thomas. *Welt ohne Krankheit. Geschichte der internationalen Gesundheitspolitik 1940–1970.* Göttingen, Ger.: Wallstein, 2017.

Zubok, Vladislav M. *A Failed Empire: The Soviet Union in the Cold War from Stalin to Gorbachev.* New Cold War History. Chapel Hill: University of North Carolina Press, 2007.

——. "The Soviet Union and European Integration from Stalin to Gorbachev." *Journal of European Integration History* 2, no. 1 (1996): 85–98.

Zubok, Vladislav, and Constantine Pleshakov. *Inside the Kremlin's Cold War: From Stalin to Khrushchev.* Cambridge, Mass.: Harvard University Press, 1996.

INDEX

Abdel-Rahman, Ibrahim Helmi, 108–9
abortion, 185
Action Against Hunger, 169
Adenauer, Konrad, 119
Afghanistan, 85, 171
AFL. *See* American Federation of Labor
AFL-CIO. *See* American Federation of Labor-Congress of Industrial Organizations
Africa, 70–71, 75–77, 83–84, 86, 132, 136, 141, 144–45, 150, 153, 178
agronomy, 160
Albania, 47, 49, 57, 69, 83, 97, 112, 174
Algeria, 129–30, 178, 237n55
Allied military organizations, 31
Alma-Ata Declaration (1978), 141–42
Altman, Henryk, 235n20
American Federation of Labor (AFL), 52, 64, 65, 115, 124, 199–200
American Federation of Labor-Congress of Industrial Organizations (AFL-CIO), 189, 192
American Relief Administration (ARA), 16–17, 19, 20
Amnesty International, 165, 188, 193
anticommunism, 20–21, 42–43, 87–92, 97

antifascism, 9, 12–13, 23–27, 32–33, 36, 79
anti-Semitism, 14, 41
Appell, Geneviève, 63
ARA. *See* American Relief Administration
Arab Countries, 85, 160
Armenians, 84
Aron, Raymond, 102, 104
Asia, 7, 38, 77, 83–84, 88–89, 136, 144–45, 153, 170, 1738
Aswan Dam, 85
Atlantic Charter, 12, 28, 30, 32–33, 36, 123, 134–35
Atomic Energy Commission, 117
Aubert, Théodore, 88
Austria, 4, 73, 95–96, 105, 127, 198
Avramović, Dragoslav, 96

Bácskai, Tamás, 176
Bahro, Rudolf, 182
Balkans. *See specific countries*
Bank for International Settlements, 30
Bauer, Peter Tamas, 168–69
Belarus, 19
Belgium, 50 , 53, 71
Berlin blockade, 12

INDEX

Berlinguer, Enrico, 181
Berlin Wall, 173
Bevin, Ernest, 51
Bidault, Georges, 51
Biermann, Wolf, 182
Blair, Tony, 193
Blanchard, Francis, 189–90
Bogomolov, Oleg, 172–73
Bolivia, 71
Boumédiène, Houari, 143
Bowlby, John, 61
Brandt, Willy, 32, 99, 107, 149–50, 166, 168–69
Brazil, 84
Bretton Woods, 12, 29, 31, 36, 42–43, 47
Bruce, Stanley, 132–33
Bruce Report, 132–33
Bruckner, Pascal, 169
Brundtland, Gro Harlem, 186
Brunner, Karl, 168
Bulgaria, 31, 47, 155–56, 155–57, 158, 243n125
Bundy, McGeorge, 101–2, 106–7
Burma, 69
Business and Industry Advisory Committee, 148

Canada, 18, 19, 27, 56–57, 60, 137, 141
capitalism. *See specific topics*
Carter, Jimmy, 171
Cassin, René, 123
Catholicism, 89, 185, 192
Central Asia, 84
Central Europe: Atlantic Charter and, 32–33; Balkans and, 20–21; CoCom in, 54; communism in, 44; Czechoslovakia and, 23; diplomacy with, 116–17; Eastern bloc and, 200; Eastern Europe and, 73–74; Germany and, 14; Latin America and, 84–85; Middle East and, 198; Rockefeller Foundation in, 21–23; USSR and, 44, 196–97; Western Europe and, 26; after World War II, 17–18
Central Intelligence Agency: in Africa, 71; Dulles for, 69; in Europe, 89; Ford Foundation and, 88, 192; Guatemala

and, 147; ICFTU and, 64; unions to, 218n114; U.S., and, 52, 163
CEPES. *See* European Center for Higher Education
children, 26–27, 45, 58–63, 60–61, 80, 208n45, 213n39
Chile, 135, 147, 181
China: Africa and, 141; Chinese model, 140–43; Comecon and, 153; communism in, 38, 124, 140; Egypt and, 133; in geopolitics, 97; Global North and, 151; Great Britain and, 182–83; India and, 19, 77; to Rockefeller Foundation, 132; Russia and, 2–3; socialism in, 177; Taiwan and, 46–47; in UN, 49; USSR and, 179–80; WHO and, 141–42
Chisholm, Brock, 56–57, 140–41
Christian, Michel, 236n38
Christian Democrats, 61, 182
Churchill, Winston, 11–12, 17, 28
Ciszewski, Jan, 33
Citrine, Walter, 64
Clayton, William, 51
Clementis, Vlado, 64
Cobden, Richard, 76
CoCom. *See* Coordinating Committee for Multilateral Export Controls
Cole, Sterling, 108
Colombia, 130, 139
colonialism, 77, 144–45
Comecon. *See* Council for Mutual Economic Assistance
Comintern, 41, 76–78, 88–89
communism: in Africa, 178; to Canada, 56–57; capitalism and, 226n8; in Central Europe, 44; in China, 38, 124, 140; in Cold War, 63, 161–62, 176–79; to Comecon, 154; communist internationalism, 76–80, 165–66, 173–82; Communist Party of Germany, 59; in Czechoslovakia, 11–12, 23–24; in Eastern Europe, 63–64; ECOSOC and, 59–60; *Eurocommunists*, 181; in Europe, 51, 163–64, 182; in France, 79–80, 181, 185; to GDR, 191; geopolitics of, 7, 20,

44–45; in Germany, 76, 89; to Global South, 87, 152; to House of Un-American Activities Committee, 20–21; ideology of, 105, 200; to ILO, 45; International Anticommunist Entente, 88; marginalization in, 45–46; Marshall Plan and, 66; Marxism and, 180; in Middle East, 181; to NATO, 54–55; to Nazis, 89–90, 97; neoliberalism and, 170–73; politics of, 120–21, 124–25; propaganda against, 50; in Romania, 157; in Second World nations, 40–49, 161; to Social Democrats, 24, 157; socialism and, 32–33, 64; in South Africa, 77; to U.S., 134–35; in USSR, 11, 15, 41, 102, 177; WFTU and, 114–15, 180; women in, 78; in Yugoslavia, 35. *See also* anticommunism

concentration camps, 24

Conference on Security and Cooperation in Europe (CSCE), 9–10, 112–13, 122, 126, 190. *See also* Helsinki conference

Congo, 70–71, 75

convergences: cooperation and, 112–13; in Europe, 101–6, 113–22; at Helsinki conference, 122–28; at Vienna Institute, 106–12

cooperation, 112–13, 118–22, 178, 230n58

Coordinating Committee for Multilateral Export Controls (CoCom): in Central Europe, 54; Embargo, 108; ILO and, 156; list, 71; Marshall Plan and, 9; NATO and, 55; UN and, 6; U.S., and, 158, 198–99

Cotton, Eugénie, 79

Council for Mutual Economic Assistance (Comecon): in Asia, 177; China and, 153; communism to, 154; Eastern bloc and, 116–17; Eastern Europe and, 119, 175–76; EEC and, 95, 121; GDR and, 158; ILO and, 140; NATO and, 239n69; OECD and, 105, 171; for socialism, 6–7, 32; to Stalin, 40–41; Third World nations for,

85–86, 152; UNECE and, 57–58; USSR and, 51–52, 73; Warsaw Pact and, 75

Cox-Reece Commission, 43–44

Croatia, 96

CSCE. *See* Conference on Security and Cooperation in Europe

Cuba, 133, 146

Cuban Missile Crisis, 71, 97–98, 99, 117

cybernetics, 110, 156

Cyrankiewicz, Józef, 24

Czechoslovakia: Central Europe and, 23; communism in, 11–12, 23–24; cooperation with, 178; GDR and, 120–21, 199; Greece and, 19; Hungary and, 118, 157; ideology in, 22–23; to ILO, 159; IMF and, 48; National Insurance Act in, 26; Poland and, 1, 4, 11–12, 20, 35, 42, 52, 55–56, 63–65, 174; politics in, 25, 32, 46; Prague Spring in, 173, 181; reform in, 81; Switzerland and, 34; U.S., and, 216n86, 242n121; USSR and, 26, 78, 80, 124–25; Yugoslavia and, 34

David, Jean-Paul, 89

David, Myriam, 63

Davis, Angela, 82

Debré, Robert, 62

Declaration of the Rights of Child (1959), 60–61

decolonization, 10, 84, 96, 131, 133–34, 233n2

de Gaulle, Charles, 99, 154

Delaney, Philip, 124

Deng Xiaoping, 77

Denmark, 55

Department of Commerce, U.S., 54

détente, 99, 116, 126

development, 28–30, 47–48, 82, 132–42, 147–49

Diebold, William, Jr., 53

disarmament, 182–84

dissent, 109, 180, 184–87

Di Vittorio, Giuseppe, 180

Doctors Without Borders, 165, 169

Dubček, Alexander, 174

Dulles, Allen, 69

Dulles, John F., 90

INDEX

Eastern bloc: to AFL, 199–200; Central Europe and, 200; in Cold War, 80–87; Comecon and, 116–17; diplomacy with, 108–9; to ECOSOC, 184–85; elitism in, 121; end of, 173–76; Europe and, 71–72; GDR and, 92; Global South and, 160; Mongolia and, 69; NIEO to, 144; in pan-European plans, 128; socialism in, 92–93; trade with, 72–73; UN and, 105–6, 151; to U.S., 90; USSR and, 87–88, 111

Eastern Europe: anticommunism to, 20–21; Central Europe and, 73–74; Comecon and, 119, 175–76; communism in, 63–64; culture of, 56–58, 63–66, 153–54; diplomacy with, 103–4; embargoes against, 54–56; in Geneva system, 45; geopolitics in, 9; Germany and, 28–29; Global South and, 31; Health Division of, 22–23; Hungary and, 170–71; to ILO, 199–200; industrialization in, 230n64; Marshall Plan and, 49–54; Middle East and, 159; Myrdal on, 172; Nazis to, 16; Poland and, 33–34; Social Democrats in, 25; social justice in, 24; U.S., and, 101, 120; USSR and, 34, 41–42, 81–82; Western Europe and, 32, 72, 127

ECA. *See* Economic Cooperation Administration, U.S.

ECAFE. *See* United Nations Economic Commission for Asia and the Far East

Economic and Social Council (ECOSOC), 6, 26, 42, 59–64, 62, 136–37, 184–85

Economic Cooperation Administration, U.S. (ECA), 50, 52–55

ECOSOC. *See* Economic and Social Council; United Nations Economic and Social Council

ECSC. *See* European Coal and Steel Community

EEC. *See* European Economic Community

Egypt, 71, 83, 85, 133

Einstein, Albert, 117–18

Eisenhower, Dwight D., 49, 68, 80, 93, 108, 117

Eisnerova, Dagmar, 44

Eklund, Sigvard, 106–7, 106–8

embargoes, 6, 49, 54–56

Emergency Economic Committee for Europe, 31

employers, 86–87

Employers' Confederation of Europe (UNICE), 148

Engels, Friedrich, 184

environment, 184–87

epistemology, 110–12

Erban, Evžen, 25–26, 159

Erhard, Ludwig, 167

établi movement, 180

Ethiopia, 19, 96, 178

Europe: to AFL, 115; Central Intelligence Agency in, 89; Cold War and, 30, 99–101; communism in, 51, 163–64, 182; convergences in, 101–6, 113–22; CSCE, 9–10; Eastern bloc and, 71–72; economics in, 13–16; *Eurocommunists*, 181; European Coal Organization, 31; European Convention on Human Rights, 123–24; G77 countries and, 177–78, 195, 197; GDR and, 2; Great Britain and, 19; Hapsburg dynasty in, 199; after Helsinki conference, 112–13; human rights in, 122–28; ILO in, 132–33; industrialization in, 226n8; international organizations in, 126–27; Lóczy-Pikler model in, 62; after Marshall Plan, 104–5; Middle East and, 19; Radio Free, 90; reconstruction in, 21–27, 35–37; revolutions in, 77; Social Democrats in, 188; socialism in, 61–62; trade in, 53–54; UN Commission for Europe, 100; to UNCTAD, 176–77; UNRRA in, 18–20; U.S., and, 16–17; USSR and, 4, 119; after World War I, 195; after World War II, 11–13, 20–21, 28–35. *See also specific countries*

European Center for Higher Education (CEPES), 113–14

INDEX

European Central Inland Transport
  Organization, 31
European Coal and Steel Community
  (ECSC), 47, 56
European Economic Community (EEC),
  72, 95, 121, 150, 171
Europe Recovery Plan. *See* Marshall
  Plan
Evans, Luther, 43

Fadeyev, Nikolai, 152
FAO. *See* Food and Agriculture
  Organization
fascism, 12–13, 23–27, 32–33, 36, 116
Federal Bureau of Investigation, 42–43, 90
Federal Republic of Germany (FRG):
  anticommunism in, 97; Canada and,
  137; culture of, 63; France and,
  126–27; GDR and, 60, 72, 185;
  Hallstein Doctrine in, 38–39; to ICC,
  119–20; Nazis and, 224n84; reputation
  of, 61; socialism in, 175–76; in
  UNECE, 38–39; U.S., and, 4, 167;
  USSR and, 171
fellowships, 22, 26, 156
feminism, 184–87
Final Act. *See* Helsinki conference
Finland, 4, 47
First World, 10, 70, 149–53, 160, 193
Food and Agriculture Organization
  (FAO): ILO and, 35–36, 85; as
  international networks, 27;
  international organizations with, 13;
  Poland to, 14–15, 60; Third World
  nations to, 151; UN and, 21; UNDP
  and, 138; UNECE and, 31; WHO and,
  45, 155
Ford, Gerald, 149
Ford Foundation, 7, 69, 88, 90–92,
  100–105, 154, 157, 173, 188, 192
foreign policy, 79–80
France: communism in, 79–80, 181, 185;
  culture of, 25–26; diplomacy by, 120;
  FRG and, 126–27; General
  Confederation of Labor in, 64–65;
  Germany and, 99; Great Britain and,
  4, 55; Italy and, 11, 50, 179; nuclear

weapons in, 182–83; politics in, 14;
  Programme comun in, 181; socialism
  in, 224n85; Switzerland and, 62
František, Klaus, 26
FRG. *See* Federal Republic of Germany

G77 countries, 130, 146–47, 149–50, 154,
  177–78, 195, 197
Galbraith, John Kenneth, 103
Galenson, Walter, 139
Gass, Ron, 105
GATT. *See* General Agreement on
  Tariffs and Trade
GDR. *See* German Democratic Republic
General Agreement on Tariffs and Trade
  (GATT): economics of, 32, 47–48, 71,
  128; Global South and, 145–46,
  177–78; IMF and, 175; OEEC and, 94;
  politics of, 170; UNECE and, 97, 118;
  World Bank and, 94, 200
General Confederation of Labor,
  64–65, 180
Geneva system, 18, 28, 45
geopolitics: in Africa, 70–71, 75; of
  antifascism, 23–27; China in, 97; of
  Cold War, 12, 36–37; of communism,
  7, 20, 44–45; in Eastern Europe, 9;
  employers in, 86–87; Germany
  in, 116; Great Britain in, 17; of
  industrialization, 34–35; of
  internationalism, 70–75, 87–92; of
  NIEO, 10, 154–58; OEEC in, 56–58; of
  pan-European plans, 28–30; religion
  in, 88; Third World nations in, 137–43,
  149–53; of trade, 33–34; WHO in, 43;
  after World War II, 13–16, 35–37
German Democratic Republic (GDR):
  Comecon and, 158; communism to,
  191; Czechoslovakia and, 120–21, 199;
  development in, 82; Eastern bloc and,
  92; economics in, 170–71; Europe and,
  2; FRG and, 60, 72, 185; Hungary and,
  80; ideology in, 153; ILO and, 175–76,
  191–92; Indonesia and, 85; leadership
  in, 182; Lutheranism in, 184;
  socialism in, 59; UN and, 31; USSR
  and, 38–39, 155

INDEX

Germany: anticommunism in, 20; Berlin blockade, 12; Central Europe and, 14; in Cold War, 38–39; communism in, 76, 89; Communist Party of Germany, 59; Eastern Europe and, 28–29; France and, 99; in geopolitics, 116; to ICC, 119–20; Jews in, 15–16; Nazi prisoner camps in, 15; reconstruction in, 33; Red Cross in, 14; U.S., and, 16; USSR and, 33–34, 60; after World War II, 46–47
globalism: AFL in, 65; anticommunism in, 20–21; capitalism in, 76; civil servants in, 8; in Cold War, 1–2; dissent in, 184–87; economics of, 71–74; elitism and, 5–6; G77 countries in, 130, 146–47, 149–50, 154; global health, 140–43; human rights in, 187–93; ideology of, 162; ILO in, 30–31, 94; internationalism and, 163–73; nuclear weapons in, 117–18; pacifism and, 182–84; race relations in, 125–26; U.S., in, 91
Global North, 131, 143, 146, 151
Global South: capitalism in, 200–201; in Cold War, 10, 125, 131–32, 187–88; communism to, 87, 152; Eastern bloc and, 160; Eastern Europe and, 31; economics in, 148–49, 169; to EEC, 150; GATT and, 145–46, 177–78; human rights in, 123–24; international organizations in, 4–5; politics of, 86; raw materials in, 178–79; trade and, 78, 153; to USSR, 82, 97; to World Bank, 142. *See also* Third World
Gomułka, Władysław, 174
Gorbachev, Mikhail, 163, 172, 174–75, 177, 182
Gramsci, Antonio, 180
Grant, John, 22–23
Great Britain: Canada and, 18; China and, 182–83; Europe and, 19; France and, 4, 55; in geopolitics, 17; International Computers Limited in, 158; Italy and, 54–55; Poland and, 34; reconstruction in, 29; U.S., and, 20, 36–37, 65, 164–65

Great Society, 101–2
Greece, 11, 14–15, 19–20, 62
Greenpeace, 186–87, 193
Greenwood, Arthur, 28
Gromyko, Andreï, 42
Guatemala, 147
Guevara, Che, 152

Haberler, Gottfried, 164–65, 168
Hallstein Doctrine, 38–39
Hammarskjöld, Dag, 68, 137
Hapsburg dynasty, 199
Havana Charter, 145
Health Commission, 22
Helsinki Accords, 188, 191–92
Helsinki conference: convergences at, 122–28; cooperation at, 230n58; Europe after, 112–13; politics of, 113–22, 186; Vienna Institute and, 101
Helsinki process, 109, 165
Herren, Madeleine, 205n16
Ho Chi Minh, 77
Hoffman, Paul, 133
Honecker, Erich, 174
Hoover, Herbert, 20
Hoover, J. Edgar, 90
Horvart, Branko, 94
Hot Springs conference, 18
House of Un-American Activities Committee, 20–21, 42–43, 79
Hromádka, Josef Lukl, 23
human rights, 121–28, 143–44, 165, 187–93, 190, 231n77
Hungary: Cold War and, 31, 47, 80–81; Czechoslovakia and, 118, 157; Eastern Europe and, 170–71; Poland and, 61–62, 71, 171; Romania and, 156–57, 175; USSR and, 70, 91–92

IAEA. *See* International Atomic Energy Agency
ICA. *See* International Cooperation Administration
ICC. *See* International Chamber of Commerce
ICFTU. *See* International Confederation of Free Trade Unions

INDEX

ICPE. *See* International Centre for Public Enterprises
IIASA. *See* International Institute for Applied Systems Analysis
ILO. *See* International Labour Organization
IMF. *See* International Monetary Fund
India, 19, 77, 85–86, 108, 115, 144, 156, 178–79
Indochina, 77, 129–30
Indonesia, 85, 144–45
industrialization, 29, 34–35, 110, 226n8, 230n64
Institute for the Socialist World Economic System, 172
Institute of Industrial Cybernetics and Robotics, 156
International Anticommunist Entente, 88
International Atomic Energy Agency (IAEA), 80, 106–7, 106–8
International Centre for Public Enterprises (ICPE), 96
International Chamber of Commerce (ICC), 6–7, 71, 119–22, 127, 147–48, 167
International Christian Union of Business Executives (UNIAPAC), 148
International Computers Limited, 158
International Confederation of Free Trade Unions (ICFTU), 7, 64–65, 78, 115, 189–90
International Cooperation Administration (ICA), 93
International Group of Democratic Socialists, 32
International Institute for Applied Systems Analysis (IIASA), 100, 107–8, 111, 127–28
internationalism: Cold War and, 68–70, 75, 92–98, 187–93; communist, 76–80, 165–66, 173–82; geopolitics of, 70–75, 87–92; globalism and, 163–73; ideology of, 40–45; liberal, 45–49; NGOs in, 195; socialist, 249n2; Sovietization and, 80–87; in Third World nations, 10, 222n253
International Labour Organization (ILO): AFL and, 124; agronomy by, 160; archives, 24; CoCom and, 156; in

Cold War, 66, 142; Comecon and, 140; communism to, 45; conferences, 26, 29, 86–87, 190; Czechoslovakia to, 159; diplomacy by, 114–15; Eastern Europe to, 199–200; ECOSOC and, 64; in Europe, 132–33; FAO and, 35–36, 85; GDR and, 175–76, 191–92; in globalism, 30–31, 94; history of, 63–64; human rights to, 123; ICFTU and, 65, 115; ideology of, 130–31; League of Nations and, 46, 209n58; OECD and, 149; in Poland, 25, 175, 235n20, 242n109; Rockefeller Foundation and, 28; socialism to, 214; UNECE and, 73; UNESCO and, 100, 138; USSR and, 1, 48, 57, 59–60, 68–69, 125; WFTU and, 64–65; WHO and, 7, 57, 140; World Employment Programme, 139; after World War II, 46
International Law Commission, 168
international mobilizations, 187–93
International Monetary Fund (IMF), 6, 31, 47–48, 92–93, 164, 170, 175
international networks, 21–27
international NGOs, 70, 130–31
International Peace Movement, 183
International Women's Year, 79, 82, 177, 184
Iraq, 178–79
Ireland, 209n58
Italy, 11, 14, 19, 47, 50, 54–55, 64–65, 179–81, 180

Japan, 181
Jdanovism, 11–12
Jenks, Wilfried, 114
Jews, 14–16, 120
John Paul II (pope), 190
Johnson, Lyndon B., 101–2, 106–7
Joliot-Curie, Frédéric, 79

Kafka, Franz, 44
Kaldor, Nicholas, 33, 84, 103
Kalecki, Michał, 84, 136
Kallos, Ödön, 175
Kemp, Arthur, 20

INDEX

Kennan, George F., 51, 54
Kennedy, John F., 134
Kennedy, Stetson, 233n95
Keynes, John Maynard, 135–36
Khane, Abd-El Rhaman, 109
Khrushchev, Nikita, 68, 75, 83, 120
Kirkland, Lane, 189
Klump, Brigitte, 191
Klump, Klaus, 191
Kollontai, Alexandra, 59
Korean War, 80
Koudriatzev, Anatoly, 57, 216n87
Kreisky, Bruno, 32, 107

Lal, Deepak, 170
Lalonde, Marc, 141
Lange, Oskar, 173
Latin America: Africa and, 77; Balkans and, 198; Central Europe and, 84–85; Cuba and, 133; Economic Commission for Latin America, 135; economics in, 165; OECD and, 239n69; UNECLA, 83–84; U.S., and, 30–31, 125; USSR and, 84; in World War II, 133
Laugier, Henri, 42
League of Nations, 18, 21–23, 28, 30, 44–46, 129, 140, 195
Lebanon, 130
Lehman, Herbert, 17–18, 29
Lenin, Vladimir, 120, 152, 180
Leontief, Wassily, 168
Lester, Sean, 209n58
liberal internationalism, 45–49, 75–76, 195
liberalizing trade, 30–31
liberal socialism, 193
Liberman, Evsei, 103
Lie, Trygve, 43, 68
Lóczy-Pikler model, 62
Lodygensky, Georges, 88
Lumumba, Patrice, 71, 75, 83
Lutheranism, 184

Mahalanobis, Prasanta Chandra, 103
Mahler, Halfdan, 141
Malinowski, Władysław, 84, 136, 147
Maliţa, Mircea, 157
malnutrition, 15, 23

Manoilescu, Mihail, 84, 198
Maoism, 177, 179
Marshall, George, 11, 49–50, 49–51, 54
Marshall Plan: CoCom and, 9; Comintern and, 78; communism and, 66; Eastern Europe and, 49–54; Europe after, 104–5; OEEC and, 39; Truman and, 133; UNRRA and, 6, 49; in Western Europe, 11–12, 21, 35, 71
Marx, Karl, 76
Marxism, 59, 86, 151, 173, 180, 185–86
Mastanduno, Michael, 216n82
M'Bow, Amadou Mahtar, 130
McCarthy, Joseph, 43, 68–69
McCarthyism, 20–21, 42–43, 65
McDonald, John, 158
McNair Committee, 48–49
McNamara, Robert, 137, 139, 149–50
Mexico, 177
Middle East, 19, 83–84, 159, 181, 198
Milward, Alan, 50
Minc, Hilary, 32
minorities, 125–26
Molotov, Vyacheslav, 47, 51
Mongolia, 69
Mont Pelerin Society, 167–68
Moral Rearmament, 88
Morgenthau, Hans, 16
Morse, David, 1, 23–25, 23–27, 26, 56, 216n86, 242n121
Mošna, Zdeněk, 157
Mozambique, 130
Mudaliar, Ramaswani, 124
multilateralism, 3, 66–67, 112, 167, 201
multinational corporations, 115, 143, 147–49
Münzenberg, Willi, 76
Muslim culture, 83–84
Myrdal, Alva, 43, 107
Myrdal, Gunnar: on Eastern Europe, 172; Kaldor and, 103; poverty to, 149; reputation of, 13, 32–35, 42, 45, 72, 95, 196

Nasser, Gamal, 85, 96, 145
National Bank of Yugoslavia, 96
National Institute of Hygiene, 22

INDEX

nationalism, 90–91
National Management Development Centers, 156–57, 173
National Resources Planning Board, 30
national space, 3–4
NATO. *See* North Atlantic Treaty Organization
Nazis: barbarism by, 123; in Central Europe, 17; communism to, 89–90, 97; concentration camps by, 24; to Eastern Europe, 16; FRG and, 224n84; legacy of, 14; prisoner camps of, 15; reconstruction after, 15–16; to U.S., 28–29; USSR and, 89; to Western Europe, 14; after World War I, 28
Nehru, Jawaharlal, 96, 145
neoliberalism, 10, 166–73, 167, 193, 200–201
Netherlands, 183–84
New Deal, 16–18, 30, 134
New International Economic Order (NIEO): in Cold War, 149–53; geopolitics of, 10, 154–58; history of, 144–47, 237n55; multinational corporations and, 147–49; neoliberalism and, 200–201; politics of, 166; socialism to, 158–62; support for, 164; Third World nations for, 6, 143–44, 195; UN and, 167–68; UNCTAD and, 177–78
NGOs. *See* nongovernmental organizations
NIEO. *See* New International Economic Order
NIPKIP. *See* Research Institute for Instrument Design
Nixon, Richard, 154
Noll-Wagenfeld, Meike, 191
Non-Aligned Movement, 96, 143, 145, 176
Non-Capitalist Path of Development, 151
nongovernmental organizations (NGOs): in Cold War, 3; history of, 4–5; Human Rights Watch, 122–23; ICC and, 6; international, 70, 130–31; in internationalism, 195; multilateral organizations and, 7; pan-European plans of, 100; WFTU and, 7

North Atlantic Treaty, 39–40
North Atlantic Treaty Organization (NATO), 54–55, 183, 239n69
North Korea, 38
Norway, 43
Novotný, Antonín, 24
nuclear weapons, 117–18, 182–83, 186–87

OECD. *See* Organisation for Economic Co-operation and Development
OEEC. *See* Organisation for European Economic Co-operation
Office of Foreign Relief and Rehabilitation Operations (OFRRO), 17–18
Ohlin, Göran, 105
oil, 144, 178–79
Olof Palme Peace March, 184
OPEX programme, 137
Organisation for Economic Co-operation and Development (OECD): Business and Industry Advisory Committee, 148; Comecon and, 105, 171; history of, 50; ILO and, 149; Latin America and, 239n69; politics of, 6–7, 134; research by, 104–5; socialism to, 94–95; UN and, 93
Organisation for European Economic Co-operation (OEEC), 39, 53–54, 56–58, 57, 94, 134
Origin of the Family, Private Property and the State, The (Engels), 184
Orlov, Pavel, 57
Orlov, Yuri, 188
Ottoman Empire, 198–99
Owen, David, 135–36

pacifism, 182–84
Padevět, Krel, 157
Pakistan, 163
Palme, Olaf, 150, 184
pan-European plans: diplomacy in, 100–101; Eastern bloc in, 128; fascism and, 36; geopolitics of, 28–30; hegemony in, 196–97; of NGOs, 100; politics of, 30–31; of UNECE, 27, 40; after UNRRA, 31–35

INDEX

Partial Nuclear Test Ban Treaty, 117–18
Peace and Freedom movement, 89
Peace Movement, 79–80, 183–84
Pelt, Adrian, 45
People's Republic of China. *See* China
perestroika, 174–75
Perkins, Frances, 28, 30
Peru, 177
philanthropy, 21–22, 43–44
Philippines, 19
Pikler, Emmi, 62–63
Piłsudski, Józef, 17
Planning, 12, 27–28, 30, 73, 81, 86, 102–5, 127, 135, 167, 171, 185, 196, 199, 201
Poland: aid in, 23; ARA in, 17; Czechoslovakia and, 1, 4, 11–12, 20, 35, 42, 52, 55–56, 63–65, 174; diplomacy with, 46; Eastern Europe and, 33–34; economics in, 21; to FAO, 14–15, 60; Great Britain and, 34; Hungary and, 61–62, 71, 171; ILO in, 25, 175, 235n20, 242n109; Jews in, 14; leadership in, 31–32; National Institute of Hygiene in, 22; nationalism in, 90–91; reform in, 81; Romania and, 127, 185; Solidarność in, 189–93; Stalin and, 15; UNICEF in, 213n39; World Bank and, 48; Yugoslavia and, 15–16, 19, 23, 26, 62, 73, 92, 154
Popular Front, 181
poverty, 149–50
Prebisch, Raùl, 48, 84, 135, 146, 152, 198
prisoner camps, 15
Pro Deo, 88
Protestantism, 184
Pugwash movement, 117–18, 182–83

race relations, 125–26
Radio Free Europe, 90
Rajchman, Ludwik, 18, 22–23, 62
RAND Corporation, 107
Rapacki, Adam, 116–17
Reagan, Ronald, 163, 166, 169, 171
reconstruction, pan-European, 13, 15–16, 21–27, 29–33, 35–37, 49
Red Army, 17, 80–81, 163
Red Cross, 14
reform, 81, 218n114

refugees, 60–61, 70
Reinalda, Bob, 205n16
religion: in geopolitics, 88; Marxism and, 151; Protestantism, 184; to Social Democrats, 189; Third World nations and, 141. *See also specific religions*
Research Institute for Instrument Design (NIPKIP), 155–56
Roberts, Alfred, 124
Rockefeller Foundation, 13, 21–23, 28, 35–36, 43–44, 91, 132, 140
Roemer, Milton, 140
Romania: Bulgaria and, 243n125; during Cold War, 31, 47, 71; communism in, 157; Hungary and, 156–57, 175; National Management Development Centers in, 156–57, 173; Poland and, 127, 185; reform in, 81; socialism in, 241n100; USSR and, 185; Yugoslavia and, 118
Romer, Milton I., 43
Roosevelt, Franklin D. (FDR), 1, 12, 16–17, 24, 29
Röpke, Wilhelm, 167
Rosé, Adam, 53–54
Rosenstein-Rodan, Paul, 29, 35, 84
Rosner, Jan, 25
Ross, Frederick Leith, 17
Rostow, Eugene, 32
Rostow, Walter, 32–35, 53–54, 134
Roy, Manabendra Nath, 77
Rudzinski, Alexander W., 46
Rudziński, Jacek, 31–32
Russell, Bertrand, 117–18
Russia, 2–3, 81–82, 88, 195
Russian Soviet Federative Socialist Republic, 185

Saillant, Louis, 78
Sakharov, Andrei, 187–88
SALT I Anti-Ballistic Agreement, 117–18, 183
SALT II Anti-Ballistic Agreement, 183
Le Sanglot de l'homme blanc (The tears of the white man) (Bruckner), 169
Saudi Arabia, 163
Sauvy, Alfred, 70, 144
Sawyer, Charles, 54

INDEX

Schaff, Adam, 109
Schmidt-Kolmer, Eva, 62
Schönbaum, Emil, 25, 208n49
Schröder, M., 120
Schroeder, Gerhard, 193
Schumpeter, Joseph, 135–36
Second World: Cold War to, 4;
communism in, 40–49, 161;
economics in, 49–56; First World
nations and, 10, 70, 149–53, 193;
history of, 38–40, 66–67;
international organizations in,
56–66; marginalization of, 74–75;
Third World nations and, 154–62;
USSR and, 195
Seers, Dudley, 139
Serrarens, Petrus, 48
Shuil, Jan, 65
Singer, Hans, 138–39
Social Democrats: communism to, 24,
157; in Eastern Europe, 25; economics
of, 135, 196; in Europe, 188; history of,
9; International Group of Democratic
Socialists, 32; multilateralism to, 201;
NIEO to, 168; politics of, 193,
200–201; religion to, 189; Third
World nations and, 166
socialism: capitalism and, 94; in China,
177; in Cold War, 124; Comecon for,
6–7, 32; communism and, 32–33, 64;
in Eastern bloc, 92–93; economics of,
85–86, 154–58; elitism in, 157–58; in
Europe, 61–62; in France, 224n85; in
FRG, 175–76; in GDR, 59; to ILO, 214;
Institute for the Socialist World
Economic System, 172; liberal, 193;
neoliberalism and, 167; to NIEO,
158–62; to OECD, 94–95; in Romania,
241n100; socialist internationalism,
249n2; Socialist International
Women, 59; in Third World, 75;
Third-Worldism and, 96–98; to U.S.,
158–59; in Yugoslavia, 92–94
social justice, 18, 24, 29, 148, 151, 161, 165,
184–87
social science, 102–4
Solidarność, 189–93

Solid Fuel Division of Supreme
Headquarters Allied Expeditionary
Force, 31
Sorokin, Pitrim, 102
South Africa, 77
South Korea, 38
Soviet Society of Friendship and
Cultural Relations, 85
Spitz, André, 61
Sputnik 1, 69
Stalin, Joseph: Comecon to, 40–41; death
of, 67–68, 71, 95, 97; in diplomacy,
212n16; elitism to, 41–42; leadership
of, 15, 25–26, 77–78, 81; Morgenthau
and, 16; Poland and, 15; reputation of,
51; Western Europe to, 50
Štampar, Andrija, 44, 141
Stańczyk, Jan, 21
Stanovnik, Janez, 95
Staples, Eugene S., 99, 101–2, 104–6,
114–15
Stein, Oswald, 25, 208n49
Stockholm Appeal, 80
Suez Canal, 70
Sweden, 35, 107, 137
Switzerland, 4, 34, 54–55, 57–58, 62, 167–68
Syria, 178

Taft-Hartley Act, 65
Taiwan, 38, 46–47
Taubert, Eberhardt, 89
Thant, U, 69, 71, 117, 134
Thatcher, Margaret, 166, 169
Third World: Cold War to, 5–6; for
Comecon, 85–86, 152; development
in, 132–42, 147–49; to FAO, 151; First
World and, 160; in geopolitics, 137–43,
149–53; ideology of, 168–69;
independence of, 128;
internationalism in, 10, 222n253;
leadership in, 197–98; for NIEO, 6,
143–44, 195; religion and, 141; Second
World and, 154–62; Social Democrats
and, 166; socialism in, 75; Third
Worldism, 70, 96–98, 169, 176; USSR
and, 83–87; in Vienna Institute,
108–9; Yugoslavia and, 9

Thomas, Albert, 30, 206n20
Tinbergen, Jan, 102–3, 168
Tito, Josip, 92, 96
Tomášek, Pøemysl, 48
tourism, 158
trade: bilateral, 34, 82; with Eastern bloc, 72–73; in Europe, 53–54; free, 7; geopolitics of, 33–34; Global South and, 78, 153; ideology of, 34–35; liberalizing, 30–31; oil, 178–79; reform in, 218n114; UN Conference on Trade and Development, 47–48; UNCTAD, 6; to UNECE, 71–72; unions, 114–15; with USSR, 32. *See also* World Federation of Trade Unions
travel grants, 22
treaties, 94–96
Treaty on the Non-Proliferation of Nuclear Weapons, 117
Truman, Harry S., 11, 20, 42, 93, 131, 133
tuberculosis, 15
Tuomioja, Sakari, 95
Turkey, 11, 31

Ukraine, 15, 19
UN. *See* United Nations
UNCTAD. *See* United Nations Conference on Trade and Development
UNDP. *See* United Nations Development Programme
UNECE. *See* United Nations Economic Commission for Europe
UNECLA. *See* United Nations Economic Commission for Latin America
UNESCO. *See* United Nations Educational, Scientific and Cultural Organization
UNIAPAC. *See* International Christian Union of Business Executives
UNICE. *See* Employers' Confederation of Europe
UNICEF, 45, 208n45, 213n39
UNIDO. *See* United Nations Industrial Development Organization
Union of Soviet Socialist Republics (USSR): in Afghanistan, 171; in

Africa, 86; at Bretton Woods, 47; Central Europe and, 44, 196–97; China and, 179–80; Comecon and, 51–52, 73; Comintern and, 41, 76–78, 88–89; communism in, 11, 15, 41, 102, 177; Czechoslovakia and, 26, 78, 80, 124–25; Eastern bloc and, 87–88, 111; Eastern Europe and, 34, 41–42, 81–82; Europe and, 4, 119; foreign policy of, 79–80; FRG and, 171; GDR and, 38–39, 155; Germany and, 33–34, 60; Global South to, 82, 97; Greece and, 62; Hungary and, 70, 91–92; ILO and, 1, 48, 57, 59–60, 68–69; imperialism by, 12–13; India and, 108, 178–79; International Labour Organization (ILO) and, 125; international philanthropy in, 21–22; Jews in, 120; Latin America and, 84; Nazis and, 89; perestroika in, 174–75; Red Army, 17, 80–81, 163; reputation of, 163; Romania and, 185; Second World nations and, 195; Sovietization, 80–87; Third World nations and, 83–87; trade with, 32; to UNECE, 16; U.S., and, 1–2, 20, 23–24, 36, 40, 67, 95, 233nn94–95; Western Europe and, 92; Yugoslavia and, 19–20. *See also* Russia
unions. *See specific organizations*
United Nations (UN): antifascism to, 12–13; Atlantic Charter and, 123; Charter, 58–59; Children's Fund, 26; China in, 49; CoCom and, 6; Cold War and, 7–8, 49, 70–75; Commission for Europe, 100; Commission on Human Rights, 125–26, 165, 187–88; Conference on Food and Agriculture, 18; Conference on Trade and Development, 6, 47–48, 136, 144–47, 146–54, 161, 166, 177, 195; Conference on Women, 177; Convention on the Elimination of all Forms of Discrimination Against Women, 79; Eastern bloc and, 105–6, 151; Environment Programme, 186; Expanded Programme of Technical

INDEX

Assistance, 73; FAO and, 21; G77 countries and, 146–47; GDR and, 31; hegemony of, 56; High Commissioner for Refugees, 70; history of, 194–201; Industrial Development Organization, 100; intergovernmental organizations to, 6; international organizations and, 9, 70; international societies to, 3–4; membership in, 23, 144–45; Morse and, 26–27; NIEO and, 167–68; OECD and, 93; Security Council, 37, 38, 40; Technical Assistance Committee, 136; Universal Declaration of Human Rights, 122–23; universalism, 96–97; WHO and, 68; after World War II, 135. *See also specific topics*

United Nations Conference on Trade and Development (UNCTAD), 6, 176–78

United Nations Development Programme (UNDP), 85, 103–4, 131, 133, 136–38, 155–60, 236n29

United Nations Economic and Social Council (ECOSOC), 124

United Nations Economic Commission for Asia and the Far East (ECAFE), 83

United Nations Economic Commission for Europe (UNECE): Comecon and, 57–58; environment to, 186; FAO and, 31; FRG in, 38–39; GATT and, 97, 118; ICC and, 121–22; ILO and, 73; pan-European plans of, 27, 40; politics of, 115–16; reconstruction to, 13; reputation of, 6, 106, 215n73; Rockefeller Foundation and, 35–36; trade to, 71–72; UNESCO and, 113–14; UNIDO and, 108–9; UNRRA and, 9, 31–35; USSR to, 16; Western Europe to, 42; World Bank and, 84

United Nations Economic Commission for Latin America (UNECLA), 83–84, 147

United Nations Educational, Scientific and Cultural Organization (UNESCO): CSCE and, 113; human rights to, 143–44; ICC and, 127; ideology of, 7–8; ILO and, 100, 138; politics of, 43; UNECE and, 113–14; UNICEF and, 45; Vienna Center, 110–11; WHO and, 85, 130–31

United Nations Industrial Development Organization (UNIDO), 6, 108–9, 138, 155–56, 159–60, 236n38

United Nations Relief and Rehabilitation Administration (UNRRA): ARA and, 16–17; Bretton Woods and, 36; ECOSOC and, 26; end of, 20–21, 31–32; in Europe, 18–20; in Greece, 15; international networks after, 23–27; Marshall Plan and, 6, 49; OFRRO and, 17–18; pan-European plans after, 31–35; Rockefeller Foundation and, 13; UNECE and, 9, 31–35; WHO and, 21

United States (U.S.): anticommunism in, 42–43; Canada and, 19, 27, 60; capitalism in, 235n20; Central Intelligence Agency and, 52, 163; to Churchill, 17; citizens of, 18; CoCom and, 158, 198–99; communism to, 134–35; Congress, 11, 30–31, 50–51; Congressional Joint Economic Committee, 69; culture of, 65; Czechoslovakia and, 216n86, 242n121; Department of Commerce, 54; Eastern bloc to, 90; Eastern Europe and, 101, 120; ECA, 50, 52–55; envoys, 104; Europe and, 16–17; FRG and, 4, 167; Geneva system in, 18; Germany and, 16; in globalism, 91; Great Britain and, 20, 36–37, 65, 164–65; health care in, 213n28; hegemony of, 5–6; ideology of, 54–55; imperialism, 44; Latin America and, 30–31, 125; McCarthyism in, 20–21; Nazis to, 28–29; New Deal in, 16–17, 134; policymakers in, 50–51, 57; propaganda, 48–49; socialism to, 158–59; South Korea and, 38; Switzerland and, 57–58; Turkey and, 31; USSR and, 1–2, 20, 23–24, 36, 40, 67, 95, 233nn94–95; in Western Europe, 34; WHO and, 164; World Bank and, 92–93; Yugoslavia and, 106

United States Agency for International Development, 93
UNRRA. *See* United Nations Relief and Rehabilitation Administration
U.S. *See* United States
USSR. *See* Union of Soviet Socialist Republics
Uzan, Marc, 50

Vanek, J., 25
Velebit, Vladimir, 95, 147
Vienna Institute, 101, 106–12
Vietnam, 129–30, 179, 181

Wałęsa, Lech, 189–90
Wallon, Henri, 63
Warsaw Pact, 39–40, 75, 78, 174, 180, 183
Western Europe: Central Europe and, 26; diplomacy in, 4; Eastern bloc and, 105–6; Eastern Europe and, 32, 72, 127; ECOSOC in, 62; Marshall Plan in, 11–12, 21, 35, 71; Nazis to, 14; to Stalin, 50; to UNECE, 42; U.S., in, 34; USSR and, 92
WFTU. *See* World Federation of Trade Unions
White, Harry, 42–43
WHO. *See* World Health Organization
Wildmann, Leo, 25
Willy Brandt Report, 166, 168–69
Wilson, Woodrow, 77
women, 58–63, 78–79, 82, 177, 184–87
Women's International Democratic Federation, 59, 78–79, 180, 184
World Bank: Atlantic Charter and, 135; GATT and, 94, 200; Global South to, 142; IMF and, 6, 31, 47, 164, 170; leadership at, 149–50; National Bank of Yugoslavia and, 96; Poland and, 48; subsidized loans by, 137; surveys, 139; UN Development Programme and, 85; UNECE and, 84; U.S., and, 92–93

World Council of Churches, 23, 183–84
World Federation of Trade Unions (WFTU), 7, 59–60, 64–65, 78, 114–15, 180
World Festival of Youth, 80
World Health Organization (WHO): Canada and, 141; children to, 61; China and, 141–42; conferences, 44; FAO and, 45, 155; in geopolitics, 43; ILO and, 7, 57, 140; UN and, 68; UNESCO and, 85, 130–31; UNIDO and, 6; UNRRA and, 21; U.S., and, 164
World War I, 19, 28, 195
World War II: Central Europe after, 17–18; children after, 58–63; Europe after, 11–13, 20–21, 28–35; geopolitics after, 13–16, 35–37; Germany after, 46–47; Global South after, 131; Havana Charter after, 145; House of Un-American Activities Committee after, 42–43; ILO after, 46; Latin America in, 133; multilateralism after, 167; refugees after, 60–61; Roosevelt in, 24; Russia after, 88; UN after, 135

Young Men's Christian Association, 23
Yugoslavia: communism in, 35; culture of, 69–70, 96–98; Czechoslovakia and, 34; Greece and, 20; Health Commission in, 22; Italy and, 14; Non-Aligned Movement in, 145; Poland and, 15–16, 19, 23, 26, 62, 73, 92, 154; Romania and, 118; socialism in, 92–94; Switzerland and, 4; Third World nations and, 9; Ukraine and, 15; U.S., and, 106; USSR and, 19–20; Yugoslav Federal Council for the Coordination of Scientific Research, 105; Yugoslav model, 94–96

Zedong, Mao, 38
Zelenka, Anton, 25–26, 46, 159
Zetkin, Clara, 59